Jewish Immigrant Associations and American Identity in New York, 1880–1939

Thomas J. Wilson Prize

Jewish Immigrant Associations and American Identity in New York,

1880–1939

DANIEL SOYER

Harvard University Press
Cambridge, Massachusetts
London, England
1997

The map on pp. x–xi is copyright © by Carta, The Israel Map
and Publishing Company Ltd. All rights reserved.

Library of Congress Cataloging-in-Publication Data

Soyer, Daniel.
Jewish immigrant associations and American identity
in New York, 1880–1939 / Daniel Soyer.
p. cm.
Includes bibliographical references and index.
ISBN 0-674-44417-5 (alk. paper)
1. Jews, East European—New York (State)—New York—Societies, etc.—History.
2. Immigrants—New York (State)—New York—Societies, etc.—History.
3. Jews—New York (State)—New York—Societies, etc.—History.
4. New York (N.Y.)—Ethnic relations. I. Title.
F128.9.J5S69 1997
974.7′1004924′006—dc21   96-47483
CIP

Designed by Gwen Nefsky Frankfeldt

Contents

Note on Orthography and Transliteration

Yiddish words, phrases, titles, and names of organizations, places, and persons have been rendered according to the transliteration scheme of the YIVO Institute for Jewish Research, except that no attempt has been made to standardize nonstandard orthography. Hebrew words, phrases, and titles have been transliterated according to a modified version of the ALA/LC 1948–1976 romanization table. Hebrew words in the text have been spelled according to their modern pronunciation, even if they are also commonly used in Yiddish. But Hebrew words that appear as integral parts of Yiddish titles or phrases are spelled as they are pronounced in Yiddish. Foreign words are italicized only the first time they appear, at which point they are explained.

European place names in the text follow the main entry in Mokotoff and Sack, *Where Once We Walked: A Guide to Jewish Communities Destroyed in the Holocaust.* They do not include the diacritical marks used in the original languages. Where Yiddish or other commonly used names for a location differ significantly from the main term used in another language (Brisk [Yiddish], Brzesc nad Bugiem [Polish], Brest-Litovsk [Russian]), I have provided alternate spellings in parentheses. When referring to Jewish natives of a particular place, I use the Yiddish form (Timkovitser for people from Timkovichi). When place names appear in the names of organizations, they remain, of course, in the form used originally. To the extent possible, I have used organizational names as they appear in English in *Di idishe landsmanshaften fun Nyu York, The Jewish Communal Register,* or *From Alexandrovsk to Zyrardow: A Guide to YIVO's Landsmanshaftn Archive.* When English names are not available, I transliterate directly from the Yiddish.

A friend loveth at all times, and a brother is born for adversity.

—PROVERBS 17:17

(Quoted during a debate on mutual aid at the Satanover Benevolent Society,
New York, October 1, 1905.)

JEWISH EASTERN EUROPE
1830-1914

⊛ Provincial Capital	★ Major City
⋯ Border	• Settlement
⋯⋯ Provincial Border	
▨ Congress Poland	▨ Pale of Settlement

km

0	100	200

© carta, JERUSALEM

POLTAVE
Poltave

KHERSON

Black Sea

Dnieper

Perevaslev

Shpole

Nikolayev

KIEV

Talne

Kiev

Uman

Odessa

Rizhin

Barditshev

Chichelnik

Zvihil

Zhitomir

Mezhbizh

Letitshev

Nemirov

Tultshin

Bratslav

PODOLIA

Dniester

BESSARABIA

ROMANIA

Kishinev

Bar

Kamenets-
Podolsk

Prut

Yas

Danube

Satanov

Strusov

Husiatin

Chortkov

Sadeger

Chernovits

Ostre

Kremenets

Rovne

Dubne

Tarnopol

Horodenka

Kolomay

Sokal

Brod

Lemberg

Belz

GALICIA

Sighet

Zholkve

Pshemishl

Rimanov

HUNGARY

Carpathian Mts

Munkatsh

Satmer

Lezhensk

Tomashov

Nay Sandz

Kroke
(Cracow)

Jewish Immigrant Associations and
American Identity in New York,
1880–1939

Introduction

Landsmanshaftn, associations of immigrants from the same hometown, became the most popular form of organization among Eastern European Jewish immigrants to the United States in the late nineteenth and early twentieth centuries.* Organized variously as independent mutual aid societies, religious congregations, and fraternal lodges, and reflecting a variety of political and religious orientations, landsmanshaftn provided their members with valuable material benefits and served as arenas for formal and informal social interaction. Exactly how many hometown societies existed at one time or another is unknown; estimates for New York City alone range from 1,000 to as high as 10,000. The most comprehensive survey of New York's landsmanshaftn, carried out in the late 1930s by the Yiddish Writers' Group of the Federal Writers' Project, identified 2,468 individual organizations. Assuming that another 500 had eluded their detection, the Yiddish writers concluded that the city harbored some 3,000 landsmanshaftn, with over 400,000 members. These organizations thus enrolled a quarter of New York's Jews, comprising a majority of those who were foreign-born. When the families of members are included together with one-time members who had let their affiliations lapse, the number of individuals

---

*The Yiddish word *landsman* denotes a person (man or woman, but usually man) from the same town, region, or country as the speaker. The plural form is *landslayt*. A female compatriot may also be called a *landsfroy* (pl. *landsfroyen*). A *landsmanshaft* is thus a formal organization of *landslayt,* or, more loosely, the informal community of *landslayt*. The plural of *landsmanshaft* is *landsmanshaftn*.

who were at one time connected directly or indirectly with a landsman-shaft may well be as high as one million.[1]

The principle of landsmanshaft (if not the term itself) has had a long presence in Jewish history. As early as 586 BCE, Jews in the Babylonian Exile formed separate congregations based on the towns in Palestine from which the worshipers had come. In sixteenth-century Thessaloniki (Salonika), Greece, Sephardic Jews maintained at least ten synagogues identified with their regions of origin in Spain, Portugal, and Italy.[2] More recently, landsmanshaftn arose among Eastern European Jewish immigrants in every major American city and many smaller centers as well.[3] Outside of the United States, Yiddish-speaking Jews in Paris, Buenos Aires, Israel, and other immigrant destinations established simi-lar societies.[4]

Despite the ubiquity of landsmanshaftn, New York remained their most important center of activity in the modern era. With over 1.5 million Jewish inhabitants by 1920, the city had become the greatest Jewish population center of all time.[5] Largely because of its size, New York accommodated a highly diversified Jewish community and pro-vided fertile ground for the subdivision of its immigrant population by place of origin, class, degree of religious observance, political prefer-ences, and other variables. Moreover, New York set an example for smaller Jewish settlements. Sociologist Louis Wirth noted, for example, that the "ghetto of New York has been more or less a model for all American Jewish communities," and that many inhabitants of Chi-cago's Jewish quarter had "considerable experience on the East Side of New York" before moving on to the Midwest.[6] Observers in Buenos Aires and Paris also commented on the influence of New York landsmanshaftn on similar societies in their cities.[7]

The landsmanshaft principle was in no way peculiar to Jewish mi-grants. In fact, it is one of the most common forms of immigrant organization throughout the world, and groups as diverse as Chinese in Singapore and Ibo in Calabar, Nigeria, have formed associations based on village or region of origin.[8] In America, fraternal societies were central to the lives of many immigrants and helped to define the boundaries of each emerging ethnic group. They provided what the historian Robert Harney has called a "psychic map" of ethnic identity, incorporating features drawn from both the old country and the new. Language, religion, race, politics, or origins in a given country, region, or locality might all contribute to the group's sense of itself. Societies often embodied the minutest of these distinctions, but the smaller units then frequently also constituted the building blocks for more broadly organized ethnic communities. The multilevel communal structure thus reflected overlapping layers of identity among the people who made up its constituency.[9]

Despite their many similarities, however, cultural and social differences leave their marks on the structures and activities of hometown associations of different groups and different times. For example, while Jewish landsmanshaftn were generally loose enough to allow membership to immigrants from other towns (often spouses or in-laws of *landslayt*), early Arab-American hometown societies were sometimes so exclusive that marriage to an outsider could mean expulsion from the association. Hometown clubs of immigrants from the Dominican Republic in the 1990s frequently sported baseball or softball teams, an activity common to both their native and adopted countries, while early-twentieth century Jewish societies never concerned themselves with athletics.[10]

The ways in which immigrants and their descendants forge new ethnic American identities constitute a central concern of immigration history. One issue revolves around the degree to which immigrants retain elements of their cultures of origin. Scholars have long since abandoned the notion that the act of resettlement, by removing migrants from their old-country cultural contexts, leaves them empty of any strong attachments and therefore ready on arrival to receive the imprint of their new country. But neither do immigrants transplant their old-country cultures intact to the New World.[11] Rather, adaptation to life in America consists of a complex and ongoing series of adjustments, by which, as one recent scholarly statement put it, immigrants and their children strive to reconcile the "duality of . . . 'foreignness' and . . . 'Americanness'" which they experience.[12]

In addition to accepting both continuity and transformation as features of the immigrant experience, this approach thus recognizes that ethnic identity is a socially constructed and malleable phenomenon. Moreover, individuals and groups play an active role in the creation of their own identities. Ethnicity, in this view, thus consists of a dynamic "process of construction or invention which incorporates, adapts, and amplifies preexisting communal solidarities, cultural attributes, and historical memories."[13] An exploration of this process of construction raises more specific questions about what the immigrants themselves have meant by Americanization. What have they wished to retain from their old-world cultures and historical memories? What aspects of this country's culture have they most wanted to incorporate into their own? How have "preexisting communal solidarities" contributed to the process of Americanization? How have all of these attributes been incorporated into a new sense of American identity, and what are the venues in which this new identity has taken shape?

Landsmanshaftn were at the center of this process for the immigrant generation of Eastern European Jews. As they negotiated an identity appropriate to their new situation, Jewish immigrants drew on elements from the cultures of both their old and new homes, and incorporated them into the structures and activities of their associations. While both the Old World and the New provided the immigrants with vital resources, neither one presented a unified model. The process of adaptation was therefore a contested one, and divisions among immigrants led to widespread debate within the Jewish community concerning the nature of its identity.

The various types of landsmanshaft associations reflected the diversity of influences on immigrant culture and the multiplicity of strategies for identity-construction pursued by groups of immigrants and individuals from the same hometown. Ironically, those immigrants on the extremes of right and left drew most heavily upon models they brought with them from the old country. Thus Jews committed to traditional Judaism established landsmanshaft religious congregations which consciously sought to maintain traditional forms of worship at the center of Jewish identity, and, in so doing, utilized much of the language and symbolism the congregants had known in Europe. Leftists sought to reconstruct the revolutionary parties and movements in which they had been active in Russia. These radicals espoused internationalist principles and took an active role in the formation then under way of an international socialist culture.[14] Nevertheless, they maintained both a secularized sense of Jewishness and an identification with their hometowns.

Others patterned their organizations after the mutual aid associations and fraternal lodges popular among native-born Americans and other immigrant groups. Though often overlooked, interaction among different ethnic communities could be nearly as important as the newcomers' relationship with mainstream Anglo-American society.[15] New York's Jewish landsmanshaftn clearly reflected the influence of the nearby German population, which was well established by the time Eastern European Jews began to arrive in the 1880s. Still, the conscious attempt to fashion a new form of Jewish ethnic identity was most evident in the rituals of those landsmanshaftn which became lodges of American-style fraternal orders. Patterned after the rites of the Masons and other secret societies, Jewish fraternal ritual was an expression of the participants' commitment to Jewishness in a form that seemed more compatible with American ways than was traditional Judaism.

The immigrants selected aspects of American culture which they found most appealing and most relevant to their own needs. In particular, they strongly identified with the tradition that considered American nationality to be an outgrowth of shared principles rather than common racial or ethnic antecedents. All a newcomer had to do to become an American, according to this view, was to adopt the nation's ideological commitment to liberty, equality, and republicanism. This "civic culture," as historian Lawrence Fuchs has described it, rested on the propositions that ordinary people could take part in their own governance, that citizens were entitled to equal participation in public life, and that those who entered loyally into the civic life of the country had the right to maintain their own religions and other expressions of ethnic identity. America did not apply these lofty tenets consistently, excluding from full citizenship people of African, Asian, and Indian descent, and, to some extent, women. But from the earliest days of the republic, European immigrants took full advantage of the civic culture to integrate themselves into a relatively open and democratic society without surrendering their own distinctive ethnic characteristics.[16]

This comparatively liberal conception of nationality never went uncontested; in the face of massive immigration toward the end of the nineteenth century, nervous old-stock citizens turned to an Americanism increasingly defined along cultural, hereditary, and even racial lines.[17] But while some native-born Anglo-Americans elevated the importance of personal ancestral ties to the land and its history, immigrants continued to uphold the ideal of citizenship based on the republic's abstract principles. They were often more than willing, as Fuchs has pointed out, to renounce allegiance to foreign governments to which they felt little sense of loyalty in the first place. They found it much harder, emotionally and practically, to give up their languages and religions, their memories of old-country landscapes, and their sense of kinship with others who had come from the same places.[18] Putting the civic culture at the core of American nationality allowed the immigrants to reconcile their conflicting loyalties. In the immigrant conception of Americanism it was no contradiction to write, as one landsmanshaft publication did about a leader of the Federation of Polish Jews of America: "Mr. Rosenberg is an American with all his being, and he would certainly sacrifice himself for the American flag. He would, without a doubt, go into battle this very day if it were necessary to fight for America. But at the same time, he has continued to feel the necessity for us to unite as Jews who come from one country, from that place where we absorbed the scent of the same earth, where we were born."[19]

Jews, in particular, eagerly adopted the American civic culture as their own, espousing an ideology based on voluntarism, democracy, and equalitarianism, and integrating these values into their patterns of communal organization.[20] The structure of the landsmanshaftn clearly incorporated their members' devotion to the civic culture of their adopted country. Characterized by a commitment to internal democracy and equality, and delineated by the societies' constitutions and by-laws, this structure had more in common with American models than with either the oligarchical traditional Jewish associations or the conspiratorial revolutionary organizations in the Russian Empire (from which most of the landsmanshaft members had come). The immigrants themselves sometimes explicitly compared their societies with the government of the United States, and participation in associational affairs often rewarded the members with an enduring education in the ideals of democratic citizenship.

Nearly all landsmanshaftn also provided their members with vital material benefits such as medical care, income support, and burial. A typical feature of immigrant societies everywhere, since newcomers can seldom count on established local social networks to cover their needs, the principle of mutual aid nevertheless took on special meaning for Jewish immigrants in the United States. They viewed material abundance as one of the chief attributes of American society, attractive not only because it offered an easier life but also because it promised social mobility and a blurring of the rigid class and caste distinctions they had known in the Old World.[21] At the same time, however, American conditions posed significant dangers. The lack of a social "safety net" left working-class people always on the edge of economic disaster. Moreover, in the context of this country's wealth, poverty carried a much stronger stigma of personal failure than it did in Eastern

Europe.[22] Eager to profit from America's abundance, Jewish immigrants nevertheless felt insecure in the face of the vicissitudes of industrial society.

By providing a modicum of material security, mutual aid guarded landsmanshaft members against economic exigencies and enabled them to take advantage of American opportunities. Devised to deal with adversity, mutual aid also afforded a chance to break free from the paternalism of traditional Jewish charity as practiced in Europe (and in America as well). It therefore represented in itself a form of independence which the immigrants closely associated with the American ideal. Significantly, however, society members guaranteed their independence collectively, not as rugged individuals.

The role of the societies in furnishing benefits reinforced their mostly male character, as one of the ways in which a man provided materially for his family. The majority of societies accepted men only, although there were also some women's and mixed organizations, as well as "ladies' auxiliaries" to the men's groups. Society benefits comprised an integral part of the family economy, and men saw membership in a society as one of their duties toward their wives and children. Then, too, most of the models available to the societies for emulation, including both traditional Jewish voluntary associations and American fraternal organizations, were all-male in composition. Even full participation in the much admired civic culture was largely limited to men. At least in part because of this exclusivity, as the historian Paula Hyman has argued, Jewish immigrant men defined their communal identity through affiliation with the myriad of organizations they formed, while women concerned themselves more with less formal neighborhood networks.[23]

Nevertheless, women participated in many landsmanshaft activities, most notably formal social events, but also in much of the informal socializing that accompanied regular meetings. In this respect landsmanshaftn in America differed from both traditional Jewish associations and American fraternal orders, whose social activities were usually highly segregated. Though fewer in number, independent women's societies, which often counted men among their founders and officers, provided benefits to unmarried women and supplemented those of married members. Both women's societies and ladies' auxiliaries also engaged in a wide range of charity and community work.

The degree to which the landsmanshaftn served as vehicles for their members' integration into American life indicates the importance of the "active participation by the immigrants in defining their group identities."[24] Most historians have seen Americanization as a process imposed on more or less resisting immigrants by outside forces, including educators, settlement house workers, social reformers, industrialists, trade unionists, and consumerist culture.[25] The landsmanshaftn, however, demonstrate that many immigrants adopted aspects of American social life independently, suggesting that the newcomers exercised a high degree of agency in their growing identification with American society. That this process of adjustment took place within the comfortable confines of groups defined by old-country identities, speaking the immigrants' language, and made up of familiar faces from the old hometown made it easier to experience, though more difficult for outside observers to perceive. Despite their apparent foreignness, therefore, the landsmanshaftn actually furthered their members' Americanization.

New Jewish immigrants Americanized largely within the context of a broader American Jewish community. As the Eastern European Jewish population in New York developed its own infrastructure, some contemporary observers mistakenly identified the landsmanshaft with an early stage of evolution, doomed to extinction with the advent of more advanced forms of communal life.[26] The staying power of the landsmanshaftn, and the role they and their members played in furthering movements and organizations with wider agendas, indicate the degree to which the immigrants maintained their identification as landslayt from a given town even as they developed a new consciousness of themselves as members of a larger American Jewish community.

The ways in which the landsmanshaftn responded to World War I demonstrate the continuing significance of their native places for society members. At the same time, the efforts of immigrant organizations to aid their war-ravaged hometowns revealed to the immigrants themselves the extent to which they had grown estranged from their origins. The war and the ensuing restriction of immigration to the United States further solidified the separation between the immigrants and their landslayt in Europe, but had the paradoxical effect of reemphasizing the immigrants' identification with the old home. During the interwar era, nostalgia for the hometown became a more prominent feature of landsmanshaft activity than it had been in the societies' period of formation, when their most important role was to help their members adjust to American life. With the immigrants well settled by the 1920s, they had the time to engage in collective reminiscing, as well as the resources to become the chief benefactors of their less fortunate brothers and sisters still in the Old World.

In a sense, the landsmanshaftn came full circle. Beginning with the natural identification of groups of immigrants with their hometowns and fellow townspeople, they returned to those ties on a more abstract and symbolic level in the years after World War I. In the meantime, however, much had changed in the immigrant Jews' sense of themselves and their place in the world. No longer greenhorns, anchored to American soil by citizenship, institutions, native-born children, property, and years of experience, the immigrants had become different people from what they had been when they first arrived. Their hometown associations had played an important part in that process, by providing them with the material and emotional support necessary to undergo the transformation. In so doing, the societies reflected all of their members' experiences and all of the influences brought to bear on them in both Old World and New.

⌣ 1 ⌐

The Old World

The vast majority of Jews who emigrated to America in the late nineteenth and early twentieth centuries were the products of a distinctive East European Jewish culture. Although they came from various lands, the Russian and Austro-Hungarian empires as well as the Kingdom of Romania, the Jews of Eastern Europe shared a common way of life different from that of their Christian neighbors. Their faith gave the Jews a separate calendar and also influenced their dress and food, setting them apart from the peoples around them. Their everyday language was, for the most part, Yiddish, while the people among whom they lived spoke Polish, Ukrainian, Lithuanian, Romanian, Belorussian, Russian, and other languages. And while most of their Gentile compatriots were peasants who lived in agricultural villages, most Jews were town-dwellers and earned their bread as artisans and petty traders.

Their old-country backgrounds naturally influenced the ways in which Jewish immigrants ordered their community once they reached the New World. To begin with, the landsmanshaftn took their names from the cities and towns of Russia, Poland, and Romania from which their immigrant members had come. Like many people in pre-industrial Europe, Eastern European Jews identified very strongly with the specific localities in which they lived. But Jews had additional reasons for this sense of attachment to the little towns and big-city neighborhoods in which they made their homes. A small minority in each country, Jews often formed a large majority in these places, which therefore took on an especially Jewish character. In order to understand the immigrants' attachment to their places of origin, it is important to examine the special meaning the small Jewish town held in the minds of its inhabitants and expatriates.

Moreover, local Jewish communal structures supplied the Jews with a great deal of organizational experience before they reached America. But the immigrants did not always find in Eastern European Jewish society the appropriate models for organizing in the New World. On the contrary, memories of widespread corruption and social inequality in many traditional communal institutions led many Jews, once they reached the United States, to shy away from any form of communal organization that smacked of centralism and coercive power. On the other hand, many Jews continued to view more positively the extensive network of autonomous voluntary associations which had traditionally provided a variety of services to the community. By the late nineteenth century, however, newer forms of organization, from political movements to mutual aid societies, challenged these traditional structures of European Jewry with the promise of a more egalitarian and democratic associational life.

The process of social change that gave rise to new forms of organization in Eastern Europe also led to mass migration overseas. The flow of immigrants from all of the far-flung corners of Jewish Eastern Europe converged in the streets and tenements of New York. Differences in Yiddish dialect, styles of religious observance, and customs extending even to food preparation, reinforced regional and local loyalties—even, or perhaps especially, when Jews from a variety of places came to live in such close proximity to one another.

For the most part, East European Jewry originated in an earlier mass migration from the German lands and Bohemia to medieval Poland. The influx began in the thirteenth and fourteenth centuries and continued to the middle of the seventeenth. By 1764, Polish Jewry numbered some 750,000, 10 percent of the population. Shortly thereafter, with the partitions of Poland between 1772 and 1795, most of Polish Jewry became subjects of the Russian tsars. Other Jews, including those of Galicia, came under the control of the Habsburg Empire.[1] In each of these states and at different times the Jews experienced very different political conditions. Nevertheless, they continued to share much of the same culture, together with Jews in other regions of Austria-Hungary and parts of Romania.

With over five million Jews in 1897, the Russian Empire contained by far the largest Jewish community in the world. Ironically, Russia had for some time attempted to keep itself free of Jews, and it continued its hostile attitude even after inheriting a large Jewish population from a dismantled Poland. The most important feature of this antisemitic policy was the creation of the Pale of Settlement, the area in the western part of the empire where the state permitted Jews to settle. As finally delineated in 1835, the Pale of Settlement included parts of the Baltic provinces, Lithuania, Belorussia, the Ukraine, and "New Russia." In addition, the law allowed Jews to live in the Kingdom of Poland, which was not technically part of the Pale. According to the Russian census of 1897, there were some 5,189,401 Jews (defined by religion) in the Empire, of whom 4,874,636 lived in the Pale of Settlement and Poland, where they made up 11.46 percent of the population.[2]

The tsars periodically decreed additional restrictions on Jewish residence. The authorities viewed with particular displeasure the Jewish presence in the villages, because they considered the Jews to be a major cause of demoralization and unrest among the Christian peasantry.[3] In the first half of the nineteenth century a number of government orders uprooted Jews from their places of residence.[4] Though many of these edicts were not especially effective, they did make life in the rural areas uncertain and helped crowd the Jews into urban centers.

The archetypical Jewish settlement throughout Eastern Europe was the small town, known in Yiddish as the *shtetl* (diminutive of *shtot*, or city). Continuing the original settlement patterns of Polish Jewry, these towns came to occupy a prominent place in Jewish consciousness.[5] By the late nineteenth century the first generation of modern Yiddish writers had begun to mythologize the shtetl. Fictional towns, such as Sholem Aleichem's Kasrilevka, became more famous than the majority of real ones. The most important feature of the shtetl myth was that the towns were completely Jewish communities, almost hermetically sealed off from the Gentile world. Though the early literary observers of the shtetl often had reformist motives and sought to depict the narrowness of small-town life, later generations focused on the shtetl as the lost idyll of a simple and harmonious community destroyed by the onrush of the modern world. In much of Yiddish literature, the shtetl also became a metaphor for the Jewish condition as a whole.[6]

The real towns were important as part of the background for the American landsmanshaftn. They not only supplied the American associations with members, but later became themselves the focus of the organizations' activities—as recipients of aid and subjects of nostalgia and memorialization. The similarities in the shtetl experience provided a common foundation for many of the ways in which the immigrants in America related to their places of birth, while the diversity encouraged continuing identification with specific towns.

There was more than a grain of truth to the image of the integrally Jewish town, but the reality of the shtetl was quite a bit more complicated. Essentially, the shtetl served the surrounding agricultural population as a market town, linking its own small hinterland to the larger markets of the city. Regular contact with the non-Jewish peasants as well as communication with the wider world were therefore normal features of shtetl life. Yet the fact that the peasantry was entirely Gentile while the population of the town was mostly Jewish certainly did give the shtetl a special Jewish character. In 1897, for example, Jews constituted two thirds of the Belorussian Svisloch's 3,099 inhabitants; the rest were Belorussians, Poles, a "score" of Russian officials, and about a dozen Moslem Tatars.[7] The tendency for the Jewish population to concentrate in the center of town, with the non-Jews residing at the periphery, further enhanced the impression of the shtetl as an inherently Jewish place.[8] As one memoirist recalled, with only a little hyperbole, his own hometown in Lithuania: "At the time I came into the world [1863], Wylkowiski was a one-hundred percent Jewish town. There were hardly any non-Jews, with the exception of a few officials stationed there. And life in the shtetl, like its population, was one-hundred percent Jewish."[9]

The essentially urban Jews remained distinct from the Christian peasants, whose illiteracy and living conditions did little to encourage acculturation of the Jewish inhabitants to the local language and culture. Indeed, both shtetl Jews and local non-Jews differentiated strongly between the two communities, a separation reinforced not only by cultural dissimilarities but by the negative attitudes of each group toward the other.[10]

The shtetl's urban status did not depend primarily on its size, which in the late nineteenth century could range from a few hundred people to 10,000 or more, but on its function as a market and small-scale manufacturing center.[11] The geographic center of the shtetl was almost always the marketplace, often surrounded by rows of stores, from which four or five main streets led out toward the suburbs. An irregular network of smaller streets and alleys, with or without names, bisected the larger streets. Conditions varied considerably from town to town. In Svisloch, "on rainy days the mud was ankle-deep and crossing the [unpaved] market was no pleasant undertaking."[12] But three of Svisloch's five main streets were paved with cobblestones, and a sidewalk around the market place was added after 1904. In addition to their names in the official language, the streets carried Yiddish names used by the Jewish population. These sometimes referred to a physical characteristic of the street itself ("Crooked Street," for example), or to an important landmark that stood on it ("Synagogue Street" or "Mill Street"). In any case, the Yiddish street names reinforced the Jewish atmosphere of the town.[13]

Just as the town's streets spread out from the marketplace, so the week's activities revolved around market day (apart from the Sabbath). In the Galician shtetl of Kolbuszowa market day was Tuesday, and peasants began to arrive the previous night, sleeping under their wagons in the market square. Different parts of the square were devoted to different sorts of goods: produce in one section, textiles in another, and so on. Trading in livestock took place separately on Commerce Street off of the main square. Typically, peasants sold their produce to the townspeople in the morning, then bought ready-made goods or availed themselves of the services of Jewish artisans in the afternoon, and returned home in the evening. Jewish vendors, too, made the rounds, selling their wares at fairs throughout the region. On market days locals thus came into regular contact with both Jews and non-Jews from beyond the borders of the town itself, belying the myth of insular shtetl detachment from the rest of the world.[14]

In addition to being the center of retail business, the small town linked the local economy to wider markets. Shtetl Jews served as intermediaries between the agricultural village and the industrial city.[15] Svisloch, for example, was connected economically to Bialystok. The town's commission merchants made weekly trips to the city, where they sold agricultural products bought from the peasants. On their return trips they brought merchandise ordered in advance by shtetl retailers.[16]

By the late nineteenth century, shtetlekh exhibited considerable variation. Some were more industrialized, others less so. Zagare, Lithuania, for example, had several small factories producing buttons and hatchets.[17] Svisloch also possessed a number of factories, and seventy percent of the Jews there drew their livelihood from the leather industry, directly or indirectly, as manufacturers, workers, artisans, or merchants.[18]

Other shtetlekh drew considerable prestige from traditional Jewish religious activity, either as seats of institutions of higher learning (yeshivahs), or as homes to Hasidic dynasties.[19] A contemporary observer noted the vast difference between the Galician towns of Miedzyrzec (Mezrich), an up-to-date center in the process of industrialization, and Biala, dominated by a Hasidic rebbe's court. While the two towns were only half an hour apart by train, there was "a difference of at least a century" between them.[20]

Housing styles also varied considerably, helping to make each town's personality unique in the minds of its current and former residents. Only 14 of 1,000 houses were made of brick in Zagare, and in Tyszowce the tallest structure had three stories. In Svisloch, in comparison, "many of the houses were substantial two-story brick structures, adorned with balconies."[21] Regional styles influenced shtetl architecture as well. In the Romanian shtetl of Stefanesti, for example, many of the houses were "built in the style of peasant huts, with thatched roofs and a *prispa,* a sort of built-in bench surrounding the outside walls."[22]

Jews also came to New York from the larger cities of Eastern Europe. In the cities the Jews generally constituted a smaller percentage of the population, but their separate neighborhoods possessed much the same Jewish character as did the small towns. Some urban Jewish communities dated from the early period of Jewish settlement in Poland. The first Jews arrived in Vilna, for example, in the fourteenth century. Originally restricted to residence on three streets, one of them actually called Zydowska, or Jewish Street, the Jewish population quickly outgrew these boundaries. By 1897 Vilna was home to 64,000 Jews, 45 percent of its total population.[23] Despite its expansion, the Jewish quarter of Vilna remained as crowded as it was vibrant, with multi-family tenements each inhabited by as many as fifteen families. A dense network of streets and alleys, Jewish Vilna was, in the words of one observer, "a hive of swarming humanity, struggling manfully in a hostile environment for a decent existence."[24]

Demographic concentration enabled both small-town and big-city Jews to feel at home in a country in which they were a small minority.[25] The specific localities in which Jews were dominant culturally and socially acquired a variety of deep associations and mythologies all their own. Vilna, with its tradition of learning, came to be known as the Jerusalem of Lithuania, nearly raising it to the status of Zion itself. Smaller towns and cities also entered Jewish folklore, which assigned to each a specific character. Special nicknames were devised for natives of hundreds of towns, each name supposedly based on a particular idiosyncrasy of that place. The inhabitants of Svisloch were Sislevitsher Krupnik, after the potato-barley soup eaten almost every day by Jews there; Kelemer Sleepers were so named for allegedly sleeping through a nighttime visit by the Tsar to their town; natives of Zamosc became known as heretics because the numerical value of the Hebrew spelling of their town's name equaled that of the word "heretic"; the rocking and shaking of Hasidim in prayer led to the name Belzer Jelly; and Glovner Doughballs were so called because people from Glowno were said to speak as if they had doughballs in their mouths.[26] Eastern European Jews clearly identified themselves, and each other, with the localities in which they lived.

The Jewish communal structure, largely an inheritance from medieval Central Europe, further reinforced local loyalties. The basic unit was the local community, known as the *kehillah,* of which all permanent residents of a given town or city were automatically members. As a corporate body, the Jewish community enjoyed a great deal of autonomy, including the right to levy taxes and enforce Jewish, and even sometimes civil, law among its members. In larger communities, the kehillah might employ a whole staff of civil servants, from rabbis and scribes to watchmen and street cleaners. Always, however, the community's autonomy was dependent on the ultimate sanction of the secular authorities, for whom it collected taxes and policed the Jewish population. Each local kehillah enjoyed a considerable degree of independence, though communities often cooperated on issues of common concern. In the late sixteenth century larger confederations, such as the Polish Council of the Four Lands and the Lithuanian Council, provided some degree of centralization. Still, the individual kehillot retained their primacy.[27]

By the nineteenth century the traditional Jewish community found itself under attack from within and from the outside. The disappearance by the end of the eighteenth century of the central Jewish confederations reflected the decline of the Polish state itself. The autocratic Russian regime was uncomfortable with the autonomous corporate Jewish communal structure inherited from Poland. The *kahal* (the governing body of the local kehillah) continued for a time as the governing agency of the Jewish community, but was closely regulated by the non-Jewish authorities, who attempted to turn the structures of

Jewish autonomy into instruments of the state's control over the Jewish population. The government gradually constricted the kahal's ability to act independently, while at the same time increasing its burdensome role of collecting taxes and, after 1827, of conscripting military recruits from the Jewish population.[28] In compelling this sort of cooperation, the regime helped to undermine the legitimacy of the kahal in the eyes of large numbers of Jews.

The infamous decree of 1827, instituting a punitive draft designed to force the assimilation of the Jews, was an important benchmark in the decline of the traditional structures of Jewish authority. Under the terms of this edict, the army inducted a specified number of Jews for twenty-five years of service. Each recruit's term began at the age of eighteen, but the "cantonists," as they were called, could be taken as early as age twelve for an additional period of preliminary training. The government delegated responsibility for meeting the quota of Jewish recruits to local Jewish communities, which often resorted to unsavory methods, including kidnapping, to provide the required number of conscripts. Moreover, the communal leadership often gave over the children of the poor in the place of those of the wealthy and used its power of impressment as a means of maintaining social control. The masses of poor Jews bitterly resented these practices, which further weakened the kahal's already shaky position.[29] The government officially abolished the kahal in the Pale in 1844 (in Poland there was some continuity) and the harsh system of military service in 1855, but a sense of alienation from the communal elite "rankled in the heads of the Jewish masses for generations."[30] Indeed, the Jewish "masses" took this distrust of any form of centralized Jewish authority with them when they went to New York, where they resisted attempts to establish communal forms resembling the coercive structures of the Old World.

With the decline of the kahal, the organizational locus of the Jewish community devolved upon the network of voluntary associations known as *hevrot* (singular, *hevrah*). Such societies devoted themselves to a variety of purposes, including religious study and worship, charity, education, and the regulation of occupational interests.[31] Since the hevrot lacked the stigma the kahal had acquired by mid-nineteenth century, they retained the respect and loyalty of a larger portion of the Jewish public.[32] Later, some Jewish immigrants in America, particularly those of a more conservative bent, saw in the hevrot a valid model for the organization of their own societies. But the American hevrot resembled their European counterparts mainly at a symbolic level, in nomenclature and forms of ceremony. The actual structure of the European associations proved much less applicable to the American context.

The European hevrot adapted to the fluctuations of Jewish communal life. When there was a strong centralized authority, the associations were subordinate to the kahal, which often regulated them very closely, and for which they carried out much of the day-to-day work of social welfare. Often, however, the hevrot both preceded and survived the creation of a centralized community. This was especially true of the burial society *(hevrah kadisha),* whose functions of preparing the corpse for proper Jewish burial and maintaining the Jewish cemetery were the first requirements of a nascent Jewish community.[33]

The hevrah kadisha was usually the most prestigious society in a given locality. Its moral authority derived from the religious belief that ministering to the dead was one of the most noble and spiritually significant activities.[34] In time, the hevrah kadisha also acquired a great deal of secular status, and its membership usually consisted of the community's most wealthy and powerful men. High dues, the provision that a new member be accepted only with the unanimous consent of all current members, and discrimination in favor of sons and sons-in-law, all helped to keep the hevrah kadisha exclusive.[35] Its authority was such that after the kahal was officially abolished in Russia, the hevrah kadisha often unofficially assumed its leadership role in the community.

A constitution and set of by-laws governed the life of the hevrah. The by-laws, called *takkanot,* were kept in a record book, together with the names of members, minutes of meetings, and a record of important events in the history of the association and community.[36] The fact that these important documents were usually written in Hebrew, the holy tongue and traditional juridical language of the Jewish people, served to sacralize the association and enhance its legitimacy in a highly religious culture. On the other hand, the practice also meant that many association members, whose spoken language was Yiddish, may not have been able to read or understand their hevrah's records. Hence there clearly was a premium on learning in the selection of leadership, and a limitation on the common members' ability to influence the course of organizational events.[37] The usual American practice of reading the minutes of the previous meeting and having the membership approve them would have had little meaning in such circumstances.

Other practices also stressed the holiness of the hevrah and grounded its practical purposes in the sacred texts of Judaism. The record book, or *pinkas,* was itself a kind of ceremonial object, often with an illuminated or ornamented front page with a biblical or rabbinic quotation relating to function of the society.[38] Even social events assumed a sacred character. Most hevrot held two banquets a year, usually on such symbolic dates as the 7th of Adar, said to be the anniversary of Moses' death. The festivities often included a scholarly discourse or sermon, the singing of special hymns, the reading of Psalms, and the performance of symbolic dances and dramatizations.[39]

Many associations maintained their own places of worship apart from the main synagogue. By meeting separately to pray, members cemented their ties to one another and increased their sense of identification with the group. Occasionally, small changes in the liturgy, such as a different melody or an additional psalm, helped to further this process. Rival religious groups, craft guilds, and wealthy individuals also organized their own synagogues, reinforcing the tendency to small independent houses of prayer.[40]

In addition to their religious and social functions, many hevrot served as the basic social welfare agencies of the Jewish community. Some societies, such as the hevrah kadisha, provided their services to everyone, setting their fees along an informal sliding scale. Others assisted only the needy. Societies for giving food to the hungry, clothing to the paupers, shelter to the homeless, interest-free loans to indigent artisans and traders, dowries to destitute brides, education to poor boys, and so on, all had the character of charity, in which giving flowed, as sociologist Natalie Joffe put it, "in a descending spiral, never in a closed circle of bestowal and reciprocation."[41] Social welfare in Jewish Eastern Europe thus differed markedly from the mutual aid model which prevailed among the landsmanshaftn in the United States.

The distinction between charity and mutual aid is an important one for understanding the differences between the Old-World Jewish hevrot and the New-World landsmanshaftn. In a system of mutual aid, members of an association contribute equally, each with the expectation that he or she will at some time benefit from the group's assistance. Participants in a mutual aid society usually see their undertaking as a collective manifestation of a spirit of independence and egalitarian democracy. The traditional mechanisms for providing for social welfare, on the other hand, confirmed the reigning social hierarchy of wealth, learning, and descent.[42]

Few members of hevrot received significant material benefits from their societies. Members of the hevrah kadisha might be guaranteed burial free of charge, but this was more of an honorific perquisite than a vital need; the burial society served the entire Jewish community, not just its own associates, and in any case, its members were generally among those who could afford its highest fees. The benefits of belonging to an association resided in the fellowship, the prestige, and the spiritual uplift associated with performing good works. Whatever mutual aid a traditional association extended to its members was likely to be of a spiritual, rather than material, nature. Thus many societies regularly recited prayers and read Psalms for their sick or deceased comrades.[43]

A relatively small number of hevrot did provide special assistance to members in time of need.[44] Craft guilds, in particular, usually included mutual aid among their primary functions. They not only regulated trade and provided vocational training, but also aided sick fellow tradesmen and established funds for the assistance of their widows and orphans.[45]

Hevrot derived revenues from regular dues, special assessments among members, fees for services to the public, fines for missed meetings and other infractions, and bequests. Some societies required contributions from members on the birth or marriage of a daughter, or the circumcision of a son. In earlier times, the kahal sometimes authorized the hevrot to levy a special tax on the entire community.[46] With money left over from their regular activities, societies often contributed some sort of ritual object or fixture to the town's main synagogue, or contributed to its upkeep. This practice emphasized the individual association's loyalty to the larger Jewish community, and also served to increase the society's prestige.[47]

Concern for personal honor also played a significant role in the internal culture of hevrot. In traditional society the distribution of honors was bound up with a hierarchy of standing and deference, and was often played out at religious services and other public gatherings. At hevrah banquets, for example, members sat in order of their status in the community. And on holidays congregants sometimes went to the homes of their leaders to pay them homage. Some societies or congregations actually came into being simply for the purpose of enabling their members to receive honorific assignments during worship. Even in the social welfare associations, it sometimes seemed that concern for prestige and honor outweighed the charitable purposes for which the societies were founded.[48]

Membership and election procedures encouraged the rotation of office holding, but they were hardly democratic in any modern sense. A candidate for membership paid an initiation fee and was often obliged to provide a feast for the group. Most associations mandated a period of "apprenticeship" of up to three years, during which a new member had no right to vote or hold a position of leadership.[49] Elections were indirect. Most often, several electors were chosen by lot from among the qualified members (generally, only married men). These, in turn, selected officers for the coming six months or year.[50] Such procedures held little appeal to the mass of Jews who emigrated to America, and they later sought to infuse their associations with a more democratic spirit.

Full membership in most of the traditional associations was limited to men, though women did play marginal roles in some. Many burial societies, for example, included women to tend to female corpses, and societies for visiting the sick sent women to look after female patients. The Psalm readers' society in Kartuz Bereze had female members who paid dues and met separately to read Psalms. In other localities women supplied books or candles for study. In no case, however, were they full members with the right to vote or hold office. Neither did they take part in social activities like the annual banquets, which were all-male affairs.[51] Yet women sometimes participated in less formal types of mutual assistance. When Sara Rabinowitsch investigated conditions in Mogilev around the turn of the century, she found that older women, who had "already begun to think of death and the next world," would sometimes organize a kind of informal fund with an indefinite membership drawn from among women living on the same street. The participants would collect money in charity boxes and hand it over to the organizer, who would distribute the funds to members in need.[52]

By the time Rabinowitsch returned to her hometown of Mogilev to study the organizations of the Jewish working class, the network of traditional voluntary associations was facing a severe crisis. Social and economic changes in the second half of the nineteenth century had set in motion a great migration of Jews from small towns to big cities, from the depressed northwestern provinces of the Pale to the developing south, abroad to Western Europe, and overseas to the Americas and elsewhere. Social changes also brought about a number of serious challenges to the Jewish communal system from new types of organization which had not existed before. Among these were political parties, labor unions, and mutual aid societies, all of which also affected the new Jewish communities established by the emigrants.

Industrialization throughout Eastern Europe combined with more efficient systems of transport to undermine much of the Jewish economy, particularly in the small towns. Local Jewish artisans had produced for a narrow market consisting of the peasants and townspeople of a proscribed area; they now found it difficult to compete with nascent consumer-goods industries manufacturing cheaper goods for distribution over a much wider area. Successful competition with large-scale producers required larger amounts of capital, which only a few independent craftsmen were able to accumulate. This led to a process of social differentiation in which some marginal small producers were driven out of business and forced to become employees of more successful colleagues. The local industrial sector, however, was not sufficiently developed to absorb the masses of proletarianized craftsmen who needed work. Moreover, many owners of larger factories, even Jews, refused to hire Jewish workers, mainly because they considered them less reliable than Gentile workers.

Local Jewish merchants suffered from similar pressures. The railroad opened up the field for systematic competition with more efficient businesses, and the availability of factory-made goods at set prices undermined the role of Jewish merchants as intermediaries between village and city. Moreover, urbanization of the general population led to increased competition from a growing non-Jewish middle class, and to the exclusion of Jews from some industrial and commercial sectors. At the same time, periodic agricultural crises and the generally depressed conditions of the peasantry further damaged Jewish interests. The expansion of railroad lines also undermined the livelihoods of many small-town Jewish transport workers.[53]

While a few manufacturers and financiers were able to take advantage of the changing economy to become wealthy, the others were either proletarianized or reduced to a marginal existence. One study by the Jewish Colonization Association (ICA) showed that in 1898 fully 18.8 percent of the Jewish population in the Pale of Settlement applied for public assistance so they could celebrate the Passover holiday. In Galicia nearly 10 percent of the Jewish population were beggars or without an occupation, and nearly twice as many people were dependent on each economically active Jew as depended on each working non-Jew.[54]

Explosive population growth, which outpaced the economy's ability to absorb the increase, led to further overcrowding in traditional Jewish trades and businesses. The Jewish population grew over 500 percent in Russia between 1800 and 1897 (from 1,000,000 to 5,189,000). In Galicia it expanded from 250,000 in 1800 to 811,000 in 1900, and in Romania from 135,000 in 1859 to 266,000 in 1899. In all cases the growth of the Jewish population outstripped that of the general population. The situation in Russia was further aggravated by the prohibition of Jewish migration from the Pale to the interior.[55]

A comparison between two adjacent provinces, one inside the Pale of Settlement, the other just outside it, illustrates dramatically the economic implications of the population explosion when joined with restriction of residence. In Smolensk Province, outside the Pale, there was one tailor for every 542 inhabitants, while in neighboring Mogilev, within the Pale, there was one tailor for every 70 residents. For cobblers the ratios were one per 280 in Smolensk and one per 127 in Mogilev.[56] Overcrowding in the trades naturally increased competition among Jewish artisans, which, in turn, further depressed their already meager incomes.

Many Jews responded to economic uncertainty by moving. One stream of migration led from small towns to small cities, and from there to larger ones, often within the same province. The Jewish populations of some cities where there had long been Jewish communities rose sharply—Vilna's Jewish population grew from 7,000 in 1797 to 63,996 in 1897. In Warsaw, where severe limitations on Jewish residence had kept the community small, the growth was even more dramatic—from 3,532 (4.5% of the population) in 1781 to 219,141 (33.9%) in 1897. In some cases Jews participated in the growth of new cities. For example, in 1793 Lodz was a sleepy village with only 11 Jews among its 193 residents. By 1897 it had become the Polish Manchester, and its 98,677 Jews made up 31.8 percent of the city's inhabitants.[57]

The similar growth of Odessa, at the extreme southern end of the Pale, highlights another trend in Jewish migration—the movement from the depressed northwest (Lithuania, Belorussia) to the booming regions of New Russia. While the northern provinces contained some of the most congested areas of Jewish population, the southern ones offered improved possibilities of employment.[58] There was also movement within the older areas of the Pale. Volhynia's Jewish population more than doubled between 1847 and 1897, and many Jews migrated from the northwest to Congress Poland, where wages were higher and opportunities greater in growing industrial centers.[59]

Movement, especially to the big cities, weakened the mechanisms of communal social control and strengthened the trend away from traditional modes of Jewish life. This was particularly pronounced in places like Odessa, which was something of a frontier city where the Jewish community lacked established institutions.[60] But the impact of movement away from traditionalism was felt even in the small shtetlekh, particularly within the working class. In Stoczek, for example, where many of the men had spent time working in Warsaw, by the time they returned, often after a stay of months or years, many had given up traditional Jewish dress and strict observance. They, in turn, influenced others in the same direction.[61]

Increased social tensions within the Jewish community often put the traditional associations under great strain. Established societies faced challenges from new groups, even within the context of conventional forms of organization. In Lutomiersk, for example, a society of tailors established as an auxiliary of the burial society to sew shrouds revolted against what it considered the extortionary practices of the hevrah kadisha. The tailors usurped the burial society's functions and began to inter corpses. Eventually a truce was achieved, but only after the tailors' society extracted conditions that enabled it to share in the prestige of the more exclusive group. According to the terms of the agreement, all members of the tailors' organization became members of the hevrah kadisha while maintaining a separate existence, retaining the privilege of sewing shrouds, and receiving one third of the hevrah kadisha's income.[62]

As class lines hardened, workers began to form their own independent organizations. Many craft guilds split into separate associations of journeymen and masters. Most of the new journeymen's hevrot patterned themselves after the old organizations, adopting their religious, social, and economic functions. However, many of them also took on the role of defending their members' interests against those of the master craftsmen. By the late 1880s artisans and industrial workers, including women, began to form *kassy*, organizations which were at first primarily intended for self-help but soon came under socialist influence and evolved into strike funds and trade unions.[63]

A new emphasis on mutual aid reflected the growing spirit of self-reliance among workers, artisans, and small traders. Some traditional associations, such as the hevrah of Psalm sayers in Kozlov, actually evolved into mutual benefit societies.[64] In Wloclawek in 1862, dissatisfaction with the established *bikur holim* society and hevrah kadisha led a group of 44 residents to form a separate hevrah to take care of sick members.[65] Jewish factory workers, clerks, and servants also set up mutual funds, sometimes with the help of their employers, sometimes independently.[66]

Jews also began to develop new forms of organization that differed from the old hevrot in their secular inspiration and purposes. Followers of the Haskalah, the Jewish Enlightenment, created their own associations that engaged in both mutual aid and cultural endeavors. These organizations no longer appealed to religious sentiment to justify their activities but instead viewed art, morality, politics, and even pure sociability as ends in themselves. Secularization also affected the use of language in two almost paradoxical ways. While some organizations sought to transform Hebrew into a spoken language and vehicle for modern cultural expression, others adopted Yiddish or the local tongue as their official language of record.[67]

By the turn of the century, several modern political movements vied for the support of the Jewish public.[68] In 1897, radical intellectuals and workers founded the General Jewish Workers' Alliance in Russia and Poland (Lithuania was added to the name later), known in Yiddish as the Bund. The Bund worked energetically for a program stressing revolutionary socialism, and played an important role in the development of a secular Jewish culture in the Yiddish language, which it championed as the vernacular of the masses. Representing a decisive break from Jewish tradition, the movement actively partook of the new international socialist culture then evolving in Europe. The Bund attracted a large and devoted following among the emerging Jewish proletariat and Jewish youth.[69]

The second pole around which modern Jewish politics revolved was Zionism. The Zionist movement sought to ameliorate the Jewish condition through the establishment of a Jewish homeland in Palestine, and, unlike the Bund, appealed overtly to ancient Jewish symbols and sentiments. Nevertheless, by stressing political action to achieve national liberation, Zionism too represented a dramatic break from the past. In time some Zionists combined their nationalism with religious orthodoxy, others with socialism.[70] Other groups attempted to synthesize various forms of socialism and Jewish nationalism and also attracted many adherents, particularly from among the younger generation.[71] Followers of these ideologies brought their enthusiasms with them when they emigrated, and in many cases the movements found echoes in American landsmanshaftn organized on ideological lines.

The same economic and social factors that prompted internal migration and new communal structures also spurred movement abroad. The flow of Eastern European Jews to Western Europe and overseas began as a trickle in the 1870s and increased to a torrent in subsequent decades. Some 2,500,000 Eastern European Jews left their native lands between 1881 and 1914, mostly to the United States, which received 75–80 percent of Russian Jewish emigrants.[72] While the Jewish flow followed a pattern similar to those of other European streams of migration, the Jews emigrated in proportionately greater numbers than any other European people except the Irish. They also tended to move in family units, thereby including more women, children, and elderly people, and had less of a propensity to return home once they reached their destinations.[73]

Antisemitism also played an important role in prompting Jewish emigration, especially in Russia and Romania. Spurts of emigration from Russia occurred after the wave of pogroms that followed the assassination of Tsar Alexander II in the spring of 1881, and after the infamous pogrom at Kishinev in 1903. In the long run, however, the terror of pogroms played less of a role in influencing migration patterns than did the government measures that directly affected the Jewish economy. In Russia, the so-called May Laws of 1882 stimulated emigration by expelling Jews from the villages and thereby increasing congestion in the towns.[74] In Romania, too, draconian limits on Jewish occupations beginning in the 1880s induced many to leave the country.[75]

A unique feature of the Romanian emigration was the organization of special mutual aid societies by young workers, artisans, and clerks who set out on foot for the port of Hamburg. Altogether, several thousand emigrants participated in this movement, which gave the participants experience in organization and formalized ties between emigrants from the same town, much as the landsmanshaftn were to do once they settled in America. The groups, known collectively as *fusgeyers,* called themselves "The Road-Walkers of Berlad," "Daughter of My People" (a women's group), "Bucharest Foot Wanderers," "Wandering Jew," "One Heart," and "Romanian Exodus." Before leaving some groups gathered in the synagogues and swore to share whatever material resources they had. They also issued publications in which they appealed for help and explained their reasons for leaving.[76]

Jewish immigration to America thus ran in several streams that met in New York to create a large community with diverse regional origins and local loyalties.[77] The largest tributary flowed out of tsarist Russia, with over 1.5 million Jews leaving for America between 1881 and 1914, including Lithuanian (from Lithuania and Belorussia), Polish, Bessarabian, and Ukrainian Jews. Not surprisingly, a disproportionate number of the Jewish emigrants from Russia came from the depressed northwestern areas near the Prussian border.[78] The next largest group, some 380,000 individuals, came from Austria-Hungary, primarily from Galicia, but also from Bukovina (like Galicia part of Austria) and Hungarian areas. About 80,000 Romanian Jews also made the journey to America, comprising about 4 percent of the overall immigration. Finally, many if not most of the nearly 39,000 Jews who arrived in the United States during that period from other countries had also originated in Eastern Europe.

The Eastern European legacy provided one set of parameters for the establishment of Jewish life in America. The Jews had developed strong attachments to the thousands of cities and towns where they had lived, and which they had made, to a great degree, their own. While some of the largest Jewish communities were the creations of the nineteenth century, Jewish roots in many places reached back for hundreds of years. Thrown together in the congested immigrant neighborhoods of the New World, it is not surprising that they retained a strong sense of identification with their native towns. The process of chain migration often even strengthened this bond, as earlier immigrants assisted the passage of relatives and friends, and landslayt helped one another adjust to their new surroundings.

When they set out to create new communal structures, even those immigrants who looked to Europe for inspiration had a number of models from which to choose. Participation in a variety of traditional voluntary associations (the hevrot) gave Eastern European Jews a great deal of organizational experience. But by the late nineteenth century, many judged the old arrangements inadequate and set out to revolutionize Jewish society. Socialists, Zionists, and others not only created new ideologies but new organizational forms as well. Immigrants brought these divisions with them to their new homes, where, ironically, the most conservative and the most radical members of the community most often based their associational lives on European precedents.

However, not all immigrants relied on Old-World experience. While many admired the traditional institutions of Jewish society or remained caught up in the ideological ferment of Europe, others looked to America for guidance. Such American phenomena as fraternal orders, mutual aid societies, and democratic aspirations thus formed the other important context for the development of the landsmanshaftn.

⌣2⌐

The New World

When Eastern European Jews arrived in America, they encountered a society in which voluntary associations played a vital role. Alexis de Tocqueville recognized the ubiquity of such organizations in American life during his visit to the United States in 1831–32. "Americans of all ages, all conditions, and all dispositions constantly form associations," he wrote. "They have not only commercial and manufacturing companies, in which all take part, but associations of a thousand other kinds, religious, moral, serious, futile, general or restricted, enormous or diminutive." For every purpose, from entertainment to temperance, noted the Frenchman, Americans set up a society. Indeed, it seemed to Tocqueville that associational life lay at the very foundation of the country's political system and even of its national identity.[1]

More strongly than any other organizational form, the fraternal order influenced American culture at the time when the large influx of East European Jews began. Modeled after the Masons and the Odd Fellows, hundreds of secret societies proliferated during the "golden age" of fraternity between the Civil War and the turn of the century. By 1901 close to 600 orders enrolled some five million members.[2] Most of them were middle-class native-born white men; smaller numbers of women also joined mixed organizations or formed women's auxiliaries to all-male groups. The orders also achieved widespread popularity among African-American, immigrant, and working-class men. In fact, the fraternal form permeated society, and a vast array of American organizations, from trade unions to temperance groups, took on the trappings of secret societies.

In addition to their social functions, fraternal organizations provided mutual aid to their members. This had both material and symbolic significance in a country whose people regarded self-reliance highly. By the end of the nineteenth century most mainstream orders and nearly all ethnic fraternals offered their members various sorts of life insurance and other benefits. Immigrants also organized tens of thousands of local mutual aid societies to protect themselves against the ravages of illness and indigence in life and the degradation of anonymity in death. The most basic of immigrant organizations, these groups often played an important role in the construction of larger and more elaborate ethnic institutions.

Immigrants typically patterned their organizations after those most prevalent in American society. In striking ways, the Jewish landsmanshaftn reflected the influences of the surrounding culture more clearly than they mirrored Jewish communal traditions (or innovations) in Eastern Europe. In particular, numerous hometown societies adopted the rituals and symbolism of the secret fraternal orders widespread in the late-nineteenth century United States. In many respects, the structure and communal role of the Jewish organizations also resembled strongly those of the mutual aid societies formed by nearly all ethnic groups.

Fraternal rites and common methods of mutual assistance entered the Eastern European Jewish community by several routes. A small number of immigrants from Russia, Galicia, and Romania had direct contact with American secret orders or organizations heavily influenced by fraternal culture. Another source was the large and vibrant New York German community, especially in the early years of mass Eastern European immigration. Many Yiddish-speaking Jews lived in close proximity to the Germans and adopted associational practices from their neighbors. Most important for the Eastern European Jews who came at the end of the century was the German-speaking Jewish community already in existence, with its own network of fraternal orders and mutual aid societies. Even before the Eastern Europeans arrived, these secular organizational forms had gained importance vis-a-vis the synagogues. Moreover, the Jewish community had begun to subdivide by country or region of origin as early as 1825. This process continued with the explosive growth of New York's Jewish population after 1880, when landsmanshaftn based on individual towns became the dominant type of organization.

All of American fraternal culture, including its ethnic manifestations, traced its origins to Freemasonry. The order started in seventeenth-century England, where gentlemen inspired by new ideas of scientific rationalism and seeking a synthesis of religion and Newtonian naturalism began to join guilds of stonemasons. Eventually, the "accepted" masons outnumbered the actual artisans and established their own lodges. In 1717, the formation of the Grand Lodge of England gave shape to the new movement and facilitated its spread to the Continent as well as to the British colonies in the New World.[3] Colonial American Masonry served mainly as a social club for the mercantile elite. But in the early nineteenth century large numbers of urban professionals, successful tradesmen, and thriving farmers entered the order and infused it with their own values of sobriety and self-restraint. Significantly, this new middle-class element also greatly enhanced Masonry's ritualistic aspects.[4]

Ironically, the "craft" which had originally extolled the virtues of the practical artisan developed an elaborate hierarchy of "degrees," or symbolic levels of membership, full of aristocratic pretension and pomp. Ritual "work," including the initiation of new candidates and the conferral of new degrees, became one of the central attractions of lodge meetings. The special costume (the artisan's apron) worn by members, the mystical opening ceremony, the specially appointed lodge room with its altar and open Bible, and the secrecy of passwords and signs distinguished the gathering from the "profane" world outside and lent an air of solemnity to the proceedings. Members of the order gained honor and distinction by climbing the hierarchy of degrees. Some special orders were open only to Masons who had reached a certain rank. Organizations like the Ancient Arabic Order of Nobles of the Mystic Shrine (the famous Shriners) and the Independent International Order of Owls (where each local "nest" was headed by a "Sapient Screecher") provided further opportunity for fanciful ceremonies and extravagant regalia.[5]

Anti-Masonic agitation of the 1820s and 1830s proved a serious but temporary setback for the order. Sparked by the alleged murder of a former Mason who had revealed the lodge's secrets, the movement fed on popular fears of conspiracy, as well as on religious objections to the Masons' somewhat heterodox philosophy and practice. Membership in the order plummeted. By mid-century, however, Freemasonry had recovered. Between 1850 and 1860, membership tripled from 66,142 to

193,763. The Masons continued to grow throughout the last half of the nineteenth century and were three quarters of a million-strong by 1897.[6]

The Odd Fellows followed the Masons closely, both chronologically and in terms of influence. Like Freemasonry, Odd Fellowship originated in England, but unlike the older order, the Odd Fellows were at first a working-class convivial society brought to the United States by artisans and mechanics. In the 1830s and 1840s a more middle-class element, including ex-Masons made homeless by the near collapse of their former order, entered the Odd Fellows and introduced to it a new ethic of sobriety and self-improvement. Advancing the cause of ritualism as well, the new members brought Odd Fellowship closer in line with Freemasonry. By 1897, the Independent Order of Odd Fellows, the American branch of the movement, counted 810,000 members.[7]

Inspired to a great extent by the Masons and Odd Fellows, American men had fashioned a wide array of secret societies by the late nineteenth century. Their activities centered on elaborate, dramatic, and colorful rituals. Though the orders strove for originality, the ceremonies and symbolism often betrayed common sources and many bore the stamp of Masonry, in both form and content. The fraternal genealogy grew tangled, as many founders gained organizational and ceremonial expertise through previous affiliation with one or more other fraternals. Dr. Darius Wilson alone intitiated at least four societies: the Knights of Honor, the Royal Arcanum, the American Legion of Honor, and the Royal Society of Goodfellows. When accused of plagiarizing the constitution of the Knights of Honor from that of the Ancient Order of United Workmen (AOUW), he answered that he had indeed copied the document from the AOUW, which had taken it from the Odd Fellow's Grand Lodge of Ohio, which had borrowed it from the Grand Lodge of the Masons.[8] Practiced brothers thus passed along rituals, symbols, mottos, passwords, handclasps, secret signals, and regalia, which became the stock in trade of all orders.[9]

Many orders struggled for years with unsatisfactory ceremonies until their leaders discovered a successful formula. Some organized around exotic motifs that permeated their activities. Ideally, the theme provided both exciting drama and an opportunity for moralistic instruction. Many initiation rites required that the candidate, clad in special (often scanty) attire, and sometimes blindfolded or bound, make a symbolic journey around a darkened and specially prepared lodge room. Led on this journey by a guide, the applicant met with various obstacles, including symbolic violence or threats of violence, even of death. Each of these encounters aimed to impress upon the novice basic lessons in the morality and philosophy of the order, as well as the seriousness of the commitment he was making by joining. Biblical themes, such as the binding of Isaac, the story of the Good Samaritan, the friendship of Jonathan and David, or the selling of Joseph, were perhaps the most popular sources of inspiration, while many societies favored allusions to knighthood and the Middle Ages.[10]

The themes and motifs of the initiation rites appeared in other activities as well. Opening and closing rituals at meetings, funeral services, degree-granting ceremonies, installation of officers, and founding ceremonies for new lodges all enabled the brothers to reiterate the sacred vows and lessons of their order. Exotic motifs influenced the names of local lodges (tribes, hives, tents, grottos, aeries, forests, groves, and so on) and officers (Sachems, Master Workmen, Grand Knights, Dictators, Noble Grands, and so on). In addition to lending color and drama, these themes also underscored the orders' frequent, though transparently false, claims to ancient origins. Masonry claimed no fewer than nine or ten different origin myths, the most common relating to the death and burial of Hiram Abiff, chief architect of Solomon's Temple. Similarly, the various Forestry orders traced themselves back to Robin Hood, the Odd Fellows to Roman soldiers in Wales, and the Woodmen to the dawn of civilization.[11]

Fraternal rituals served a number of social and cultural purposes. They helped to bind members together by giving them a sense of common experience, added a feeling of purpose to idle socializing, and sacralized serious but otherwise secular endeavors.[12] Initiation rites also helped participants make difficult transitions from one status to another. As the historian Mark Carnes has argued persuasively in regard to white Protestant men, fraternal ritual "provided solace and psychological guidance during young men's troubled passage to manhood in Victorian America." According to Carnes, this passage was a particularly difficult one for young men entering adult male status, having been raised by their mothers in the Victorian home. Moreover, the general perception that the mainstream Protestant churches had been infused with a feminine ethos led many man to look to the fraternal ritual for an alternative religious experience.[13]

Other groups besides white Protestant men also found fraternal organization and ceremony useful. Perhaps half a million women chose to enroll in women's and mixed-gender orders or in auxiliaries to all-male brotherhoods. Like other women's associations of the period, lodges contributed to the expansion of their members' sphere of public activity. But while they helped to blunt female opposition to male fraternalism, the form continued to be a primarily masculine one. Affiliated women's orders seldom developed the elaborate rites of the men's groups, and they remained subordinate to their male counterparts. In some cases the larger masculine orders were reluctant even to recognize their sister organizations. Still, most of the important men's orders had allied women's groups, the largest of which was the Order of the Eastern Star. Made up of Master Masons and their wives, widows, sisters, and daughters, the Eastern Star enrolled 160,000 members at the turn of the century, the majority of them women.[14]

African-American fraternalism corresponded to the larger white movement and shared many of its features. Like the white orders, black orders ultimately derived much of their culture from Freemasonry. Indeed, notwithstanding white Masonry's failure to recognize them, the black lodges had as valid a claim to Masonic legitimacy as the white. A lodge attached to the British military in Boston initiated the first fifteen African-American Masons in 1775. Led by Prince Hall, an immigrant originally from the West Indies, the black group eventually received its own charter from the Grand Lodge of England as African Lodge no.459. Prince Hall Masonry, as it came to be called, expanded first to other cities in the Northeast, then to the Midwest. Finally, after the Civil War, the order experienced its greatest growth, spreading to southern cities and eventually to the countryside.[15]

Like their white equivalents, the black Masons served as a model for a long list of imitators and competitors. Some of these African-American orders, including the Grand United Order of Odd Fellows and the Knights of Pythias of North and South America, Europe, Asia, and Africa, were black versions of orders popular among whites. Others, such as the Independent Order of St. Luke, the Grand Order of True Reformers, the Knights of Tabor, the Grand United Order of Galilean Fishermen, the Grand Order of Wise Men and Women, and the United Order of the Good Shepherd, were active only among blacks.[16]

Organizations formed to espouse a variety of causes and promote a range of interests cast themselves as fraternal orders and adopted their own elaborate ceremonies. Nativism, temperance, labor, white suprem-acy—all had spread their fraternal wings in the second half of the nineteenth century. The Order of United American Mechanics, the American Protective Association, the American Protestant Association, the Patriotic Order Sons of America, and the Junior Order, United American Mechanics espoused anti-Catholicism and nativism. Temper-ance had its champions in the Good Templars, the Sons of Temperance, and the Independent Order of Rechabites. The largest Union veterans' organization, the Grand Army of the Republic, acted as a fraternal order, as did the first incarnation of the Ku Klux Klan, which derived much of its "solemn and mysterious" ritual from the Knights of Malta.[17]

Many trade unions in the late nineteenth century used the lodge system and employed secret ceremonies to foster a sense of solidarity within their ranks. The largest of these workers' organizations, the Knights of Labor, which peaked at over 700,000 members in 1886, grew directly out of the fraternal tradition, though the exact origins of its rite were disputed. Created in 1869 by former members of a dis-banded Philadelphia garment cutters' union, the Knights adopted se-crecy partly as a defense against retaliation from employers. The first Master Workman, Uriah Stephens, belonged to the Masons, Odd Fel-lows, and Knights of Pythias, and composed the union's ritual. Other prominent knights later attributed the rites to either the Pythians or the Masons.[18]

Many working-class immigrants, including at least a few Yiddish-speaking Jews, first discovered fraternal ritual in the Knights of Labor. Long-time union activist Abraham Rosenberg later recalled that when he joined the Knights in 1885 with a group of Jewish cloakmakers, the veteran members drew a circle in chalk on the floor, placed a sword on the table and hung a globe by the door. The strange ritual evidently terrified the immigrants. "Seeing the sword, many of us thought that we would either all be slaughtered or inducted into the army," wrote Rosenberg. "Many of us had already bid their lives farewell."[19] Many Catholic workers also enrolled in the Knights, despite the church's ban on secret societies. Grand Master Workman Terrance Powderly, himself a Roman Catholic, sought continually to modify the ritual and make it more acceptable to Catholic sensibilities.

Fraternal ritual appealed to immigrant men as much as it did to the native-born, and the rites of ethnic orders paralleled those of the mainstream societies. In some ways, however, immigrants and natives used the ceremonies and symbols in different ways. Although immigrant and native rituals resembled each other in most respects, they meant something different to immigrants, who came from other cultures and therefore faced divergent questions of identity, than they did to native-born Americans. Immigrant initiation rites aimed largely at reconciling lingering loyalties to native lands, languages, and religions with the deep desire to integrate fully into American life. Immigrant fraternalists thus intended explicitly, though not always fully consciously, to invent new "ethnic traditions" that would express harmoniously both aspects of their personalities. Indeed, to many groups, including the Jews, the very act of expressing their particularity through such a quintessentially American medium as fraternal ritual seemed a major step toward that goal.

Given their church's opposition to secret societies, the avid interest in fraternalism expressed by Roman Catholic men underscores the powerful attraction exerted by this organizational culture in the late nineteenth century. The church hierarchy's vociferous antagonism to secret orders dated back to 1738, when Pope Clement XII issued the first of a number of papal pronouncements condemning the deism of the Masons and the oaths required of new initiates. American bishops reiterated their specific objection to oaths binding new members "to secrecy, especially not to divulge a communication to be subsequently made, and upon whose nature they can pass no reasonable judgement when they undertake the obligation." A further objection concerned the aspect of secrecy itself, which, the church argued, would prevent a Catholic fraternalist from being fully open with his confessor. Moreover, the church suspected many secret orders of subversive social and political goals. Indeed, an 1861 pastoral letter of the Provincial Council of New York called secret societies "one of the most fatal snares laid to entrap innocent youth."[20]

Nonetheless, many Catholics defied the ban and joined lodges. Some made their way into the general orders. Many more organized their own societies, which adopted the trappings of fraternal ritual but maintained their loyalty to the church. The Ancient Order of Hibernians (AOH) and the Clan na Gael, established by Irish immigrants, demonstrated the appeal of the fraternal system and its adaptability to a variety of ends. Members of both the Clan and the AOH expressed their commitment to the cause of Irish nationalism through a ceremonial medium foreign to Ireland but native to North America. During the Clan na Gael's initiation rite, written by Mason, Odd Fellow, and Pythian James Sheedy, the candidate's hands were tied behind his back, and members used a sword to impress upon the newcomer the necessity of force in the struggle against England. Despite the ritual's proclamation of ethnicity and national purpose—"Irishmen banded together for the purpose of freeing Ireland"—a group of prominent exiles who arrived in America in 1871 found the ceremony quite foreign.[21]

While the Hibernians and Clan na Gael espoused Irish nationalism, the Knights of Columbus strove explicitly to reconcile its members' Catholicism with their ardent Americanism. The Knights' ritual used the voyages of Christopher Columbus as a motif to underscore the Catholic contribution to America from the moment of discovery. The ceremonial for the fourth degree, known as the "Sir Knights," emphasized the Columbian order's commitment to good Catholic citizenship: "Proud in the olden days was the boast, 'I am a Roman Catholic'; prouder yet today is the boast, 'I am an American citizen'; but the proudest boast of all times is ours to make, 'I am an American Catholic citizen.'" The Knights faced considerable opposition from some Catholic clergy and lay leaders, but they rejected the charge made by one prominent Catholic editor that their order was "little more than a hodge-podge of Masonic apery diluted with religion." Indeed, they preferred to see their movement as a weapon against the proscribed secret societies in the battle for the hearts of American Catholic young men.[22]

German immigrants too participated actively in a variety of fraternal orders, both together with native-born Americans and separately in their own organizations. Many German immigrants, particularly those in the upper middle class, belonged to Masonic, Odd Fellow, and Druidic lodges. The largest German-American order was the Orden der Hermanns Soehne (Order Sons of Hermann), brought into existence in 1840 partially in response to nativist sentiment. The order took as its model an "ancient Teuton warrior," and adopted as one of its goals the fostering of German language and culture. By 1896 the Hermanns Soehne claimed 90,000 members. A second society, the German Order of the Harugari, had similar aims and took its name from legendary ancient Germanic tribes of forest dwellers.

At least two German lodges resulted from splits in general orders to which German-Americans had previously belonged. These cases bring to light some of lines of influence between "mainstream" and ethnic fraternal culture. From its very beginning the Improved Order of Red Men, though its symbolism was quintessentially American, included a large number of German members, many of whom met in their own lodges where they performed the pseudo-Indian rituals in the German language. By 1850, however, in the midst of the nativist upsurge, the order divided largely along ethnic lines, as English-speaking members adopted a less tolerant attitude toward cultural diversity within the organization. The resulting German-American order, the Independent Order of Red Men, continued to use the old ritual. Likewise, the Improved Order, Knights of Pythias, left the similarly named general order when the latter outlawed the use of the German language in 1895.[23]

Jews, many of them German-speaking, also participated in the nineteenth-century boom of fraternal orders. Some joined the general orders, including Masonry, which, despite its Protestant overtones, attracted many Jews with its universalistic and liberal religious ideal. The Masons' use of Old-Testament imagery and Hebrew words helped Jews to feel at home in the order, even as many Jewish businessmen identified strongly with the craft's middle-class constituency. Individual Jews joined general lodges, while others joined all-Jewish or mostly Jewish branches of the Masons, Odd Fellows, Knights of Pythias, Harugari, and Hermanns Soehne.[24]

Other Jews found the fraternal idea appealing but preferred to implement it within the confines of their own religious and ethnic group. By the 1880s Jewish fraternal societies enrolled more members than any other Jewish organizations in America. B'nai B'rith (Sons of the Covenant) was the first and largest, with 25,000 members in 1880, followed by Independent Order Free Sons of Israel with 11,000, Kesher shel Barzel (Bond of Iron) with 9,000, and Improved Order Free Sons of Israel with 3,300. Other orders established in the nineteenth century included the Independent Order of True Sisters (closely allied with B'nai B'rith), Order Brith Abraham, Independent Order Sons of Benjamin, American Star Order, Improved Order of B'nai B'rith, Independent Order Brith Abraham, Order Ahavas Israel, Independent Order Free Sons of Judah, Independent Order Sons of Abraham, Independent Order of American Israelites, Independent Western Star Order, and Knights of Zion.[25]

Each of these orders shared in the general fraternal culture but infused it with its own ethnic content. Masonic elements (the all-seeing eye, for instance) vied with Judaic symbols such as the menorah and the tablets of the law. Bible stories furnished much of the material for their initiation narratives. The names of the orders included allusions to the patriarchs and Jewish peoplehood together with the very fraternal and very American word "independent." The maze of overlapping memberships in both Jewish and non-Jewish orders once again explains the diffusion of ritual and symbolic features, as experienced fraternalists transported their favorite ritual elements into the new lodges they joined.[26]

Independent Order B'nai B'rith set the pattern followed by other Jewish fraternals. It was founded on New York's Lower East Side in 1843 by twelve young German-speaking Jewish immigrants, several of whom had been Masons or Odd Fellows. Indeed, they appear to have been motivated to establish an exclusively Jewish lodge partly by a number of recent instances of discrimination within those two orders. In any case, the new fraternity combined Jewish symbols, including the menorah, with a hierarchy of six degrees and a typical array of rites, regalia, and passwords. Even the Hebrew titles accorded to officers— Grand Nasi Abh (sic, President), Grand Aleph (Vice President), and Grand Sopher (Secretary)—were reminiscent of the exotic terms used in other orders.[27]

By removing the locus of Jewish identity from the synagogue, B'nai B'rith helped to create a new kind of secular Jewish culture based on a fusion of American and traditional Jewish symbols. Their lodge enabled B'nai B'rith members to maintain a Jewish affiliation and pledge their fealty to what they considered the best traditions of the Jewish people while at the same time participating in the most American of activities. The ritual proclaimed the compatibility of Jewish and American values. B'nai B'rith thus served, as the historian Deborah Dash Moore has written, to "bridge the gap from immigrant status to American status," a transition many "sons of the covenant" made with enviable success. The fraternal framework also promised to transcend the growing religious rift between Orthodox and Reform Jews, supplying a meeting place broad enough to embrace a wide spectrum of Jewish practice and belief. In theory, B'nai B'rith represented a Judaic version of Masonic universalism, though, like the Masons, it often fell short of the ideal.[28]

The other Jewish orders played similar roles, but each catered to a different constituency. B'nai B'rith remained an organization of German and English-speaking Jews, attracting only a few Eastern Europeans. Kesher shel Barzel consisted mostly of immigrants from Poland.

Some orders, such as Brith Abraham and its offspring, Independent Order Brith Abraham, acted as links between Jews from Central and Eastern Europe. Started by German-speaking immigrants from Germany and Hungary, they opened their doors to Yiddish-speaking newcomers, eventually absorbing a considerable number of landsmanshaft lodges. In this way, fraternal culture spread into all corners of the Jewish community.[29]

The fraternal principle of aid to brothers and sisters in times of need also attracted many to the orders. Organizations that offered a formal package of benefits differed from those which, like the Masons, preferred to emphasize the spontaneous nature of charity arising from the love of one's comrades. Most of the immigrant societies belonged to the former category—understandably, given the newcomers' need to construct new communal mechanisms for social support. In B'nai B'rith's early years, for example, its lodges provided their members with a sick benefit of three or four dollars a week, funeral expenses, and a thirty-dollar death benefit with a pension of one dollar a week for widows of members (plus fifty cents for the oldest child and twenty-five cents for each additional child up to the age of 13).[30] Native organizations such as the Odd Fellows, Foresters (several factions of which led independent existences), United Ancient Order of Druids, Independent Order of Rechabites, and Knights of Pythias also made available a regular list of benefits. Masons rejected the institutionalization of mutual aid but visited their sick, provided funerals and burials for out-of-town fellows, took up collections to aid indigent associates, and voted stipends to aged members.[31]

Beginning in 1869, the Ancient Order of United Workmen (AOUW) became the first fraternal organization to combine all the ritual features of the older orders with a standard and centrally administered system of life insurance. Founded by John J. Upchurch, a Mason and member of several other orders, the AOUW adopted such Masonic symbolism as the all-seeing eye and the square-and-compass. In addition to symbols, however, the AOUW offered a cash $2,000 death benefit financed by a uniform one-dollar assessment on each member. The combination of fraternalism and insurance proved very popular. Not only did the AOUW attract over 300,000 members by 1895, but many other fraternals imitated the successful formula. By the turn of the century more than half of American secret societies had an insurance feature, and they became a rapidly growing sector of the fraternal world.[32]

The rise of benefit orders corresponded with the public's growing acceptance of life insurance. Earlier religious and cultural objections to this form of insurance gave way in the late nineteenth century to a belief that the practice was a moral and efficient method of providing for widows and orphans. Nevertheless, people some still resisted the valuation of human life in cold monetary terms spelled out in an impersonal contract. But benefit plans as part of a web of brotherly obligations in the context of fraternal organizations were easier to accept. The appeal to the values of mutual aid, combined with the relatively low cost of fraternal coverage, explains why in 1895 fraternal organizations had more insurance in force than did the commercial companies.[33]

In one respect, fraternal practices lagged behind those of the commercial insurance companies. Many orders persistently rejected suggestions to adopt scientific actuarial tables or rates graduated by age. As M. W. Sackett, a contemporary observer and participant in the fraternal movement, explained, "They looked upon a graded assessment as a violation of the principle that perfect mutuality be accorded one brother to another."[34] Unfortunately, this unsound fiscal policy often led to instability, and many orders collapsed under the burden of aging memberships and falling revenues. The following process repeated itself any number of times: as the members aged, death rates increased, insurance assessments rose, and younger individuals hesitated to join, producing a vicious circle of increasing costs and decreasing income.[35]

Many leaders of the benefit orders recognized the need for measures to protect their memberships from the instability caused by flawed insurance practices. The Royal Arcanum adopted graduated rates as early as 1877, and others later followed suit. The National Fraternal Congress (NFC), a federation of fraternal insurance societies set up in 1886, first raised the issue of scientific rate structures in 1895, and eventually produced its own actuarial table. The NFC (and several similar federations) pressed affiliated societies to reform their insurance practices. Many organizations also attempted to build large reserve funds as buffers against sudden surges of claims.[36]

Orders usually attempted to safeguard their treasuries by regulating eligibility for membership. To the traditional standards concerning a candidate's character, they added health requirements. Virtually all the orders fixed limits on the age at which a new member could be admitted and required a medical health certificate. A few denied entrance to workers engaged in dangerous professions and to residents of areas deemed unhealthful. The Modern Woodmen of America, for example, recruited only in the upper Midwest (except for certain large cities) and barred railroad workers, miners, gunpowder factory workers, baseball players, aeronauts, sailors, football players, and submarine operators.[37] Although character standards varied from order to order, admission procedures were aimed at admitting only worthy and morally upstanding men. A candidate needed the endorsement of several members, and the lodge appointed a committee to investigate his background. Only after the committee reported on his fitness did the brothers vote on admission. A unanimous ballot was necessary for acceptance.[38]

A multitude of local immigrant mutual aid societies fulfilled many of the same functions as the fraternal orders, from which they copied both admissions procedures and varying amounts of ritual. In time some of the local societies even became branches of the larger fraternal bodies, though most remained unaffiliated. Both societies and lodges provided an important measure of material security to their largely working-class members. They took care of sick members by granting them a sum of money weekly to make up for lost wages and sent visiting committees to inquire into patients' needs. Societies contracted with doctors to treat members and their families for low annual fees, and a few even built their own hospitals and clinics. Numerous associations offered such additional services as disability or unemployment insurance, aid in finding employment, and low-interest loans. Death benefits were invariably central to the appeal of the ethnic societies. They provided appropriate funerals, often requiring all members to attend, and burial, often in their own cemeteries. Like the beneficiary orders, ethnic mutual aid societies proffered payments to survivors, ranging from small amounts raised by a tax on the members (usually one dollar per member) in the case of independent societies, to a fixed benefit of as much as $2,000 in the case of larger orders.[39]

In addition to their material benefits, societies furnished venues for social interaction and generated ways to acquire self-esteem and competence on a variety of levels. Members looked forward to informal socializing before and after regular meetings. Other events—balls, picnics, lectures, and sporting events—were typical elements of American organizational life.[40] Election to societal office brought honor to immigrants with few other opportunities to acquire recognition. The organizations adjudicated disputes and enforced a sense of decorum and morality both inside the meeting hall and out. Constitutions contained provisions against the use of foul language and the slander of another member, and denied benefits for venereal disease or for injuries arising out of "arguments, drunkenness or acts of rowdyism."[41] High participation rates, at least in terms of formal affiliation, illustrate the centrality of the societies in the lives of many immigrants. The associations often enrolled a majority of eligible individuals in a given community.[42]

The pool of eligible individuals was usually restricted to men; the degree of women's participation depended in part on the attitudes of each ethnic group. Anglo-American culture shared with most ethnic cultures limits on the public role allowed to women, and the benefits offered by mutual aid societies made them an especially male province. Men acted in their capacities as chief family providers when they joined a benefit society. The name of an Italian society in Utica, New York, is most explicit: the Società Capi dei Famigli Italo-Americana di Mutuo Soccorso (Italian-American Society of Heads of Families for Mutual Aid).[43]

Immigrants from the same region or locality in the old country frequently organized their own independent societies or fraternal lodges. (The Jewish landsmanshaftn constitute just one example of this phenomenon.) The larger the ethnic group, the finer were the distinctions made between natives of different villages and towns.[44] Acquaintance in the old country was a logical point of departure for the organization of recent arrivals, but such ties persisted long after the immigrants had adjusted to life in the New World. In some cases, it appears, the importance of hometown ties even increased after a period of time in America. As Stanley Nadel has reported, associations based on occupation dominated New York's "Kleindeutschland" in the 1850s. Only in subsequent decades did its inhabitants renew old ties, transforming "a nostalgic sense of identity with a place in Germany into a living social network."[45]

Many immigrants had extensive experience with associations in their lands of birth, and some historians, seeking to stress a high degree of cultural continuity between the Old World and the New, have pointed out instances in which immigrants attempted to recreate in America the societies they had known in Europe.[46] For the most part, however, immigrant organizations in the United States resembled each other so remarkably that it is hard to escape the conclusion that they were largely American in form, if not in inspiration. Their membership requirements, leadership structures, benefits, activities, even, in many cases, their names all followed a like pattern.[47] Significantly, immigrant associations closely paralleled those of African-Americans, another group excluded from mainstream American society, though not so foreign to it. Whether commonalities between the organizations of European immigrants and American blacks reflect interaction between the two groups remains unclear. But their similarities reveal they both followed an American model.[48]

Different immigrant groups influenced each other more obviously, especially when they had some sort of linguistic, religious, or political affinity. Already rooted communities transmitted their organizational cultures to newer ones in two ways. First, individual ethnic pioneers often affiliated with congenial groups until enough of their own com-patriots arrived for them to organize independently. Early Italian arri-vals in San Francisco, for example, joined the churches and societies of the predominantly Catholic French residents.[49] Second, large and well-organized communities set examples for nascent nearby groups. In New York, the impressive German associational network influenced the Czech and the Jewish communities, which clustered near the German neighborhoods.[50]

Immigrant societies reflected religious and political divisions among the populations they served. Slovaks, for example, chose secular, Catholic, Lutheran, and Calvinist organizations. Much of the Polish-American community lined up behind either the militantly Catholic Polish Roman Catholic Union, or the nationalist and anti-clerical Polish National Alliance. In predominantly working-class communities socie-ties sometimes lent crucial support to unionization efforts and strikes. A well-developed communal network of organizations could spell the difference between success and failure in labor struggles. Thus Irish workers in Troy, New York, who sustained a vibrant associational life, organized trade unions much more quickly than did French-Canadian workers in nearby Cohoes, who lacked such a web of affiliations. Since some trades harbored concentrations of immigrants from particular countries or regions, unions even sometimes evolved out of ethnic mutual aid societies.[51]

Despite all of these divisions, immigrant associations played a central role in overcoming regional, religious, and class differences, and in defining their respective ethnic communities. Societies often partici-pated in public ethnic rituals, which, like their own organizational ceremonies, helped delineate the boundaries and cultural contents of group life. Drawn from both old-country and New-World sources, these rituals often fused a collection of particularistic village or regional affiliations to shape a broader American ethnic identity. For instance, the *festa* of the Madonna del Carmine, brought to New York in 1882 by a society of immigrants from a town in the province of Salerno, soon emerged under the auspices of the Catholic Church as a major annual event which drew celebrants of all regional backgrounds. By absorbing the faithful from other regions in Italy, the cult of the Madonna of 115th Street helped create an Italian-American community. Likewise, German immigrant *vereine* contributed to the public pageantry which engendered a sense of German-American "communitas" despite religious and regional differences among their members.[52] Nevertheless, as the persistence of regional and village associations shows, immigrants retained a sense of local loyalties alongside newly assumed wider identities.

Mutual aid societies helped build ethnic communities on the practical level as well. They often preceded other communal institutions and were sometimes the driving force behind the establishment of larger structures such as church bodies and national fraternal orders. The national ethnic organizations centralized the provision of benefits along the same lines as the nonethnic fraternal benefit orders. In addition, they became leading actors in the cultural and political affairs of their communities, sponsoring ethnic cultural activities, citizenship programs, and language schools. National organizations also developed a corps of educated and sophisticated leaders able to represent the interests of their groups in broader arenas.[53]

Jewish life in America reflected the centrality of mutual aid societies and lodges in the creation of ethnic identity even before the arrival of large numbers of Jews from Eastern Europe. In fact, voluntary associations laid the foundations for many Jewish communities in America. This was especially true of smaller centers, where benevolent societies often predated synagogues. In the absence of any other institutions, these societies provided burial, health care, charity, and religious services. Inevitably, they became social centers as well, molding local Jewish residents into cohesive communities. In many places religious congregations emerged out of or alongside the early associations, but in small towns mutual aid societies or B'nai B'rith lodges often remained the only Jewish organizations.[54]

In New York, North America's largest and oldest Jewish community began with a religious congregation. Nevertheless, mutual aid societies took on increasing importance as the nineteenth century progressed. Moreover, as the population expanded, it subdivided along geographical lines as immigrants from various countries organized their own synagogues and associations. By the 1860s small numbers of Jews from Russian Poland began to form congregations and societies named for their hometowns. The handful of landsmanshaftn established before 1880 set the precedent for the thousands that were formed during the ensuing period of mass immigration from Eastern Europe.

Congregation Shearith Israel held undisputed dominance over the city's Jewish community until 1825. Constituted by the first Jews to arrive in New Amsterdam in 1654, Shearith Israel governed the Jewish population's religious life, regulated its morals, adjudicated disputes, arranged for burial, and distributed charity. Early Jewish associations remained affiliated with the congregation. The first such society about which there is significant information was the Hebrah Gemilut Hasidim, founded before 1785. Benefits accorded to its members included care during illness, burial, and a *minyan* (the required quorum for prayer) and compensation for loss of wages during *shivah*, the seven-day mourning period prescribed by Jewish law. The Hebrah also engaged in charitable work and held an annual celebration. When it disbanded in 1790, its assets reverted to Congregation Shearith Israel. The Hebra Hased Vaamet, which provided burial to its own members and to members of the Congregation, followed in 1802.[55]

In 1825 the process of division by nationality began when German and Polish Ashkenazim broke away from Shearith Israel, which followed the Sephardic ritual, and started New York's second synagogue, Congregation Bnai Jeshurun. By mid-century Jews with origins in different countries gathered separately in their own synagogues: English Jews in Shaarey Tefilah, Dutch in Bnai Israel, Polish in Shaarey Zedek, Beth Israel, Beth Abraham, and Beth Elohim, and the more numerous Germans in Anshe Chesed, Rodeph Shalom, Shaar Hashomayim, Emanu-El, Shaarey Rachamim, Neveh Zedek, Bnai Zion, Aderet El, and others. The "Germans" further divided by region of origin. By the 1830s, these congregations had taken over from Shearith Israel the duty of burying deceased indigent Jews from their respective countries.[56]

At first New York's Jewish mutual aid societies formed within the synagogues, but by the 1840s they began to act more independently. For example, the Hebrah Gmilut Hassed, also known as the Hebrew

Mutual Benefit Society, started in 1826 as part of Congregation Bnai Jeshurun. When the congregation split in 1845, the society remained intact, so that it now included both members and nonmembers of its parent congregation. In the 1850s societies began to control the burial of deceased members. When in 1859 the Hebrew Mutual Benefit Society acquired its own cemetery, it became possible for the first time to receive a Jewish burial without recourse to a synagogue. Increased secularization of the Jewish population and lower dues further encouraged the independent societies' expanded role. These included associations based on country of origin such as the Netherland Israelitish Sick Fund Society (1859) and the Société Israélite Française (1873), as well as craft groups such as the First Hebrew Bakers Sick Benevolent Society (1872) and the Purim Lodge of the Knights of St. Crispin, a shoemakers' organization.[57]

The internal culture of the Jewish societies in the nineteenth century duplicated that of their non-Jewish counterparts. Members gathered annually at balls, banquets, concerts, and theater parties. Likewise, the banquets were often open only to men and their fundraising pitches were punctuated by toasts and ample consumption of alcohol. In all of their undertakings the associations evinced a great love for pomp and celebration. All sorts of ceremonies, from the dedications of communal buildings to the installation of rabbis and society officers, attracted large crowds.[58]

An Eastern European Jewish community began to take shape as early as mid-century. The first Russian congregation, the Beth Hamedrash, was founded in 1852. Soon immigrants from Russian Poland and Galicia fashioned synagogues and mutual aid societies bearing the names of their home cities and provinces. The oldest Eastern European landsmanshaft benefit association on record was the Krakauer Society, Chebra Raufei Chaulim of the State of New York, incorporated in 1855. Among the earliest landsmanshaft congregations were Chevrah Kadisha B'nai Israel Kalvarier Congregation (1862) and the Chevrah T'hilim Anshei Viskover (1860 or 1864). More congregations and societies followed in the 1870s, as the trickle of immigration quickened. Before 1882, Eastern European immigrants incorporated some eighty-seven landsmanshaftn. Seven of these consisted of natives of Cracow, including the first women's association, the Cracower Ladies Society (1868).[59] These early efforts laid the groundwork for the thousands of landsmanshaftn that arose later.

When Yiddish-speaking Jewish immigrants began to arrive in the United States in large numbers after 1881, they discovered an American society in which voluntary association formed the very basis for all aspects of communal life. American experience strongly influenced the choices made by the newly arrived Eastern European Jews as they developed their own communal structures. The fraternal orders of native-born Americans, other ethnic groups, particularly the nearby Germans with their well-developed *vereinwesen,* and the established Jewish community with its congregations and benefit societies divided by country of origin, all reinforced the ideals of voluntary association, mutual aid, and fraternalism. The new immigrants soon adopted these elements and put them to use in varying combinations with traditions brought along from the old country.

Charter members of the First Independent Storoznetzer Bukowiner Sick and Benevolent Association, founded in 1903. (Photo courtesy of YIVO Institute for Jewish Research.)

Satanov, a shtetl in Ukraine, just over the border with Galicia. Immigrants from Satanov in New York founded the Satanover Benevolent Society in 1903. (Photo courtesy of YIVO Institute for Jewish Research.)

Lodz, a major industrial center in Poland; the photo was probably taken in the 1920s or 1930s. There were at least fourteen Lodzer landsmanshaftn in New York, reflecting the size of the city and the mix of its Jewish population. (Photo courtesy of YIVO Institute for Jewish Research.)

CONSTITUTION

— of the —

KOLOMEAR
FRIENDS ASSOCIATION

Organized January 31st, 1904

107

Reiter & Reiner, Printers, 102-4 Attorney St., N. Y.

The constitution of the Kolomear Friends Association,
organized in 1904. Landsmanshaftn commonly issued
their constitutions in the form of small booklets in
Yiddish and English. (Photo courtesy of YIVO Institute for Jewish Research.)

A composite portrait of the officers of the United Wilner Ladies Relief in celebration of the organization's fifteenth anniversary. It was not uncommon for women's societies to have male officers. (Photo courtesy of YIVO Institute for Jewish Research.)

Delancey Street, 1908. The sign on the second-floor fire escape (just left of "Corsets") indicates that the tenement building is home to the First Lemberger Congregation, a landsmanshaft synagogue. (Photo courtesy of the Municipal Archives of the City of New York.)

In Brisk, sitting under Polish and American flags, United Brisker Relief delegates Jacob Finkelstein (first from left) and H. Kleinberg (third from left) distribute relief money from America, 1921. (Photo courtesy of YIVO Institute for Jewish Research.)

THE LOWER EAST SIDE

25 Public School 63
26 Music School Settlement
27 Asch Building
28 Astor Library
29 Cooper Union
30 Hebrew Technical School for Boys
31 Labor Temple
32 Rand School
33 Hebrew Charities Building
34 Metropolitan Life Building
35 Madison Square Garden
36 City College

Boundaries of sub-ethnic districts
······ Hungarian
─┼─ Galician
←o─o→ Rumanian
∿∿∿ Levantine
─ ─ ─ Russian

Shaded blocks indicate Tenth Ward

0   ¼ MILE

1 Newspaper Row
2 World Building
3 Chatham Sq. Library
4 Beth Israel Hospital
5 Israel Elchanan Yeshiva
6 Seward Park Library
7 Forward Building on Yiddish Newspaper Row
8 Educational Alliance
9 Henry St. Settlement and Clinton Hall
10 Machzike Talmud Torah
11 Hebrew Sheltering House
12 Hebrew Technical School for Girls
13 Home for Aged
14 Jewish Maternity Hospital
15 Young Men's Benevolent Association
16 Camp Huddleston Hospital Ship School
17 Beth Hamedrash Hagadol
18 Pro-Cathedral Mission
19 University Settlement
20 Grand Theater
21 Yiddish Rialto
22 Thalia Theater
23 People's Bath
24 Police Headquarters

Map by Samuel H. Bryant from *The Promised City* by Moses Rischin. (Courtesy of Harvard University Press.)

~ 3 ~

Landsmanshaft Culture and Immigrant Identities

Jews from all over Eastern Europe met in New York. Though they shared the same culture, spoke the same language, and appeared to outsiders to be a homogeneous group, they sometimes seemed very different to one another. Old-country folklore and prejudices concerning regional characteristics carried over to the New World, where they became more noticeable in an environment in which Jews from a variety of places interacted on a daily basis. When asked by a journalist what she thought of her Russian-Jewish neighbors, one Galician woman responded: "A strange sort of people. You can't understand a word they say. They always shout and talk with their hands . . . And their cooking! Dishes which one should never even see in a Jewish house! They put sugar in everything and call everything by the wrong name . . . Oh, leave me be, its simply impossible to get along with them."[1] As eminent a figure as David Blaustein, director of the Educational Alliance and himself an immigrant from Russia, subscribed to some of the common stereotypes of the day. Russians, he believed, were "intellectual," Galicians "emotional," Romanians "materialistic," and Hungarians "imaginative."[2] Some commentators attributed distinct character traits even to residents of neighboring towns. Natives of Pinsk, for example, were said to be "active [and] lively," while those who hailed from Pinsk's twin city of Karlin were "lazy [and] phlegmatic."[3]

Geographic origin had more than just symbolic significance. Established immigrants often brought newly arrived friends and relatives into the shops where they worked, creating concentrations of compatriots in various factories, trades, and even entire industries. In the early years men's tailors hailed mainly from Suwalki Province in Poland, pressers from Bessarabia in the southwest corner of the Pale of Settlement, furriers from Pukhovichi in Belorussia, pocketbook makers from Warsaw, and neckwear makers from Hungary. In the 1880s, before the labor movement gained strength and stability, workers did not always distinguish sharply between landsmanshaft society and union. Locals in several trades organized along landsmanshaft lines.[4]

The same migratory chains that brought compatriots together in the workplace also fashioned small regional neighborhoods within New York's main immigrant Jewish quarter on the Lower East Side. Hungarians lived above Houston Street between Avenue B and the East River. Galicians settled between Houston and Broome streets, east of Clinton along Attorney, Ridge, Pitt, and Willet. The Romanian quarter included Chrystie, Forsyth, Eldridge, and Allen streets between Houston and Grand streets on the north and south, and the Bowery and Allen Street to the west and east. The rest of the Lower East Side belonged to the "Russians," a broad category of Jews from the diverse areas of the Pale.[5]

These regional sections changed over time as the entire Jewish quarter expanded and as various streams of immigration altered the composition of the Eastern European Jewish community. To be sure, the neighborhoods were hardly monolithic; thus Galicians, for example, may have constituted only a large minority of residents on any given street in the Galician quarter.[6] Nevertheless, each regional neighborhood possessed a unique atmosphere. Observers writing in the Yiddish press thought the Romanian Quarter was "distinguished by its liveliness."[7] Galician and Hungarian areas, on the other hand, had an air of piety. "When you walk through the streets of the Jewish quarters of New York on a Friday evening," wrote one journalist, "and you see winking at you from the windows the monotonous, but quietly eloquent and modestly sparkling Jewish Sabbath candles, and you hear the sadly joyous singing of the Jewish Sabbath songs—then you know that for the most part you are walking past the tenement houses in which the [Austro-Hungarian] Jews live."[8]

Immigrants congregated informally with fellow-townspeople in a variety of settings. Restaurants catering to natives of various localities in Europe dotted the Lower East Side, where one could eat "familiar dishes" among "familiar people" and feel "very much at home."[9] Street corners often served as gathering places for immigrants seeking out their landslayt. Looking for compatriots from the Galician city of Lvov (Lemberg)? "Do you want to meet a Lemberger landsman, a newly arrived greenhorn who can tell you all the latest news from that city, or a 'yellowed' older immigrant who already knows how to make a transfer on the streetcars or cheat the ticket-chopper on the elevated? If so, go to the northeast corner of Clinton and Rivington streets. There you can find out about jobs, familial scandals, landslayt parties and other things which may interest you." Opposite the Lemberger corner, where people took pride in their big-city sophistication, was the Tshortkover corner, where the Hasidic rebbe's court was the topic of discussion. Galicians from Stanislavov, Kolomyya, Ternopol, Przemysl, and Bobrka all had their own corners, while natives of the Belorussian town of Oshmyany met near Cohen and Silverstein's soda stand at the corner of Pike and Henry. Bricklayers from the industrial center of Bialystok gathered, together with other Jewish tradesmen, at Hester and Essex in the Lower East Side, or at Stone and Pitkin avenues in Brownsville, Brooklyn.[10]

Eventually, these casual gatherings of compatriots gave rise to formal societies. Natives of the town of Kaluszyn regularly gathered on the corner of Allen and Stanton, where many of them lived. One evening two friends got to talking at a party for the circumcision of a landsman's son and decided to organize a society. Two weeks later, 45 men signed up as members of the Independent Kalushiner Benevolent Association. The Shater Progressive Benevolent Association was organized by twelve landslayt who were accustomed to meeting at a bench in Central Park. Other societies got started at funerals and holiday celebrations.[11]

Developing out of the informal interaction of people who had been acquainted in Europe, the landsmanshaftn appear to have been, in Irving Howe's words, the "most spontaneous" of the immigrants' institutions.[12] They had roots in the residential, work, and social networks which took shape naturally during the process of resettlement. Their members' common origin in the same European locality—a "primordial" identity which assumed even more significance once the emigrants left their places of birth and recongregated in America—served as the societies' chief unifying factor.

On second glance, however, the landsmanshaftn turn out to have been anything but spontaneous. In fact, when it came time to establish a formal association, the founders had to choose from a wide variety of organizational types. The very fact that even small hometowns were often represented by a number of societies indicates that factors other than common geographic origin were also at work. Some elected to form religious congregations to continue as best they could along the path of traditional Eastern European Judaism. Others organized radical groups reflecting the party divisions of the Russian revolutionary movement. Immigrants who looked to America for inspiration found it in the fraternal lodge, whose influence reached the landsmanshaftn most directly through the Jewish orders. German organizational culture, transmitted by German-Jewish fraternal orders and the nearby German immigrant community, influenced the Eastern European associations as well.

Ritual and nomenclature helped differentiate the various sorts of landsmanshaftn, each of which represented an alternative strategy for dealing with life in the immigrants' new surroundings. Despite their diversity, however, all of the landsmanshaftn embodied their members' gradual Americanization. Rituals often celebrated the promise of upward mobility in status, even as democratic procedures realized on a small scale the most cherished aspects of American civic culture. All of the landsmanshaftn, from right to left, shared the same underlying structure, patterned largely after American (and immigrant German) models. Considerable cross-fertilization also jumbled the distinctions among societies. Even Orthodox congregations adopted a few fraternal trappings, while radical cells soon recognized that their immigrant members' immediate material needs were as important as the course of the revolution in Russia, if less romantic.

Membership policies demonstrate the multiplicity of influences on the landsmanshaftn, as well as the degree to which the societies quickly moved away from their early "spontaneity." In principle, the hometown associations welcomed all landslayt. But in fact ideological divisions and other factors regulated admissions as well. Place of birth did not always play a determining role, and many landsmanshaftn included a high percentage of non-landslayt in their ranks. Most societies also restricted membership to men only; in this respect, the landsmanshaftn followed nearly all of their potential models, including traditional Eastern European Jewish hevrot and contemporary American fraternal orders.

Establishing a landsmanshaft was a more difficult undertaking than simply making a suggestion at a party. A handful of dedicated organizers often had to work long and hard to gather the landslayt together, by way of informal contacts and modern means of communication. Advertisements in the Yiddish press frequently announced the existence of new associations and called on compatriots to come forward. "Shishlivitser landslayt awake!" read one such notice. "Come and join the society which has just been founded, by the name Shishlivitser Benevolent Society."[13] Such tactics sometimes brought results. After the Satanover Benevolent Society advertised in the newspapers, "many of the landslayt who had not belonged gathered together, and the Brother President presented the society to them . . . in the brightest colors." Several joined on the spot.[14] However, when the three founders of the Chigriner Progressive Benevolent Society discovered that their landslayt needed more prodding to come to meetings, they went door to door to "awaken the landslayt, like the sexton used to awaken the townspeople for the [predawn] prayer of *slikhot*."[15]

Even after the idea of forming a society arose, landslayt might disagree about what sort of organization to establish. On the Lemberger corner, for example, a compatriot known as "Red," already resented for flaunting his recent success in business, proposed the formation of a congregation to be known as Anshey Lemberg Number One. His fellows balked, however, evidently considering the formation of a hevrah (religious society) beneath their level of urban sophistication. Rather, proud of their Habsburg origins and their military service to the Empire, they intended to found a secular association with the unwieldy name of First Lemberger Gentlemen's and Ladies' Support and Sick and Death Benefit Society Under the Patronage of the Godly Late Austrian Empress Elizabeth (or so reported a cynical journalist for the *Jewish Daily Forward*).[16]

The name of a society was, however, no laughing matter, for it signaled the organization's political, religious, and cultural character.[17] Thus when Samuel Schoenfeld joined Adler's Young Men [sic] Independent Association Number One, he asked his uncle, already a member, why the society had such a long name. The older man replied that each word had significance. The Adler society actually consisted of landslayt from Kaunas (Kovno) in Lithuania, but its Americanized organizers sought to project an image of urbanity and polish. As chief rabbi of London, Adler epitomized English-speaking refinement combined with loyalty to Judaism. He was a "good Jew," according to the uncle, "it would bring honor to the society to call it by his name." On the mundane level, the society was "independent" because it did not affiliate with an order. But the word resonated with the democratic aspirations of the immigrants, and it was "also a nice word, reminiscent of the Declaration of Independence." Finally, the founders referred to their society as "Number One" in anticipation of the inevitable splits led by disappointed office-seekers. Apparently, Adler's Young Men successfully projected the desired image. Schoenfeld remembers that when he joined in the 1890s, the society already had about 200 members: "No 'greenness' was apparent [in the society]. The members looked like American young people. They came to the meetings in clean, well-pressed clothing and looked like modern people. The atmosphere impressed me. It was refined."[18]

Names of organizations often denoted both the age cohorts and the social aspirations of the organizations' founders. Religious landsmanshaftn usually included a Hebrew phrase of the sort often used in synagogue titles, followed by the word *anshey,* meaning "people of," followed by the name of the members' hometown. Many associations, especially in the earlier years, styled themselves *krankn untershtitsung fareynen,* a term reflecting a strong German linguistic influence. In English, these societies often called themselves "sick benevolent societies" or simply used the abbreviation "K.U.V." ("V" is for *Verein,* "society" in German). After 1900 English names, often including the words "young men's" or "progressive" (or both), signaled members' desire to be part of the modern world and of American society. For the most part, to be "progressive" simply meant having a vague sort of forward-looking attitude and an up-to-date way of doing business (more modern insurance practices perhaps). Sometimes, however, the term did denote a degree of social liberalism or political radicalism. The Chigriner Progressive Benevolent Society considered itself such because it counted a number of women among its early members. The Progressive Slutzker Young Men's Benevolent Association's self-identification referred to its broad educational program, as well as its decidedly left-wing politics. Other societies preferred to keep their names more neutral. After deciding to name their organization after their hometown in the Ukraine, for example, the founders of the Satanover Benevolent Society rejected proposals to include the words "progressive" and "Zion," which might have indicated a more traditional or nationalistic philosophy. Instead they chose a wording which would leave their society's orientation open and perhaps allow a broader range of land-slayt to feel comfortable about joining.[19]

A few societies actually changed their names, hinting at a redefinition of their members' personal identities, and, by dropping the explicit link with their hometowns, perhaps displaying a degree of Americanization. Thus the Independent Young Men of Poniewiez became the Manhattan Young Men's Association in 1901, and ten years later the Ekaterinoslaw Ladies' Charity Society became the Ladies' Charity Society of New York. In contrast, when well-known communal activist Joseph Barondess suggested that his society alter its name from Oshmener Brothers to American Brothers, the majority of members rejected the proposal.[20] Evidently, they remained proud of their town of origin and still felt the need to retain an explicit link to it.

Even when a landsmanshaft continued to identify with its home-town, its name differentiated it from other societies of landslayt from the same place. Groups created as many organizations as were necessary to enable all of the townspeople to find their appropriate niche. Natives of the Ukrainian town of Proskurov (later Khmelnitskiy), for example, formed the First Proskurover Sick Benevolent Society (which soon disappeared) in 1897, the Proskurover Zion Congregation and Kranken Unterstitzungs Verein in 1900, the First Proskurover Young Men's Progressive Association in 1904, the Proskurover Ladies Benevolent Society in 1909, and the Proskurov-Yarmolintser Workmen's Circle Branch 355 in 1910. During World War I all of the societies combined in a United Proskurover Relief to aid the hometown. Proskurovers continued to found new societies during the 1920s and 1930s, including the Proskurover Yugent, an International Workers' Order (IWO) branch, a Ladies Auxiliary of the Progressive Young Men, and an Independent Proskurover Society in Brooklyn. The Proskurover Yugent, made up of former Russian university students, soon split, some members joining the Workmen's Circle, some the IWO, and some forming a new organization, the New Nook, which dropped its landsmanshaft name if not its orientation.[21]

Big-city origins did not diminish the impulse to get together with one's landslayt. Indeed, the greater numbers of immigrants coming from a given city produced a higher degree of social differentiation and encouraged the multiplication of landsmanshaftn.[22] Tens of societies represented each of the larger cities. Immigrants from the Polish textile center of Bialystok created a sizable and remarkably active group of landsmanshaftn. Before 1914 Minsk was the one to lead the way, with some thirty different societies incorporated in New York County. Land-slayt debated the merits of their respective organizations; here is a scene observed at a restaurant catering to immigrants from Minsk:

> There sits a young man with a strange button in his lapel. He seethes and agitates among the Minsker for his sick-benefit society. He boasts that it pays better death benefits than any other society. For a member it pays to die.
>
> Another young man, also a Minsker, jumps up and denies everything. He demonstrates conclusively that the other society isn't worth a thing, but that his is the true Minsker society. It gives a nice present when a member gets married. . .
>
> So everyone is screaming at the top of his lungs for his society, until one man stands up and with an air of importance displays his Workmen's Circle button.
>
> "Now this is a society," says the young man pointing at the button in his lapel. "All your societies are splinter societies. I belong to the Work-men's Circle."[23]

Two of the largest of all landsmanshaftn, the Minsker Independent Benevolent Association and the United Minsker Benevolent Association, reached the thousand-member mark in 1912.[24]

Four general categories may be distinguished among the landsman-shaftn, although the lines drawn between them were not fixed and there was considerable variation within each camp. Before 1900 religious congregations and fraternal lodges predominated. Secular mutual aid societies became more popular after about 1900, as did ideologically committed societies made up of immigrants who had been active in the revolutionary movement in Russia. Even in these later years, however, religious congregations and fraternal lodges continued to attract new-comers. Moreover, the conservatism of even the most traditional con-gregations masked their absorption of considerable levels of American values and practices.[25]

Landsmanshaft Congregations

In 1872 some 29 Jewish congregations worshipped in New York. By 1914 there were as many as 800, the growth attributable almost en-tirely to Eastern European Jewish immigrants, and in great part to the establishment of landsmanshaft congregations.[26]

The hundreds of religious societies on the Lower East Side and in other immigrant neighborhoods occupied a variety of spaces, with landsmanshaft synagogues concentrated in the districts where their compatriots predominated. Most rented rooms in tenements or meeting halls, and a weekday dance or wedding hall might become a house of prayer on the sabbath.[27] Larger congregations converted whole tenement buildings into synagogues. Only a few, perhaps sixty or seventy out of the hundreds of functioning congregations on the Lower East Side, owned buildings built for the purpose of worship: converted churches, synagogues abandoned by older congregations that had moved uptown, or new structures built by the congregations themselves.[28] Many landsmanshaftn rented space from others, and any one address might house several places of worship.[29]

Dedications of new synagogue buildings received thorough coverage in the pro-Orthodox Yiddish press. Each such occasion served as a kind of demonstration to impress both the Jewish public and the surrounding population. First, the synagogues defined the immigrant neighborhoods as Jewish territory better than any other type of structure. Secondly, they symbolized the persistent vitality of Orthodox Judaism in a community where the defenders of tradition often felt under siege by secular forces. When the Chevrah Midrash Anshei Makover of Poland laid the cornerstone for its two-story *shul* (synagogue) at 203 Henry Street, the Kutner Congregation sent a present, and a band accompanied the speeches under American and blue-and-white Jewish flags.[30] Eventually, landsmanshaft congregations built some of the grandest synagogues on the Lower East Side. Chevrah Kadisha B'nai Israel Kalwarier, one of the oldest Eastern European congregations, confirmed its position as a leading downtown synagogue in 1904 when it erected a $75,000 building on Pike Street, with seats for more than 1,000 worshippers in the main sanctuary and 500 more in the study hall.[31]

The "ansheys" considered themselves guardians of old-world traditionalism, and they defended it against the challenges of secularism. As one religious landsman recalled during his society's thirtieth anniversary celebration, when "the tide of radicalism flooded the East Side, when Yom Kippur Balls and the denial of God were considered the main signs of modernism and progress," the religious landsmanshaftn set out "to stand on a truly Jewish foundation, with truly Orthodox . . . principles."[32] The very language of their constitutions, which, like their names, often contained a heavy admixture of Hebrew words and references, reminded members and others of the hevrah's links to the Jewish religious tradition.[33]

Landsmanshaft congregations differed from other societies in their central concern with religious observance. Their constitutions often mandated that services be held according to local custom. One such document, for example, stipulated that the "society shall have a synagogue for prayer every day and on the sabbath and holidays according to the custom of the Jewish people of Lubeshov and Yanova."[34] At the Tshortkover Shul on Attorney Street, the men kept their Galician *shtraymlekh* (round fur-trimmed hats) locked in cabinets during the week. On Saturdays they donned their distinctive headgear, let their *pe'ot* (sidelocks) loose from behind their ears, and "prayed with enthusiasm, just like at the [Hasidic] rebbe's prayer house in the old home."[35] More than the formal aspects of the service, perhaps, the atmosphere in the landsmanshaft synagogue allowed worshippers to express themselves religiously in ways that seemed familiar and natural.

The cantor and preacher helped determine the tone of worship, and landsmanshaft congregations sometimes turned to landslayt to fill these roles. The arrival of the old Monasterzhisker Cantor, Shimon Leyzer, enabled Chevrah Yad Charutzim Monesterzisker to get started in 1891, and the Bialystoker Shul later imported a well known preacher from Bialystok.[36] Most smaller congregations, however, did not employ any professional clergy at all but depended instead on local lay talent to lead prayers and give sermons. In many cases they elected a member to serve as cantor for the high holidays and other special occasions.[37]

Yet few of the larger congregations, which were more likely to engage full-time clergy, hired landslayt.[38] For a synagogue with aspirations beyond its own circle of compatriots, a fine cantor was an important drawing card in a city where a sizable turnout for services could not be guaranteed. Committees conducted extensive searches, advertised in the newspapers, and held auditions for cantors. When a hevrah found a suitable prayer leader, it broadcast his qualifications (which did not necessarily include nativity in the same city as most of the members) in an effort to attract worshippers. In 1891, for example, Mishkan Israel Anshei Suwalk, one of the oldest Eastern European congregations, announced that it had hired Cantor Yankev Moyshe Behr, formerly of Brody in Galicia and the Hungarian Congregation on Norfolk Street, and recommended that whoever wanted "to have pleasure and hear some Torah, sacred song, and prayer should come in time and provide himself with a seat."[39]

As the laity's position of authority over the clergy indicated, the landsmanshaft shuls had adopted many American practices, despite their self-perception as defenders of Old-World religion. In fact, the Orthodoxy of the landsmanshaft hevrot often took on a defensive tone. Even within the congregation it could not be assumed, as it could be in Europe, that all members adhered strictly to Jewish law. Many of the faithful, it appears, violated the law quite openly. Newcomers must have been startled to read in the constitution of their Orthodox synagogue that a "cantor (or prayer leader) who goes to pray at the pulpit may not be a man who shaves or who is a desecrator of the Sabbath."[40]

Despite their loyalty to Orthodox Judaism and use of terminology familiar in Europe, the congregations absorbed a great deal from their American environment. Some religious societies even adopted lodge customs. The Ershte Radimnoer Khevre Bney Mordkhe Menakhem, for example, instituted an initiation ceremony in which new candidates received instruction in the society's "mysteries," which consisted of little more than a series of hand and gavel signals. Before swearing never to reveal the hevrah's secrets, however, the new member was "assured that these do not violate your obligations to God, your family, your neighbors, or the state in which you live."[41]

Most important, landsmanshaft congregations aggressively adhered to American democratic principles. Frequent meetings, open discussions concerning matters of administration, access to leadership positions even for those without pedigree or education, and the primacy of the lay leadership over the rabbinate all distinguished the downtown shul from its counterparts in Eastern Europe. At least one contemporary Orthodox observer, the acerbic Rabbi Moses Weinberger, harshly criticized the new conditions. In America, Weinberger lamented, leaders were recruited

> by inspecting everyone who displays haughtiness and greed, talks big, leaps forward to barge into other people's conversations, has a tall and handsome appearance, and cannot speak gently to his fellow human beings. First, such a one is made a trustee, then a treasurer, then a secretary, then a judge of minor matters, and from there he is raised to [the highest religious court] the *Bes Din Hagadol*. He is placed at the head

of the community, given a golden scepter, which in this country is in the shape of a mallet, and with it he rules his people; he is at once their ruler and judge.[42]

In other words, politicians held sway in America, not scholars or aristocrats.

What seemed to Weinberger the height of boorishness, however, appeared to many religious Jews to be not only the right to express their opinions publicly but also the power to influence the course of events in their community. In addition to the usual set of society officers, congregations elected functionaries to maintain the synagogue and preside over services. These officials *(gabaim)*, whose function was to distribute honors during prayer, as well as a paid caretaker *(shamas)* were called by their familiar Hebrew titles. But in Europe it was a small committee chosen by lot from among the limited number of qualified electors that selected the administrators; in America the full membership filled the positions by majority vote.[43]

The voice of the laity extended well beyond synagogue administration to questions of ritual and interpretation of the Torah. A shortage of qualified clergy allowed ordinary Jewish men to occupy positions of spiritual leadership, especially in smaller congregations that could not afford to employ rabbis and relied instead on their own members for inspiration and guidance. Even Weinberger expressed grudging admiration for the simple workers who acted as spiritual leaders within their congregations: "Remarkably, these meetinghouse orators always know how to illustrate their words with tales of their trials and tribulations—those encountered during their many long days at the machine shop and factory." Newcomers from Europe, Weinberger wrote, were "filled with wonder at what they see: tailors, shoemakers, and tanners standing tall and expounding Torah to the multitude."[44] While Weinberger may have felt these lay preachers were unseemly, their peers seemed to enjoy listening to their exhortations. Indeed, worshippers at the Timkovitser Shul reported finding one such sermon by a member "very pleasant to hear."[45]

The members of landsmanshaft (and other immigrant) congregations thus infused their traditional religious practice with a degree of egalitarianism and democracy rare in the places from which they had come. While Orthodox Judaism found it difficult to plant roots in American soil, and strict adherence to Jewish law declined, still tens of thousands of Jewish immigrants joined synagogues. American conditions actually provided many of the faithful with the opportunity to exercise a greater role in both worship and congregational politics than would have been possible in Europe. More than even its own members may have realized, the landsmanshaft shul was as much a product of the New World as of the Old.[46]

Fraternal Lodges

Many landsmanshaftn affiliated with the popular Jewish fraternal orders and helped them reach their peak in the second decade of the twentieth century, with more than half a million members nationwide.[47] Not all orders welcomed the hometown societies (or East Europeans in general). B'nai B'rith, for example, remained almost exclusively German-Jewish and rejected the bond of landsmanshaft as being antithetical to its ideal of Jewish unity.[48] However, other fraternal orders actively recruited hometown lodges. Some 42 of the 88 New York City lodges of Independent Order B'rith Sholom (established in 1905 by Eastern Europeans) carried the names of cities, regions, or countries. So did some lodges of Independent Order Ahavas Israel, Independent Order Free Sons of Judah, Independent Order Sons of Benjamin, Independent Western Star Order, Order Brith Abraham, and Order of the United Hebrew Brothers.[49]

The Independent Order Brith Abraham (IOBA), one of the orders most hospitable to landsmanshaftn, grew to be the largest Jewish fraternal organization around the time of the First World War. At its height, IOBA claimed 210,000 members across the country, including 90,000 in New York City. Fully one-third, or 121 out of 354, of its New York branches were landsmanshaftn. IOBA's founders, mainly German and Hungarian Jews, left the Order Brith Abraham in 1887, accusing the older group's leadership of being undemocratic and incompetent. Of the 27 lodges that met at IOBA's founding convention on the Lower East Side only one bore the name of a town, though others, such as the Kronprinz Rudolf and Kaiser Franz Joseph lodges, revealed their members' Habsburg origins. From the start, however, Russian and Polish Jewish immigrants joined the order, often with their landsmanshaftn.[50]

Why would a landsmanshaft join a fraternal order? In return for higher dues, about $14–18 a year as opposed to $4–6 in the independent societies, the lodge acquired the order's high social prestige together with better and more secure benefits.[51] The Jewish orders derived their status primarily from their close resemblance to truly American institutions such as the Masons, Odd Fellows, Elks, and similar groups that flourished in the late nineteenth century, the heyday of American fraternals. Like members of the American organizations, young men joined Brith Abraham with the hope of advancing their business or professional careers, and in so doing furthered the order's image as American, "progressive," and successful.[52]

The Jewish orders regarded the Americanization of their members as one of their most vital missions. Using strikingly similar language, fraternal leaders argued that the lodge trained its members for better citizenship in both the Jewish community and the American polity. "The lodges of the various orders have been and still are the most valuable schools through which our immigrated Jews pass," wrote Leo Wolfson, First Vice Grand Master of the Independent Western Star Order.

> Many have learned their English at their lodge meetings. Others have acquired there their knowledge of parliamentary procedure and decorum at public meetings. Many of our best known public men and speakers have begun their careers modestly, in filling an office in their lodge or joining the debates at the meetings. In fact most of our people gain their connection with and knowledge of American Jewish activities, and take an interest in the same, through their affiliation with the Jewish fraternal orders.

Grand Masters Samuel Dorf, of Order Brith Abraham, and Max Stern, of Independent Order Brith Abraham, agreed. Dorf called the lodge room a "school" in which members "learned the language of the country [and] became Americanized." Stern likewise termed the lodge "the school of humanity," with a duty to introduce the immigrants to "American civilization."[53]

Significantly, immigrant lodge brethren Americanized each other without the interference of native social workers or reformers. Most of the leaders themselves had come to this country from Russia, Austria-Hungary, Germany, or Romania. And while the orders boasted that they brought Jews from all of these parts together under one roof, many of the individual lodges consisted entirely of compatriots from the same European town or region. A leader such as Wolfson, himself active in Romanian landsmanshaft affairs, acknowledged the contribution of hometown societies to the growth of the orders and saw no contradiction between the retention of local loyalties and the Americanizing mission of the orders. In fact, among familiar faces from home and in their own dialects, many immigrants engaged in the same activities that captivated large numbers of American men at the time.

The Jewish fraternal orders also developed elaborate rituals and regalia, which enhanced their American image and high social standing. Fraternal ceremonial entered the immigrant community through the older orders that already included more Americanized elements, as well as through occasional encounters with American organizations like the Knights of Labor. Articles in the Yiddish press further educated the immigrants concerning the history and genealogy of European and American fraternal orders.[54] One journalist noted the ubiquity of fraternalism among the native born. "It is hard to find an intelligent American who does not belong to a secret order," he wrote, and Jews, who had known little of such matters in Eastern Europe (especially in Russia, where secret organizations were illegal), borrowed much of their fraternal practice from Americans.[55]

The ritual of Independent Order Brith Abraham stressed both fealty to Jewish tradition and enthusiastic American patriotism. Clearly patterned after the popular fraternal rites of the day, it used the biblical motif of the life of Abraham as well as such Jewish symbols as the Star of David and the Old Testament to strengthen the feeling of attachment to an ancient heritage. Yet the props, costumes, and dramatic structure of the Brith Abraham ritual were all utterly foreign to the Jewish tradition they purported to represent.

IOBA's initiation ceremony was particularly dramatic.[56] The Binding of Isaac formed the rite's central motif, with the candidate playing the role of Isaac. Blind-folded and bound, the candidate wore a white robe "from shoulders to feet" and carried a bundle of wood on his back. In the center of the lodge room stood an altar covered with an American flag, on top of which lay a Bible, which was opened as the meeting began and closed when the meeting adjourned. Blue and white ribbons formed a Star of David on the floor, and the lodge officers sat at the points. At the beginning of the ceremony the brothers rose, stood along the blue and white outline, and linked arms. As the president passed under the crossed swords of the "conductor" and "marshal," the candidate entered the lodge room, accompanied by a "guide" carrying a staff with a six-pointed star at the top.

As the guide led the candidate to the stations around the room, the initiate received various general moral lessons. In the course of the ceremony the novice also proved his bravery and faith in the face of the impending sacrifice by refusing offers to stop the proceedings. After acknowledging his belief in God and in God's power, the candidate came before the altar on which several pieces of wood lay next to a bowl of burning alcohol. As the ceremony headed toward its climax, the president granted the initiate one more chance to turn back. But the guide answered for the newcomer, reaffirming his faith. The president, playing the role of Abraham, then put his hand on the blindfolded candidate's shoulder as if ready to carry out the sacrifice. At the last possible moment, the ex-president, playing the part of the biblical angel, called out:

> *Ex-President:* Abraham, Abraham.
> *President:* Here am I.
> *Ex-President:* Lay not your hand upon your son; nor do the least unto him; for now I know that you fear God, seeing as how you did not withhold your only son from Him.
> *President:* Remove the bonds. My soul rejoiceth. For now I know that they who seek admission into the lodge fear God, seeing that they held not back their very lives, in obeying the commands of the Lord.

The president then swore in the candidate as a member of the Independent Order Brith Abraham, and removed the blindfold. On the altar lay a cloth with representations of a heifer, a she-goat, a ram, and a dove. The marshal pointed to each picture with his sword and explained its meaning. The new brother received instruction on the secret handshake, the password, and other fraternal lore. Quoting from the story of Abraham, the lodge officers lectured him on the equality of lodge brothers, the importance of peaceful relations within the lodge and among nations, the centrality of brotherly love, and the virtues of faith.

The central lessons of the ritual emphasized both commitment to Judaism and enthusiastic patriotism for the United States. As the president made clear to the candidate toward the end of the ritual, the Brith Abraham conception of Americanism stressed its civic aspects and linked the country's acceptance of the immigrant with the newcomer's adoption of an American ethos: "Never has there been for us Jews an opportunity as that presented to us in America. Our very existence here depends on our loyalty to our new home. Our Order preaches obedience to the laws of the land, fealty to its constitution, and devotion to its history and traditions. Be a loyal member of Brith Abraham. Be a true and devoted Jew. Be no less a true American."

Published in Yiddish, as well as in English and German, the IOBA ritual evidently appealed to the many Eastern European immigrants who formed landsmanshaft lodges. It is striking that the lodge brothers chose to express their loyalty to Judaism in a manner so outside the Jewish liturgical tradition. In fact, some Orthodox commentators protested vociferously against the "gentile spirit" of the IOBA ceremonies. The Orthodox Yiddish daily *Tageblat* considered the ritual "thoroughly contrary to the Jewish spirit and . . . simply a desecration of God's name." The editors objected particularly to the use of the story of Abraham and Isaac and its transformation into a "comedy," and a "gentile comedy" at that.[57] Many members undoubtedly failed to see the contradiction and continued to attend both lodge meetings and synagogue services.

While the landsmanshaft synagogue retained the aura of the old country, the fraternal order promised its members a new kind of Jewish-American identity. Like all initiation rites, the IOBA ritual explicitly bestowed a new status on the newly initiated brother: "As Abraham left all behind him that he might worship the one living God, so you, my brother, upon being admitted to the Order, leave behind you all that may hinder your complete realization of the highest truths of your profession as a member of Brith Abraham." For those immigrants who wished to embrace the New World and its manners, the Jewish fraternal order offered a way very much in keeping with the current native trends of the late nineteenth and early twentieth centuries. It was all the more convenient and reassuring, if slightly ironic, that this ritualistic initiation into a new identity could be carried out in the company of one's landslayt.

Fraternal ritual offered other advantages as well. For one thing, it provided better secular entertainment than the traditional Jewish service, so it appealed to some as a more satisfactory, less tedious way of professing one's Jewishness. Moreover, the fraternal ritual was in the vernacular, making it accessible to people whose Hebrew and traditional education might not have been adequate, but who may have aspired to higher status in the new country. Finally, the ritual itself called for the abolition of differences based on *yikhes,* defined as "pride in family" in the English version of the ritual, but perhaps better understood as pedigree. The rites thereby held open the promise of integration into a new Jewish community in which old standards of status would not apply.

Ideological Orders

After 1900 several politically oriented orders competed with the conventional fraternals for the allegiance of the Jewish public. The ideological orders resembled their rivals in many respects, but their focus was on a commitment to socialism, or Jewish nationalism, or a fusion of the two. Immigrants frequently brought with them from Europe a dedication to one or another of these causes, and once in America they formed hometown associations with comrades from the old home. At first, many of these political landsmanshaftn, especially those comprised of former revolutionaries from Russia, remained oriented toward helping their respective movements abroad. Soon, however, they turned their attention to the immediate needs of their members as they settled into their new homeland.

The oldest and largest of the political fraternals was the radical Workmen's Circle (Arbeter Ring in Yiddish), originally founded as a mutual aid society in 1892 and reorganized as a national order in 1900. By 1917 it boasted some 25,000 New York members in 240 branches, at least 143 of which were landsmanshaftn.[58] Landsmanshaftn also comprised the majority of New York branches of the labor-Zionist Jewish National Workers' Alliance, founded in 1911. The Zionist B'nai Zion had but a single "camp" bearing the name of its members' hometown.[59]

The Arbeter Ring's working-class organizers sympathized with radical ideas but felt impatient with the factional squabbles between anarchist and socialist intellectuals. Rejecting the obscure ideological interests of the intelligentsia, the founders of the Arbeter Ring focused on concerns similar to those that occupied the Lower East Side's other societies: material aid in times of need and fellowship to counteract the loneliness of the immigrant. But the founders of the early Workmen's Circle chose to organize along the lines of class and political orientation rather than geographic origin. As class-conscious workers, they also refused to join an ordinary lodge which might also count bosses and foremen as members. Moreover, the radical mutual aid association

differentiated itself from other societies and lodges by explicitly rejecting fraternal ritual as reactionary and unbecoming to a progressive
workers' organization.[60]

Nevertheless, the early Workmen's Circle clearly drew much of its
internal culture from the fraternal world. The ten founders of the
original society, two of whom had been members of Order Brith Abraham, retained some of the practices common among other lodges and
societies. They adopted a password, for example, choosing the French
"mon ami" in honor of the Paris Commune. (This was later changed
to the Yiddish "mayn fraynd.") They also retained the initiation lecture
in which new members were instructed in the organization's principles
and lore. Subsequent Arbeter Ring leaders placed their organization
clearly within the fraternal tradition and attempted to educate the
members in the history of the fraternal movement, from the English
friendly societies to American secret orders.[61]

At the same time, however, the Workmen's Circle presented itself as
a radical alternative to the more conventional orders, and sought to
distinguish itself by proclaiming its greater devotion to principle. A
careful distinction in terminology helped to differentiate the Workmen's
Circle from the "bourgeois" orders. New recruits were told: "We call
each other 'friend,' and not 'brother,' as in other societies, and we
require that our members be true friends to each other."[62] The Workmen's Circle radicals argued that the rites of the other orders masked a
basic hypocrisy. As one convention report put it, "In all benefit societies
the members call each other 'brother' . . . They talk about brotherhood
within the four walls of the society, but in the real world outside they
strengthen the evil order of dog-eat-dog and hurry-up—the order of a
kingdom for one derived from the horrible poverty of thousands.
Therefore, their calling one another 'brother, brother' is nothing more
than a Purim masquerade. It is the brotherhood of Cain to Abel."[63]

The Workmen's Circle also rejected Jewish religious ritual; individual
members were allowed freedom of conscience in regard to their belief
in God, but branches were required to remain secular. While it would
have been loath to admit it, however, the Workmen's Circle, like socialists elsewhere, developed its own set of rituals. In place of the Holy Ark
of the synagogue or the American flag-draped altar of Independent
Order Brith Abraham, Workmen's Circle convention halls were be-
decked with red banners, and in place of traditional prayers or invitations into the "tent of Abraham," Arbeter Ring members sang socialist

hymns in Yiddish. They even developed a calendar of festivals, including May Day and the anniversary of the Paris Commune.

In 1900 the Arbeter Ring's three existing branches, joined by a formerly independent society in Brooklyn, reorganized the Circle as a national, multi-branch fraternal order. The new order invited sympathetic societies to enlist, promising to "become for the Jewish workers and their friends that which the large orders are, without the reactionary characteristics, ceremonies and nonsense, which make the orders unbearable for the progressive worker and citizen." After stating the conditions for affiliation and explaining the method of assessments used in determining membership contributions, the proclamation expressed support for the "solidarity of the workers" and their "struggle against oppression and exploitation."[64] In the meantime, the Workmen's Circle proposed to provide the Jewish immigrant worker with the material benefits needed to survive in the present social order.

By soliciting the support of independently formed societies, the Workmen's Circle opened itself up to branches espousing a variety of principles and identities. Anarchists and social democrats organized their own branches, as did workers in the same trade or industry. Landsmanshaftn joined as well and eventually made up more than half of the order's New York branches. A Minsker society in Brooklyn became Branch 6 in 1901, but the first landsmanshaft to retain its name within the order was the Homler Progressive Society, which affiliated as Branch 20 in 1902.[65] Many other radical hometown societies followed the Homler into the order, but the period of fastest growth in landsmanshaft branches came after the suppression of the Russian Revolution of 1905. Between 1906 and 1910 at least 85 newly founded landsmanshaft branches contributed to the Arbeter Ring's period of greatest expansion, when its membership nearly quadrupled to 31,581.[66]

Before they enlisted in the Workmen's Circle, the left-wing societies were as strongly oriented toward the Old World as the landsmanshaft hevrahs. Radical newcomers often formed their landsmanshaftn along European party lines. Former members of the Bund, Russia's largest Jewish revolutionary party, established their own hometown clubs, which banded together in December 1903 at the behest of visiting representatives of the party in Russia to form the Central Federation of the Bund in America.[67] Among the active constituents of the Bundist Federation was the Dvinsker Revolutsionerer Imigrantn Untershtitsung

Fareyn, organized by landslayt from Daugavpils (Dvinsk), Latvia, in 1902. Like many of the societies founded by former revolutionaries, the Dvinsker Fareyn at first concerned itself far more with aiding its comrades back in Russia than with helping its members make their way in America.[68] Other radical landsmanshaftn that eventually became part of the Workmen's Circle began with similar orientations.[69]

The youthful immigrants who formed the radical landsmanshaftn also continued the cultural revolution that had already begun to transform their Jewish identities in Europe. Radical ideologies, together with the secularization of Jewish life, combined to produce in many of the youth a strong desire for worldly knowledge. Thus when a group of radicals, both men and women, from the neighboring towns of Halta (Golta) and Bogopolia (later Pervomaisk) in the Ukraine formed the Golter-Bogopolier Yugnt in 1908, education came first on their list of priorities. Over the next few months meetings of the Golter-Bogopolier always included readings of selections from modern Yiddish literature. Poems by the "proletarian poets" Morris Rosenfeld and David Edelshtat were especially popular, as were stories by Sholem Aleichem and I. L. Peretz. The landslayt also debated such questions as "Can trade unions go hand in hand with socialism," "Do the workers have a right to the wealth," and "What is realistic drama?"[70]

It was not long before the radical groups began to orient themselves more toward the practical needs of the immigrants in America. As each radical society "little by little turned its face toward America," in the words of one participant, it adopted the elements of mutual aid common to most landsmanshaftn. This move, which often seemed necessary to maintain the interest of the members, appeared to some to threaten the radical identity of the organizations by diverting their attention from larger political issues and implying acceptance of the current social order. Affiliation with the Workmen's Circle offered a way to serve the immediate material needs of the immigrant members and maintain socialist credentials at the same time.[71]

Once in the Workmen's Circle, the landsmanshaft branches participated fully in the activities of the order. Affiliation with a larger body organized on ideological grounds seems to have diluted the landsmanshaft nature of some of the branches. After the Kremenchuger Radical Association became Branch 63, recalled one organizer, non-landslayt prevailed over the actual Kremenchuger and voted to send money to revolutionary parties in other towns in Russia.[72] The Zerdover Educational Society, Branch 301, was already the outcome of the merger between the most disparate of landsmanshaftn, united only by their radicalism and common interest in self-education: the Ukrainian Golter-Bogopolier Yugnt and the Central Polish Zheradover Progressive Young Mens (sic). When it joined the order, the branch dropped the Golter name (Bogopolia had already been jettisoned) and over the years enrolled a large number of non-landslayt. Nevertheless, both the Kremenchuger and the Zherdover continued to identify with their core-groups' hometowns.[73]

In fact, old-country party divisions often faded more quickly than landsmanshaft orientations. Lodzer Branch 324 started out as the Lodzer Bundisher Untershtitsung Fareyn, but gave up its specifically Bundist orientation when it merged with another radical Lodzer landsmanshaft. For a time, conflict between the Bundist and non-Bundist factions threatened the unity of the group, as many original branch members resented proposals to share the branch's quarterly contribution to the Bund with other revolutionary organizations, and, subsequently, to eliminate it altogether.[74] Even so, the branch held together and sectarian squabbles eventually quieted down. Likewise, Bialystoker Branch 88 absorbed a number of different political tendencies and its old-country party lines became blurred; yet the landsmanshaft character of Branch 88 remained strong, and it remained active in the broader Bialystoker landsmanshaft community.[75]

Independent Societies

Most landsmanshaftn remained independent of the larger fraternal orders. The independent societies catered to a wide range of members, and the most successful managed to balance the needs of young and old, religious and secular, radical and conservative. Often, however, landslayt clashed over the direction of their societies, sometimes dividing over political differences, sometimes along the lines of age or length of time in America. These conflicts occasionally led to splits or to changes within the organization. In 1911 dissidents broke away from the Independent Kalushiner Benevolent Association and formed the Kalushiner Young Men's (sic), which soon joined the Workmen's Circle. Other radical elements stayed in the parent organization and by 1913 had enough strength to abolish some of what they saw as "conservative forms," including greeting signs, closed doors, and the practice of blackballing.[76]

Whether radical or conservative, the independent societies provided an arena for status mobility among the landslayt. While their common origins laid the basis for unity, the members' social position in the old country did not necessarily determine their present role in the society. Often a subject of comment in immigrant literature, reversals of status and the jumbling of social distinctions could seem to some immigrants disorienting and even unfair. Conversely, others considered these changes a fulfillment of the democratic promise of America. "The society abolished the ascribed social distinctions *(yahsanut)* familiar from home," wrote one landsmanshaft historian in a passage full of specific references to the status hierarchy of his hometown: "Those who were born on the outskirts behind the bathhouse became the equals of those who were raised on Zupraner Street and attended the district school. The tailor's or the shoemaker's apprentice was as respected in the society as the young man known in the home-town for his refinement. The Oshmener society was the melting pot which remolded us and made us into better and different people."[77]

As was the case in both lodges and congregations, the fraternal ritual adopted by the independent societies stressed the theme of mobility and democratic access to honor and station. The Satanover Benevolent Society's ceremonial elements invoked good fortune and undoubtedly expressed the brothers' hopes for their own lives as well as for their society. The association first adopted as its password the Hebrew phrase *ken yirbu* ("may they increase," see Exodus 1:12), which it changed several years later to the English "successful." One can only speculate as to whether the transition from Hebrew to English reflected a shift in the members' point of reference from the Bible to modern America (later passwords reverted to Hebrew). Interestingly, however, none of the passwords were in Yiddish, the language in which the society transacted its business, kept its records, and, presumably, socialized informally. Perhaps both the Holy Tongue and the local vernacular were felt to possess a sense of dignity which Yiddish lacked, or perhaps their strangeness lent the ritual feature of a password more of an air of mystery.[78]

Officers' regalia and the imposing ritual made a deep impression on new candidates. They conveyed the message that regardless of anyone's old-country status or current position, he (or, only very occasionally, she) could eventually become a society officer, even a president, the highest aspiration appropriate to a republican country. For Jewish immigrants from Eastern Europe, where remote and threatening gentile government officials often wore uniforms and other insignia of office, the sight of a fellow Jewish townsman wearing the accoutrements of power as he presided over a meeting could appear bewildering at first. This was the impression of William Bakst at his own first society meeting.

> When I was brought to a meeting to be installed as a new member, and when the inside-guard led me to the president so that I could give the oath that I would never, God forbid, reveal the secrets of the society and that I would be true to its goals, when I set eyes on Gershke Yankls with a red sash across his chest, standing there giving three strong raps of the gavel, and all those present responding by standing, I became so scared that I didn't even know what they were telling me to repeat. The "regalia" that the president wore scared me most of all. For me, a greenhorn just out of the yeshivah who had never in his life attended a meeting, the red sash gave the impression of a high government official. When he gave a rap with the gavel, everyone stood up, and that simply scared me.[79]

However unnerving at first, this transformation of ordinary Gershke Yankls into "worthy brother president" ultimately provided a great deal of the society's appeal, even after the immigrant's basic social and material needs were met.

Ceremony added an air of gravity to meetings, along with an element of organizational elan. Like many societies, the Satanover instituted a set of hand and gavel signals, including a "greeting signal" (right hand to the left breast when entering a meeting in progress), "voting signal" (lifting the right hand), and a series of gavel commands (one rap meant a call to order, all brothers were to sit; two raps, the officers were to stand; three raps, all brothers were to stand).[80] A banner, "blue on each side and white in the middle, an indication of the Jewish flag," and a button with the Satanover's anchor emblem identified the society and its members in public. The badges were distributed with ceremony and the wish that they "turn hate and enmity to love, loyalty and fraternity in the hearts of all brothers, and that the society progress." The assembled brothers greeted this pronouncement with applause.[81]

A peculiar, heavily Germanized form of Yiddish inherited by the societies from the fraternal orders also seemed to many members to inject a degree of solemnity, even grandeur, into landsmanshaft meetings. Many Yiddish speakers saw this kind of language, widespread in the late nineteenth-century Yiddish press and stage, as a sign of culture, refinement, and modernity. At a time when Yiddish was only beginning to form a vocabulary for new political, social, technical, and cultural concepts, Yiddish-speaking Jews often found it natural to borrow words from the language they considered to be the normative model for their own dialect.[82] As one society activist replied heatedly to a journalist who challenged him on his use of "German" during meetings, "What do you want, that I take the floor in the society and speak the plain mother-tongue *(proste mame-loshn)?!*"[83]

Like the rituals, the societies' strange jargon underscored the transition from the Old World to New. New arrivals were unlikely to understand all that was going on. But once a member mastered the lingo, he could participate fully in society affairs and ceased to be an utter greenhorn. William Bakst recalled that soon after he had enrolled, the president appointed him to the standards committee to investigate a new candidate. At the following meeting the investigators reported their findings. Generally, if an applicant was found suitable for membership, he was pronounced *ginstik,* from the German *günstig,* meaning "favorable." When Bakst heard the first committee-member say *ginstik,* he misunderstood and answered that he too found the candidate *dinstik* ("Tuesday"). The brothers burst out laughing, and Bakst left the meeting dejected, wondering "when and where my Oshmener lads had learned the German language." Within a year, however, he had become so proficient in society ways that some landslayt nicknamed him the "Speaker of the House."[84]

By the 1920s the German-Yiddish jargon had lost its appeal, and many societies carried out their meetings and rewrote their constitutions in idiomatic Yiddish. In part this reflected the maturity of Yiddish as a language suitable for communal affairs. In other respects it represented a trend away from ritualism current not only in the Jewish organizations but among non-Jewish fraternals as well. Perhaps, too, the ritualistic lingo had outlived its usefulness as an initiation rite once the immigrants had become well-settled in both America and their landsmanshaftn.[85]

Religion played a more ambiguous role in the culture of the independent societies than did secular ritual. This largest and most varied category of landsmanshaftn naturally embraced a wide range of attitudes and approaches. Some independents included the maintenance of a synagogue among their primary functions.[86] Others, such as the Gluboker Benevolent Association, sometimes rented halls for Rosh Hashanah and Yom Kippur services. The Association actually absorbed the much smaller Gluboker hevrah and thus acquired the hevrah's Torah scroll.[87] Many organizations, however, would have seconded the Satanover Society's response to a group of landsfroyen who offered to present a Torah scroll to the men. In rejecting the proposed gift, the brothers argued that their society had been founded for mutual aid, not for having "shuls and Torahs."[88]

Many landslayt thus applied an important aspect of American civic culture to their own societies. Not necessarily antireligious, the Satanover landslayt had come to see religion as a "private matter," best left alone by their own little model of the general polity.[89] Each member had the right to worship as he pleased, but the society itself needed to remain above potentially divisive issues if it was to fulfill its function of holding together a group of compatriots for whom faith was no longer a unifying force. Although many landsmanshaftn included both believers and freethinkers, most did require their members to be Jewish. As the constitution of the Gluboker Association stated, "The candidate [for membership] must be an Israelite and of Jewish descent. But it is immaterial whether the aforementioned is religiously inclined or not."[90]

Despite their differences, lodges, congregations, branches, and independent societies all shared the same basic structure. Remarkably uniform, this structure had little in common with traditional Eastern European patterns. Rather, the immigrants appeared intent on forming associations of a type with which they had little prior experience. They received instruction in this undertaking from Yiddish intellectuals who looked to both mainstream and German-American organizational life for guidance. Once the Eastern European newcomers had gained some experience in these matters, they were able themselves to transmit the organizational culture to less experienced compatriots through a web of overlapping affiliations.

Landsmanshaft constitutions all followed more or less the same formula, with small variations according to the type of society.[91] Societies frequently distributed their constitutions to their members in the form of small booklets written in highly Germanized Yiddish and sometimes in English. The constitution generally regulated all aspects of society life, including the organization's name, purpose, and official language. It provided for regular and general meetings, prescribed the manner of selection and duties of members and officers, and defined the material benefits to which a member was entitled in case of sickness or death. By-laws usually stressed the equality of members and the necessity of decorum in maintaining democracy.

Landsmanshaft leaders who needed advice in running their societies could refer to any one of a number of Yiddish-language manuals that instructed them in the arts of organization and the rules of order. These publications ranged from slim elementary pamphlets in the simplest language to technical treatises on parliamentary procedure. A pamphlet entitled *For Every Member* gave step by step instruction on how to set up a society, from calling the first meeting to making a point of order.[92] In fact, as he became more experienced in organizational matters, a member could graduate from one of the 18- or 32-page beginners' booklets to the full-fledged 137-plus-page manual of parliamentary practice. Instructions were also offered by the Yiddish press.[93]

Despite one journalist's complaint that it was out of date and difficult to apply to small organizations, *Cushing's Parliamentary Practice* appears to have been the most popular of the full parliamentary manuals. First published in 1850 by a Massachusetts legislator and lawyer, Cushing's Rules appeared in at least two Yiddish editions, in 1900 and 1914. One publisher of Cushing's went so far as to call it the *shulhan arukh* of societies, in reference to the traditional code of Jewish law.[94]

The left-wing *Arbeiter Zeitung* published what was perhaps the first Yiddish-language organizational handbook in 1891. Claiming to have been "compiled from the best books on parliamentarism," it stressed the need for Jewish immigrants to learn about organizations from more experienced members of American society. In the introduction the anonymous compiler noted that both native-born Americans and Germans had a proclivity for organization, and stressed the Jewish immigrants' unfamiliarity with the norms of associational life. "There is no other country in the whole world where associations are so widespread as in the United States of America," claimed the introduction, echoing Tocqueville. "It would be hard to find an American or German who does not belong to some sort of union, lodge or club." The writer noted the value of uniting with others for common interests and hailed the growing importance of organizations in the lives of Jewish workers. Parliamentary rules were important, the writer asserted, because they helped keep order and save time and gave all members an equal opportunity to speak. "All English and German associations thus adhere strictly to parliamentary rules" and should serve as an example for Russian and Polish Jews, who "in their homeland had almost never heard of such things."[95]

Another introductory manual linked the American form of government directly with society administration: "The government of this great republic is run exactly the same way as a society, like a big society. It also has its constitution and officers: the President with his secretaries . . . Congress is the meeting place of the entire people, and since it is impossible for the whole people to meet in person, everyone sends a delegate which he elects." The writer thus presented the democratic administration of a voluntary association as an appropriate, even logical, extension of the form of governance of the republic which the immigrants had adopted as their home. In the process, the societies gained some of the federal government's aura of prestige and grandeur.[96]

Jewish intellectuals, whether radicals, nationalists, or acculturationists, believed in the value of discipline. The unruliness of the landsmanshaftn worried them constantly, and they frequently tried to impress upon the public the advantages of decorum. Not only was disorder inefficient, they argued, but it was unbecoming to equal citizens of a free country. They felt that turmoil in the Jewish societies represented a holdover from the Old World and was an embarrassment before the non-Jewish world.[97] An advertisement in the Yiddish press for one edition of *Cushing's Parliamentary Practice* warned that failure to adhere to proper parliamentary procedure could lead to dire consequences: "Very often the honor of all of Israel is at stake, since the members don't know how to run their meetings and they therefore get into fights among themselves, and the scandals wind up in court."[98]

Whether or not the manual writers were right that Eastern European Jews initially lacked organizational expertise, many activists had acquired proficiency in it by the turn of the century. The more knowledgeable landslayt taught those with less experience how to set up and run their organizations. Some landsmanshaft founders had participated in other societies before their fellow townspeople had the numbers or initiative to form their own associations. In a circular announcing the founding of a Shpoler society in 1902, the organizers lamented that "while every community founds its own society, we Shpoler are scattered among the many New York hevrot, societies and lodges."[99] The objection of a member of the Satanover Benevolent Society to a proposal that all brothers wear the society button illustrates how common multiple affiliations were. "If I belong to six or seven societies," he complained, "and each one decides to make buttons, I'll have to walk around with buttons stuck to me from head to foot."[100]

Landsmanshaft borders were, in fact, distinctly permeable. While some societies mandated that candidates come from the regions around the towns whose name they bore, many left membership open to others as well.[101] Even when a society's constitution stated that only landslayt might affiliate, ways could be found to accept other desirable candidates. The rules of the Timkovitser Congregation allowed only those from a ten-mile radius around Timkovichi to become members. Nevertheless, the congregation admitted a candidate from Slonim, beyond the constitutional limit, by a special vote. On another occasion, it was suggested that a candidate from Grodno Province, "farther than our constitution allows . . ., come to services on a Sabbath, and if a large number of brothers meet him there, it will be possible to accept him." Between 1906 and 1916, 85 (60%) of the 142 candidates whose places of origin are listed came from Timkovichi. Another 8 (6%) were "Timkovitser sons-in-law" (that is, men married to women from Timkovichi), and 10 (7%) were Rozever landslayt, whose own hevrah had merged with the Anshei Timkowitz. Some 39 (27%) came from other places altogether.[102]

In all other respects the rules and procedures for the admission of new members resembled those of many non-Jewish fraternal orders and societies (except in the requirement that candidates and their wives be Jewish). Membership was generally open only to men between eighteen and forty-five years of age (though the exact age span might vary), in good physical and mental health, of respectable moral character, able to provide for their families, and in the country six months or longer. To join, a candidate had to be sponsored by a current member and had to hand in a written application with a small fee. A committee appointed by the president then investigated the candidate's character. If it found him suitable and the society doctor certified his good physical condition, the members voted on his acceptance. Many societies retained the practice of blackballing, in which three negative votes meant rejection (often with the right to reapply after six months). In practice, however, societies admitted most candidates and blackballing was rare.[103]

In restricting membership to men, landsmanshaftn followed the examples set by most of their available models, including both traditional European Jewish hevrot and modern American fraternal orders. Even the democratic American polity excluded women from active participation. Not surprisingly, women sometimes expressed a degree of alienation from the organizations, viewing them as wastes of money and time better spent on the family.[104] Nevertheless, women were much more of a presence in the American Jewish societies than they were in either the traditional hevrot or the Masonic-type orders.

Independent Order Brith Abraham counted women among its members, although their status in the largest Jewish fraternal organization was somewhat ambiguous. Only wives of "brothers" could join the order, and there was no initiation ritual for women members.[105] On the other hand, one social worker familiar with the downtown lodges noted that "wives often attend[ed] the meetings and always the functions." He described the Jewish lodge room as a place where men and women could have "natural . . . and healthy social intercourse," a far cry from those fraternals (like the Masons) which explicitly aimed to provide men with an escape from the presence of women.[106] In 1917 the *Jewish Communal Register* identified 9 female lodge presidents out of a total of 462. IOBA itself had eight separate "ladies'" lodges in New York, including one landsmanshaft, the Czernowitz Bukowiner Ladies' Lodge 17.[107]

Women were more likely to be active in independent mutual aid societies than in fraternal lodges. A few of the societies that considered themselves "progressive" enrolled both male and female members, as did some branches of the radical orders. Other associations consisted entirely or mainly of women, as demonstrated by the 55 female presidents of independent mutual aid societies noted in the *Jewish Communal Register* and the 48 ladies' landsmanshaftn founded before 1919 listed in the WPA's 1938 survey. These women's societies offered all of the same benefits as the men's, including sick and death benefits, and undertook many of the same kinds of social events.[108]

Significantly, however, many of the women's associations had male organizers and presidents. Paternalistic feelings of responsibility for the welfare of their landsfroyen motivated much of the masculine involvement in women's associations. The societies provided vital material benefits in times of need, and women (particularly single women and widows) unprotected by a husband's membership in a landsmanshaft were especially vulnerable. More extensive education and greater organizational experience of men may have also contributed to their leadership role. Tellingly, the only two women of the seven incorporators of the Nowoselitzer Ladies' Sick and Benevolent Society were both illiterate.[109]

Some women formed "ladies' auxiliaries" to the men's organizations; these groups seem to have become widely popular only in later years.[110] Auxiliaries carried out social and charitable functions, but did not necessarily provide material benefits. Instead, they contributed to the cultural and social lives of the individual landsmanshaftn and represented their members' interests to the men's societies. In 1912, for example, the sisters who attended services at the Timkovitser synagogue requested that the brothers supply them with several *taytsh-khumoshim* (Pentateuchs in Yiddish translation) and prayer books. Two years later the Hevras Noshim (Women's Society) Ahavath Zedek Anshei Timkowitz donated a Torah scroll to the congregation. At a meeting after the scroll was presented, the men's president "summoned the sisters, who were meeting in their room, and in the name of all the brothers, thanked them for the precious and holy gift . . . which they presented to the congregation, and wished them health and a long life, and that they should keep in mind giving more such presents." In return, the congregation agreed to President Leah Kanter's request that it honor the women with a plaque bearing the names of sisters who had contributed time and money to have the scroll made.[111]

While wives and daughters participated actively in the social activities of the landsmanshaft, men considered the more formal aspects of association life to be their province, being the primary breadwinners for their families. The organizations provided important material benefits, and men saw membership as one way in which they provided for the well-being of their wives and children. The socialist *Jewish Daily Forward* explained why a (male) radical should join a society: "We have been convinced that a socialist should not forget his obligations to his wife and family any more than any non-socialist . . . We have therefore realized that a socialist must belong to a lodge as much as any other poor person."[112] At least one writer in the "bourgeois" press concurred, arguing only half-facetiously that women would drop their objections to all those evening meetings if they only knew what important business their husbands discussed there.[113]

The membership history of the Zerdover Educational Society, Branch

301 of the Workmen's Circle, seems to confirm the view that women's participation correlated inversely with the societies' benefit function. Women comprised nearly a third of the members of one of the branch's predecessor organizations, the Golter-Bogopolier Yugnt, so long as it remained interested primarily in cultural activities. When the Golter-Bogopolier merged with the Zerdover and affiliated with the Workmen's Circle (thereby transforming itself into a society with a major benefit component), the complexion of the membership changed. Although the branch continued to accept women as members, only four applied on their own between 1909 and 1916, compared to 230 men.[114]

Representing the consolidation of informal networks that arose naturally in the process of migration, landsmanshaftn nevertheless embodied all of the political, religious, and cultural divisions within the immigrant community. The societies expressed these differences largely through the use of various sorts of ritual and symbol. While some associations of compatriots consciously attempted to draw from an old-country heritage, itself riven by conflict between traditionalists and radicals, others enthusiastically adopted the most popular organizational forms of the New World.

At the same time, however, the landsmanshaftn reflected a number of common influences and hopes. Most shared an emphasis on the possibility of upward mobility, in status if not in wealth, and all subscribed to the promise of an open and democratic society in which members participated equally. Their basic structure, derived from American sources and democratic in form, incorporated the immigrants' eager acceptance of the civic culture of the United States. (Even the socialist Workmen's Circle appealed to the "worker and *citizen*" (emphasis added) in its first declaration of principles.) Moreover, all kinds of organizations used varying amounts of fraternal ritual to underline their commitment to these ideals.

The landsmanshaftn also contributed to the immigrants' struggle for personal independence by providing their members with health care, financial assistance, and dignity at death, as well as an invaluable arena for comfortable social interaction. These benefits, both material and emotional, were central to the societies' mission and help to explain not only their membership policies but also their role in the Americanization process.

— 4 —

Brothers in Need

Landsmanshaftn of all types and persuasions offered essentially the same system of mutual aid. Each society met its members' basic material needs by providing a set of benefits that included medical care by an affiliated doctor, reimbursement for wages lost during illness, a form of life insurance, the cost of a funeral, and burial in the society's cemetery. The organizations also shielded the immigrants against indigence by granting emergency assistance and dispensing small interest-free loans. In addition, the associations offered less tangible benefits, including, most importantly, the casual sociability of regular meetings and the more formal social interaction that took place at society-sponsored balls, picnics, and theater outings. Set in place from the earliest years of mass Eastern European immigration, this array of material and nonmaterial benefits remained virtually unchanged well into the twentieth century.

Society benefits helped members and their families avoid dependence on charity and thereby enabled the immigrants to maintain a sense of dignity even during hard times. To ask for charity was to admit inadequacy, and recipients were exposed to invasive meddling by their benefactors. Charity therefore reinforced social hierarchy and vitiated the American promise of free and equal citizenship. Moreover, as Michael Katz has noted, "In the land of opportunity, poverty has seemed not only a misfortune but a moral failure."[1]

While charity spelled dependence and hierarchy, the ideal of mutual aid stressed reciprocity and democratic control. Equals engaged in mutual assistance with the assumption that each would take his or her turn at both receiving and giving. The immigrants also gained mastery over crucial aspects of their lives through their associations. By hiring their own physician, for example, the members of a society not only escaped the indignities of the public dispensary but also entered into a relationship in which their power matched that of the caregiver.

The principles of mutual aid thus reflected commonly held American ideals of masculine independence and self-reliance. Landsmanshaft benefits were designed to be part of the "family wage" with which a male household head provided an adequate living for his wife and children. In the absence of government social insurance programs, society benefits allowed workers and owners of small businesses to ensure a modicum of material security for themselves and their families. Significantly, however, the landslayt did not equate independence and self-sufficiency with rugged individualism. Rather, they responded collectively to the challenges posed by life in industrial society.[2]

Social events also furthered the immigrants' pursuit of both individual and collective dignity. Society members could make any occasion an arena for the allocation of individual honors. They brought their propensity for honors with them from the Old World, where it occupied an important place in Jewish social life. The distribution of distinctions acquired added urgency in America, since immigrant workers and small shopkeepers found them in short supply. The societies were one venue where the members might receive public recognition for their accomplishments and contributions. The American societies further improved over the Old World by adding an element of democracy to the bestowal of individual honor. While personal distinction in Europe demanded deference from people of lesser rank, in America it required the acknowledgment of one's peers.

Balls, banquets, and picnics also strengthened the standing of the group as a whole. The festivities expressed the organization's vitality, as well as its ability to take care of the material and emotional needs of its members. Further, social interaction helped create the sense of solidarity necessary to sustain the societies in their role as benefit providers. Even when members shared roots in an East European hometown, the steady round of social activities constantly reinforced ties that might otherwise have withered with time.

When the landslayt themselves later recalled their motivations for establishing societies, they often linked material needs with less tangible ones. As recent immigrants, they remembered, they had never felt more lonely and isolated than when faced with sickness, unemployment, or death. Interweaving the themes of material crisis and the need for companionship, one landsmanshaft chronicler described the plight of the early immigrants, who "did not have where and with whom to pass the little leisure that they had. When one took sick he had no one to care for him or to lend him a helping hand. And when one of the friendless ones passed away, the Hebrew Free Burial Society buried him in the Jewish 'Potter's Field' cemetery. Unable any longer to bear such lonesomeness, these landsmen united and founded this society."[3]

Jewish immigrants associated both the loneliness and the physical uncertainty with America. One landsmanshaft publication wrote of the need to organize in a country whose motto seemed to be "help yourself" (no one else will help you).[4] Jacob Massel, a Yiddish journalist and communal activist close to the landsmanshaftn, wrote that in Europe an individual could depend on family and friends in times of need, and that long-term face-to-face relationships with landlords and storekeepers mitigated the personal effects of economic hardship. In America, by contrast, merchants and landlords demanded payment on time, a high rate of geographical mobility made it difficult to form stable ties with neighbors or co-workers, and nobody could count on the help of strangers. American conditions, concluded Massel, made mutual aid societies "entirely a necessity."[5]

While the socialist poet Abraham Liessin did not share Massel's idyllic perception of Old-World Jewish life, he agreed that American circumstances required mutual assistance and organized benefit societies, something most Eastern European Jews had learned only after they reached these shores. Moreover, he too linked material want with emotional needs. "In no other civilized country in the world," wrote Liessin, "is the struggle for existence so infused with unexpected and fearful dangers as in the United States. And in no other country are the feelings of insecurity, of loneliness, of fear for tomorrow so well developed . . . That is why the United States is the classic country of all sorts of insurance societies."[6]

Whether or not Massel's description of conditions in Eastern Europe corresponded to reality, many immigrants shared his feeling that both social networks and communal institutions (like the hevrah kadisha) had been natural, even eternal, aspects of East European Jewish life. In comparison, America seemed to lack such deeply rooted arrangements. If they wished to establish any sort of community in their new home, the immigrants would have to "help themselves."

By forming mutual aid associations, the landslayt transformed a necessity into an opportunity to embrace the American promise of self-reliance and independence. Seeking to avert dependence on either traditional Jewish or modern American modes of charity, immigrants used their landsmanshaftn to accomplish collectively what they could not have done individually. They thereby created a mechanism for dealing with life's vicissitudes. As Massel put it, "After all, who wants to turn to charity as soon as one is forced to spend several weeks or months in bed?"[7]

The landsmanshaftn's espousal of collective self-reliance did not go uncontested. In the years before the turn of the century, both Orthodox and radical observers criticized the practice of mutual aid. Rabbi Moses Weinberger argued from a traditionalist standpoint that charity was a morally and practically superior method of relieving distress. He contrasted true charity, by which he meant that those with means gave freely to those in need, with what he saw as a highly conditional form of assistance. In fact, he considered landsmanshaftn and similar beneficial societies to be merely a second-rate form of charity in which benefits were "only paid out at the end, essentially as repayment of a loan." Not only did "those who contributed nothing to the fund receive nothing," but, Weinberger contended, society members who fell behind in their dues forfeited any claim to support they might otherwise have had: "But hark! The treasurer has his book open: 'For two quarters you have made no additional payment to your account.' So instead of receiving his principal back, the erstwhile contributor is dismissed that very night from the society. Membership, fellowship, and fraternal love all cease instantly. The bonds of friendship dissolve forever."[8]

Arguing from an entirely different set of assumptions, early Jewish socialists and anarchists also opposed the immigrants' mutual aid societies. The leftists too based their antagonism on grounds of principle and practicality. First, they scorned organizations not primarily intended to further the class struggle. As Bernard Weinstein, long-time leader of the United Hebrew Trades, later recalled, most radicals believed "that to get caught up in such trifling matters would impede the social revolution."[9] Secondly, they feared that the workers' limited dues money and organizational energies would go to the more popular societies, not the fledgling unions and radical parties.

While the intelligentsia harbored doubts, however, the rank-and-file eagerly embraced the principle of reciprocal assistance. The many religious congregations which also provided a regular set of benefits attested to the popularity of mutual aid among Orthodox Jewish immigrants. Radical societies were fewer in the early years, but the growth of the Workmen's Circle after 1900 demonstrated the appeal of benefit societies to socialist workers as well. Eventually both traditionalist and radical intellectuals came to favor mutual aid for precisely the same reasons as the broader public. Y. Weintraub of the Workmen's Circle expressed most succinctly the ethos shared by all associations, from the most conservative to the most radical. "The main advantage of the current benefit societies," he pointed out, "is that they are not charity organizations. There is no class of givers and no class of takers who are not also givers." While charity as practiced in the Jewish communities of Europe demeaned its recipients, Weintraub contended, "The Jewish orders and benefit societies in America root out the deeply ingrained feeling of powerlessness, and plant in its place a feeling of self-reliance."[10]

Organizations safeguarded the self-respect of needy members. Many society constitutions prohibited any member from reproaching another for having accepted aid from the association. The Independent Drobniner Benevolent Society underscored the severity of such an infraction by suspending violators for three months. The Ponevezher levied a small monetary fine for the first offense, but a second transgression brought an appearance before the society's "court."[11] When some society members began to donate their sick benefits back to their organizations, a Yiddish journalist decried the practice as a threat to the dignity of poorer landslayt. He described what might transpire in such a case: "Brother president," the recovered patient would begin, "and my dear brothers. I am alright. I do not need, God forbid, the benefit. You understand, I am a businessman, you know. I am alright and I hereby donate the money, you know, to the lodge." While the benefactors in these cases received the accolades of their lodge brothers, poorer members were made to feel like beggars when they kept the benefits due to them. The writer therefore called on Jewish societies to forbid this practice so that benefits would continue to be seen as a right and not a handout.[12]

As the historian Susan Glenn observes, Jewish men, who made up the bulk of official landsmanshaft members, increasingly staked much of their self-respect on their role as chief breadwinners for their households.[13] In fact, the average Russian Jewish man in 1911 brought home considerably less than was needed to support a family, and minimum standards of living were maintained only with the help of additional income from wives and older children. Nevertheless, the male head of the household was still likely to be the main earner. Since society benefits enhanced their ability to provide a secure living for their wives and children, men came to see membership as an "obligation to their families."[14] Coverage usually extended to wives, to daughters until they married, and sons up to the age of 18 or 21. Many societies also provided widows with some sort of benefit package, though this frequently covered only the costs of funeral and burial.[15] Women and children thus profited directly from their men's society affiliations, but they themselves usually had no formal voice in organizational affairs. Rather, the man, as head of the household, represented the family in the deliberations of the association.

Some women's and mixed societies provided similar benefits to women, many of them undoubtedly single or widowed, who supported themselves or their families. However, these benefits reflected the inferior earning power of female workers. Women generally paid lower dues and received smaller compensation than their male counterparts. For example, the Workmen's Circle at first established women's branches without any benefits at all, though Ladies' Branch 1 decided in 1901 to institute its own sick payment of $3 a week (half the regular amount paid by the order). Later, the order introduced special categories of female membership with lower benefits at less cost. Only after 1908 could women join as "class-one" members, although they retained the option of a cheaper "class-two" membership.[16]

Clearly, the material benefits offered by landsmanshaftn and other mutual aid societies contributed to the welfare of both men and women. Although no study ever measured the precise economic effect of association membership, contemporary observers generally agreed that the organizations helped many immigrants escape indigence and appeals to charity.[17] Yiddish editor Peter Wiernik reported that many of the pathetic cases who turned to him for assistance prefaced their stories by declaring apologetically, "I do not belong to a society."[18]

Material society benefits fell into three main categories: those associated with death, those dealing with illness and health care, and those providing general financial assistance.

Death Benefits

Benefits related to death were of great significance to the landsman-shaftn. In part, the importance of funerals and interments reflected the strong continuing influence of Jewish tradition even among secular groups.[19] But the stress placed on these ceremonies also derived from the immigrants' aspirations to an American standard of living, as well as from their preoccupation with a sense of both individual and collective honor. The societies' simple form of life insurance, called "endowment," aimed on a practical level to ease the financial burden on survivors.

The societies assured members and their families of a proper Jewish funeral and burial. In fact, practices associated with death and bereavement were often the most traditionally Jewish features of society life. Even otherwise secular societies helped their members observe the traditional custom of "sitting shivah," the seven-day mourning period prescribed by Jewish law, and more religiously inclined societies organized their own internal hevrah kadishas, with all the honorific trappings of the European burial societies. As a friend told Zvi Hirsch Masliansky when the popular preacher first arrived in America in 1895, "Death sustains the life of American Judaism."[20]

Death was not solely a Jewish preoccupation, however. Many working-class New Yorkers agreed with sociologist Robert Chapin that "burial constitute[d] an essential part of the American standard of living."[21] As Louise Bolard More reported, immigrants (other than Jews) spent more money on elaborate funerals than did the native-born, perhaps in deference to American expectations. Both immigrant and native-born workers, she concluded, exhibited a "desire to have a 'decent' or even fine funeral and an abhorrence of pauper burial."[22]

Membership in a society was not necessary in order to secure a proper Jewish burial in New York, since a charitable organization, the Hebrew Free Burial Society, provided them free of charge to the indigent after its founding in 1888. The landsmanshaftn, however, sought to help their members elude a demeaning resort to charity even after death. Moreover, when it came to burial, any potential disgrace fell not only on the "recipient" himself but also on the survivors, including the

deceased's landslayt, for failing to provide him with a dignified departure from this world. Burial benefits therefore constituted a major
motivation behind the founding of many societies. As one memoirist
recalled, the death of a landsman from Kamenets Litovsk prompted his
compatriots to form a society:

> After all of his acquaintances had gathered to pay him their final respects,
> they found to their shock and dismay that they did not have the means
> to bury him, and after many difficult and painful debasements, they were
> forced to bury him in the cemetery of the Hebrew Free Burial Society
> *(Hesed shel Emet).* With pain in their hearts, the Kamenetser landslayt
> returned from the funeral of their compatriot and friend, whom they had
> left in a strange cemetery among the unfamiliar graves of strangers, to
> which it would even be hard to get, and on which a friendly tear would
> never fall. Then several noble and empathetic people decided that such a
> thing should never happen again.[23]

As the Kamenetser example illustrates, many Jewish immigrants
demonstrated an aversion to interment by and among strangers, even
Jewish ones. Indeed, they placed much importance on burial among
their compatriots, in a place where acquaintances and friends could
watch over them. In this respect, the Jewish newcomers differed little
from those nineteenth-century middle-class Americans who saw "the
grave as a home in which the deceased rested with family and friends."
The continuing centrality of death in the Jews' consciousness, however,
contrasted dramatically with the increasing marginality of death among
the native-born middle class.[24]

To ensure that the dead remained part of the community, landsmanshaftn maintained their own cemeteries. The societies bought lots from
the commercially maintained Jewish cemeteries in the New York area,
and allocated the graves as needed to their members. By the 1890s a
society might respond to an advertisement in the Yiddish press, such as
the one placed by Mount Neboh Cemetery in 1891, announcing "cemetery plots by installment" from $100, and promising "for societies and
lodges, special low prices, easy terms."[25] The burial grounds themselves
lay in remote areas of Brooklyn, Queens, and Staten Island, but the
offices were on the Lower East Side. In fact, the acquisition of a
cemetery was often among a new society's first acts.[26]

Though located outside the center of the city, the Jewish society
cemeteries more closely resembled the tenement districts than they did
the "lawn" or "park" cemeteries then fashionable among the American
middle-class. With their "open meadows ranging over gently rolling

hills," these cemeteries discouraged the fencing-in of private plots and sometimes even the erection of tombstones. Their designers strove "to provide quiet and seclusion for mourners."[27] Jewish immigrant cemeteries looked quite different, quickly becoming a muddle of fences and gates as each society marked off its territory. Furthermore, they were allowed to get quite crowded. Seclusion and privacy in mourning were not part of the aesthetic of death which the immigrants had brought from the old country.

Landsmanshaft cemeteries, however, did not play quite the same role as Jewish burial grounds in Europe. Combining concern for a proper Jewish burial with an interest in worldly honors and a modern indulgence in sociability for its own sake, the societies used their cemeteries for both religious and secular purposes. Usually the only real estate the organizations or their members owned, the cemeteries symbolized a new rootedness in American soil as much as they represented a loyalty to an ancient heritage. Besides, many landslayt must have thought, why wait to put to good use the land in which they had invested their money?

The cemeteries thus grew into important centers of social activity and supplemented the meeting hall as places of honors and ceremony.[28] Outings to the cemetery with food and drink became a favorite activity for many landsmanshaftn. In the spring of 1905, for example, the Satanover Benevolent Society appropriated three dollars for liquor and sent out invitations for an excursion to "post the sign and have a bit of amusement."[29] The uses to which the societies put their burial grounds sometimes angered both middle-class Jewish reformers and defenders of traditional observance. Societies retained the old custom of visiting graves on the ninth day of the Hebrew month of Av, the traditionally observed date of the destruction of the ancient Temples in Jerusalem, but, as one Orthodox critic complained, "The law of fasting and mourning is overlooked . . . Jews go the cemetery, but they do not mourn or fast; they go to have a merry picnic."[30] At the prompting of Zionist leader Joseph Barondess, the New York Kehillah convention passed a resolution in 1912 condemning this practice. The community leaders sent a letter to local Jewish cemeteries requesting that they not "allow the Jewish name to be disgraced by permitting unseemly sights to take place in the sacred precincts." Washington Cemetery, one of the most popular with societies, responded, however, that it was powerless to stop the thousands who descended on the graves on *Tisha B'Av.*[31]

Societies commonly erected elaborate fences around their cemeteries.

The stone arches and cast-iron gates demarcated each association's property and proclaimed the group's existence to the silent denizens of adjacent plots and their frequent living visitors. Each society sought to protect its honor and image by keeping up with its neighbors. The First Prailer Sick Benevolent Association, for example, contracted in 1914 with the Richmond Borough Marble and Granite Monumental Works to build an arch and gate "the same as the Bacauer Society" for $675.[32] The construction of a gate also afforded an opportunity to hand out individual honors and raise funds with ceremony and celebration. When the Satanover Society auctioned off the honor of having one's name inscribed on its gate, the structure's permanence ensured that this would be perhaps the most expensive honor a brother could buy. (Inscriptions brought between $6 and $45, depending upon their placement.) After the Satanover completed their gate in 1917, "there took place the finest ceremony appropriate for the dedication of a cemetery gate, and the brothers and friends who came to take part in our celebration had a fine time."[33]

A deceased member's funeral constituted the most important ceremony associated with death and the cemetery. All organizations arranged and paid for funerals. The funeral confirmed once and for all the dead one's honorable place in the landsmanshaft community and gave the surviving members a chance to pay their last respects in the knowledge that they too would be accorded this final dignity. Typically, the Independent Mlaver K.U.V. covered expenses up to $30 and provided a hearse and two carriages. The Mlaver also required their members to "accompany the body to the ferry or bridge," and to dress respectably and behave decorously while doing so. Brothers who did not attend a funeral were fined.[34] Like many landsmanshaftn, the Satanover Society had its own banner to drape over the coffin at funerals. Black with white fringe, it bore a six-pointed star and the society's anchor symbol.[35]

Some religious landsmanshaftn maintained a semi-autonomous burial society and followed the tradition of according it special honor. The hevrah kadisha of the First Soroker Bessarabier Mutual Aid Society kept its own traditional *pinkas* (record book), which included the hevrah's by-laws *(takkanot)* and minutes, the names of deceased society members, and an introduction of a philosophical nature in Hebrew on life and death and the human desire to be remembered after passing on. Like other landsmanshaft hevrah kadishas, the Soroker hevrah held an annual banquet, for which it received a subvention from the larger society. The hevrah's members also retained the exclusive right to be called to the Torah in the society's synagogue on certain holidays, and to present gifts to the congregation in its own name.[36] Membership in the hevrah kadisha carried both privileges and responsibilities. The Timkovitser Congregation actually fined two brothers for insulting the burial society, but it also punished hevrah members who failed to fulfill their duties.[37]

In time the organization of funerals and burials in early twentieth-century America underwent a transformation. The introduction of the undertaker, and with it the commercialization of death, began with the need to transport the body over long distances to cemeteries located in outlying areas. Congregations and other societies made agreements with carriagemen, some of whom evolved into undertakers who provided a full line of services to their clients. Sanitary regulations and the use of factory-made coffins encouraged the growth of a funeral industry among Jews. Eventually, even the process of preparing the body for burial according to Jewish law *(taharah)* was transferred to the funeral parlor. Though some societies continued to maintain a hevrah kadisha which carried out the ritual preparation, others left this to the undertaker.[38]

In addition to covering funeral costs, societies paid five dollars in "shivah benefits" to cover wages lost by bereaved members during the seven-day mourning period. Even nonreligious societies provided this benefit, thereby enabling Jewish immigrants to adhere to custom when economic pressures made it difficult. According to Jewish tradition, the grieving family remained at home for one week and received visitors who came to console them. The society, too, would send a "shivah committee" to call on the mourners, and religious congregations supplied a quorum of ten men for prayer each day.[39] In this respect Jewish immigrant custom contrasted starkly with the emerging middle-class American view articulated by one cemetery superintendent in 1901: "When a death occurs in a family, the sanctity of the home should be respected. The privacy of the family should not be intruded upon by the public."[40]

Besides funeral costs and shivah benefits, societies provided their members with a form of life insurance, which they called "endowment" or "death benefit." Most independent associations offered the widow or heirs of a deceased brother one dollar for each member of the society. In many societies a surviving husband received half that amount on the death of his wife, reflecting the lesser loss of family income when a woman passed away. The amount of the benefit thus directly paralleled the size of the organization. For example, the First Prailer Benevolent Association paid Bella Garber $81 after the death of her husband, Julius, in 1915, while the Timkovitser Congregation disbursed $184 to a widow in 1918. Though modest and variable, Jewish society endowments compared favorably with the "industrial insurance" plans usually held by workers, which paid between $100 and $150.[41]

In contrast to the independent societies, the large orders offered fixed death benefits. These ranged from about $100 to over $1,000, but $500 policies were the most common.[42] The higher endowments made the orders attractive, but their unsound financing ultimately proved inherently destabilizing. The struggle to reform the orders' insurance practices dragged on for years and involved debates over the fundamental principles of fraternalism.

Most of the orders used the "assessment system" to raise the funds necessary to pay out the benefits promised to members. Under this arrangement the benefits dispensed in the previous quarter were tallied, and each member was assessed an equal share of the amount necessary to cover the previous quarter's disbursements.[43] As long as the members were young and the membership growing, this system seemed both fair and practical. As the membership aged, however, benefit disbursements mounted and so did assessments. Eventually, younger members came to feel that they were bearing a disproportionate share of the burden but not enjoying as many of the benefits as the older members. As costs increased, fewer new recruits joined. And as older members died, the membership shrank, further driving up costs. In addition, there was no relation between what the average member contributed during his lifetime and the benefits his survivors received. Over time, the order found itself paying out more than it was taking in.

The occasional collapse of a Jewish order brought home to many fraternal leaders the system's untenability. As Leo Wolfson, First Vice Grandmaster of the Independent Western Star Order, noted in 1917, "Every now and then a Jewish order goes out of existence and leaves in its trail thousands of widows and orphans, absolutely helpless in their greatest hour of need."[44] One of the largest Jewish orders of the nineteenth century, Kesher shel Barzel, had disappeared by 1910. By the time the Order Sons of Benjamin went under in 1911, it had shrunk from a membership high of 30,000 to just 9,700, nearly half of whom were over the age of sixty, with just 400 under forty.[45]

The most effective way to secure an order's funds was to adopt graduated rates based on actuarial tables such as the one developed by the National Fraternal Congress. Most of the Jewish fraternal leadership, together with sympathetic intellectuals, endorsed "fraternal rates" and pushed hard for their adoption. But the membership resisted.[46] The debate over fraternal rates in the Jewish orders paralleled discussions in the larger general fraternal movement. Older members opposed reforms because they believed, rightly, that their payments would increase. Many also objected to the changes as a violation of the fraternal principle that all members should share equally in all burdens and benefits. Samuel Dorf, Grand Master of Order Brith Abraham, opposed fraternal rates, believing them a commercial intrusion into the realm of brotherhood. He expressed the misgivings of many fraternalists when he argued, "If I considered Order Brith Abraham an insurance company like all other New York insurance companies, I would favor forcing each member to pay that . . . which he would have to pay to an insurance company. But our members and I consider Order Brith Abraham a Jewish benevolent body."[47] Even in the progressive Workmen's Circle, it took a ten-year battle to institute a graduated rate table. Branches like the Zerdover Educational Society, Br. 301, wavered between support and opposition, voting overwhelmingly in favor of fraternal rates in 1915 but opposing them by a narrow vote in 1917, after hearing a convincing antireform speaker. Nevertheless, the labor order finally adopted fraternal rates that same year. Other orders were also forced to reform or face extinction.[48]

Benefits and activities related to death thus stood at the center of landsmanshaft concerns. In some respects the landslayt sought to cope with death as they had in Europe, and their societies enabled them to do so by providing proper Jewish funerals and shivah payments. Even seemingly traditional practices, however, assumed new meaning in America. For example, while landsmanshaft cemeteries did not resemble those of the native middle class, neither did they conform to the Eastern European pattern. Even the hevrah kadisha, symbolically equivalent to its traditional European counterpart, now served the dues-paying membership of an individual mutual aid society rather than the entire local Jewish community.

Illness and Health Care

In an arrangement known as "contract practice" landsmanshaftn hired physicians to treat members and their families in return for a set annual fee. Working-class immigrants in many urban areas engaged doctors in this way, but observers associated the system especially with New York's Jewish societies. A report from Rhode Island, for example, noted that a number of ethnic lodges employed their own doctors, but made special mention of the practice in the Jewish immigrant neighborhoods of Providence, where "it is almost as rampant as it is in the East Side of New York." Likewise, a doctor in the Boston area, complaining of the difficulties faced by young physicians in setting up their practices, called for "a system of paid . . . contract work similar to the Jewish lodge system."[49]

The system of hiring doctors gave society members with access to primary health care. But just as importantly, it preserved the immigrants' sense of dignity and guaranteed them a great deal of power in the doctor-patient relationship. Members of societies did not have to resort to public dispensaries or hospital clinics, the other major health-care providers for the poor, which carried the stigma of charity. The services of the society doctor resembled those of a private physician in that treatment was carried out at the home, and therefore at the convenience, of the patient.

Contract medicine survived because it benefited some doctors as well. Young physicians just starting out in practice found it especially useful. By securing a number of lodge contracts, a fledgling practitioner could ensure a steady income while he built up an independent clientele.[50] Physicians who were immigrants themselves also profited from the system. Three of the doctors who served the Timkovitser Congregation between 1909 and 1918 were perhaps typical. Ranging in age from twenty-five to thirty-two, Drs. Osher Borenstein, Sol Sheyfer, and Israel Bernstein were immigrants who lived on the Lower East Side. Borenstein was even a Timkovitser landsman himself.[51] Facing social and cultural barriers to practicing outside of their own communities, ethnic doctors like these competed with one another for patients from a limited population. One 1906 study remarked on the popularity of the medical profession among Russian Jews in New York, and reported that "of late symptoms of over-supply in the market have been noticed."[52] These young immigrant or second-generation doctors formed the pool from which the societies hired their physicians.

Society practice meant long hours and hard work for the doctor. Physicians sometimes served as many as seven to ten lodges, and saw forty or more society patients a day. In addition to office hours from

8–10AM, 1–2PM and 6–8PM, the societies required their doctors to make house calls, often at odd hours over a wide geographic area. Forced to climb up and down tenement stairs in the Lower East Side, Harlem, and Brooklyn, society doctors found their patients exceedingly demanding. One angry physician described a case in which an associate answered an emergency call at eight in the morning only to find that a mother simply wanted her child vaccinated in time to register for school that day. On another occasion, a society doctor discovered that the patient to whom he had been summoned was not a family member entitled to his services, but a boarder who complained of feeling sick whenever he drank beer.[53]

Abuses of the lodge system sometimes compromised the quality of patient care. Harried and inexperienced practitioners had too little time to pay adequate attention to each case. Resentment at being over-worked and underpaid further dampened their inclination to exert themselves on behalf of their charges. One doctor later recalled hearing the story of a colleague who, tired of running up and down tenement steps, simply examined his patients from the sidewalk beneath their windows, dispensed prescriptions, and ran off to the next appoint-ment.[54] "Sad is the life of the lodge and society doctor," observed one journalist, "but sadder still is the suffering of the majority of patients who are treated by this sort of doctor."[55]

Nevertheless, contract medicine filled an important need. For the cost of just one or two visits ($2–3) from a private physician, a working-class family secured the services of a society doctor for the entire year. Inexpensive access to a physician encouraged early treatment and may well have prevented the progression of disease. If some members ex-ploited the system, a sympathetic journalist argued, it was still "better to trouble the doctor than to rely on miracles."[56] Access to regular physicians strengthened a preference already widespread among Jews and limited the use of patent medicines, folk healers, and other irregular practitioners.[57] Besides, not all the care was substandard, and some physicians who started out as society doctors went on to distinguished careers.[58]

Dispensaries—the main alternative to contract medicine—had all of its shortcomings plus the additional taint of charity. Like their col-leagues in society practice, doctors in public dispensaries faced over-whelming case loads. Patients waited for hours in crowded conditions for perfunctory examinations. Cultural differences exacerbated the mutual distrust between patients and physicians who hailed from widely different ethnic and class backgrounds. Most importantly, the dispensaries carried the unmistakable stigma of assistance tendered to the poor by their social superiors. Legislation in 1899 even made it illegal for any but the indigent to use the clinics, and administrators strove to eliminate what they termed "charity abuse" by both the nondestitute and the "unworthy poor." Recourse to a dispensary thus constituted a public declaration of indigence and exposed the patient to intrusive investigations to determine his or her eligibility for service. No wonder most immigrants avoided the clinics and preferred treatment at home.[59]

Society affiliation offered immigrant patients a way to bypass charity medicine and exert a considerable amount of control over their caregivers. The medical establishment, on the other hand, generally opposed contract practice as a violation of its preferred standard of fee-for-service remuneration. Many physicians believed that contract medicine simply put too much power into the hands of the patients at a time when the profession was struggling to establish its authority. As Paul Starr has pointed out, doctors needed to gain control over the institutions of the medical market if they were to secure the professional autonomy and high pay to which they aspired. While some doctors called for reforms in the lodge system that would give them more power, others called for its outright abolition.[60]

One Lower East Side doctor's vituperative attack on lodge practice clearly illustrates the issues of control and status involved in the contract system. Dr. Morris Joseph Clurman resented the influence of the "laymen . . . of the lowest strata of working men" who ran the societies. In his view, lodge practice seemed legitimate only so long as the members exhibited proper deference to the professionals they sought to employ. At first, he wrote, "societies would send a humble delegate to some physician and ask him to accept the office of lodge doctor for a fair and reasonable consideration." Later, competition among doctors enhanced the societies' control over the market until "the quilt had been reversed. It was the doctors who sought after the societies and not vice versa as formerly. The societies found that . . . they could well afford to discriminate and choose from the numerous candidates."[61]

Practitioners like Clurman objected especially to the method by which societies chose their doctors. Essentially, the members elected their physician every six months as they would any other officer. Because the stakes were so high, competition was fierce, and young physicians frequently joined many organizations in the hope of politicking their way into a position. Unfortunately, the system rewarded good campaigners better than it did good clinicians. Doctors curried favor with influential members, and meetings around election time abounded with medical rivals touting their own virtues and deriding their adversaries. Votes were close, and elections sometimes resembled the free-for-alls decried by Dr. Clurman and others. Disinterested observers agreed with the physicians that this process degraded the profession and damaged the quality of care. But the members remained unwilling to surrender the mechanism that guaranteed them control over their own health care.[62]

Members demanded medical care on their own terms and often complained that their doctors failed to meet the stringent conditions set forth by the societies. The organizations regularly and publicly took their doctors to task for their failures, and frequently exercised their power to hire and fire physicians to get the kind of service they wanted.[63] Landsmanshaft minutes reveal the members' perspective on the struggle for control between doctor and patient. The Satanover Benevolent Society, for example, retained five different doctors between its founding in 1903 and 1916.

When the Satanover Society first approached Dr. S. Klurman of the Kamenetser society in 1905, it appeared that the relationship between society and doctor would follow the pattern favored by the angry Dr. Morris Clurman. That is, the society respectfully requested the services of the physician, who agreed only reluctantly to serve such a small association. After the brothers finally persuaded Dr. Klurman to accept them, his profit was indeed small. Six family members signed up for medical benefits together with fourteen single members, each paying 75 cents and 35 cents respectively per quarter. Altogether, he received $9.40 quarterly to treat the members and their families.[64]

By August 1907 the Satanover had grown more assertive as consumers of medical care. In that month the society entertained a proposal to dismiss Dr. Klurman and invited the brothers to nominate a new doctor.[65] After investigating a number of candidates, the members chose Dr. Seidler of 100 East 4th Street and agreed with him to the following conditions: he was to receive $40 a year plus 25 cents for each examination of a prospective member; he was to be available from early in the morning until midnight, except for office hours, and make house calls as far north as 116th Street in East Harlem, and across the bridge in Williamsburg, Brooklyn.[66]

Satanover expected service from their doctor and did not hesitate to complain when they felt that they had not gotten what they paid for. The ink on Dr. Seidler's contract (if in fact he had one) was hardly dry when Brother Tshesler submitted a written complaint that "he called him twice and he did not come."[67] On another occasion, Brother Frankfeld "submitted a protest against the society doctor, [asserting] that he pays the society's doctor dues as a family man, and since he has a sick child he called the doctor by telephone. It was before 8PM, and he put him off until 12, and even then did not come. He was forced to call a doctor at 12 o'clock and to pay him two dollars for the visit." This time the society reimbursed the brother and deducted the amount from Dr. Seidler's regular fee. Although the members also voted to discharge the doctor, they reinstated him when he appeared at a meeting to deny the charges.[68] Dr. Seidler remained the society's doctor for some time, though complaints persisted.[69]

Even in a relatively small organization like the Satanover Benevolent Society many candidates vied for the position of society doctor. In 1911 the members finally ousted Dr. Seidler and replaced him with Dr. Theodore Dickes of Madison Street.[70] Dr. Dickes, in turn, lost his position to Dr. Jacob Marantz sometime around 1913. Dr. Dickes fought back, however, and regained his post by a vote of 11 to 10 in June 1915. The two doctors continued to do battle, but after Dr. Marantz returned to the position in December 1915, he beat back subsequent challenges by votes of 9–8 and 11–7.[71] Dr. Marantz actually won praise from the society, the first doctor to do so. The minutes record, "Since our brother L. Sagin was sick for several weeks . . . and reported that our Dr. Marantz had been devoted to him for the entire time that he was sick, better than money could buy, and since Dr. Marantz was also present at the meeting, the president thanked him from the heart in the name of the society."[72]

For a manual worker the costs of illness included loss of wages as well as doctor bills. Nearly all societies offered a "sick benefit" to make up for this potentially devastating deprivation of income. As Jacob Massel wrote, "When a poor member becomes sick, he and his family need not degrade themselves by appealing to the [United Hebrew] Charities for assistance . . . He suffers no degradation . . . because he asks no charity. He is given what he is entitled to. It is mutual aid."[73]

The standard sick benefit consisted of five dollars weekly, about half the average wage of a poor garment worker, for six to thirteen weeks each year.[74]

When a brother reported sick, a committee from the society called on him at home. The committee had a dual mission. On the one hand, it carried out the Jewish tradition of bikur holim, visiting the sick to comfort them and attend to their needs. On the other hand, it determined whether the patient had truly qualified for benefits by missing work due to illness. Some families may have found the committees intrusive (especially, as one humorous skit suggested, if they were malingerers), but a visit from landslayt, who shared the patient's cultural orientation and social standing, was undoubtedly preferable to a call by social workers from the "Charities."[75]

The societies even made it possible for ailing members to leave the city for extended stays in more healthful surroundings—one of the chief prerogatives of the middle-class sick. "Physicians in private practice," notes the medical historian Charles E. Rosenberg, "relied consistently in their therapeutics upon adjusting the regimen of their patients, especially in chronic ills." Rosenberg argues that poor patients were unable to "vary their diet, take up horse-back riding, visit the seaside, or voyage to the West Indies."[76] However, while their destinations may not have been so exotic or elegant, many landsmanshaft members suffering from tuberculosis and other chronic diseases went to "the country" with the aid of their societies. Some patients stayed at one of several Jewish sanatoria established after the turn of the century.[77]

Some societies tendered this aid on an ad hoc basis, while others adopted formal "consumption benefits." The Timkovitser Congregation belonged to the former category. On one occasion it granted a member $100 outright to go to the country for health reasons. In a second case the Congregation sent a brother to see a "professor" (that is, a specialist), and decided that if the doctor so ordered, the patient would receive $8 each week for as long as he needed to be out of the city.[78] Among the organizations with standard benefits, the First Komarover B.S. stipulated that when its physician certified that a member had to "go to Colorado" (home of the National Jewish Hospital for Consumptives), the society would give the unfortunate landsman $50, representing ten weeks' sick pay. Workmen's Circle branches utilized the order's $100 consumption benefit, and after 1910 sent their tubercular members to the Circle's own sanatorium in Liberty, New York.[79]

Financial Assistance

American society around the turn of the century offered little social insurance to the poor and near-poor. New York enacted its first workers' compensation law in 1910, but this only covered injuries sustained on the job. (It was declared unconstitutional in 1911, but a second law was passed in 1913.) Only in 1914 did the state establish a program of aid to "dependent children of widowed mothers," but this did not help intact families. Unemployment and old-age insurance were still twenty years away, and immigrant workers in small garment shops and similar industries were not among the limited number of people with private or government pensions.[80] Most Eastern European Jewish immigrants lived under or barely over the poverty line, and even common situations—illness, unemployment, the presence of young children in the household, or old age—could easily overtax their meager means. And with most garment workers facing "slack" for three or four months every year, un- and underemployment were a normal part of life.[81]

Private charitable organizations provided the bulk of relief for the destitute. By the turn of the century advanced thinkers on the subject no longer viewed poverty as primarily the result of the moral failures of the poor. Rather, settlement workers and others blamed poverty on social conditions and devoted much of their energies to reform and prevention. Nevertheless, on the practical level old attitudes and programs persisted. Professional social workers substituted dependence on impersonal bureaucracies for individual paternalism, but, as James Patterson has noted, they still sought to reform the individual as much as society.[82] Even in the best of circumstances, applying for charity compromised the petitioner's independence and sense of self-worth.

Landsmanshaftn attempted to help members "in need" without recourse to charity. Methods for dispensing assistance varied from society to society, and some had more formalized procedures than others. If a member of the First Komarover B.S. requested aid at a meeting, the president appointed a committee to investigate the petitioner's circumstances. Should the committee report that the member was "truly in need," the society dealt with the matter at the following meeting. The constitution did not indicate an amount to be given, but did limit members to $15 in aid annually. It also gave the president the right to disburse up to five dollars in an emergency situation. The Drobniner Society allowed its president to give up to ten dollars and did not require a committee report. It did, however, limit members to two relief payments each year.[83]

In some ways general relief functioned in the least satisfactory way of all the societies' benefits. It was the only benefit that employed a "means test" to determine eligibility, demanding that a member convince his fellows that he was actually destitute enough to need the money. Landsmanshaft relief thus came perilously close to resembling the charity aid that it was intended to avoid. Furthermore, societies left the amounts of aid to the discretion of the membership, and this sometimes led to arbitrary decisions in which politics and personal relationships played a large role. In the Satanover Society, for example, a brother in need might receive a grant from the treasury of five or ten dollars, a loan of as much as $15, or the proceeds from a collection among those present. In one case a member received a loan of $50, but when several brothers protested vociferously at the next meeting, order collapsed, and a "sheriff" had to bring the meeting to an end.[84]

Nevertheless, members preferred assistance from the society to dependence on alms. For one thing, the recipient of aid from the landsmanshaft did not necessarily lose his standing among the members. The Satanover Society's Brother Berman, for example, served as vice president despite his repeated appeals for relief from the organization.[85] Furthermore, aid from the society could play a constructive role, such as providing the capital to open a business. When one brother contracted a chronic illness and needed such help in 1911, the Timkovitser Congregation gave him $15 sick benefits in advance, $10 outright support, and a $25 loan, payable over two years.[86]

The personal approach, which sometimes caused trouble, also occasionally worked in favor of needy members. At a time when professional social workers had come to stress impersonal techniques and principles, the immigrants continued to value long-standing relationships with their landslayt. In fact, these sentimental ties frequently helped a member to secure access to material benefits. For example, although nonpayment of dues constituted grounds for denial of benefits or expulsion, the landsmanshaftn almost always granted a member's request for a reduction or postponement of his debt. During the depression of 1908, the Satanover Society received favorably such an appeal from its Brother Tishman: "Since he is an old brother," the minutes relate, "it would be very painful for him to be stricken from the Satanover Society. But since times are now very bad, [he requests that] the society wait a while and when things are going a little better for him he will pay everything."[87]

Interest-free loans as a form of aid have deep roots in Jewish tradition. American Jewish social workers continued to prefer loans to outright relief because, they argued, loans discouraged pauperism and encouraged a spirit of self-reliance.[88] The immigrants themselves agreed. Landsmanshaftn frequently aided members in need by lending them small amounts, and about a third of the societies created formal loan funds which provided start-up capital for new businesses as well as assistance to those who were simply strapped for cash.[89] The size of the funds varied considerably, but figures from one of the largest illustrate their popularity. The Husiatiner K.U.V. reported a fund of $3,000 in 1916, with loans of $10 to $100 amounting to an annual circulation of $5,000 to $6,000.[90] Assuming that most of the individual transactions were small, this would indicate that more than one hundred members took advantage of the fund each year. Fund regulations also differed in their details, but not in their main provisions. The Meretzer Relief Association allowed a member to borrow up to five dollars on his own signature, and an additional five with a second brother as guarantor. Loans of $10 to $50 required the endorsement of a member or nonmember with "an open business." The directors of the fund, however, had the right to accept an endorser without a business if they knew him to be a "prosperous and honorable man." The association required borrowers to repay loans over a twenty-week period.[91]

It is impossible to evaluate with any precision the degree to which society benefits maintained the good health of the Jewish population or effectively kept society members off the relief rolls. As measured by several important indices, including general and infant mortality, Jews were in fact healthier than most other New Yorkers, particularly those living in similar conditions of poverty and overcrowding. Both contemporary observers and later historians have attributed this advantage to specific Jewish cultural and religious traits, as well as to improvements in public sanitary conditions.[92] Nevertheless, it seems plausible that regular primary care contributed to New York Jewry's relatively sound physical state. Sympathetic social workers also credited the mutual aid societies with helping their members avoid charity. Noting that the number of families dependent on the assistance of the United Hebrew Charities had fallen steadily since 1901, the prominent social worker Morris Waldman wrote of the societies in 1917: "They are increasingly responsible, there is little doubt, for the gradual diminution in the need for charitable relief."[93] While many other factors were certainly also at work, there is no question but that the societies enabled their members to maintain their sense of dignity and independence in sickness as well as in health.

Nonmaterial Benefits

Intangible benefits proved to be as important as any payments received by members when in need. These included social interaction in a comfortable atmosphere, escape from the drudgery and worry of tenement and shop, the conferral of collective and individual honors, the safe venting of anger and resolution of disputes, and the sense that the immigrants had their lives under control.

Landsmanshaft socializing was closely related to society ritual. Together they strengthened the bonds among members and the sense of solidarity evident in the material benefits. In addition, such undertakings as balls, picnics, and theater parties reflected the substantial secularization of Jewish life. Unlike the banquets of traditional Jewish associations in Europe, many of these affairs had no other rationale besides sociability for its own sake. As one outside observer noted, "The history of the Jewish race is one long record of oppression and repulsion, by which, if such a thing were possible, the very capacity for enjoyment might have been destroyed. Decidedly, however, it has not been destroyed. Whatever may be true of the Jew in Russia or Rumania, when he once becomes acclimated in the New York Ghetto, he has a very good time."[94] Events that raised funds for good causes were partial exceptions to just having a good time, and so were some of the activities of the religious societies. The congregations distinguished themselves from more secular groups by celebrating such traditional Jewish occasions as the completion of a new Torah scroll.[95]

Landsmanshaft socializing also differed from both the traditional Jewish pattern and the practice of the largest American fraternal orders by including women. While the material benefits and organizational business were male preserves, entire families participated in the more social aspects of society life. Women frequently took part even in the informal socializing which accompanied regular meetings. As for major social events, both men and women invariably attended and enjoyed them together.[96]

Much socializing occurred informally before, after, or even during meetings. The landslayt took the opportunity to tell each other of their troubles, receive news from the old country, and simply converse in a relaxed atmosphere. No wonder that for many immigrants "a meeting of the society . . . was a holiday, for which one would prepare and to which one would look forward like the arrival of the nearest and dearest thing."[97] Maintaining decorum always presented a problem, but members did not want to change. The Satanover Society, for example, rejected a proposal to fine members who "carry on private conversations and are not attentive."[98]

Similarly, religious services of downtown synagogues were as much an opportunity to meet with landslayt as to worship. As one visitor reported, "The old women, and still more the old men, when they meet in the Synagogue enjoy themselves socially quite as much as religiously. They talk all through a large part of the service, but no one seems to be disturbed by the conversation and hand shaking."[99] Indeed, attendance at synagogue services and meetings provided many immigrants with their major "means of social gratification."[100]

The societies also organized social interaction in a number of more formal ways. In winter, the East Side witnessed hundreds, if not thousands, of balls and other entertainments given by all kinds of organizations.[101] On one randomly selected Saturday in November 1908, a reader of the *Forward* could choose from among ten advertised balls, two literary evenings, a dinner/concert, and several lectures and meetings. If he or she cared to plan in advance, the paper also featured announcements for at least 19 upcoming balls. All of the dances were sponsored by landsmanshaftn. The Lomzer Young Men's Benevolent Association, for example, announced a masquerade ball with two halls, two bands, and a $125 first prize for best costume. The Lomzer event was the most expensive to attend, at 25 cents for admission and 25 cents for hat check; those of the Novaridoker Progressive Association, Branch 146 Workmen's Circle (15 cents for ticket and hat check), and the Musher and Baranowitcher Benevolent Association (25 cents for gents, 15 cents for ladies, with hat check), were cheaper. The Minsker crowd had a choice of two affairs: at the Minsker Loan Association or at the Minsker Young Friends Benevolent Association, which sponsored a "color-light ball." The Novoridker Young People Association promised to donate 50 percent of the proceeds of their ball to the victims of a recent fire in their hometown.[102]

The elegant society dances provided the landslayt with a momentary escape from their difficult day-to-day existence. Gimmicks such as colored lights, confetti, "Bengali lanterns," and "perfume balls" created a fantastic atmosphere far removed from the realities of the gritty city streets, the crowded tenement, and the noisy factory. This form of entertainment, which the Yiddish press traced back to seventeenth-century French aristocracy, also symbolized for the immigrants a personal, if ephemeral, transcendence of class barriers.[103] At the ball of the Brailer Young Men's Benevolent Association, a participant reported, "one forgot completely that these were simple workers who suffered through their days in the shops."[104]

The balls made a statement by the landslayt, to themselves and to the wider world, that they were dealing successfully with their new American environment. At the Brailer affair, as at other society functions, "Uncle Sam's fortunate banners . . . tenderly waved a consolation to the brooding flags of Zion" and set a decidedly upbeat and optimistic tone. The showy evenings celebrated the societies' ability to take care of their own and demonstrated that the immigrants had formed a prosperous and united community independent of uptown benefactors. "It is a pity," opined the Brailer observer, "that there was no representative of the United Hebrew Charities present to see how the East Side for the most part takes care of itself, without noise, without drums and without trumpets."[105]

Landslayt of all ages enjoyed themselves at the hometown association balls. These functions gave married and older immigrants a chance to indulge in the era's passion for dancing even after they had outgrown New York's many commercial dance halls.[106] The affairs had something for everyone, mixing contemporary European and American dance styles with old-fashioned Jewish steps. Nearly 4,000 "young men and women, boys and girls, but also old folks," attended the 1902 function of the Minsker Independent Benevolent Association, where "young and old amused themselves each in their own manner. Young couples danced the modern American and also a couple of Minsker dances, and old men and women danced *dreydlekh* and *'hopkes.'"[107]

Landsmanshaft balls thus also offered a respectable alternative to the many dances sponsored by "pleasure clubs" or commercial halls catering mostly to single young people. Though highly popular, these had an aura of social adventure, if not unsavoriness. By contrast, the presence of several generations and the close acquaintance of many of the revelers made the society affairs settings at which young women in particular could safely enjoy themselves and meet other people their age. Bella Feiner found the balls a congenial place for having fun, and also, significantly, recalled that they helped overcome the barriers among immigrants from different towns and regions: "I loved life and was anxious to go to dances. After all, 'youth is youth.' I didn't go to dance halls but to organizations of towns in Europe. The town organizations invited each other to affairs. That is how we melted, mixed. I went to a Rumanian affair, a Russian affair. We met different young people."[108]

The functions helped boost each society's sense of organizational elan and also attracted new members. The affairs usually featured an imposing members' or "couples' march," which demonstrated ceremoniously the sponsoring group's strength and unity.[109] Landslayt who were not already members might attend and find inspiration to join. The balls of the Satanover Society barely covered expenses, but the "results" as reported by the arrangement committee included the number of candidates nominated, as many as twenty-two in 1913.[110]

Like all landsmanshaft activities, balls served as occasions for the distribution of individual honors. The officers and organizers of a successful event received special attention at the event itself and afterwards as well. The committee that planned the Minsker ball marched several times around the room, "and when they finished, the members took their leader, Mr. Joseph Leder, by the hands and to the strains of the 'Marseillaise' danced with him around and around the hall." The names of both officers and committee members also appeared in the newspaper.[111] The Satanover Society generally honored committee members by adding their names to the organization's honor roll, or by presenting them with "resolutions with golden letters." The Satanover also funded their affairs by auctioning off individual honors in the form of special ball offices, including floor manager, "first couple march," "second couple march," treasurer, assistant floor manager, banner carrier, American-flag bearer, and cashier.[112]

Picnics were the summer equivalents of the winter balls. Working-class organizations representing all of New York's ethnic groups sponsored excursions to the country or outlying areas of the city. The societies could run their own outings, or they could buy tickets to the many large picnics arranged by fraternal, social, trade-union, and political organizations and advertised to the general public through posters and newspaper advertisements. Tickets were relatively inexpensive, and one study found that three quarters of the city's working-class families went on such outings at least once a summer. Despite the rise of commercial recreations such as amusement parks, beginning in the 1890s, the organizational picnic remained a central feature of society activity well past the turn of the century.[113]

The appeal of the picnic was simple: a cheap one-day family vacation from the hot city summer. For residents of the immigrant "ghetto," the excursion by subway, tram, train, or boat also constituted a kind of adventure outside the confines of their accustomed neighborhood. Yiddish humorist Z. Libin described the thrill and the potential terror of one such outing. In this story Sam the capmaker convinces his wife that they should attend his society's upcoming picnic. They do nothing but work and struggle, he tells her. Why should they not have a little pleasure as well? "The summer is almost over," he says, "and we haven't even seen a single blade of grass; we sit here day and night and sweat in the dark." Furthermore, he argues, it won't cost much; only about 80 cents altogether for the family ticket (30 cents), carfare, and food for the family of eight.[114] Unfortunately for Sam and his family, their outing ends badly: the milk bottle breaks and spoils the food, they never find the other lodge members, and it starts to rain. They retreat home and swear never to go on another picnic. Readers must have identified with Sam's desire for some fresh air, his difficulties in organizing a large family for an outing, and his and his wife's anxieties about leaving their familiar neighborhood. But his haplessness in overcoming these obstacles provided the story's humor. Although more than one Yiddish humorist adopted the disastrous picnic as a subject, most immigrants negotiated the topography of their new homeland quite effectively.[115] Excursions must have been successful, for societies and other organizations continued to sponsor them year after year.

Theater parties, known as "benefits," formed the third important component of the landsmanshaft social calendar. Both societies and theaters gained from these events, with the society receiving a major social event, a focus of activity for months before, a venue for the distribution of honors, and, if all went well, a profit. (Earnings went to the treasury or to aid a needy brother or some other cause, hence the term "benefit.")[116] The Yiddish theater, in turn, received a substantial intake and an audience for the performance. Perhaps even more importantly, the society outings helped develop an audience of regular theatergoers.

Within ten years after the first Yiddish stage production in America took place in August 1882, the benefit system had become a mainstay of support for the theater. The various companies appealed for group patronage in the Yiddish press before each season. In 1892, for example, the Rumanian Opera House at Second Avenue and Houston Street announced its coming attractions and issued a call to organizations: "Notice! Lodges, hevras and societies who want to save half their money, and to have a sure profit, should hurry as quickly as possible to buy their benefits."[117] Associations bought blocks of tickets at discounts of between 50 percent and 80 percent. They would then sell the tickets to members, friends, and the public. The benefits took place primarily on week nights, when an audience was more difficult to attract, but there were some on weekends as well. Writing in 1901, Yiddish playwright Jacob Gordin figured that the three Yiddish theaters then in existence gave some 480 weekday benefit performances each year, with over 600 societies in attendance.[118] Since societies also bought smaller discount blocks on weekend nights, the total number of theater parties was undoubtedly even higher.

Commentators with different points of view blamed the societies for what they saw as the sorry artistic state of the Yiddish theater. Ironically, both Jacob Gordin, a crusading exponent of dramatic "realism" and secular enlightenment, and the Orthodox *Tageblat,* which considered Gordin's own work to be "filth" and "degeneracy," openly criticized the benefits. Gordin believed that they helped transform the theater into a "circus," while the *Tageblat* saw them as the mainstay of "Gordinism."[119] One friendly nonimmigrant observer agreed that the benefits "lower[ed] the tone" of the Yiddish theater, but nonetheless valued the boisterous ebullience of the typical Yiddish audience. From this viewpoint, the societies added to the main spectacle:

It is on the "benefit" nights that the Yiddish theatre is best worth visiting, provided the play is not the thing. The audience is made up of family parties and neighbor-groups; from the grandsires to the infant and boarder the whole tenement house is there with its luncheons and its bedlam . . . Altogether they are joyous occasions, these benefits. Presents are passed over the footlights to the "stars," the officers of the society strut out before the curtain between acts and make "spitches," the member who sold the greatest number of tickets has a gold-medal pinned on his palpitating bosom, and all bathe in a sea of ecstasy, with a feeling of good deeds well done, philanthropic purposes well served—if the "benefit" is a success.[120]

For the landsmanshaftn, the play was probably less the thing than the financial success of the benefit and the honor it brought to both the group and the individual organizers. The Satanover Benevolent Society decided to buy tickets to the People's Theater in 1906 because it was "easier to sell the tickets," and it offered a cash prize to any brother who distributed $15 worth.[121] In subsequent seasons, the Satanover landslayt attended the Kalish, Windsor, Thalia, and Adler theaters, generally on a Saturday night. The brothers almost always proclaimed the theater outing a great success, and the chairman of the arrangement committee usually received an award, such as a place on the society's permanent honor roll.[122]

The landslayt used balls, picnics, and theater parties to confer honors on one another, but they hardly needed any special occasion to do so. The bestowal of honors was, in fact, one the most important benefits accorded by the societies to the immigrants, and it permeated all of the organizations' activities. Eastern European Jews brought a hunger for honors with them from the old country, but while wealth, learning, and pedigree determined distinction in Eastern Europe's hierarchical Jewish society, America seemed to promise the ordinary person freer access to honor and recognition. Yet the newcomers found that immigrant life offered few opportunities to achieve distinction. Shop workers and small businessmen seldom received much recognition from their own community, much less from society at large. Only in their own associations could they expect acknowledgment of their contributions and accomplishments.

Within their organizations, the immigrants democratized the bestowal of honor by conferring it by majority vote. Indeed, election to office constituted the most important means by which a brother might acquire distinction. Installation night provided the most obvious forum for giving recognition to active members, as outgoing officers received thanks for their service and new ones took their places on the dais.[123] At regular meetings even the reading of the minutes could be an occasion for paying tribute to officers, since many societies read their names aloud at the beginning of each gathering.[124]

Ceremonies conferring honors were closely bound up with the societies' ritualism. The officers' regalia enhanced their dignity, as did the president's power to wield the gavel and command the meeting. The honor accorded to the officers diffused throughout the lodge, devolving by association on the rank-and-file as well. Writing of the fraternal orders, B. Rivkin perceptively noted: "Of all the privileges which the order granted to the lodge, the most important was autonomy in assigning honors. It gave the chairman of the lodge the right to call himself 'president' and dressed him in epaulets with red braids and a medieval military hat with feathers. It gave him the right to give out honors and titles, and put a gavel in his hand with intricate incantations and slogans."[125] This was equally true of the independent societies, though Rivkin underestimated the degree of democracy inherent in the distribution of distinctions. They were awarded not by an imperious president but by the membership as a whole.

Small impromptu ceremonies to recognize this brother or that by adding his name to the honor roll, or by presenting him with a medal, proclamation, engraved beaker, or candlesticks, pervaded society life. When in 1906 the Satanover Benevolent Society awarded a medal to its first secretary, Brother Bass, it did so with great fanfare. The minutes relate:

> The committee consisting of Brothers Liptzin, Hilberman and Tasler, in charge of the medal for Brother Bass, brought it to the society today. And the committee showed the medal personally to all the brothers. Then the brother president introduced Brother S. Bass, [enumerating] the good deeds which he performed from the first period after the society was founded until the present, and all that he has accomplished from the first day until now, and honored him with the honor of having the president pin on him the medal, on which is engraved our emblem, an anchor, on which is written "Satanover Benevolent Society." In addition it has Brother Bass' name, and under that the year in which it was presented. And it was enthusiastically received with brotherly applause, and with friendly hand greetings, full of heartfelt love and loyalty from one brother to the other.[126]

The brothers thus heard Brother Bass honored twice: once during the ceremony itself, and again at the next meeting, when the secretary read the minutes.

Religious congregations adopted the new ways but also retained old-country methods of acquiring distinction. They followed the traditional practice of auctioning off certain honorific roles in the service, and also allowed members to purchase honor by donating ritual objects to the synagogue. So that less affluent members of the congregation might enjoy this distinction, the Timkovitser Congregation raffled off the opportunity to do this on at least two occasions. Both times the winners were wives of members. One, "Brother Zev Grunem Rabinovits's wife, Khatshe," received a silver beaker to present to the shul, while the other won the honor of giving a silver breastplate for the Torah.[127]

The matter of individual honor assumed added importance because it impinged on the collective honor of the group. The landsmanshaftn attempted to replace many traditional mechanisms of social control lost in the course of migration. Like the mutual aid societies of other ethnic communities, the Jewish associations regulated the behavior of their members not only to protect the associations against bad insurance risks, but also to make sure that behavior reflected well on the moral standards of the group. Thus many societies refused benefits to those with "immoral diseases" and reserved the right to expel members convicted of crimes.[128]

The associations found it impossible to enforce absolute harmony, but they did attempt to contain dissension within the confines of the group. Historian Abraham Karp has even suggested that immigrant societies "provided members with a safe place to release their hostility."[129] As Karp notes, members insulted one another and charged each other with various infractions, after which the society "peace committee" would pass judgment, levy fines, and restore unity. The Timkovitser Congregation was expert at this process, turning instances of discord into opportunities for honor by sentencing wrongdoers to present gifts of Bibles to the synagogue.[130] At all events, the landsmanshaftn sought to prevent disputes from reaching the public eye and, especially, from going to court. Given the potential material and emotional stakes, it is not surprising that they did not always succeed.[131] Nevertheless, most landslayt lived in relative concord with each other and their societies.

Under American conditions Jewish immigrants from Eastern Europe experienced both insecurity and opportunity. Lacking well-established communal structures and social networks, the immigrants' vulnerability to illness, death, or financial crisis exacerbated the sense of loneliness they often felt in their new home. Accepting the American value of self-reliance, they realized that they could only live up to that ideal by banding together in associations. The landsmanshaftn provided their members with vital assistance in overcoming both material and emotional obstacles through extensive programs of mutual aid and social interaction. Moreover, the societies enabled the immigrants to exercise a degree of democratic control over some aspects of their lives that would have been impossible in the Old World.

Landsmanshaft members attained collectively, through their associations, the independence and dignity that would have been difficult for them to achieve individually. This they achieved first of all by avoiding dependence on charity for medical care, burial, and income support. But they reinforced their achievements symbolically with their balls, picnics, and theater parties, events which signaled to the world that the immigrants were coping successfully in their new environment. In addition, these occasions, as well as ordinary meetings, provided arenas for the bestowal of the individual honors desired by the immigrants but in short supply in the outside world.

Landsmanshaft mutual aid was directed inward toward each society's own members. But the hometown associations were not isolated islands oblivious to the surrounding society. Rather, their concern for honor required awareness of broader standards, and many organizations exhibited interest in larger communal issues.

⌣ 5 ⌐

The Building Blocks of Community

As the Jewish population of New York grew and matured at the beginning of the century, various conceptions of Jewish community vied for the allegiance of the public. Efforts to consolidate the community and provide some sort of unified structure contended with clashing interests and ideologies. Traditional leadership groups, such as the Orthodox rabbinate and wealthy philanthropists, competed with the labor movement, the fraternal orders, and other mass organizations. Vocal adherents of such competing ideologies as Zionism, socialism, and Americanism (and various syntheses of the three) debated the nature and future of Jewish identity. On a more practical level, charities sponsored by Eastern Europeans arose alongside those sponsored by the older German-Jewish community to create an impressive infrastructure of social-service, educational, and medical institutions.

Despite its reputation for insularity and resistance to outside influence, the landsmanshaft world reflected this ferment. While some contemporary observers lamented that the "Anshe Kowno and Anshe Jitomir and the 'Men of every Russian Hamlet' lead separate existences," and subsequent historians described the landsmanshaftn in the years before the First World War as "completely isolated, provincial, and clannish," the societies in fact participated in a variety of larger communal endeavors. While most societies lacked a consistent ideological orientation, they were far from constituting what Irving Howe characterized as a "nonideological oasis" in the midst of a politically charged community. Rather, all of the debates of the surrounding environment echoed within the lodge room.[1]

Notwithstanding their locked doors, passwords, and "inner watches," the societies were surprisingly open to all kinds of outsiders. Proponents of diverse movements recognized that gaining the support of the Jewish public meant winning over the hometown groups, and on meeting nights the public halls at which the various organizations gathered teemed not only with landslayt attending to their business but also with delegations seeking support for their causes and charities. Depending on their orientations, landsmanshaftn regularly contributed to educational institutions, political causes, and philanthropies ranging from the small old-fashioned Maskel el Dol (Aid to the Poor) society and the Mizrachi (Religious Zionist) movement to the Socialist Party's Meyer London Campaign Conference, and the Peter Kropotkin Jubilee Committee.[2]

Beyond these occasional small contributions, a number of organizations and movements sought to involve individual societies in Jewish communal affairs in a more permanent way. Hundreds of hometown associations became branches of fraternal orders and landsmanshaft country federations, such as the Federation of Galician and Bucovinean Jews of America. These larger bodies nurtured leaders who used their base of support in the landsmanshaftn to play a wider role in the Jewish community. The orders and federations also gave voice to the mix of sentimental Jewish nationalism and enthusiastic American patriotism which formed the inchoate philosophy of many of the smaller organizations.

Less successful were some more far-reaching experiments that aspired to unite New York Jewry in overarching structures similar to those that had once dominated the local Jewish communities of Europe. Leaders of such ambitious undertakings as the New York Kehillah appealed for landsmanshaft support, and many societies did in fact join them. Ultimately, however, landsmanshaftn and other societies zealously guarded their independence and rejected affiliation with centralized communal structures. Memories of the corrupt and iniquitous kahal system in Europe conditioned the Jewish public's reluctance to create a new central community. American conditions of voluntarism enabled the grass-roots associations to escape the discipline such a system would necessarily have imposed. Indeed, the autonomy of their societies symbolized for the members the American promise of opportunity, equality, and democracy, and any structure that threatened to create a European-style oligarchy aroused distrust.

The hometown associations proved much more willing to support movements that promised to help the members in their day-to-day concerns without demanding that the societies surrender their autonomy. Only a few landsmanshaftn fully accepted the labor movement's socialist ideology, and most of these had affiliated with the Workmen's Circle. However, when the labor movement successfully identified itself with the practical interests of large numbers of their members, the other societies came willingly to its support. Likewise, many landsmanshaftn enthusiastically backed such practical social welfare agencies as the Hebrew Sheltering and Immigrant Aid Society (HIAS). All segments of the Eastern European community, whatever their political or religious leanings, had shared the experience of immigration and naturally sympathized with an organization which assisted newcomers and lobbied against restriction.

In Search of a United Community

The earliest effort to create an overarching structure for the New York Jewish community drew on the support of some landsmanshaftn, but failed in the end because of seemingly irreconcilable landsmanshaft differences and the inability of centralized Jewish institutions in America to discipline a diverse population. In 1887 the Association of American Orthodox Hebrew Congregations hoped to strengthen traditional Judaism in New York by establishing order in the city's chaotic religious sphere. In particular, the Association's affiliated synagogues sought to standardize marriage and divorce proceedings, and above all to regulate the production of kosher meat. To accomplish these goals, the Association, which included a number of prominent landsmanshaft congregations, imported Rabbi Jacob Joseph from Vilna to serve as Chief Rabbi of New York.[3]

After an auspicious beginning, the undertaking ran into a series of obstacles that proved insuperable and soon led to the Association's collapse. Adherents of Reform Judaism, immigrant radicals, and Americanized Orthodox circles all refused to acknowledge the Chief Rabbi's authority. The regulation of kashrut proved more difficult than expected when butchers resisted Rabbi Joseph's control and consumers objected to higher prices caused in part by the fees he collected for giving his approval to meat. These fees, in fact, reminded many people of the infamous *korobka,* the onerous tax imposed upon kosher meat by the Russian government. An anti-korobka campaign soon arose led by an unlikely coalition of butchers, radicals, and disaffected Orthodox rabbis.[4]

Tensions also developed between non-Hasidic "Lithuanian" Jews represented by Rabbi Joseph, on the one hand, and Galician and Hungarian Jews, mainly Hasidim, on the other. To mollify the latter group, "who were beginning to murmur that the association was run by and for Lithuanian Jews," the Association offered Rabbi Joshua Segal, a Galician who had been in New York since 1875, the post of *av bet din* (head of the rabbinical court). He refused to be a subordinate of the newly arrived Chief Rabbi, however, and turned down the position. By October 1888, a year after Rabbi Joseph's arrival, the Congregations of Israel Men of Poland and Austria, a body of twenty congregations, had named its own chief rabbi and formed its own rabbinical court, which met at the Sarayer Shul on Hester Street.[5]

As Rabbi Joseph's authority declined, congregations began to drop out of the Association. For a time, Rabbi Joseph depended for his support on the very butchers he was supposed to supervise, until even they dispensed with his services in 1895.[6] The Chief Rabbi died in poverty in 1902, and was rescued from obscurity only by the famous riot which took place at his funeral. Neither the original Association of American Hebrew Orthodox Congregations nor its Galician rival survived the rabbi.

Over the next two decades, organizations that did not aim to establish centralized authority over the Jewish community successfully incorporated large numbers of societies. The fraternal orders were the first, absorbing hundreds of landsmanshaftn. As lodges of an order, landsmanshaftn came into intimate contact with one another and also participated in the general work of some of the largest Jewish organizations of the day.[7]

The fraternal orders supported Jewish charitable undertakings and, increasingly, took stands on political issues. On a number of occasions in the first decade of the twentieth century, Independent Order Brith Abraham (IOBA) and other orders "championed publicly the interests of Jewry as a whole." In the wake of the Kishinev pogrom, for example, IOBA donated $1,500 to the victims and appealed to President Roosevelt to intervene. Subsequently, the orders worked actively against immigration restriction and protested Russia's refusal to honor the American passports of Russian-born Jews visiting the Empire.[8]

As the mainstream orders assumed more responsibility for leadership in Jewish communal affairs, they gradually adopted a nationalist political perspective. By the second decade of the century, a number of orders embraced Zionism officially. Independent Order Ahavas Israel, the Western Star Order, Independent Order Brith Abraham, and Brith Sholom had all endorsed Zionism by early 1914.[9] Many landsmanshaft lodges thus took at least symbolic part in one of the major Jewish political movements of the day. Additional societies joined the explicitly Zionist orders: B'nai Zion and the Jewish National Workers' Alliance.

Although more loosely knit than the fraternal orders, several federations or *farbandn* of landsmanshaftn from the same countries or regions became the most durable and inclusive organizations linking the small associations with broader trends in Jewish life. The first and largest of these was the Federation of Galician and Bucovinean Jews of America, founded in 1904, followed by the Federation of Russian-Polish Hebrews of America (1908), the Federation of Hungarian Jews in America (1909), the Federation of Bessarabian Organizations (1911), and the Federation of Oriental Jews of America (1911). Roumanian Jews formed two rival factions: the Federation of Roumanian Jews in America (1909) and the American Union of Roumanian Jews (1916).[10] Encompassing hundreds of individual hometown societies, with tens of thousands of members, the federations brought the landsmanshaftn into closer collaboration with one another, harnessed their considerable energy for wider social goals, and created a new layer of immigrant Jewish leaders.

The motivations behind the establishment of the landsmanshaft federations varied. To some extent, the smaller groups came together because of perceived slights at the hands of the numerically dominant Russian Jewish immigrants. As Dr. Samuel Margoshes, journalist, educator, and sometime president of the Galician and Bucovinean Federation, put it, the federations were "offensive and defensive alliances, a sort of Verein zur Abwehr des Anti-Galizianerismus or Anti-Rumanierismus, as the case might be."[11] When they addressed this issue at all, however, the federations did so indirectly, by raising the prestige of their respective groups through the establishment of institutions to serve the whole community. Following the lead of the Federation of Galician and Bucovinean Jews, most of the farbandn undertook to maintain health-care or social-welfare facilities, the largest of which were the Galicians' Har Moriah Hospital and the Russian-Polish Federation's Beth David Hospital.[12]

The federations were intermediate entities between what the historian Josef Barton has called the "little tradition of communal leadership" and organization, represented by the myriad of individual societies, and the "larger tradition of national leadership," which sought to create a more fully integrated ethnic community.[13] Specifically, they developed a group of leaders who transcended their landsmanshaft origins and played active roles in the wider immigrant Jewish community. Most of these leaders fit the description of "ethnic brokers," men who were conversant enough with American society to be able to negotiate it on behalf of their followers. In the Jewish context, however, American society often appeared synonymous with the so-called "uptown" Jews, "prosperous, Americanized or native born, and sharing common German origins for the most part." The uptown leaders were mostly businessmen "of means and social standing" with whom few successful Eastern Europeans could compete. Aspiring immigrant leaders, therefore, often depended upon an organizational constituency for their authority. The landsmanshaft federations, together with the fraternal orders, provided such bases of support for individual leaders moving into the higher councils of American Jewish leadership.[14]

The leaders of the country federations embodied the organizations' fusion of American and Jewish values. Successful businessmen and professionals, these individuals constituted "a type of truly democratic servant of the people, a type which possesses American energy and Jewish loyalty."[15] They included physicians such as Dr. Solomon Neumann (co-founder and Honorary President of the Galician Federation), Dr. Max Moskiewitz (founder of the Polish Federation) and Dr. Pierre Siegelstein (dissident Romanian leader), lawyers such as Leo Wolfson (President of the Romanian Federation) and Leo Lerner (President of the Bessarabian Federation), and even politicians such as Assemblymen Solomon Sufrin and Charles Flack (both Romanians). Many of the leaders had come to America at a relatively young age and had acquired an American education. Of the six federation presidents listed in the *Jewish Communal Register,* for example, Joseph Gedalecia, of the Sephardic Federation of Oriental Jews of America, had immigrated at the age of eleven, Jacob Carlinger of the Russian-Polish Federation at twelve, Samuel Goldstein of the Romanian Federation at fourteen, and Siegelstein, then President of the American Union of Roumanian Jews, at fifteen or sixteen. Samuel Margoshes of the Galician Federation had arrived at the age of eighteen and attended Columbia University and

Jewish Theological Seminary, where he earned a doctorate. The Bessarabian leader, Leo Lerner, had come at the advanced age of 32, but had graduated from the law school of New York University.[16]

The federations provided these leaders with a broader sphere of action than they would have had in their separate landsmanshaftn. What the *Tageblat* wrote of the Galician Federation could also be applied to the others: "The Federation has called forth new powers among the Galician Jewish public in New York; it has created new activists, new good and devoted communal workers which were entirely unknown before."[17]

The federations also articulated a philosophy of Jewish life, more latent than expressed within their constituent associations, which combined declarations of loyalty to the United States with support for the ideals of Jewish nationalism. The farbandn always saw themselves as a step toward the eventual unity of all American Jews. The Federation of Galician and Bucovinean Jews of America argued that it was expedient that "the Jews from each country . . . unite among themselves, because they understand and know each other better," and this would make it "easier to arrive at the main goal of uniting all Jews."[18] At its 1906 convention the Galician Federation even appointed a committee to negotiate with the Independent Order Brith Abraham concerning the establishment of a united communal organization.[19] Like the Galician Federation, the Federation of Roumanian Jews in America promised to work for Jewish unity. One journalist assured readers that the Romanian Federation stood "on a solid national base and does not intend to create its own little sectarian prayer-house. The Federation strives to go hand in hand with all other Jewish organizations created for Jews and Jewish interests."[20]

Indeed, at a time when the official Zionist movement in America was still weak, the landsmanshaft federations provided a reservoir of mass support for the Zionist ideal. Jews from Galicia and Romania had a particularly strong reputation for sympathy with the Jewish national movement, leading one Galician journalist to write that among the "other Jews of New York, it is practically accepted that a Galician is the same thing as a Zionist."[21] The Galician Federation officially endorsed the Zionist Basel Program at its 1906 convention, and the Romanian Federation did so in 1911.[22] Another sympathetic writer noted that the Galician Federation had brought 600 societies and thousands of members into the movement. If the federations had not been so active, he suggested, the Zionists would just demand more from each body.[23]

The federations expressed their commitment to Zionism most clearly at the symbolic level. The blue and white Jewish flag hung at federation conventions, which often opened or closed with the singing of *Hatikvah*. The annual gatherings also heard such prominent Zionist speakers as Shmaryahu Levin and Louis Lipsky. More concretely, the federations contributed to the Jewish National Fund (JNF) to further Jewish settlement in Palestine, and urged their branches to do so as well. At the 1914 Galician Federation convention "pretty girls" interrupted the proceedings by selling flowers for the JNF, and the following year the Federation voted to pay the shekel (dues in the Zionist movement) for each of its member societies.[24]

The landsmanshaft federations considered Jewish unity, even nationalism, to be entirely consistent with an ardent commitment to America. Even as it adopted resolutions in favor of a Jewish homeland in Palestine, the Galician Federation set out "to educate its members . . . in the knowledge of true citizenship and patriotic American principles."[25] Whatever role they envisaged for the Jewish state in the future, very few of the immigrants planned to leave the United States for Palestine. In 1905, when the Galicians sponsored a mass rally to celebrate the 250th anniversary of Jewish settlement in America, *Der amerikaner,* then the Galician Federation's unofficial organ, went so far as to speak of America in terms of the promised land. "[W]ho should be more happy with this holiday," the editors asked rhetorically, "than the Jews of the East Side who have been freed from Exile, thanks to those first Jews who blazed a trail for us here?"[26]

The need to demonstrate loyalty to America became all the more pressing when the United States entered World War I in 1917. Opposition to American involvement in the war had run high in the immigrant Jewish community, fueled both by hatred of the old Russian regime and by the warm feelings of many Galician and Hungarian Jews toward the Habsburg rulers. On the last day of November 1916, just months before America's entry into the war against the Dual Monarchy, thousands of Jews had attended a memorial meeting at Cooper Union for the late Emperor Franz Josef called by the Galician and Hungarian Federations.[27] But once war was declared, the Galician, Romanian, and Russian-Polish federations, as well as the Romanian Union, all declared their loyalty to President Wilson and sought to demonstrate that they were "loyal citizens of their new home—America."[28]

By 1917 a number of movements had been actively promoting the consolidation of Jewish communal life for over a decade. The downtown community heard the first rumblings of the movement to call a representative American Jewish Congress, while uptown Jews formed the elitist American Jewish Committee in 1906. Also organized in 1906, the Federation of Jewish Organizations hoped to gather all of the smaller Jewish societies under one roof. It attracted some 400 affiliates, mostly by lobbying and campaigning on behalf of liberal immigration laws. The Federation also concerned itself with such issues as discrimination against Jewish American passport holders in Russia, the mistreatment of immigrants on Ellis Island, crime in the Jewish community, political corruption, and "white slavery" among Jews.[29]

Although it made only minimal demands on its affiliated societies and never became the powerful communal center it aspired to be, the Federation did help draw some societies into broader spheres of political action. The Satanover Benevolent Society, for example, maintained membership for a number of years and heard regular reports on the coalition's activities against immigration restriction, as well as on a proposal to create "a general Jewish federation with the aim of taking part in the political affairs of the government of the United States." Through the Federation, the Satanover landslayt first joined in the protest against the police commissioner's assertion that Jews were more involved in crime than other groups, the affair that eventually led to the formation of the New York Kehillah.[30]

In 1908 the movement toward general organization of the Jewish community received a push forward after New York City Police Commissioner Theodore Bingham claimed in a newspaper article that Jews committed half of the crime in New York. All sectors of the Jewish community expressed outrage; the Federation of Jewish Organizations and a number of other groups called protest meetings, while leaders of the American Jewish Committee worked behind the scenes to elicit a retraction from the commissioner. The incident emphasized to many the need for an ongoing body to represent the interests of New York Jewry. A series of meetings in September 1908 resulted in a call for a conference of "representative Jews of the city" to meet in Clinton Hall on October 11th and 12th for the "purpose of forming a permanent organization to foster the interests of the Jews in every proper way."[31]

As one of the largest Jewish combinations then in existence, the Federation of Galician and Bucovinean Jews of America played an instrumental role in the movement which led to the establishment of the New York Kehillah. The Federation's President Bernard Semel was one of the six signers of the conference appeal, and its office provided the committee with an interim address. The initiators anticipated that "much, very much good could be accomplished if we had a *proper Jewish Community,* which united the Russian, German, Galician, Hungarian and Roumanian Jews." Nevertheless, they assured the public, "the [resulting] organization will *not interfere* with the internal affairs of the orders, federations, societies, etc." Constituent groups would operate as before, with complete autonomy, but would speak with a united voice on issues of common concern.[32]

Overcoming objections by the Federation of Jewish Organizations and the misgivings of the American Jewish Committee, the Clinton Hall conference endorsed the establishment of a permanent Jewish community structure. The Committee of 25 appointed after the Clinton Hall Conference included five men closely associated with the landsmanshaft federations. Semel was now joined by fellow-Galician Dr. Solomon Neumann, Dr. Max Moskiewitz of the Russian-Polish Federation, and Romanian leaders User Marcus and Dr. Pierre Siegelstein. Together with thirteen representatives of a reluctantly reconciled AJC, the Clinton Hall committee issued a call to a founding convention for a New York Kehillah (Jewish Community) which would bring "harmony and a proper sense of solidarity in place of the deplorable conditions which now exist."[33]

Some 222 organizations, including 77 landsmanshaftn, sent delegates to the first Kehillah Convention, which was held over several weekends in February and March, 1909. Altogether, over one third of the participants represented individual hometown societies or the larger country federations. The Federation of Galician and Bucovinean Jews, then at the peak of its influence, had by far the largest delegation, with 37 members. The Galician Federation's Har Moriah Hospital sent an additional three of its own. Many of the other delegates represented non-landsmanshaft mutual aid societies, congregations, and fraternal lodges. Socialist organizations such as the Workmen's Circle (with the exception of one lone branch) absented themselves, refusing to help promote Jewish unity across class lines.[34]

Despite the large landsmanshaft representation at the convention, their leaders did not fare well in the elections for the first 25-member Executive Committee. While three, Bernard Semel, Solomon Neumann, and Pierre Siegelstein, won places on the committee, another seven went down in defeat. Two factors explain this relative lack of success. First, only the Galician Federation was well established by the time of the founding of the Kehillah. Second, as Arthur Goren, the historian of the Kehillah, has pointed out, the vote of the predominantly downtown delegates expressed their confidence in the prestigious uptown elite. Undoubtedly, too, Joseph Barondess and Order Brith Abraham Grand Master Samuel Dorf, both popular figures in the societies and lodges, drew some of their support from landsmanshaft delegates.[35]

Despite their poor showing, a number of top landsmanshaft leaders remained active in the Kehillah and served on its Executive Committee at one time or another. William Fischman, a Galician cloak manufacturer and president of the Galician Federation from 1912 to 1913, acted for many years as the Community's treasurer. Many prominent figures not elected to the Executive Committee became members of the larger (and largely powerless) Advisory Committee. Samuel Margoshes, of the Galician Federation, and Joseph Gedalecia, of the Federation of Oriental Jews, ascended to the leadership of their respective organizations after having served on the Kehillah's professional staff.[36]

One prominent Galician, Bernard Semel, emerged from the landsmanshaft sector to play an especially important role. A member of both the Doliner K.U.V. and the First Bolechower K.U.V., and president of the Federation of Galician and Bucovinean Jews from 1907 to 1911, Semel had come to America at the age of fourteen and worked his way up from pushcart peddler to respectable woolen merchant. At the time of the founding of the Kehillah, Semel was thirty years old and had already achieved something of a reputation as an "energetic worker and . . . convincing speaker." He served on the Kehillah Executive Committee throughout its existence, becoming a close associate of Rabbi Judah L. Magnes, the Kehillah's guiding light. At various times Semel headed the Community's Bureau of Industry and its Committee on Information and Service. He devoted himself especially to the reform of Jewish education, a field in which he continued to work after the Kehillah's demise.[37]

Supporters of the Kehillah realized that their organization could only speak, as intended, for the entire Jewish community if it involved the city's thousands of small societies and congregations. They set out to reach unaffiliated organizations through pamphlets, newspaper advertisements and articles, circulars, and neighborhood meetings.[38] An advertisement in the press that year asked, "Is your synagogue, society or lodge connected with the Kehillah of New York?" and went on to argue, "All good Jewish organizations strive to protect Jewish interests and introduce a more secure Jewry to this city. But this goal cannot be reached until we all unite and concentrate our forces in a central body which will have the power and the authority to deal with all communal problems and improve our living conditions as Jews."[39]

The Kehillah never fully succeeded in these efforts. Consensus was difficult to achieve in the fractious world of Jewish communal politics, and it was impossible under American conditions of voluntarism to compel dissenters to participate in the larger community. Thus many Orthodox Jews wondered why they should allow Reform rabbis like Judah Magnes to regulate their affairs, and most radicals refused to take part in a body based on the concept of Jewish unity above class interests.[40] Magnes summed up some of the difficulties in his report to the Kehillah's convention in 1912:

> Some will not join us because we deal too much with the problem of Jewish religion, some because we do not deal with the problem sufficiently. Some hold that we have no right to concern ourselves with problems of Jewish education, and others again contend that this should be our exclusive field of work. Some complain that we have neglected the field of philanthropy, while others oppose us because they regard us as intruders upon their spheres of activity. Some claim that we have not given enough attention to labor disputes, while others hold such questions to be beyond our jurisdiction.[41]

In 1914 Dr. Magnes admitted that "fewer than half of New York's 3,500 Jewish organizations" had affiliated with the Kehillah.[42] In fact the Kehillah never attracted more than about a tenth of that number of organizations; 341 organizations were represented at the 1915 convention, one of the largest the Kehillah held. Generally, landsmanshaftn contributed about one quarter of the Jewish Community's affiliates, with the Federation of Galician and Bucovinean Jews consistently sending the largest delegation. But most societies, including most landsmanshaftn, did not respond enthusiastically to appeals to join the Kehillah.[43]

The Kehillah had difficulty activating even its own affiliates, let alone those organizations standing on the sidelines. At various times, delegates complained that the Kehilla was neither getting its message across nor fulfilling its democratic promise.[44] One rank-and-file supporter reported in 1915 that, in an effort to enlist more groups into the Jewish Community, he had visited many society meetings, and "found that the public is very much estranged from the work of the Kehillah and therefore has no interest in joining." Judge Leon Sanders, President of HIAS and Grand Master of the Independent Order Brith Abraham, put it even more bluntly. "Once a year," he charged, "you call upon the organizations to send their delegates. Do you know what they say when they receive your invitations? . . . Aha! The Kehillah is here again. The whole year we do not see them; now they want us to give them five dollars for every man we send them."[45]

Despite the energetic and often excellent work of its professional staff in such areas as Jewish education and industrial relations, the Kehillah failed to demonstrate to the societies its usefulness in relation to their own particular needs. In fact the Kehillah did very little for them, never even acting on several proposals that would have aided the societies directly.[46] Had the Kehillah more actively pursued such programs to assist the individual societies, the societies would perhaps have taken more interest in the activities of the Kehillah.

Indeed, the Kehillah sometimes even seemed to interfere with the cherished autonomy of the landsmanshaftn. In 1912, for example, the Federation of Bessarabian Organizations decided to follow the example of the larger Galician, Russian-Polish, and Romanian federations, all of which sponsored (or had already undertaken to establish) hospitals or other social welfare institutions intended for the community at large. The Bessarabians, believing that there was a need for an orphanage close to the neighborhoods from which the children had come, resolved to build such an institution on the Lower East Side. The Executive Committee of the Kehillah, however, thought that "there was no need for any new institutions of this kind" and tried to persuade Bessarabian leaders to drop the idea.[47] Two years later, when the Bessarabian Federation seemed determined to go ahead with its plan, a motion was introduced at the Kehillah convention that "the Kehillah take steps to prevent the establishment of new Jewish orphan asylums, or hospitals unless a thorough investigation and hearing shall satisfactorily show that such new institutions are needed." The major proponents of the measure, including Louis Marshall and Cyrus Sulzberger, argued strenuously that no new institutions were needed, least of all in "crowded residential sections of the city" like the Lower East Side. A few delegates, including at least two affiliated with landsmanshaftn, spoke against the motion, contending that the Kehillah had "no right to meddle in such matters." The resolution passed, but two years later the Bessarabians opened the Hebrew National Orphan House anyway.[48]

The Kehillah also met with limited success in its efforts to mediate disputes involving landsmanshaftn. In 1910 it formed a Committee on Conciliation "for the purpose of adjusting amicably and outside of the courts, disputes which arise among members of congregations, societies and lodges." One of the committee's first cases concerned a widow who charged her late husband's society with failing to pay her the proper death benefit.[49] Soon, however, the committee reported that it would no longer hear cases involving individual societies. Rather, the Executive Committee resolved that the Conciliation Committee would only "concern itself with matters affecting the Jewish Community at large."[50] But in this area too the Kehillah failed, unable to resolve the ongoing feud between opposing factions of Romanian Jews. The refusal of one of the Romanian leaders, Pierre Siegelstein, to agree to Kehillah mediation although he was a member of its Executive Committee only underscored the umbrella group's ineffectualness.[51]

By 1917 even Magnes had to conclude that the attempt to place the Kehillah's professional bureaus under the direction of the constituent assembly had failed. The fact that the bureaus raised most of their funds from sources outside of the affiliated organizations simply enhanced their independence. In 1917, therefore, Magnes moved that the bureaus be severed from the Kehillah in the hope that it would then become a wide-open forum in which all voices within the Jewish community could be heard and an authoritative consensus formed. Over the course of the next year, the Kehillah was completely restructured on the basis of individual membership and district elections. The 1918 convention proved lively, but it could no longer make even the pretense of controlling a communal bureaucratic apparatus. The Kehillah soon withered, a process furthered by Magnes's identification with militant pacifism during World War I.[52]

The onset of war itself helped to undermine the Kehillah by redirecting the attention of much of American Jewry to the plight of Jews in the war zones overseas. Magnes's address to the Kehillah's 1915 convention began by emphasizing the war in Europe and the need for the Jews of America to exercise leadership in the crisis.[53] But the Kehillah, argued Magnes, could not be the vehicle through which American Jews would come to the aid of their brothers and sisters in Europe. As the Kehillah's abdication of any responsibility for the most burning issue of the day became apparent, dissatisfaction grew. As early as February 1915, the *Tageblat* reported that "very few" delegates had come to a recent meeting, "and the majority of them bitterly attacked the Kehillah for its inactivity in this critical moment."[54]

During the war, organizations that seemed better attuned to the needs of the day began to attract more attention. In addition to relief activities, the movement for an American Jewish Congress gathered momentum. As envisaged by its supporters, the American Jewish Congress would in many ways resemble the Kehillah. It would be a democratically elected deliberative body which would speak authoritatively for American Jewry. However, unlike the Kehillah, the Congress would be national in scope and engage itself in national and international political matters. Specifically, its Zionist and Labor Zionist proponents expected it to play a major role in securing Jewish rights in Europe and, eventually, a Jewish homeland in Palestine after the war.[55]

For a time Congress supporters hoped that the Kehillah would take the lead in the organization of this national Jewish body. Here, however, they ran into fierce opposition by the American Jewish Committee, of which the Kehillah was officially the New York branch, but which claimed for itself the exclusive right to speak for American Jewry on national and international questions. In 1915 and 1916, the Kehillah was the venue for debates and negotiations between the Committee, led by Louis Marshall, and the "democratic" faction led by the Zionists and supported mainly by East Europeans. Several landsmanshaft leaders sided outspokenly with the pro-Congress group, taking part in the caucus which demanded that the Kehillah sever its ties with the American Jewish Committee and endorse the Congress movement. When their demands were not met, the pro-Congress forces walked out of the Kehillah's 1916 convention.[56]

Hometown societies discussed the Congress movement at their meetings and many came to support it. The Galician, Russian-Polish, and Romanian federations all became early backers of the Congress. Some individual societies, such as the Timkovitser Congregation, affiliated with the movement as well and sent delegates to various pre-Congress conferences and rallies.[57] Within the Galician quarter, the Austro-Hungarian Zionists and a newer group known as Young Galicia joined the Federation of Galician and Bucovinean Jews in agitating for the

Congress. Mass meetings sponsored by the Galician Farband featured prominent speakers from the whole Zionist spectrum, together with Federation leaders. (When it seemed that the Federation's support might waver in the face of American Jewish Committee opposition, the other groups pressured it to continue its backing of the movement.)[58]

Eventually, the American Jewish Committee agreed to go along with the Congress on condition that it disband after hearing reports from its delegates to the European peace conferences. Accordingly, in May and June 1917, some 335,000 American Jews in over eighty cities voted for delegates to an American Jewish Congress, which would, in turn, select American Jewry's representatives to the international deliberations.[59]

Some landsmanshaftn organized to elect their own people to the Congress and to place their demands on its agenda. A number of important New York landsmanshaft figures attended the gathering and helped look out for the interests of their respective landslayt.[60] Bernard Semel chaired the Commission on Galicia and Solomon Sufrin headed the committee on Romania. Jacob Carlinger, of the Russian-Polish Federation, served as Honorary Financial Secretary of the Congress and received official thanks for his diligent organizing work. At the assembly's last session, Jacob Pfeffer, founder of the Galician Federation, caused a stir when he moved to make the American Jewish Congress a permanent body. (He was ruled out of order.)[61]

In 1920, after hearing the report of its delegation to the European peace talks, the American Jewish Congress heeded its original agreement with the American Jewish Committee and disbanded. It was reconstituted shortly thereafter, to become an activist organization devoted to defending the civil rights of Jews at home and abroad. But it never again acted as the constituent assembly of a (nearly) united American Jewry.[62]

The Labor Movement

Both the Kehillah and the American Jewish Congress endeavored to organize American Jews into a unified polity on the assumption that they shared a single set of national, or at least communal, interests. Not all Jews agreed, however, least of all the "self-conscious Jewish labor community" which had gained the support of many immigrants in the first decades of the twentieth century.[63] Led by a socialist intelligentsia, the labor movement had a vision of Jewish society in which class interests were at least as important as those of ethnicity. Jewish labor built its own institutions, including the *Jewish Daily Forward,* the Workmen's Circle, trade unions, and radical parties. However, rather than remain aloof from the community at large, the labor movement exerted its influence in all aspects of Jewish life. By the time labor lawyer Meyer London was elected to the House of Representatives on the Socialist Party ticket in 1914, the movement's influence had spread beyond the boundaries of the working class to all classes of immigrant society.[64]

The Workmen's Circle formed the main bridge between the labor movement and the landsmanshaft world. The order's branches encouraged their members to join the unions in their trades, afforded them strike benefits when they walked off their jobs, and disciplined scabs.[65] The branches could also be counted on to donate to strike funds even when no members were involved. Between 1909 and 1913, Zerdover Branch 301 supported at least 26 strikes, from that of the shirtwaist-makers to that of the Singer Sewing Machine representatives. They even gave to non-Jewish unions, such as the "German bakers" and the "Philadelphia car strikers."[66]

Other landsmanshaftn, like the Progressive Slutzker Young Men's Benevolent Association and the Kolomear Young Friends, remained independent but maintained close ties to the labor movement. The Slutzker Young Men considered themselves "progressive" because they believed that their society "should enlighten [its] members in all important matters and aid outside worthy causes in general." The society's program of "enlightenment" included lectures by such socialist luminaries as Jacob Panken, Meyer London, and Abraham Shiplikoff, and its stated goals made it clear that the members considered trade unions to be "worthy causes." The association excluded strikebreakers from membership and remained proud that, during the great strikes of 1909 to 1914, it "not only helped its own members and the general strike fund of the unions but also conducted an educational campaign for the unions in maintaining the morale of its strikers."[67]

The old-country heritage, in this case a radicalizing factor rather than a conservative one, heavily influenced the Kolomear Young Friends, founded in 1904. Many of the Kolomear immigrants had already acquired a deep commitment to socialism in their Galician hometown of Kolomyya, which was known for its pious prayer-shawl weavers as well as its strong workers' movement. The "young friends"—some religious and some free-thinking, some of them businessmen and others laborers—imparted a socialist tone to their organization but never joined the secularist Workmen's Circle. During the cloakmakers' strike of 1910, the Kolomear Friends contributed to the strike fund and also offered weekly benefits to their striking members. Between 1910 and 1914, the Kolomear distributed $1,675 in strike pay, more than they gave out in any other type of benefit.[68]

Some scholars have viewed the Old World as a uniformly conservative influence and argued that the landsmanshaftn expressed their isolation and backwardness most clearly through hostility toward the labor movement. "The Old World antipathy toward New World Society," Michael Weisser has written in his study of the hometown associations, "was most evident in the groups' conservative attitude toward trade unions and other labor issues." In a more sophisticated argument, the historian Moses Rischin has contended that the landsmanshaftn "obstructed labor organization" by binding boss and worker together in a paternalistic relationship. Fictional works of the period, such as *Forward* editor Abraham Cahan's *The Rise of David Levinsky* and Sholem Asch's *Uncle Moses,* agree that manufacturers used the societies to manipulate their landslayt employees and prevent them from organizing independently. Cahan's cloak manufacturer, Levinsky, hires only landslayt from his hometown of Antomir and organizes the Levinsky Antomir Benevolent Society, moves which he admits "afforded me a low average of wages and safeguarded my shop against labor troubles." Likewise, Asch's Moses Melnick employs only his fellow Kuzminer Jews and doubles as patriarchal head of the landsmanshaft congregation. When one worker considers joining the union, Uncle Moses responds, "Not here, my friend . . . This is not an ordinary shop which admits union men. Here we are landslayt, family."[69]

In reality, however, landsmanshaft ties sometimes reinforced worker solidarity against the bosses. Even at the end of Asch's novel the workers do indeed organize a union under the leadership of a young Americanized landsman, a socialist lawyer named Charlie. Significantly, when they finally organize against their "benefactor" and boss, Uncle Moses' workers meet in the Kuzminer synagogue that he had built for them.

The reefer makers' strike of 1907 provides a dramatic example from real life of an industrial conflict in which workers took militant action against their paternalistic landslayt bosses. The reefer trade, the manufacture of cheap coats made entirely by machine, was comparatively new. It had been built almost single-handedly by Philip Weinstein, a former cloakmaker, and his brother, Max, a former clothing salesman. The firm of Weinstein Brothers, founded in 1901, remained the largest in the industry at the time of the strike. The brothers hailed from Pukhovichi, Minsk province in Belorussia, and the trade they established retained a close connection with towns in that region. The names of the companies illustrate the family ties among the manufacturers. In addition to Weinstein Brothers there were Weinstein and Levy, Weinstein and Co., Weinstein and Arbes, Philip Rosenberg, Adolf Rosenberg, Edelman and Shapiro, Shapiro and Shulman, Shulman and Shor, Fried and Shor, Miller and Fried, Berman and Feinman, Holtsberg and Feinman, Feinman and Blauenson, Lipshitz Bros., Lipschitz and Fried, and so on. The work force, too, consisted of landslayt from Pukhovichi, Smilovichi, Dukora, Berezino, and Cherven (then Igumen or Ehumen). Since the trade required less skill than work in other lines of ladies' clothing, newcomers found ready employment in the trade. Many of the workers had never worked in any other shop than the one against which they struck in 1907.[70]

The reefer makers first struck against their landslayt bosses in 1905 to demand an end to a 16-hour workday and other abuses.[71] The employers sought to avert a strike by emphasizing their common origins with the workers. According to one Igumener landsman and union official, the manufacturers "took to throwing parties, giving out beer, organizing societies, promising sick benefits and buying cemetery plots for the workers; acting nice and promising the world-to-come in order to con them out of the present world." The climax of the campaign came at a party thrown by Weinstein Brothers in a hall behind a Lower East Side saloon. With tables laden with herring, corned beef, bread, and other delicacies, and beer flowing on tap, the bosses called on the workers to form a landsmanshaft. In the "middle of a fiery speech by one of the bosses," recounted the same union leader, "a union committee walked in and broke up the party. The poor bosses did not know that most of those present were unionists who had been waiting for the raid." The workers marched out of the hall singing revolutionary anthems.[72] The union won the ten-day strike, but little changed in the industry until two years later.

The expiration of the agreement in 1907 set the stage for a showdown between International Ladies' Garment Workers' Union Local 17 and the manufacturers' association. The union demanded an end to the practice of requiring workers to supply their own machines. The bosses responded by revoking recognition of the union. The bitterly fought eight-week strike began on March 22 with a walkout of the 125 workers at Weinstein Brothers, and within two days, over 1,500 reefer makers left their jobs.[73] Eventually, the intervention of Samuel Gompers and the conservative Yiddish newspaper, the *Tageblat,* helped bring about a settlement. On May 16, the *Forward* proclaimed "Complete Victory for the Reefer Makers, Hurrah!"[74] The settlement resulted in a number of improvements. Most importantly, the strike extended union recognition beyond the life of one contract and guaranteed a closed union shop. The Jewish labor movement had won an unprecedented victory.

Far from bringing the sides closer together, the fact of shared nativity gave the strikers additional moral and material ammunition against the bosses. The *Forward,* speaking for the strikers, taunted the Weinsteins for their lowly old-country pedigree, poked fun at the close family relationships among firms—"Holtzberg and Feinman, Feinman and Berman, Berman and Krutshik, Krutshik and Pintshik, Pintshik and Shmintshik"—and sneered at "our brothers in Israel, the former moochers and current allrightniks of the reefer trade, the little parvenu bosses of Spring Street, Lispenard Street and Walker Street."[75] The bosses had instituted a degree of exploitative paternalism, but this too backfired at the time of the strike. Thus local 17 discovered that many workers had banked part of their wages with their bosses. The union persuaded its followers to put their notes in the hands of its lawyer, Meyer London, who threatened to turn them over for collection. Faced with bankruptcy, the manufacturers lost their enthusiasm for continuing the confrontation.[76]

The landsmanshaft societies most closely connected to the reefer industry came to the aid of the strikers. The Puchowitzer Young Men's and Young Ladies' Progressive Association resolved to "support the courageous reefer makers financially and morally and that the members should work with all their might with the reefer makers and for the reefer makers."[77] Not surprisingly, the Socialist Federation of Humener, Bereziner and Shmilevitzer contributed to the strike fund. Less expected support came from the Independent Ehumaner Benevolent Society and even from the conservative Congregation Anshe Puchowitz, which gave the comparatively large sum of $25, showing that groups across the ideological spectrum assisted their striking landslayt.[78]

The financial support of the community, including a broad range of landsmanshaftn, contributed greatly to the success of the strike. Societies of all kinds responded to the union's appeals and demonstrated that they could provide the labor movement with the resources it needed to overcome its wealthier adversaries. The union spent $18,000, a large figure for that time, over $7,700 of which was raised through the *Forward*. The paper called on the whole community to aid the reefer makers. "Let the whole Jewish quarter take the strike in its hands!" it urged. "Let the whole Jewish quarter support the fighters! Let us see who is more powerful, the entire Jewish quarter or the association of reefer bosses."[79] Landsmanshaftn contributed significantly, their $1,449 coming in 309 donations. Participating societies predictably included associations of recently arrived revolutionaries from Russia, but they also included nonradical groups like the Independent Kiever Benevolent Society, Zembrover Young Men's Benevolent Association, and the First Yedinitzer Young Men's and Young Ladies' Benevolent Educational Society, as well as lodges of the "bourgeois" fraternal orders—Order Brith Abraham and Independent Order Brith Abraham—and religious congregations such as the Agudas Akhim Anshe Smila, Khevre Menakhem Mendel Anshe Dubrov, and Congregation Anshei Mozir.[80]

The reefer strike set the stage for the "great revolt," which rocked the immigrant Jewish community between 1909 and 1914. General strikes by shirtwaist makers in 1909–1910, cloakmakers in 1910, furriers in 1912, men's tailors in 1913, and others, established the unions as powers to be reckoned with in the garment industry and other Jewish trades. Entering the "revolt" with 5,000 members in 41 constituent organizations, the United Hebrew Trades, a federation of predominantly Jewish unions, claimed 250,000 members in 111 affiliates by 1914.[81]

Public support was crucial to the success of each of the general strikes. Particularly when labor managed to equate its program with the needs of the whole population, many landslayt societies willingly provided vital support to the cause. The largest and most successful battle, that of the cloakmakers, reportedly cost the union $246,000.[82] The *Forward* raised large sums of money and published lists of contributors. The socialist daily continually exhorted its readers to come to the aid of the strikers, urging organizations to make strike support "the chief topic of discussion, the first point on your agendas."[83] In one article during the furriers' strike, the *Forward* implicitly recognized the potential social power of the landsmanshaftn and editorialized on the role of the societies in industrial disputes:

> Nine thousand furriers are on strike—a whole army. They come from all ends of the earth, from various regions, and they belong to various societies, associations and organizations. These organizations, branches and societies can and must be the first to help their members who are participating in the great, glorious, bitter struggle of the furriers against the fur magnates. Every landslayt society, every Workmen's Circle branch can and must care for the several members who are in need of bread and other necessities of life . . . This is their duty.[84]

Landsmanshaftn responded by donating significant sums of money. The outpouring of sympathy from the community for the cloakmakers in particular was tremendous, and landsmanshaft contributions to the strike fund reflected the general enthusiasm for the strike. The home-town societies provided $4,643 in 600 separate gifts, and Workmen's Circle branches, many of them also organized on a landsmanshaft basis, added over $6,000 in almost 500 donations.[85]

The broad range of groups that participated in strike-support work illustrates the degree to which the cloakmakers' "great upheaval" became a cause for the entire immigrant community. "In all lodges, in all societies, even in conservative ones," the *Forward* reported, "committees of the strikers are very well received. Everywhere, sympathy is expressed for the great strike, and from everywhere, financial support is provided to the fighters."[86] At one point in the strike, supporters organized a fundraising conference, which included "tens of Workmen's Circle branches, unions, benevolent societies, religious congregations, conservative mutual aid societies, socialist and simply progressive organizations." Conservative groups objected to a proposed executive committee of 15 representatives of progressive organizations. "In such a matter," they explained, "in a people's cause, no distinction may be made between progressive and conservative. Everyone wants to work for the strike." In the end the conference added five seats to the committee to appease the conservative societies.[87]

In addition to contributing to general strike funds, landsmanshaftn often provided direct assistance to their own striking members. During the cloakmakers' strike, the *Forward* reported that it had received many resolutions from societies which had "taken it upon themselves to support their striking members during the entire course of the strike."[88] Some societies continued to provide strikers with the normal benefits of membership without requiring the regular payment of dues. Congregation Ahavath Zedek Anshei Timkowitz did this tentatively when it voted to "allow an extra two weeks this quarter to the brothers who are employed in the cloak trade," and more boldly in 1913 when it waived dues payments altogether for its tailor members.[89] Some societies went a step further, presenting their striking brothers with outright grants, or even weekly benefits. The Stabiner Young Men's Benevolent Association, for example, gave six dollars a week to each family man and three dollars to each single brother on strike with the tailors.[90] Morris Waldman of the United Hebrew Charities summed up the importance of this kind of aid, noting that "remarkably enough, none [of the shirtwaist and cloak strikers of 1909–1910] found it necessary to apply to the Charities for aid. Why? Because . . . after they exhausted their own scant resources, they applied to the mutual benefit societies, as well as to their unions, and received grants or loans sufficient to tide them over their emergency."[91]

By sponsoring fundraising events, landsmanshaftn served a larger cause at the same time as they carried out one of their own central organizational purposes—that of providing social opportunities for landslayt. The Ekaterinoslaver Young Men's Club, for example, held a ball and concert for the shirtwaist strikers, and the Bialystoker Young Men, perhaps of a more serious bent, staged a lecture and literary evening for the same cause. Volozhiner and Pinsker young men each held "confetti balls" for the benefit of the cloakmakers, while the proceeds of an earthier picnic given by the Orsher Young Friends Association went to help the furriers. Several societies from a given region also got together to organize special conferences to raise funds for strikers: Galician societies worked for striking dry goods clerks in 1909, and Bessarabian, Mohilever, and Volhynian organizations for the furriers in 1912.[92]

Societies expressed their support for organized labor in other ways as well. The Zgierzer Sick Benevolent Association voted to print its rule book at a union printer. Among the organizations that pledged in 1907 not to smoke cigarettes without a union label were the Brisker Benevolent Society, the Horodoker Progressive Educational Society, and the Shavler Progressive Benevolent Society. Minsker Young Friends refused to eat in nonunion restaurants, and the Kamenets Podolier Untershtitsung Fareyn vowed not to attend the People's Theater until its managers met the actors' demands.[93]

When striking workers and struck bosses belonged to the same society, however, that landsmanshaft did not always back the trade union movement so eagerly. Often, a bitter struggle for the soul of the organization took place. During the furriers' strike, the *Forward* reported on several groups in which member employers blocked aid to member strikers. The Melnitzer Benevolent Society, in the words of the newspaper, "covered itself with shame. When its striking members demanded that their dues payments be postponed, member bosses did not permit it. The 'worthy brothers' were not able to refuse the honorable gentlemen, and the poor strikers were stricken from the rolls. This is what you call a benevolent society!"[94] Divisions arose in other societies even without intervention by landslayt bosses. The president of one landsmanshaft wrote to the *Forward*'s popular advice column that his society had been unable to donate to the cloakmakers' strike because of a previously imposed freeze on disbursements. To his chagrin as a "friend of the workers," the brothers also defeated a motion to tax themselves, on the grounds that if a member wanted to contribute to the strike, he could do so as an individual.[95]

In one important instance, the reluctance of many landsmanshaftn to back a strike demonstrated the limits of society support for the labor movement. During the predominantly female shirtwaist strike of 1909–10, the mostly male society membership apparently shared the prejudices that led many men in the ILGWU to see the women's locals as "a drag on the international."[96] Bias against the young women strikers, most of whom were not members of landsmanshaftn, and mistrust of feminists and upper-class women from outside the immigrant community who supported the strike, combined to dampen society enthusiasm for the strike. Though 213 associations did donate over $1,400 to the strike fund, this was proportionately less than they contributed to either the reefer makers' strike two years earlier or to the cloakmakers' strike the following year.[97] There were even examples, the *Forward* reported, of outright hostility on the part of some landsmanshaftn. When Socialist Party member G. Bress went to sell strike-support stamps at the ball of the Suwalker Benevolent Association, he was thrown down the stairs by two security guards and the chairman of the arrangement committee, who shouted after him, "Enough begging!"[98]

Still, when their own members were involved, most independent landsmanshaftn supported strikes and unions. The Satanover Benevolent Society willingly assisted its own members on strike. Brother Klein received $20 when he was "reported . . . in need" in 1913. But the brothers were particularly enthusiastic about the furriers' strike of 1912. The society made a substantial $15 contribution to the strike fund and waived the dues of striking members until the conclusion of the walkout. The Satanover society's interest in the furriers' strike probably resulted from the involvement of a number of its own members in the dispute. A partial membership roster lists a fur cutter and a fur tacker, and fragmentary notations of occupations of candidates for membership between 1909 and 1914 show a furrier and another fur tacker. The roster also contains two "fur dealers," possibly employers, although this is not certain. In any case, the presence of six individuals connected with the fur trade in such incomplete membership records indicates that there was likely an extensive link between the Satanover and the industry.[99]

At other times, when the financial interests of the society conflicted with principle, the Satanover were not so generous with their support. In April 1911 the Satanover boldly voted to show sympathy for striking clerks by closing their account with Jarmulowsky's Bank. However, they prudently attached a proviso to wait until the end of the quarter in July, so as not to lose interest on the money. There is no indication that the group ever did withdraw the funds. Most shockingly, the landslayt voted in 1912 to print their constitution at a nonunion printer, "$18 for 300 booklets."[100]

No matter how flawed their commitment might have been, however, the landsmanshaftn clearly lent widespread and vital assistance to the Jewish labor movement at critical times. Moreover, even if they did not fully align themselves with any coherent ideological position, the record shows that, at the very least, landsmanshaft members avidly debated and acted upon the major issues facing the Jewish population.

The Social Welfare Model: HIAS

Social service provided a third model of Jewish communal organization. This conception of the Jewish community as a network of philanthropic agencies ultimately proved more durable than either the attempts to form a united Jewish polity or the socialist labor alternative. By the first two decades of the century, Eastern European Jews had begun to build their own social welfare institutions to rival those run by the well-established German Jews. Many of these remained small, but some, like the Hebrew Sheltering and Immigrant Aid Society, grew into important large-scale service providers. Concentrating on the practical needs of the population, they were able to draw support from all sectors of the community.

Some landsmanshaftn formed philanthropic organizations to aid needy compatriots. Agencies based on country of origin included the Roumanian Hebrew Aid Association and the United Austrian Hebrew Charity Association. Landslayt from large cities, such as Bialystok and Cracow, also had their own charitable groups. The Bialystoker Bikur Cholim, for example, provided medical care to indigent landslayt. Unlike most landsmanshaftn, this organization enrolled no permanent members but relied for its funding on the proceeds of its annual ball and similar events. The Bialystoker Ladies Aid Society Tomkhey Aniim and the United Krakauer Charity Aid Society likewise aided needy landslayt.[101]

A few landsmanshaft groups also sponsored educational institutions. Galician Jews supported the Downtown Talmud Torah, which was sometimes referred to as the "Austrian" Talmud Torah, but a few institutions even bore the names of specific towns. The largest of these was the Talmud Torah Anshei Zhitomir, which started out modestly in 1912. In 1915 it moved to its own building at 337 East 4th Street, and by 1917 it had a staff of seven teachers and an enrollment of 482 boys and 103 girls.[102]

One social welfare agency emerged from the welter of small associations to become a major institution. The Hebrew Sheltering and Immigrant Aid Society, known by the acronym HIAS, came into being in 1909 after the merger of two organizations which had originated among the Eastern European immigrants on the Lower East Side. Both the Hebrew Sheltering House Association and the Hebrew Immigrant Aid Society (also called HIAS) had depended for much of their support on hometown and other societies, and the combined organization continued to do so after 1909. Because it dealt with the practical and political problems of immigration, around which the community stood united, HIAS uniquely commanded the allegiance of the entire range of landsmanshaftn, from right to left.[103]

Established at a meeting at Pythagorean Hall on East Broadway in November 1889, the Hebrew Sheltering House Association was a self-consciously Eastern European effort. Dissatisfaction with the work of the established United Hebrew Charities (UHC), which the organizers felt to be condescending to the new arrivals and insensitive to their needs, motivated the founders. The new association began its work the following year by opening a shelter for homeless immigrants. Led by Yiddish publisher Kasriel Sarasohn, the Hebrew Sheltering House attracted the support of many immigrant associations. By 1906–1907 the House had expanded its work and added such wealthy "uptown" Jewish philanthropists as Jacob Schiff to its list of contributors.[104]

The original Hebrew Immigrant Aid Society, founded in 1902, was also closely bound up with the landsmanshaft, or at least the fraternal, sector. In that year members of the Rabbi Jochanon Lodge 144 of the Independent Order Brith Abraham, which may have been joined by, or have been itself a society of landslayt from the city of Zhitomir, heard of a Jewish immigrant who died at Ellis Island and had been given a pauper's burial. Determined to provide a proper Jewish burial to immigrants who died at the immigration station, a delegation from the lodge went to the island to investigate. So horrified were the delegates at the conditions they found there that they decided to form an organization to aid new arrivals and work energetically for their interests.[105]

The founding of HIAS came at a time of great concern within the Jewish community over the treatment accorded newcomers at Ellis Island. Reports that the station had begun to apply immigration regulations restrictively prompted a campaign by five prominent Jewish fraternal orders for a more liberal interpretation. At the same time, discontent with the United Hebrew Charities, whose representative at Ellis Island did not speak Yiddish and seldom appealed a deportation ruling, resurfaced within the Eastern European community. The new immigrant aid organization was therefore able to win widespread financial and moral support by appealing directly to societies as well as individuals. The Kamenets Podolier Untershtitsung Fareyn became one of its first endorsers when it donated ten dollars in response to a visit from a HIAS representative. Many brothers also signed up as individual members and pledged to "help the Hebrew Emigrant Aid Association [sic] to do away with the bad laws and to ameliorate the condition of the emigrants on Ellis Island."[106]

By the beginning of 1903, HIAS had begun its work and had stationed a representative at Ellis Island. The new organization aggressively appealed deportation cases, provided translation and interpretation services, investigated conditions on arriving ships, helped new arrivals search for relatives, provided immigrants with transportation to their final destinations, opened an employment bureau, and published advice on American customs and immigration laws. In 1909 HIAS and the Hebrew Sheltering House Association, by then located across the street from one another, merged. Morris Waldman, who helped to bring them together, noted that the leadership of both organizations shared common Ukrainian origins and predicted "a compatible marriage . . . in view of the close landsmannschaft relation between the people on the two boards."[107]

The combined Hebrew Sheltering and Immigrant Aid Society (still usually referred to as HIAS) expanded the pace and scope of its work, opened branches at several other important ports of entry, and established contact with Jewish relief agencies in Europe. The organization also undertook a political role, lobbying from its office in Washington against restrictive immigration laws. Statistics for the first ten years of the combined organization's activity give some idea of how many individual lives HIAS directly affected: From 1909 through 1918 HIAS handled 28,884 potential deportation cases (winning admission for 22,760 of these), placed 21,145 workers in jobs, sheltered 32,202 immigrants and "wayfarers" in its dormitory, assisted 64,298 immigrants to acquire naturalization papers, helped 84,023 people reach destinations outside of New York, and gave advice to 750,000 information seekers. In addition, HIAS sponsored 188 lectures in its building and conducted 337 English and citizenship classes.[108]

Landsmanshaftn and similar organizations accounted for a significant percentage of the agency's revenues. This was especially true of the early premerger years, when upwards of 40 percent of HIAS's small income came from societies and lodges. Later, as the merged agency's budget grew, the percentage declined, but in 1914 lodges and societies still accounted for just over 15 percent of HIAS's income of $121,000.[109]

Representatives of HIAS visited the meetings of many kinds of landsmanshaftn, often eliciting an enthusiastic response. At one gathering, the HIAS delegate "made such a good impression on [the members of the Hatsiler Society] with his speech that the president, Mr. Sam Gottlieb, undertook as his duty to recruit as many members as possible for the institution, and right on the spot influenced six members of the society to join the sheltering society as members and pay their dues."[110] The Satanover Benevolent Society responded to a visit from a HIAS representative by appointing a committee to look into the agency. When the investigation committee reported that HIAS's "work is very good," the society took out the standard five-dollar organizational membership.[111]

In special circumstances many societies readily increased their backing for HIAS. In 1908, for example, the Bialystoker Young Men's Association organized a conference of societies to drum up support for the immigration agency, which had suffered during the economic crisis. Twenty-three societies responded to the Bialystokers' reminder that "many [landsmanshaft members] have come in direct or indirect contact with this society or with its representative on Ellis Island."[112] During World War I groups as diverse as the Timkovitser Congregation and the Zerdover Workmen's Circle branch responded to HIAS appeals for increased contributions to deal with war-related emergencies.[113]

The range of organizations that contributed to HIAS's work was unique for the period. As the Bialystoker Young Men noted in their appeal, HIAS came into contact with a large proportion of New York's Jewish immigrant population. Individuals who had not themselves received assistance from the agency knew relatives and friends who had. All members of the community, of every political or religious orientation, shared the experience of having arrived in a new country, and nearly all fervently supported a continued liberal immigration policy. HIAS's donor lists include the names of hundreds of independent mutual aid societies, religious congregations, union locals, and fraternal lodges. Though the socialist Workmen's Circle officially endorsed HIAS for the first time in 1908, many of its branches had already contributed earlier. By 1913 the HIAS Membership Committee rightly boasted that its 2,621 contributing organizations (1,682 of these in New York) gave it "a larger constituency than any other institution of American Jewry." Furthermore, continued the report, "There are all varieties of Jewish organizations represented, lodges, chevras, charities, federations, labor unions, etc. This is the best evidence of the democracy of our society, of the widespread popular interest there is in our work."[114]

Landsmanshaftn thus reflected all of the enthusiasms and biases of the Jewish immigrant community as a whole. Far from the backward "oases" of passive insularity portrayed by scholars such as Howe and Weisser, the societies formed a crucial reservoir of mass support for a range of communal undertakings—from the Kehillah to the labor movement and HIAS. Hundreds, if not thousands, of landsmanshaftn participated at one time or another in the various movements and charitable causes that engaged the Lower East Side and other immigrant neighborhoods of New York. Some, such as the Workmen's Circle branches on the left and the religious congregations on the right, had explicit ideological commitments. Most were less consistent, though they often evidenced a sentimental attachment to Jewish symbolism and Zionism.

A given cause could attract strong landsmanshaft support if the organization or movement making the appeal could demonstrate its practical necessity and relevance to the members themselves. At the same time, the organizations fiercely guarded their independence and resisted the efforts of larger bodies to subordinate them. HIAS and the trade unions thus won widespread support because they directly touched the lives of many members without imposing discipline on the societies. The Kehillah, on the other hand, remained remote from the daily concerns of most immigrants and was unable to overcome their suspicion of centralized communal structures.

The landsmanshaftn were not prepared to surrender what must have seemed to be the hard-won autonomy afforded them by American conditions. Yet they were more than ready to support those causes which they felt furthered their own interests and those of the community as a whole. Through their federations, they even took the initiative in establishing substantial medical and social-welfare institutions designed to serve the needs of the broader Jewish immigrant population.

～6～

Institutional Dilemmas

Each of the major landsmanshaft federations sponsored a hospital or similar social welfare institution. The Federation of Galician and Bucovinean Jews of America led the way with its Har Moriah Hospital, which it dedicated in 1908. Eager to duplicate the apparent success of the Galician hospital, the other groups followed. The Federation of Russian-Polish Hebrews of America acquired a small hospital in Yorkville in 1910, renamed it Beth David Hospital, and moved it to a new facility in East Harlem in 1913.[1] The Federation of Bessarabian Organizations opened its Hebrew National Orphan Asylum in 1914, and the Federation of Roumanian Jews its Jewish Home for Convalescents in 1916.[2]

By developing these local institutions, the federations responded to their members' primary interest in American conditions rather than in the needs of their former towns in Europe. Founders of the other federations took note especially of the early history of the Galician Farband. Established in 1904 in response to a series of fires in Galicia, the Galician alliance stagnated until it decided to build a hospital on the Lower East Side. Only after adopting this practical program of service to the local community in 1906 did the Galician Federation rapidly attract hundreds of individual societies to become the largest Jewish organization in New York. The Russian-Polish, Romanian, and Bessarabian federations followed suit, each incorporating from the start the sponsorship of a health care facility. The Romanians were a partial exception, since their federations expressed an ongoing concern with Jewish affairs in the old country.[3]

The landsmanshaft hospitals constituted a direct response to a perceived need in the Jewish community. As New York's population grew, largely as a result of immigration, the city's supply of hospital beds proved inadequate.[4] Beth Israel Hospital, at Cherry and Madison Streets, was the only Jewish-sponsored hospital on the Lower East Side, and the only such institution in the city to have been established and maintained by Eastern European Jews. In the first decade of the new century several groups undertook to found additional medical facilities on the Lower East Side, and the Galician's Har Moriah, the Hungarian-sponsored People's Hospital, and the Jewish Maternity Hospital all followed Beth Israel by 1910.[5]

Another incentive to build new facilities was that the new immigrants viewed existing institutions with deep mistrust. Hospitals often considered the moral reform of the patient as much part of their role as his or her physical cure. Moreover, this tradition of moral stewardship was very often connected to an explicit commitment to Christianity, further alienating prospective Jewish patients.[6] Even in institutions sponsored by Americanized Jews, such as New York's Mt. Sinai Hospital, the medical staff and management often treated the cultural values of Orthodox Jews and other immigrants with contempt. The lack of kosher food, for example, caused many patients great distress. "It is an open secret," the Orthodox Yiddish daily *Tageblat* reported, "that in most of the Jewish hospitals in New York the food is trefah [not kosher], and that pious Jews who do not want to eat it are ridiculed . . . The directors of the Jewish hospitals have until now remained deaf to proposals for introducing kosher food."[7] Other complaints included forcible shaving of religious patients' beards and also the beards of deceased patients. The members of Congregation Ahavath Zedek Anshei Timkowitz reacted with outrage when they learned that Mt. Sinai Hospital had cut off the beard of one of their own members after his death. They considered this action a "desecration of the body, when it was known that the brother was a truly pious Jew and never did such a thing in life," and protested that it was "certainly against the laws of the United States."[8] At the 1911 Russian-Polish Farband convention, Joseph Barondess moved the audience with his depiction of the "plight of the Jewish patient who arrives at a hospital where they understand neither his language nor his psychology."[9]

The landsmanshaft hospitals, by contrast, promised to treat their patients with dignity and to respect their cultural needs. Moreover, the institutions constituted a natural extension of the societies' mutual aid function, with its emphasis on health and the avoidance of charity. Both Jewish and non-Jewish hospitals carried the stigma of charity, and many working-class patients feared "being humiliated in the acceptance of free care."[10] By relying on the support of mass organizations like the landsmanshaftn, hospitals like Har Moriah and Beth David aimed to narrow the social gap between patients and patrons. There a society member who needed treatment might be both patron and patient and thus escape any sense of degrading dependence.[11]

While they hoped to avoid the disgrace of receiving charity, the immigrants increasingly sought to share in the prestige of giving it. The federations did not intend their institutions solely for the use of their own members. Rather, the hospital, convalescent home, and orphanage constituted the landsmanshaftn's collective contribution to the community at large. By providing these services to the Jewish population, each federation hoped to raise its group's status vis-à-vis the Americanized German-Jewish elite that funded most of the city's larger Jewish philanthropic enterprises. The presence of prominent "uptown" figures at the opening ceremonies of Har Moriah and Beth David Hospitals, together with the frequent comparisons made between the landsmanshaft facilities and Mt. Sinai, illustrate the degree to which the elite set the standards to which the immigrants aspired.

The Eastern Europeans recognized that the local Jewish establishment derived much of its stature from its charitable activities. Few downtown Jews, however, could ever hope to match the wealth of individual uptown philanthropists. By giving their institutions a broad base of support, the federations provided a way for many rank-and-file members of modest means to share in their organizations' charitable endeavors. The landsmanshaft facilities thus promised to be "democratic" in several senses of the word. First, they were to be subject to the control of the landsmanshaft membership through their delegates to the annual federation conventions. Moreover, they were to receive funding from a large number of small contributors—workers and small businesspeople—rather than a handful of wealthy benefactors. Finally, they were to embody a spirit of social equality, with funders, patients, and even doctors sharing similar social and cultural backgrounds.

Har Moriah and Beth David fit into the prevalent pattern of small hospitals founded by ethnic and religious groups in the nineteenth and early twentieth centuries. But by the time they were established this model had become less and less tenable, as the modern acute-care hospital replaced the small community facility. Increased patient load and developments in medical technology drove up costs, and many institutions found it difficult to keep pace. Hospitals that had previously cared for the poor began to seek a higher proportion of middle-class paying patients. In many older institutions conflicts arose between older patrician elements and newer elites co-opted onto boards of trustees "primarily for their money." Doctors challenged the lay leadership for control, and municipal reformers used the power of public financing to drive small facilities out of operation in the name of rational consolidation.[12]

In such an atmosphere it proved impossible to sustain the landsmanshaft hospitals on the donations of the societies and rank-and-file members. In the Galician Federation responsibility for funding Har Moriah devolved upon a small group of affluent federation leaders, who assumed practical control over the institution. These prominent landslayt, part of an emerging immigrant elite, enjoyed the prestige the hospital lent to their landsmanshaft group and sought to sustain the institution even if it lost its wide funding base. However, others in the Federation viewed this development with alarm as a threat to the democratic nature of the hospital. Similar conflicts took place in the Romanian and Russian-Polish federations.[13]

The federations overcame these factional battles, but the largest and most ambitious of the landsmanshaft institutions were seriously damaged. As the immigrant community focused its attention on the plight of Jews in Eastern Europe during World War I, the hospitals suffered further. The Roumanian Federation's convalescent home and the Bessarabian orphanage survived, but by the end of 1917 Har Moriah Hospital had closed, and the doctors at Beth David had seized the facility from the Polish Federation.[14]

Organized in 1904, the Federation of Galician and Bucovinean Jews of America was the first, largest, and most influential of the landsmanshaft federations. It united individual societies of Jews hailing from two adjacent regions of Habsburg Austria, but since immigrants from Galicia vastly outnumbered those from Bukovina, it was commonly referred to simply as the Galician Federation. The Galician Federation (or Farband) set the trends that the other country federations followed, and its history serves well as a case study.

Tensions between Galician and Russian Jews in New York partly motivated the organization of the Galician Federation. Galician immigrants reported that their Russian neighbors and co-workers looked down on them, viewing them, one young female garment worker reported, as "inhuman savages."[15] Moreover, at the beginning of the century Russian Jews controlled many of the immigrant community's most important institutions, and many observers believed that they had adapted more successfully to American life than had other newcomers.[16] Complaining of discrimination at the hands of Beth Israel Hospital and other Russian-sponsored agencies, one Galician claimed, "It is a known fact . . . that the Russian, and especially the Lithuanian, Jews, hate the Romanian and Galician Jews even more than outright Gentiles hate the Jews in general."[17] The Yiddish press condemned any expression of bigotry, though some journalists suspected that the Galicians exaggerated their plight. As Galician-American journalist Gershom Bader later admitted, "It is very possible that the Galician Jews in New York were simply too sensitive and it only seemed to them that the Russian Jews were looking down at them."[18]

Whether or not their perceptions were accurate, many Galician immigrants felt the need to raise their group's standing in the larger immigrant community, and to furnish, as Bader put it, "a kind of balm for the 'shame' of their Galicianness."[19] Paradoxically, Galician leaders also argued that they and their landslayt possessed far more organizational expertise than did those who had fled the Tsar, pointing to the experience in modern organization and political participation they had gained in the comparatively liberal Austro-Hungarian Empire. Commenting on the success of the Galician Federation, the *Tageblat* editorialized that the Galicians "stand higher than the Russians in all that has to do with organization. They come from a country that has a constitution, from a country that has the ballot box. You should not underestimate the significance of two generations of voting rights and elections!"[20]

While this background may have enabled the Galician Jews to organize earlier than others, a series of fires in Galicia itself supplied the immediate impetus for the Federation's founding. On October 2, 1903, the New York Yiddish press reported conflagrations in three Galician towns: Zolochev (Zloczow), Monastyriska, and Strzysow. In addition to reporting on the details of the disasters, the *Tageblat* noted that the towns' New York landsmanshaftn were already organizing to send relief. Congregation Yad Charutzim Monesterzisker immediately called a meeting at its synagogue on Attorney Street, at which a letter from the town was read and a committee appointed to collect contributions. The First Zlotshover Krankn Untershtitsungs Fareyn also formed a relief committee and appealed for aid from individuals and other societies.[21]

The idea of a federation of Galician landsmanshaftn emerged during the campaign to aid the unfortunate towns. Just two days after it reported the fires, the *Tageblat* suggested that the societies from the towns pool their resources and carry out a joint action.[22] Eventually, after still another blaze, this one in the town of Buchach, the Yiddish journalist Jacob Pfeffer published a call to all Galician societies to band together into one large federation. Pfeffer reminded his readers of the frequency of terrible summer fires in the small Jewish towns of Galicia. Noting the region's deep poverty, he argued that only the Jews in America had the resources to save their landslayt in the old country, and that the inefficient ad hoc method of collecting aid meant that little help reached the stricken towns. "The luckiest town is usually the one which burns down right after Passover," he wrote. "For the first one there is greater enthusiasm." Pfeffer estimated that there were some 400 Galician societies in New York, with about 40,000 members, and suggested that they create a permanent fund to respond in a more timely fashion to requests for assistance from the old country.[23]

As the movement to form a league of Galician societies took shape, its aims broadened. Within a month after the publication of Pfeffer's article, a group of fifteen associations issued a call for a convention of "Austrian" (Galician and Bukovinean) landsmanshaftn. The initiators emphasized the formation of the united relief committee Pfeffer had proposed, but hinted that the planned federation might "with time . . . accomplish many other good and useful works."[24] On June 12, 1904, 225 delegates representing 75 societies met at 96 Clinton Street and founded the Federation of Galician and Bucovinean Jews of America.[25] Shortly thereafter, the new organization enunciated a broader purpose more directly, if vaguely, related to the needs of New York's Galician community. "The aim of the Federation," according to the *Tageblat*, "is to support the members of the societies in times of need, to help unfortunate towns in Galicia and Bukovina, and in general to protect the interests of the tens of thousands of Austrian Jews in this country."[26]

Over the next year, the leaders of the new federation concentrated their efforts on recruiting members among the hundreds of Galician landsmanshaftn in New York. Dr. Solomon Neumann, a leader of the Monastirzhisker Society and the Federation's first vice president, described how "night after night for a whole year, the elected executive committee of the Federation undertook to wander among the Galicians and Bukovineans scattered around New York." Spending from three to five hours on the stump each evening, the leaders appealed to the whole range of immigrant organizations, from the "young men's" societies to Hasidic congregations.[27]

Despite their efforts, the organizers met with limited success. Many members, especially veteran officers, resisted the idea of joining a larger combination. Indeed, though President Pfeffer claimed to have seen a "complete change" over the course of the year, during which "Galician Jews suddenly awoke," the Federation appears to have grown hardly at all. Only 77 societies sent delegates to the Farband's second convention on July 23, 1905.[28]

During its first two years the Galician Federation struggled to define its role. Pfeffer's articles in the Yiddish weekly *Der amerikaner,* which he edited, increasingly emphasized Galician interests in American Jewish life over aid to the old country. Calling the Federation a "movement for recognition and unification," Pfeffer particularly stressed the need to improve his landslayt's status in the immigrant community as a whole.[29] The concern for group status and prestige paralleled the interest in honors exhibited by individual immigrants in their own societies. The Federation therefore bestowed honors on associations in much the same way that the smaller groups granted them to their members. President Pfeffer and other officers made the rounds of societies, ceremoniously presenting them with gold-plated plaques and silver gavels in return for services rendered to the cause.[30] These blandishments, however, failed to attract many societies to the Federation.

The turning point in the history of the Federation of Galician and Bucovinean Jews came in 1906 at its third convention, when the delegates considered a resolution to found a hospital. For some time, the organization had been searching for a concrete project. President Pfeffer at first favored the establishment of a shelter to house homeless newcomers and later recommended the creation of an old-age home and orphanage. Others proposed plans to maintain a Galician representative on Ellis Island, to create an employment bureau, and to establish a fund to aid general Jewish causes.[31] One delegate introduced a resolution that "the Federation energetically undertake to build a hospital on the Lower East Side." After "considerable debate," the delegates appointed a committee to study the idea.[32] When it reported back favorably, the Federation committed itself to building a hospital, "especially important and necessary now in a time of great immigration."[33] Opposed to the building of a hospital, which he saw as a distraction from the organization's proper purpose of aiding Galician Jews in Galicia and America, President Pfeffer declined reelection.[34]

For the next two years the campaign for a hospital formed the focus of Federation activity, and it brought immediate results in terms of prestige and recruitment. As the journalist Z. Kotler noted, "Charity came to the rescue and gave the Federation a raison d'etre."[35] By the beginning of 1907, the Federation had already bought two adjacent buildings at 138–140 East 2nd Street and named the future hospital Har Moriah (Mt. Moriah). A concrete project aimed at solving a local problem proved to be the key to organizational success. Membership in the Federation doubled in the course of a year, from 78 affiliated societies in August 1906 to 157 by June 1907. It continued to expand over the following year to some 261 branches with an estimated 60,000 members (plus three ladies' auxiliaries and 600 individual members). Member societies included K.U.V.s, "young men's" societies, religious congregations, and fraternal lodges, each paying $10 a year dues.[36] The Federation of Galician and Bucovinean Jews had become "one of the largest and most powerful organizations in the country," and had gone a long way toward accomplishing its implied goal of raising the status of the Galician Jews in America.[37] The 1907 convention, held in Tammany Hall, elected businessman Bernard Semel president, and it was he who presided over the growth of the Federation and the opening of the hospital.[38]

A major event on the Lower East Side, the ceremonial opening of Har Moriah Hospital in November 1908 was designed to enhance Galician prestige in the immigrant community.[39] The festivities lasted two whole weeks and, as the Galician-oriented *Yudishe vokhenblat* put it, represented "not the opening of a hospital, but the great triumph of Austrian Jewry in America."[40] Symbolically, the presence of Jacob Schiff, the premier Jewish philanthropist of the day, as well as prominent politicians and representatives of Mt. Sinai and Lebanon Hospitals, proclaimed the equality of this "downtown" enterprise with those of the more prosperous German-Jewish community. The impressive mobilization of landsmanshaft forces for the celebration also proclaimed the arrival of the Galicians as a significant presence in communal affairs.

The first day of activities began with a meeting of the Federation at the Progress Assembly Rooms at Avenue A and Third Street, followed by a parade to the hospital accompanied by the Hebrew Guardian Orphan Asylum band. There, despite cold and wet weather, thousands of people gathered in front of the building, which was decorated with flowers, American flags, and a large Zionist banner. Following a round of speeches, President Bernard Semel handed a ceremonial key to Schiff, who officially opened the hospital. In the center of the women's ward, visitors crowded around a table to be inscribed in a "Golden Book" for a donation of five to twenty dollars. Others put money into charity boxes or bought "paper bricks" for one dollar apiece. Altogether, $10,000 was raised in half a day. Other days were devoted to various constituencies, featuring member landsmanshaftn, the three ladies' auxiliaries, presidents and ex-presidents of societies (addressed by prominent Reform Rabbi Judah Magnes), individual Federation members, and affiliated doctors.[41]

Har Moriah's promise to be a democratic undertaking, sponsored and controlled by the masses of Galician Jews, was one of its strongest attractions. Newspaper accounts called the Har Moriah a "people's institution," and emphasized that it drew its support from "simple . . . East Side Jews," "workers and . . . small merchants," and the "simple poor," rather than "Jewish magnates."[42] The money was to be supplied primarily by the member societies of the Federation, as well as by individual contributions and special events such as an annual ball, picnics, and theater benefits.[43] Speaking at the opening, President Semel reported that $50,000 had already been raised. "But our real wealth," he maintained, "consists of our 60,000 members who are ready to exert themselves on behalf of the hospital whenever necessary."[44]

Moreover, the staff at Har Moriah Hospital treated its immigrant patients differently than did the city's other hospitals. Part and parcel of the immigrant community, Har Moriah respected its mores. The "aristocratic-bureaucratic spirit" would not rule there as it did in many other institutions.[45] The food was strictly kosher, and the immigrant Jew would have no trouble feeling at home from the moment he or she entered. In outward physical appearance the hospital fit right in with the neighborhood, occupying what the *Tageblat* referred to as "a simple building . . . with a simple inscription above the door," and the *For-*

ward called a "very ordinary three-story building, much shorter than the tenement houses that press upon it from all sides." The *Forward* reporter who visited Har Moriah found it much less intimidating than other hospitals. "You can open the door and enter," he wrote, "as if to your own home, without a racing heart and without fear." Moreover, the staff greeted him in a warm and friendly manner, which he had never before encountered in a hospital. In all, the *Forward* reported, "patients feel more at home here . . . It seems like the relationship between the patients and their nurses and doctors is more familiar and friendlier than is the case in other hospitals."[46] The Federation even decided that only Yiddish-speaking nurses should be hired.[47]

While they strove to make Har Moriah homey and familiar, the hospital's sponsors also took pains to emphasize the high quality of its facilities. The modest structure contained "all the latest improvements" in its light, clean, and well-ventilated patients' wards, several private rooms, a modern operating room, examining rooms, a dining room, a kitchen, a laundry, and a roof garden, as well as a dispensary and a training school for nurses. "The poor patient who arrives at Har Moriah Hospital," reported the *Tageblat,* "will be well attended, better than the rich patient at home." Altogether, the hospital accommodated between 85 and 120 patients.[48]

Despite their distrust of uptown institutions, Har Moriah's backers clearly admired and sought to emulate Mt. Sinai Hospital in regard to both facilities and staff. In 1910 the board of directors decided to install "large laboratories" in Har Moriah, "in the same style as Mt. Sinai Hospital." Har Moriah's superintendent, A. N. Spector, had formerly been one of the managers at Mt. Sinai, and the *Forward* reported that "various doctors from Mt. Sinai Hospital, as well as several well-known professors," were on the staff of the Galician hospital.[49] "It will not take more than a couple of years," Semel predicted in 1909, "for Har Moriah Hospital to become the Mount Sinai of the East Side."[50] At the same time, however, they tried to reconcile Mt. Sinai's professionalism with their own down-to-earth approach. The *Tageblat* singled out the appointment of Dr. A. Strachstein, a young physician who seemed to embody both immigrant sensibilities and high professional qualifications. Born in Kishinev, Moldavia, Dr. Strachstein came to America as a child. He attended public schools on the Lower East Side before graduating from Cornell University. A former house physician at Beth Israel Hospital, Dr. Strachstein remained affiliated there, as well as at the Daughters of Jacob Home. He was also a medical examiner for the Metropolitan Life Insurance Company, the "greatest honor for a doctor because the company employs as examiners only first-class doctors." At the same time, he remained a "lovely person." Other doctors at Har Moriah included the Galician Federation's honorary president, Dr. Solomon Neumann, his brother William, and the Lower East Side's popular Dr. Abraham Jacobi. In addition to the doctors, six graduate nurses supervised a staff of student nurses from the hospital's own training school.[51]

From the time of its opening Har Moriah Hospital served a broad cross-section of the community. The hospital admitted patients regardless of their ability to pay, and the great majority, 916 out of 1,144 in the first year, received treatment completely free of charge. The remainder contributed up to seven dollars for a week's stay. Har Moriah also accepted patients "irrespective of race, creed or color," let alone landsmanshaft. Nevertheless nearly all of the patients appear to have been Jewish, and these remained disproportionately "Austrian." During its first year of operation the hospital turned away 1,343 applicants for lack of space or because their cases did not require hospitalization. Doctors performed 546 operations, and the average length of stay was 16 1/3 days. The dispensary, which opened in September 1909, treated a total of 7,840 cases.[52]

Buoyed by the success of its hospital, the Federation of Galician and Bucovinean Jews of America enjoyed its greatest influence between 1909 and 1911. President Bernard Semel expressed pride in his organization's accomplishments and looked forward to still more. "Our Federation is praised everywhere," he wrote, "and recognized for having provided the Jewish world with an example of how to build and sustain a people's institution in the true sense of the word."[53] In 1910 the Galician Federation reached its peak, with a membership of 370 individual societies. At that time the Federation had an income of $41,585 and expenditures of $40,657, of which $31,679 went for hospital expenses and $3,500 toward the second mortgage on the hospital building.[54]

During this period, the Galician Federation's annual conventions at Tammany Hall were impressive occasions. Some 1,300 delegates attended the largest in 1910. The meetings opened with the singing of the Zionist hymn, *Hatikvah,* followed by a benediction by a rabbi and a memorial prayer by a cantor and choir. In addition to reports on the activities and finances of the hospital and Federation, the delegates heard greetings by a number of illustrious guests. These included politicians and Jewish leaders such as New York Secretary of State Samuel Koenig, Congressman Henry Goldfogle, Rabbi Judah Magnes, Samuel Dorf of Order Brith Abraham, Max Stern of Independent Order Brith Abraham, the popular preacher Rev. Zvi Hirsch Masliansky, the Yiddish writer, lawyer, and advocate of an American Jewish Congress, Abraham Shomer, and other landsmanshaft leaders such as Leo Wolfson and User Marcus of the Roumanian Federation. Joseph Barondess, the former-Socialist-turned-Zionist leader, spoke regularly at the conventions. Guests from abroad, such as Galician journalist Gershom Bader, who later emigrated to New York, also made appearances.[55]

The Galicians' annual fund-raising ball/concert also became an important fixture on the Lower East Side's social calendar. The elaborate programs featured dramatic skits in Yiddish and English, Yiddish theater songs, operatic performances, and young dancers and musicians. The second ball, for example, took place on Saturday, March 28th, 1908, in the Grand Central Palace at Lexington Avenue and 43rd Street, an address outside the immigrant neighborhoods. The lengthy program was indeed formidable. The concert featured the chorus of the Halevy Singing Society, three artists from the Manhattan Opera House, the band of the Hebrew Orphan Asylum, Herr Seifstein, lyric tenor of the Vienna Imperial Opera House, the "famous dancemaster" Professor Baraban with a special children's ballet, and stars of the Yiddish stage, Miss Minna Yuvelir, Madame Regina Prager, and Mr. Kalman Yuvelir. According to the *Tageblat* some 18,000 tickets were sold, and 5,000 people actually appeared on the night of the ball. Many could not get into the packed hall. "Despite the crowded conditions," the audience enjoyed itself immensely, and the party lasted until five o'clock in the morning. It brought in $7,600 for the hospital. Subsequent events drew as many as 10,000 and raised up to $10,000. In 1914 the performers included a comedian named George Burns.[56]

Despite its apparent success, however, the hospital almost from the beginning presented the Federation with serious problems. The small contributions of the members quickly proved insufficient to sustain Har Moriah, and a select group of wealthy landslayt quietly filled the deficit. Deep personal animosities and conflicting ambitions of leaders (particularly Ex-President Jacob Pfeffer and President Semel) compounded the fear of many members that this handful of rich individuals would seize the hospital. As early as the spring of 1909 Pfeffer and others began to accuse Semel of plotting to take the hospital away from the Farband, an allegation which would be repeated many times over the next several years. Semel denied the charges and remained in office. But Pfeffer turned the weekly *Yudishe vokhenblat,* of which he was then editor, into an anti-Semel organ, leveling a variety of vituperative charges against his rival and publicizing the activities of the antiadministration faction with evident approval.[57]

Before the 1910 and 1911 conventions the dispute flared up with renewed passion, though both sides claimed to support the same goal: securing Federation control over the hospital. In advance of each convention opposition elements called raucous protest meetings to rally their forces. At one such gathering in March 1911, some 500 people, "including several women," heard Dr. Neumann and others reiterate the accusation that a "half dozen rich men want to remove the hospital from the Federation and use it for their own interests, to give medical appointments to their friends, etc."[58] At issue specifically was the administration's proposed plan, developed with the aid of the prominent lawyer Edward Lauterbach, to overcome a legal obstacle to the Federation's ownership of the institution. Because the Federation's articles of incorporation did not permit it to operate a charitable institution, the hospital had been incorporated separately and was therefore technically independent of its sponsoring organization. To remedy the situation, the administration proposed the issuance of mortgage bonds to be held by each affiliated society in equal shares, the idea being that if the Federation could not legally own the hospital it could be a bond-holder, and thus effectively control the facility. The opposition saw hidden dangers in the plan, but the administration faction won a complete victory: the bond proposal passed and Neumann's post of honorary president was abolished.[59]

Even as they feared the removal of the hospital from Federation control, oppositionists in the Galician Farband argued that Har Moriah constituted a drain on the organization's resources. Members and sympathetic observers complained that the Farband did little other than maintain its institution. "The Federation lies smothered," Pfeffer cried, "under the heavy edifice called the hospital."[60] Ironically, the same people at times articulated the fear that a small clique would capture Har Moriah and also the opinion that the hospital was an unnecessary burden for the Federation. Pfeffer himself straddled the fence uncomfortably, now advocating that the Farband take less of a role in running the hospital, now attacking the administration for taking the facility out of the organization's hands.

The apparent contradictions in the dissidents' arguments reveal that a variety of interests lay behind their coalition. Pfeffer, who was motivated at least in part by personal pique, was joined in opposition by such intellectuals as Dr. Samuel Margoshes and the poet Reuven Iceland, who hoped that the Farband would more actively promote cultural and educational projects. Newcomers like Gershom Bader saw a need for greater intervention in Old-World affairs. (Indeed, Bader first entered the debate in the Federation while he was still living in Galicia.) But rank-and-file members and societies supplied the bulk of antiadministration forces. In contrast to President Semel and his supporters, these members were less interested in the symbolic value of the hospital as a prestigious Galician-sponsored communal institution and more in its egalitarian promise as a facility founded and staffed by the same people it served. Fear that this democratic mission was being compromised formed the basis for the accusation that a wealthy clique was out to seize the hospital. "Instead of a people's institution," the leaders of the Federation Delegates' Association complained, "it has become a sort of political machine."[61]

At the 1912 convention the delegates discovered that the hospital was $14,000 in debt, that only 120 branches of 413 had fully paid their dues, and that the societies themselves had contributed only $1,735 toward Har Moriah's annual budget of over $40,000. Voices were now raised even among supporters of the administration demanding that the Federation free itself of this institutional burden. Joseph Barondess called for a plan to save the hospital and to allow the Federation "to deal with general Jewish national work and not remain a bikur holim society." "Let the directors have the hospital, which they maintain anyway," shouted a delegate named Meyerson. "And when the Federation is rid of it, we will find a president who is able to devote himself to more useful work than maintaining 40 patients."[62]

The delegates to the 1913 convention of the Federation of Galician and Bucovinean Jews finally ousted the incumbent administration. The new leadership proclaimed itself to be at one with the "people" rather than the "wealthy," as the two factions had come to be called, and announced its intention to broaden the scope of Federation activities. As far as the hospital was concerned, the new officers confirmed that many beds had been kept empty even as members who applied for admission were being turned away. In vain did a partisan of the old administration, writing under the name "An Insider," argue that the members had been misled by a hostile press and a dishonest campaign by the organization's secretary and his partisans. Confidently, the new regime even announced that it had "won over other wealthy men" to replace the old ones.[63]

The new leadership soon discovered, however, that it was impossible to sustain such an institution with the support of masses of small donors at a time when it was difficult even for well-established local elites to maintain their hospitals. Despite claims that the Federation had done "splendidly" over the preceding year, that debts had been paid off and more patients treated in the hospital, the official figures for 1913–14 showed quite the opposite. As income dropped from $43,158 to $41,033, the number of patients treated fell from 1,200 to 1,006. Moreover, while in past years the majority of patients had received free treatment, only 250 received care without paying in 1913–14. After one year in office, the "popular" faction invited the "wealthy" old guard back into the Federation. The convention passed a resolution of apology to former President William Fischman and ended on a note of harmony.[64] The process continued the following year, as the economic downturn and war in Europe made mass fund raising even more difficult. On the last day of the 1915 convention Bernard Semel returned triumphantly to make a speech and install the reelected slate of officers.[65]

The outbreak of war in Europe had a severe effect on the fortunes of Har Moriah Hospital. From 1914 the immigrant Jewish community in America focused its attention on events in the old country, where the centers of Jewish population in Eastern Europe were being ravaged. As landsmanshaftn devoted themselves to assisting their compatriots abroad, it became difficult to raise money for institutions in New York.[66] The Federation of Galician and Bucovinean Jews began to stress war-relief work, sending funds to Europe and serving as a clearing house for information on the fate of individuals and communities there. Once the sole beneficiary of the Federation's major fund-raising social activity, its yearly ball, Har Moriah now competed with war relief for limited resources. Even at the Har Moriah ball itself, it seemed, the patrons had their minds on other matters. In 1914, "there was a feeling in the air [at the ball] that the celebration was not altogether complete.

A kind of hidden melancholy showed on people's faces, and it is no wonder given the present circumstances of war and since everyone has his kin in the old country."[67] By the end of 1916 the Federation's annual ball became a benefit solely for war relief.[68] The hospital had become almost an afterthought in Federation deliberations.

Reorganization and one last conflict over control marked the last two years of Har Moriah Hospital. In 1915 no public outcry ensued when the administration of the hospital quietly separated from that of the Federation. Revenue continued to drop at a time when inflation should have been driving it up, and the hospital treated the fewest patients (899) and turned away the most (2,149) since its inception. All of a sudden, in early 1917, the entire Board of Directors resigned together with the medical staff, throwing Har Moriah back into the hands of the Federation. This time, the Federation Executive Committee, representing the "people," charged that the "wealthy" faction, which had dominated the hospital board, was trying to destroy the hospital by abdicating responsibility for it. The former board, in turn, argued that it had resigned as a result of a "long series of unpleasantries" it had suffered at the hands of the Executive Committee, which feared that the Federation would "atrophy" without the hospital. After months of struggle, the board felt it had no alternative but to resign.[69]

At first, it appeared that the Federation would attempt to keep the hospital open, though a note of ambivalence marked its deliberations. "The attention of the nine hundred delegates" to the annual convention, reported the *Tageblat,* "is directed entirely at the question of the hospital which has caused so much trouble and unrest, not only in the Federation, but also in the entire Galician Quarter." As conditions deteriorated and debt mounted, the city's Charity Department revoked its support because of deficiencies in Har Moriah's building, which was "not modernly constructed or equipped."[70] The journalist Z. Kotler warned that it would take $60,000 a year to maintain the hospital, "a sum which the Federation is in no way able to deliver, and if the local wealthy Galicians do not take the hospital into their hands in time, it will have to close."[71]

By the time a special convention met in September 1917, Har Moriah had closed, and most participants hoped only to save the Federation itself. Everybody agreed that the hospital's demise had dealt a shameful blow to Galician pride and a few still spoke in favor of reopening the facility. But nobody proposed that the Federation maintain it. Former

President Pfeffer, who seven years earlier had raised the hue and cry that a rich clique was out to kidnap the institution, now returned to his original position and "demonstrated that the cause of the Federation's ruin was the hospital, and that the Federation was not founded for the sake of the hospital, and that it does not need it."[72] The convention reconstituted the Farband around a program of overseas relief and Jewish unity. Dr. Samuel Margoshes became president, joined on the Executive Committee by Dr. Neumann, and former presidents Semel, Pfeffer, and Bernard Turkel.[73] In the end, few regretted the decision to divest the Federation of Har Moriah. "At the conclusion of the gathering," reported the *Tageblat,* "all expressed their satisfaction with finally being rid of the hospital, which has been an affliction for the Federation."[74]

The establishment and maintenance of significant health-care facilities constituted an impressive achievement for the landsmanshaft federations. By supporting the institutions morally and financially, hundreds of societies demonstrated their desire to be of service to the wider immigrant Jewish population, and also to attain parity with the "uptown" German-Jewish elite in the realm of philanthropy. The hospitals' initial sponsorship by a broad base of modest contributors, as well as the narrow social gap among patrons, patients, and doctors, allowed many members to view them as a natural extension of the societies' central mission of mutual aid.

Unfortunately, the landsmanshaftn opened their institutions at a time when such small community-based facilities were becoming too difficult to sustain. The federations could not fund their hospitals adequately, and small groups of relatively affluent individuals assumed responsibility for doing so. For many rank-and-file society members, sponsorship and control by a small group of wealthy patrons, even if these were also landslayt, threatened to undermine the institutions' democratic nature and transform them into ordinary charity institutions. In 1917, after years of factional struggles around this issue, both the Galician and the Russian-Polish federations lost control of their institutions.

By that time World War I had grabbed the attention of the entire Jewish community and forced the landsmanshaft federations to reorient their activities and resources toward overseas relief. The hospitals suffered proportionately. Ultimately, the war also undermined the very definitions of the countries and regions whose names the federations carried. Early in the war, a journalist joked that the Federation of Galician and Bucovinean Jews might soon have to realign itself to fit new political realities: "The new sign which the Galician Federation recently made for its office reads only 'Federation Office,' because no one knows in whose hands Galicia will fall, and what name the 'Federation' will have to take. Perhaps Russia will capture Galicia and the Galician Federation will have to merge with the Russian-Polish Federation, or vice versa, or maybe Romania will conquer Galicia and the Galician Federation will become a branch of the Romanian Federation."[75] By the end of the war realignment had become a reality. When Poland gained independence, the Federation of Russian-Polish Hebrews became the Federation of Polish Jews, maintaining strong organizational continuity throughout the interwar period. The dismantling of the Habsburg Empire, however, led to the break up of the Federation of Galician and Bucovinean Jews. The Bukovinans, whose homeland was now in Romania, left to form their own short-lived federation. The Federation of Galician Jews continued, resisting merger overtures from the Polish Federation, but faded from existence by 1930.[76]

⌣7⌐

The Heroic Period

World War I was a pivotal moment in the history of the landsman-shaftn, as it was in the history of Jewry as a whole. Some three quarters of all Jews lived in the belligerent countries, and much of the fighting took place in areas of heavy Jewish concentration in Eastern and East Central Europe. The battles themselves, the economic dislocation of the war, and violence directed specifically against the Jewish population all combined to take a heavy toll on the towns and cities whose names the American landsmanshaftn bore. Hundreds of thousands were up-rooted, making their way to the large cities and the interiors of the Russian and Austro-Hungarian empires. Economic losses reached an estimated $400,000,000.[1] Moreover, the crisis extended beyond 1918, as the Russian Civil War and war between the new Soviet and Polish states continued into the 1920s.

The landsmanshaftn responded by organizing to provide massive amounts of aid to their unfortunate landslayt. This was, in the words of social critic Borukh Rivkin, their "heroic period." Societies now devoted the full range of their activities to raising money for overseas relief. Between 1914 and 1924 they sent millions of dollars to their European brothers and sisters. The increase in activity around relief work sometimes breathed new life into flagging societies. Some immigrants even founded new associations in response to events in Europe.[2]

The landsmanshaft activity was only part of the extensive relief effort undertaken by American Jewry during and after World War I. Organizations such as the Joint Distribution Committee of the American Funds for Jewish War Sufferers (JDC or Joint), formed in the early days of the war to provide emergency relief, developed into permanent bodies with a commitment to the Progressive Era's ideal of social-welfare professionalism. The landsmanshaftn often supported the general relief agencies, but relations between them were tense. The former maintained an emotional attachment to their hometowns and sometimes resented the air of bureaucratic aloofness of the central agencies. The JDC, for its part, considered the hometown associations to be important potential partners, but at the same time it strove to control what it viewed as a chaotic, wasteful, and amateurish landsmanshaft sector.

Despite these differences, the landsmanshaftn and the Joint displayed significant similarities in their approaches to overseas relief. Most importantly, the war crisis brought an unprecedented degree of unity among previously hostile segments of the Jewish community. The JDC itself was a coalition of "uptown" and "downtown" Jews, of radicals, conservatives, and professional communal workers. On the landsmanshaft level, hitherto competing organizations from the same town banded together in united relief committees to assist their beleaguered landslayt. Moreover, the professional agency and the societies alike sought to impose this very American sense of nonpartisan pragmatism on the ideologically charged and highly factionalized Jewish communities of Eastern Europe.

Overseas relief work, which since World War I has been a defining characteristic of American Jewry, provided the medium through which the landslayt demonstrated both a new sense of Americanism and a more explicit concern for their old hometowns than they had previously displayed. Paradoxically, as the hometowns became more central to official landsmanshaft activity than they had ever been, the increase in formal contact made society members more conscious of the differences separating them from those they had left behind. Not only did their material condition contrast starkly with that of their friends and relatives, but the immigrants also came to recognize definite, if only vaguely defined, psychological differences as well. During the war, the immigrants came to see themselves clearly as American Jews, a community distinct from those in the countries of Eastern Europe.

News of the early weeks of the war in August 1914 shook the immigrant Jewish community in New York. Newspaper reports were full of the names of the Jewish towns and cities from which many of the immigrants had come. In the war's first days the Germans captured the Polish towns of Kalisz, Bedzin, and Czestochowa, and moved toward Warsaw. Battles erupted near Vilna, as Polish Jews fled toward Lithuania. At the same time, Russian and Austro-Hungarian troops fought over Galicia. The Yiddish daily *Tageblat* ran feature stories on the Jewish communities of the war-stricken towns along with first-hand accounts in letters from friends and family in Europe. The letters contained vivid and frightening accounts of life under military occupation. They described not only battles but economic breakdown, shortages, confiscations, arrests, executions, and widespread hunger. Soon, the letters also began to include reports of pogroms carried out mainly by Russian forces.[3]

American Jews quickly recognized that the war in Europe gave them a special international responsibility. The immigrants shared in this sense of obligation as they came to realize that their current situation and future fate in America differed markedly from those of their brothers and sisters overseas. As the *Tageblat* editorialized, "It is important for American Jews to keep in mind that we are the only large Jewish community which is not caught up in the horrible tumult. We are the only part of the Jewish people which is living in peace and tranquility, so we should help, when we are able, the Jews on the other side of the ocean."[4] Not only were Jewish communities suffering the direct effects of the fighting, but the war had also disrupted established channels of support for poorer communities by wealthier ones. Russian Jewry could no longer count on aid from Germany, nor Galician Jewry on help from Britain and France. The Jewish community in Palestine, long dependent on assistance from Europe, was also left in a desperate state.[5]

The Eastern European immigrants' special relationship to the places from which they had come reinforced their sense of duty. No one realized better than they how necessary American relief had become for their war-stricken hometowns and regions. Consequently, the landsmanshaftn were among the first to respond to the crisis. As the Yiddish press reported, "The cry for help that is now coming from Galicia . . . has been heard in the Galician quarter of New York, and it has moved the Galicians to new activity." By August 16th, just two weeks after the war had begun, one Galician society, the Bolechower K.U.V., had already begun a campaign to raise money for relief, contributing the first $1,000 from its own treasury.[6] Neither did towns on the other side of the Russian-Austrian border escape the effects of the war. In September and October 1914, more than a dozen relief committees were organized at mass meetings called by both Russian and Galician landsmanshaftn. Tens more joined them in the following months.[7]

The enormity of the catastrophe in Europe moved landslayt to overcome the political and religious divisions which had fractured the landsmanshaft world. From right to left, religious congregations and Workmen's Circle branches combined to form united relief committees to aid their places of origin. For example, the two largest societies of landslayt from the Belorussian city of Minsk, the Minsker Independent Benevolent Society and the United Minsker Benevolent Association, formed a joint committee and invited other Minsker societies to affiliate. They were soon joined by the Minsker Young Men's Commercial Aid Society, the Minsker Hebrew American Society, and the Minsker Progressive Br. 99, Workmen's Circle, in a campaign to raise $20,000.[8] Similarly, a coalition to aid the twin cities of Pinsk and Karlin encompassed the whole range of immigrant societies, including two synagogues, two fraternal lodges, a women's charitable association, and the Pinsker Workmen's Circle branch.[9]

As landsmanshaft relief committees formed, calls arose from various quarters for a more centralized and coordinated effort on the part of American Jewry. The Orthodox sector united first, forming the Central Relief Committee for the Relief of Jews Suffering through the War (CRC) at a meeting in the offices of the *Tageblat* on October 4, 1914. Soon after, the American Jewish Committee, primarily representing wealthy Americanized Jews, established the American Jewish Relief Committee (AJRC). Finally, in the summer of 1915, labor and socialist elements formed a third central relief organization, known as the Jewish People's Relief Committee of America (PRC).[10] Although they were associated with different elements of the community, all three committees appealed for support to a broad base of societies, congregations, lodges, and other organizations. Prominent landsmanshaft figures participated in each group.

In November 1914 the CRC and the AJRC formed the Joint Distribution Committee as a common mechanism for disbursing the funds which each had raised. The PRC later also joined the JDC. While each affiliated committee continued to employ the appropriate emotionally charged language necessary to reach its own targeted constituency, each also saw the need for professional efficiency in the actual delivery of aid. The Joint, which was to become one of American Jewry's most important agencies, thus reflected a desire on the part of much of the Jewish leadership for a relief organization able to "function with the greatest directness and the least duplication."[11] The JDC aimed to apply its "scientific" and rigorously non partisan expertise to the problems of Jewish communities in Eastern Europe relating to economic development, public health, education, and even agriculture. Like other progressive professionals, JDC staffers valued a dispassionate application of training and skill to the resolution of social ills.

While the JDC strove to establish efficient distribution mechanisms abroad, each of its member committees raised funds at home. Despite the involvement of some landsmanshaft federations and leaders in its founding, the AJRC operated primarily among Americanized Jews in New York and elsewhere. The PRC drew much of its support from Workmen's Circle branches, as well as independent landsmanshaftn and other fraternal orders. Landsmanshaft religious congregations were the most likely to support the CRC, often with money pledged during synagogue services. In addition, the CRC issued five- and ten-cent stamps, which congregations bought and affixed to their High Holy Day synagogue tickets each year of the war.[12]

The landsmanshaft federations supported the JDC and at the same time attempted to coordinate relief activities on their own. All of the federations participated in the Joint's major fundraising campaigns.[13] They also provided the JDC staff with information and insight into the situations in their native countries and on the local level.[14] The Federation of Galician and Bucovinean Jews of America likewise encouraged its affiliates in their own efforts, while it transmitted collected funds via the Austrian embassy to the Viennese Israelitische Alianz for Galician Jewish refugees in Vienna and elsewhere.[15] The Farband also made a special appeal on behalf of the Galician Jewish community in Palestine, which it described as sinking in a "sea of troubles and suffering."[16] Soon, however, the Farband decided to leave most fund raising to the individual societies. It concentrated instead on helping refugees in Austria find their relatives in America, transmitting letters and publishing the names of recipients in the Yiddish press. The Federation claimed to have put 20,000 refugees in touch with American relatives during the first year of the war.[17]

The Russian-Polish, Hungarian, and Romanian federations also labored energetically on behalf of their landslayt in Europe. A visiting delegation helped convince the Federation of Roumanian Jews in America and the American Union of Roumanian Jews to set aside their differences and collaborate closely on issues of common concern. (The Union even met with President Wilson to inform him of conditions in Romania and ask that he pressure the Romanian government to grant equal rights to the country's Jews.)[18]

While they sometimes cooperated with the central agencies, the individual landsmanshaft relief committees continued to focus on the needs of their particular landslayt in Europe. Many called mass meetings to raise money and exhort the American landslayt to action. In just one week in December 1914 more than twenty rallies took place in New York, raising between $75 and $1,500 each for the war victims of various towns.[19] On one such occasion at the Mezritsher Synagogue, 415 East 6th Street, members of "all the congregations, hevrot, and societies of Jews who came here from Miedzyrzec and vicinity" heard Joseph Barondess and several rabbis speak so effectively that 162 donors contributed $503 on the spot. The meeting also resolved to send committees to call upon landslayt who had not attended the rally.[20]

One of the functions of the mass relief meetings, and perhaps their greatest draw, was the exchange of information concerning conditions in the old country. Though immigration had slowed to a trickle, the occasional new arrival was pressed into service to give an eyewitness account of events in the hometown. At the venerable Kalvarier Shul, for example, Mrs. Mary Vatkin, now of the Borough Park section of Brooklyn, reported "on the terrible suffering undergone by the Jews of Kalvarija during the battles between the Germans and the Russians which took place in and around the city." Mrs. Vatkin, who had been present during the fighting, pleaded for aid to the Kalvarier refugees now "scattered throughout various towns in Russia and Poland."[21] Like the federations, each local relief committee served as an address to which war victims in Europe could turn to get in touch with relatives in the United States.[22]

The societies now devoted many of their traditional activities to the relief effort, and their new purpose gave the old events a weightier meaning. Concerts, balls, banquets, regular meetings, and Sabbath services all became occasions at which to raise money.[23] Attendance at the annual ball now rated as a "great *mitzvah*" (good deed or commandment), in the words of the Oshminer Ladies U.V. "You will be entertained and see your landslayt and friends, and at the same time our quarters will alleviate the hunger and misery of the unfortunates in our native town."[24] A number of societies, such as the Timkovitser and the Zlotshover, also adopted the traditional Jewish practice of distributing special home charity boxes among their landslayt.[25]

Theater benefits were transformed into rallies for war relief. The Austrian consul spoke during intermission at the Strier society's benefit at Kessler's Theater in January 1915. The Yiddish actor Boris Tomashevsky, a Berditshever landsman, donated an entire performance to the Berditshever Relief, and speeches by prominent figures accompanied the play.[26] A description of the reaction to the speech by "the beloved people's orator," Zvi Hirsch Masliansky, at the Pinsker Relief's theater benefit gives some idea of the charged atmosphere at these events. According to a report, Masliansky "gave a fiery speech in which he depicted the suffering of the victims of the war in general, and of the Pinsker in particular. The speech moved everybody to tears and money began to pour from all sides. In a matter of 15–20 minutes $842.68 were raised for the unfortunates."[27]

Despite all of this activity, however, the changing zones of occupation and broken lines of communication combined to make it difficult for the relief committees to reach the intended recipients of their funds. The JDC soon arranged to transmit relief funds through existing Jewish agencies in Europe.[28] But at various times throughout the war years it was impossible to get relief funds through to specific areas, especially if they fell within the zone of battle or under Russian occupation. With Galicia in the hands of the Russians in early 1915, reported Gershom Bader, "neither the post office nor any bank" was willing to undertake deliveries there.[29] Some time later, the Pinsker Relief Committee reported to its contributors that "none of our efforts to establish contact with responsible persons in Pinsk . . . have brought results. All of the letters which the committee has sent there have been returned, and the committee has been forced to deposit in the bank the $440 which it collected."[30]

Even so, landsmanshaftn managed to send some money to their hometowns and regions. In July 1916, when the Timkovitser Congregation in New York learned from their stricken hometown's rabbi that it had become possible to reach Timkovichi, it immediately dispatched 1,000 rubles, followed by an equal amount later the same year.[31] By 1916 a number of immigrant bankers were willing and able to transmit money to war-affected regions. They aggressively solicited landsmanshaft business. The Bank of United States, for example, erected two large signs over its office on Delancey Street listing the societies and relief committees which had already availed themselves of its services. In a full-page advertisement in the *Tageblat,* the bank claimed that "many, many societies" had already each sent "hundreds and thousands" of dollars through its office in Berlin. Other immigrant bankers made similar pronouncements.[32]

The general relief organizations complained throughout the war years' however, that many societies hoarded money until they could forward it directly to their hometowns. The Galician Federation estimated that by November 1914 the individual Galician societies had accumulated some $20,000, which they refused to turn over to the Federation. The Farband argued that it needed at least part of this money to help Galician refugees stranded in Vienna and other Austrian cities. "Women and children die of starvation in the streets," it charged, "and the societies still hold the money until such time as the victims of the war are able to return to their homes."[33] A year later, the Federation estimated that the societies had sent $20,000 abroad and were holding some $40,000.[34]

It became more difficult to reach German- and Austrian-controlled areas once the United States entered the war in the spring of 1917. Although the JDC formulated an arrangement with neutral Holland for the transfer of relief funds, the smaller landsmanshaft committees were cut off from their towns and so were all the more likely to hold on to their accumulated money.[35]

The United Brisker Relief was in many ways typical of the many landsmanshaft relief committees of the World War I era. Established early in the crisis, the Brisker Relief waxed and waned in relation to developments abroad and tensions among its diverse components. Eager to help their unfortunate landslayt in Brisk (Brest Litovsk in Russian, Brzesc nad Bugiem in Polish), the American Brisker were frustrated during the war by their inability to reach the intended recipients. Some Americans became discouraged, but the majority continued to raise money in the hope of assisting in the rebuilding of the community at the conflict's end. The complete evacuation of the city's civilian population made their task especially hard. Nevertheless, even during the war itself they succeeded in sending some badly needed funds to Brisker refugees in other parts of Poland. After the war, the Brisker Relief renewed its efforts with increased energy, becoming the center of a national network of relief committees with branches in Chicago, Detroit, Cleveland, Los Angeles, and Newark.

The city of Brisk, located on the Bug River on the border of Poland and Russia, had been a major trade center between Germany and Russia, as well as an important garrison town. Its relatively prosperous Jewish community made up a majority of the city's population before World War I; in 1913 its 57,068 inhabitants included 39,152 Jews, together with 10,042 Russians and 7,536 Poles.[36] The city suffered terribly during the war. Since it was a strategic point, the Russians made special preparations for its defense, drafting many citizens to the hard labor of digging trenches and setting out barbed wire. Many residents of Brisk fled in panic to the surrounding towns. Intermittent periods of forced labor, together with German bombardment, further weakened the civilian population, which was finally expelled altogether in August 1915, as the Russians prepared for a German offensive. There were not enough trains to take the refugees into the interior of Russia, and many refugees left on foot or by horse-drawn wagon, staying nearby in the expectation that they would soon return home.

Despite their preparations, the Russians surrendered the city to the Germans without a fight. As they left, however, Russian soldiers and Cossacks looted the deserted houses and set fire to the city to obstruct the German advance. After capturing Brisk on August 25, 1915, the Germans at first allowed some civilians to return. Within weeks, however, these were again expelled, and hardly any civilians were in the city during the entire period of German occupation, 1915–1919. The former inhabitants of Brisk remained dispersed, some in Russia, some in a number of towns in the vicinity. Many lived in special barracks under German supervision, and the German-Jewish Hilfsverein assisted in their upkeep.[37]

In the fall of 1914, even before the evacuation of Brisk, the landslayt in New York began to receive disturbing news from their hometown. After some informal discussions, a coalition of some twelve or thirteen Brisker organizations called a mass meeting and established a united relief committee.[38] The societies ranged from the Brisker branches of the Workmen's Circle and Jewish National Workers' Alliance to the Brisker Shul Tiphereth Israel and lodges of the Independent Orders Brith Abraham and Brith Sholom. Jacob Finkelstein, longtime secretary of the United Brisker Relief, later recalled that meeting. "It was a very hot evening. The hall was packed; the crowd was diverse—Bundists, nationalists, and Orthodox . . . The conference was a great success. Everyone went away with the intention of creating a great relief committee for Brisk and of throwing themselves into the work to make it a success."[39]

Early setbacks, however, discouraged many members. A ball failed to raise as much money as expected, and tensions arose between some of the younger radicals and the older conservatives. Perhaps most discouraging of all was the inability of the committee to send aid directly to Brisk. Finkelstein recalled that some delegates proposed the dissolution of the committee altogether: "There is no one left in Brisk itself," they argued, "So there is no need for a relief."[40] The Brisker Relief in fact lay dormant for about a year, until a handful of members revived it in June 1916, taking over the $167.10 in the treasury of the old organization. Still, the reorganized committee could not satisfy those landslayt who looked to it to provide information concerning their relatives in Europe, much less aid the scattered refugees.

In the meantime, committee activists continued to raise money and labored to convince the landslayt that "we must not wait with our aid until after the war, when the Brisker return to Brisk, and in the meantime let them die of starvation."[41] After June 1, 1916, when the committee was reorganized, it collected $2,984 in about a year through dues, donations, raffles, collections at private and public affairs, and a ball thrown by the Harlem branch. Donations also arrived from Cleveland, Detroit, and Aplica, Alabama. By far the largest money-maker was the theater benefit, which netted nearly $1,000.[42]

Late in 1916 the committee finally established contact with landslayt in Europe, and shortly thereafter it sent its first money abroad. With the help of the Red Cross and the Hilfsverein der deutschen Juden, the Brisker Relief secured a list of refugees in the towns of Miedzyrzec, Antopol, Biala, Lukow, and Pruzhany. Soon after, a dramatic appeal appeared in the New York Yiddish newspapers from a Brisker committee in Warsaw. Signed by twenty-two individuals, the statement was addressed to "Dear brothers," and implored the United Relief to aid the refugees from Brisk through the legally constituted committee in the Polish capital. The New Yorkers responded by cabling 4,000 marks (over $700) to Warsaw.[43]

At its wartime peak in 1917, the Brisker Relief also functioned as an information agency. On Wednesday evenings at its office at 106 Forsyth

Street the organization passed on letters it received from Europe for landslayt in America. It also published in the *Jewish Daily Forward* names of located refugees and reported the latest news at its meetings.[44] The committee drew people to its 1917 annual meeting by promising, "We have much important news from Brisk which we will report to you . . . We have a letter from Brisker who are now in Miedzyrzec."[45] It also promised that landslayt would "hear greetings in person from the newly arrived Brisker" at its picnic that summer.[46]

With America's entry into the conflict, the Brisker Relief drive slowed. Not only did communication become more difficult, but many of the young mainstays of the organization entered the American army or the Jewish Legion. Up to this point, the committee had sent only $748 to Europe, less than its own organizational expenses. The rest of the money sat in a bank awaiting the end of the fighting, when it would once again become possible to establish direct contact. The activists' main accomplishment during the war was the establishment of an organizational mechanism which played its most important role in the immediate postwar period, when it funneled hundreds of thousands of dollars to landslayt in need.

When World War I came to a close in 1918, contact between American and East European Jewry resumed. The crisis faced by the Jews residing in the new states of Eastern Europe, however, did not end with the Armistice. During the Russian Civil War, counter-revolutionary forces, Ukrainian nationalists, Anarchist bands, and even some Red Army units carried out hundreds of pogroms in the Ukraine. War between Poland and the Soviet Union between May 1920 and March 1921 also severely affected the Jewish population, and the total Jewish death toll in these two conflicts reached as high as 250,000.[47] Moreover, the devastation of the economic infrastructure during the war, the breakup of the old empires with its attendant loss of markets, and anti-Jewish policies of nationalist governments all hindered the rebuilding of Jewish communal life. The lack of adequate communal institutions, many of which had ceased to function during the war years, exacerbated these problems. American relief agencies, particularly the JDC, were to play a major role in reconstructing the Jewish community, especially in Poland.[48]

After the war, the JDC began to administer its relief programs directly, as well as to train local personnel in modern methods of sanitation, child care, and economic rehabilitation. In 1919, Boris Bogen, an experienced social worker, led a team of forty uniformed American experts to Poland to help establish local relief committees, child-care institutions (there were an estimated 100,000 to 150,000 Jewish war orphans in Europe in 1921), credit cooperatives, and loan funds. Other units followed, including a group of eighteen doctors and nurses headed by Bernard Flexner, who went to Poland in 1921 to finance and reform local sanitary and health facilities. The JDC's cultural committee also backed some 1,800 educational institutions, including vocational schools. Between 1919 and 1923 the JDC raised $47,000,000 for its projects overseas, mainly in Poland and other East European countries.[49]

In addition to organized relief, American Jews sent private remittances to relatives. The large agencies such as JDC and HIAS, as well as private banks and landsmanshaftn, all transmitted such moneys to individual families. These private funds actually amounted to more than the sums given to general relief. In 1920, for example, the JDC sent $7,932,674 in private remittances to Europe (excluding the USSR), while expending $7,657,836 on its own programs. Unstable exchange rates and inconsistent regulation by the Polish government made the transmission of private money a difficult business, and often led to speculation and other abuses. Nevertheless, as one observer wrote, "Rarely will you find in Russia, Poland or Lithuania a family, which is not being helped in one way or another by relatives from overseas."[50]

Landsmanshaft relief activity also increased tremendously following the Armistice, stimulated once again by moving petitions from abroad. The National Council of Lithuanian Jews addressed the Lithuanian landsmanshaftn in America directly: "If you do not want that your friends and your relatives, men, women and children, shall perish through the conditions of the present time, extend to us your helping hand as brothers."[51] Jewish delegations from Galicia, the Ukraine, and Warsaw came in person to meet with the appropriate landsmanshaft societies and federations. Individual landsmanshaftn like the Dwinsker Dinaburger Relief Committee circulated letters they received from the Jewish communities in their hometowns.[52]

Aroused by these entreaties, landsmanshaftn formed new committees and revived old ones. At least fifty-three relief meetings or benefits took place in three days from March 6 to 8, 1920.[53] The Poloner Relief reported that its hometown faced "horror without limit," and called on the landslayt to become more involved. The committee had "recently once again undertaken the necessary relief work with renewed energy," distributing charity boxes, running a theater benefit, convening a mass meeting, and even establishing a loan fund to help people meet the expenses of bringing relatives from Europe.[54] Moreover, hundreds of landsmanshaft relief committees had already accumulated substantial amounts of money that they had been unable to distribute during the war. By the summer of 1920, a JDC staff member estimated that approximately 750 relief committees in New York had "at least $7,500,000 of available cash for Europe."[55]

Once they were able to do so, the landsmanshaftn began to send this money to their hometowns. Even a little money could prove helpful in a small town, as illustrated by a letter written in 1920 to the Narever Relief Committee from its landslayt in Narew. The writers thanked the committee for the recently sent $350, which they had used to rebuild the bath house destroyed three years earlier by the Germans, subsidize bread for fifteen weeks, hire a doctor and buy medical supplies, and maintain a public school for poor children.[56]

The Joint Distribution Committee realized that the landsmanshaftn constituted an important resource, which it hoped to harness for its work. At first, however, the JDC was reluctant to meet the one basic condition set by the landsmanshaftn for cooperation with the general relief agencies: that the money each raised go to its own town. The Joint's officers and staff based their objections on their own perception of the demands of professionalism, viewing the societies' emotional concern for their own towns as narrow, inefficient, and unjust, since it meant that places with strong landsmanshaftn in America would receive more aid than those whose landslayt were not so active. The central agency preferred to distribute resources on the basis of its experts' impartial assessment of need. Searching for a middle ground, Dr. Samuel Margoshes of the Galician Federation pressed for a combined Federation-JDC mission, with the Joint supervising the distribution of funds earmarked for specific towns.[57] But when the Federation's Bernard Semel repeated the proposal in June 1919, JDC Chairman Felix Warburg, responded curtly that Semel was "pampering to the human weaknesses of [his] constituents." "The Joint Distribution Committee," wrote Warburg, "has distributed funds according to the needs which they see in the different parts, disregarding in the appropriations for Galicia what the Galician Jews have contributed or for Lithuania what the Lithuanian Jews have contributed, and they will continue to do so."[58]

Soon, however, the Joint realized that it would have to compromise with the landsmanshaftn if it were to tap their resources. As JDC leader Paul Baerwald bluntly put it, "The Landsmanschaften heretofore wanted our aid, now we must facilitate matters for them, because only in that way can we hope to get hold of some of their money to be used for proper relief purposes."[59] A Committee on Landsmanshaftn, appointed in September 1919, stated its belief that the societies could be more effective in fund raising than the central agencies "because of the intimacy and close relationship between the soliciting organizations and contributors, and because of the strong sentimental grounds upon which the appeal is made." Moreover, the committee recommended that the JDC accede to landsmanshaft demands that it transmit funds to "the designated town or city in Europe" and give credit to the contributing society.[60] The JDC also conferred with the heads of the country federations and large societies concerning ways in which the landsmanshaftn could be drawn into general relief work.[61]

In the spring of 1920 the JDC managed to involve a number of landsmanshaftn in its campaign for "constructive" relief that would further the economic rehabilitation of Jewish communities in Eastern Europe. The centerpiece of the effort was to establish funds for interest-free loans in the affected localities. Several landsmanshaftn turned over significant amounts of money to set up loan funds in their towns with the understanding that, if necessary, the Joint would provide additional sums. Significantly, the landsmanshaftn also received the right to appoint some members to the local committees administering the funds.[62]

That summer, the JDC established a Landsmanshaft Department to coordinate its activities with those of the societies. The department was predicated on JDC's acceptance of the societies' legitimate role in relief work, but also on its conviction that the landsmanshaft relief committees needed the professional supervision of the larger agency. Samuel Schmidt, the first chief of the new department, argued that the societies were motivated by a "natural, healthy clannish instinct" which led them to wish to "render relief to their cities as far as possible directly." The JDC, according to Schmidt, had no choice but to "adopt a definite policy of full cooperation" if it hoped to win the societies' confidence. At the same time, Schmidt also expressed the professional social worker's concern that leaving the landsmanshaftn unsupervised would "only encourage the formation of unscrupulous private organizations and private individuals who will exploit them for their own private ends." He concluded that "there can be no question but that the J.D.C. is duty bound to take control of the Landsmanschaften activities."[63] The department opened an office at 98 Second Avenue, with a staff of four and a large map of Eastern Europe on which it stuck a push-pin on each town for which it had located a landsmanshaft.[64]

From its establishment in 1920 until its dissolution in 1924, the department strove to incorporate the landsmanshaftn into the JDC's efforts. Much of its work consisted of transmitting both personal and general relief funds to the JDC's Warsaw office for distribution according to the instructions of contributing landsmanshaftn. In return, the department forwarded reports on local conditions from JDC's Warsaw office to the societies, and handed over personal messages from the old country for delivery by the landsmanshaftn. The department also gathered information concerning landsmanshaft activities, publicized the work of other JDC divisions, and informed the societies of special immediate needs. Between September 1920 and September 1922, the department handled 454 remittances from 381 different landsmanshaftn, including about $680,000 in aid to individuals and $520,000 in general relief funds. In the same period it sent reports on conditions in their towns to 450 landsmanshaftn and relayed tens of thousands of individual messages.[65] In addition, the department carried out special campaigns to send flour for matzot each Passover and accepted money from landsmanshaftn for purchase of food, clothing, medicine, and other supplies for delivery to towns in the Soviet Union.[66]

The JDC most wanted to control the landsmanshaft practice of sending "delegates" with large amounts of money to the societies' hometowns. The delegate movement peaked in 1920 and 1921, becoming what one JDC staff member called "almost a mania on the East Side."[67] As a writer in the Yiddish daily *Tog* put it, "The 'delegate' has become, so to speak, an institution in the Jewish community. There is not a single landsmanshaft here in America (however small), which has not sent, is not sending, or will not send a delegate with money and letters to the landslayt on the other side of the ocean."[68] Often, the delegate to a larger town would also bring aid to smaller nearby communities. At the end of 1920, 290 American delegates were registered at the Warsaw office of the Hebrew Sheltering and Immigrant Aid Society (HIAS). In 1920 and 1921, 200 delegates went to Romania.[69]

The landsmanshaftn had their reasons for sending delegates to Europe. They most likely adopted the idea from the general relief organizations, which had sent representatives abroad during the war itself. These delegates, including the popular Rabbi Judah L. Magnes, who went to Europe in 1916 on behalf of the Joint, helped to deliver aid. But perhaps even more importantly, their first-hand reports of conditions in Eastern Europe energized relief efforts once they returned. Isidore Hershfield, who toured the front in 1916 on behalf of HIAS, spoke directly to the landsmanshaftn at a series of meetings for groups of landslayt from the towns he had visited.[70] The landslayt thus came to realize the value of personal representatives on the scene, not just to distribute aid but also to gather information on the spot.

Moreover, many landsmanshaftn distrusted the JDC, which they considered too bureaucratic and lacking in intimate knowledge of conditions in their hometowns. By sending their own representatives they hoped to bypass the large relief agencies altogether.[71] Some Bessarabian Jews, for example, argued that the Joint had "absolutely no practical idea of the relief work which should be done."[72] Many landslayt complained that the JDC was forced by government regulations to pay out remittances in local currency, which, owing to rapid fluctuations in exchange rates, often severely diminished the money's value. Some societies also feared that if they turned over their funds to the JDC, the agency would decrease its appropriation to their town proportionately.[73]

Sending a delegate provided the society or committee with a focus for its activity, and stimulated interest among its members and constituents. As a delegate prepared for departure, the organization would launch a campaign to raise funds at mass meetings and other special events. "When our Bialystoker landslayt heard that the Bialystoker Relief was going to send a delegate to Bialystok," remembered one activist, "they began to stream in with money. A couple of dozen volunteers sat day and night in the office of the Relief, and accepted money for relatives, issued receipts, and wrote letters to friends for those who could not write. It hummed like a bee-hive at the office of the Relief at 246 East Broadway."[74] Upon his return the delegate would report back on general conditions and deliver individual letters and messages.[75] This, in turn, helped spur the landslayt on to still more efforts.

A mission to Europe gave the individual delegate an opportunity not only to visit his native town and provide public service, but also to win a great deal of honor among the landslayt. The delegate was the center of attention at meetings and banquets before, during, and after his trip.[76] A Warsaw Yiddish newspaper lampooned a "typical" speech by a delegate after his return to America:

> Ladies and Gentlemen! How fortunate it is that you delegated me to our unfortunate landslayt in Europe. Like an angel from Heaven, I brought succor and alleviated the want of our suffering brothers: I comforted twelve people with the most moving words, I warmly pressed the hands of five women, I expressed admiration for four institutions, and I stroked the hair of countless children. This is the sum of my useful activities on behalf of our oppressed landslayt in Poland.[77]

Despite the parody, it appears that most delegates really did bring significant amounts of material aid to their hometowns.[78] Moreover, the delegate's direct experience of conditions in the hometown often prompted him to exert himself even more upon his return. Such was the case with Itshele Feygenbaum, who returned from a trip to Kaluszyn with renewed commitment to alleviate the town's pain. "He worked indefatigably and with fervor for the Relief," recalled a landsman, "and kept the promise he gave to his landslayt in Kaluszyn not to forget them when he returned to America."[79]

The delegates exemplified the upwardly mobile lower-level society leadership. Well-settled in America, they spoke English and most supported their families by working at white-collar jobs. Above all, their business experience and years of communal activism had given them the confidence to venture on such an arduous mission. The thirty prospective delegates who filled out questionnaires for the JDC hardly constitute a representative sample. Nevertheless they can provide a sketchy profile of the typical relief delegate. All of the delegates were men, ranging in age from 24 to 55. The majority were in their thirties, with an average age of 37.2. All were born abroad, with 20 indicating that they had been born in the town whose landsmanshaft they were representing. Only one indicated that he had been born in another city. (The rest gave general answers, such as "Russia.") Twenty-eight were American citizens, the other two having taken out their "first papers." Twenty were married and two were widowers. Of the 29 for whom occupations are indicated, only nine were blue-collar workers. Ten were agents, brokers, or salesmen, six were in business, and four were professionals. All spoke English, with other languages claimed including Yiddish (23), Russian (22), Polish (20), German (12), Hebrew (2),

French (2), Ukrainian (1), and Esperanto (1). All were literate in at least one language, though judging from the forms, sometimes imperfectly in English. Only eight answered that they had personal business to attend to in Europe—five wishing to bring parents or other relatives to America, three others hoping to visit or assist family abroad. Finally, as energetic members of the community, some delegates were acquainted with a range of prominent communal leaders (whom they named as references), from the Socialist city alderman and manager of the *Forward,* Boruch Charney Vladeck, to Rabbi Meyer Berlin of the religious Zionist Mizrachi movement.

Many societies and committees commissioned several delegations to Europe. The vigorous Zlotshover sent six between 1919 and 1922, and the Bialystoker dispatched a representative every three months.[80] Some individual delegates went abroad on more than one occasion, sometimes becoming experienced social workers in the process. Ely Greenblatt, a Harlem real estate agent, went to his native town of Miedzyrce (?) in 1920 and 1921. On his first trip he purchased food and other supplies at low prices for the community and arranged with landslayt in London to send clothing for the town's children. On his return in 1921 he brought with him a professional nurse to train local women for the town's hospital, and intended to provide seeds for vegetable gardens, the surplus produce of which would be marketed.[81]

The story of how the United Brisker Relief sent its delegates to Europe is once again illustrative of what went on in many landsmanshaftn. The Brisker refugees began to trickle back into the ruined city in May 1918. A Joint Distribution Committee survey revealed that the main commercial center had been destroyed, together with several complete neighborhoods. On February 8, 1919, the first Polish army units entered the town, driving out the last remaining German troops and making the city part of independent Poland.[82] The city rebuilt slowly, but much of the Jewish economy had been undermined and conditions remained dismal for some time. "From a large fortified city and important railroad center of former times," wrote one investigator, "Brest . . . has become transformed into an ordinary provincial Polish town. The fortifications are no more, and with the fortification and large garrisons have also disappeared the great Jewish commerce." In 1924 many people still lived in the city's synagogues, and workers in some trades, who had previously found work with the army, now faced an unemployment rate of 80 percent.[83]

In 1919–20 the Brisker landslayt in America began to receive letters from hometown individuals and institutions requesting help.[84] The Brisker Relief Committee called for a "new beginning of activity" to aid the population of Brisk. "Each Brisker," read a flyer for a mass meeting at the Brisker Shul, "is obligated at this time to ask himself: 'What have I done to stop the hunger, the massacres, the angel of death who reigns with terror over the heads of our unfortunate landslayt across the sea?'"[85]

When they learned that fluctuating exchange rates sapped much of the value out of the money they sent to their relatives abroad, the landslayt "began to pressure the Relief to send a delegate and to pay out the money in American dollars."[86] The Brisker relief committees in other cities also pressured the New Yorkers to hold a conference and send a delegate. The Cleveland landslayt endorsed the idea: it would "probably liven things up here and make it more likely that our funds will be placed in the right hands there."[87] By hosting a conference attended by representatives from other cities, the New York committee became, in effect, the central office for a network of Brisker relief committees in various parts of the country.[88] The decision of the conference to send its former chairman Philip Rabinowitch as a delegate to Brisk sparked a round of intense activity. Mass meetings in various parts of New York City netted $80,000, and, after another rally to see him off, Rabinowitch left for Europe on May 12, 1920.[89]

Rabinowitch carried out his assignment, though it was not easy. Frightened of local antisemitic bands, he almost returned to America early. After three weeks in Brisk, Rabinowitch's report to the New York landslayt revealed an intimate sense of connection to the recipients of aid and made an emotional appeal for the continuation of the committee's efforts. His letter also touched on the symbolic importance of the emissary from America to locals who were desperate to know that they had not been forgotten by their more fortunate compatriots. Long lines of people, he wrote, waited to "speak to '*Herr Delegat,*' whether or not they had money coming . . . If you saw the scenes at the distribution of money, if you saw the tears of joy and the tears of sorrow, you would understand how great a thing you have done for the unfortunate city of Brisk by sending a delegate. In one word, it can be said that the Brisker Relief Committee has saved our fathers, mothers, sisters and brothers in Brisk from certain death by starvation."[90] When Rabinowitch returned, he "received a fine reception, much prestige for the

Relief and many letters of thanks from individuals who had received money."[91] Touring the country he brought first-hand "greetings from Brisk" to meetings in New York, Cleveland, and Chicago.[92]

Letters from Brisk requested another visit, and on December 25, 1920, a second conference selected H. Kleinberg and Jacob Finkelstein to go to Europe in 1921.[93] Again, the upcoming mission supplied a focus for activity, and appeals stressed the special responsibility of American Jewry. The United Brisker Relief announced a meeting for January 22, 1921, "where all details concerning sending money and affidavits for bringing over friends" would be discussed. "All of Brisk already knows that the Brisker Relief is sending a delegate to Brisk," read the proclamation, "and the only hope of the needy in Brisk is that the delegates will come and bring them something from their friends in America . . . It is your duty, your task."[94] This time the committee amassed $110,000, including $30,000 for relief to smaller towns around Brisk.[95]

The visit of the delegation made a deep impression on both the townspeople and the delegates themselves. Transportation was difficult—there were no regular passenger trains, and Kleinberg and Finkelstein traveled in freight cars.[96] Finkelstein later recalled that it took longer to get from Warsaw to Brisk than it did from New York to Warsaw. The delegates' arrival in Brisk, however, was memorable. Near the train station, they saw craters left by heavy cannon fire during the war. Later, on a tour of the devastated city, Finkelstein discovered that nothing remained of the neighborhood of his youth. On the other hand, their landslayt gave the delegates a gratifying reception. "As we entered the city from the train station," recalled Finkelstein, "it was seven o'clock in the morning and already there were people in the streets to greet the delegates. Within an hour, almost the entire city knew of our arrival, and the street in front of Svisher's house was crowded with people who had come to greet the delegates Finkelstein and Kleinberg. A great mass-meeting took place at Sarver's Theater, where the two delegates conveyed greetings from the Brisker in America."[97]

To carry out their mission Finkelstein and Kleinberg met with a wide range of communal leaders, from the chief rabbi to the leaders of radical parties, endeavoring to remain nonpartisan in their distribution of $15,000 in general relief funds. The delegates dispensed aid to the Talmud Torah (public religious school), the old age home, the Jewish hospital, the pharmacy and clinic, the orphanage, the Great Synagogue, several smaller study houses, the schools of the Young Zion movement, and the Workers' Relief Committee. They also disbursed personal funds to over 3,000 individuals, keeping a careful record of each transaction.[98] The Americans left after a second rally at Sarver's Theater.

Upon their return Finkelstein and Kleinberg reported on conditions in Brisk and brought more than three hundred letters to relatives and friends in America. They distributed the letters and receipts for money at the office of the relief committee on East Broadway each evening until 10PM. On each receipt they noted "how your friend looks," so that even those who did not get a letter had some sort of personal report.[99] Finkelstein toured Chicago, Detroit, Cleveland, and Newark, where he met with the local committees of landslayt. The delegates also brought back an official declaration of thanks from the Jewish Community Council in Brisk, as well as photographs taken by a professional photographer they had hired. The pictures of social welfare institutions supported by the Relief undoubtedly helped to make the committee's accomplishments more real in the eyes of the landslayt, and to increase its prestige as well. Photos of Finkelstein and Kleinberg meeting with the town rabbi or distributing individual aid under the Polish and American flags surely also served to elevate the personal status of the delegates themselves.[100]

Delegate Harry Nachimoff had an even harder time reaching his hometown of Volkovysk. When Nachimoff decided in 1920 to go to Volkovysk to see his parents, the Wolkowysker Relief Society agreed to pay half the cost of his trip if he acted as its representative. Following standard practice, the society took 10 percent out of each private remittance to pay for its share of Nachimoff's expenses and to provide aid to Jewish institutions in the town. He left New York on July 8 and arrived in Warsaw on July 20. Because of the Polish-Soviet war, however, it took him sixteen weeks from his arrival in Warsaw to reach Volkovysk by a circuitous route. As the Soviets neared the Polish capital, the United States consul advised Americans to leave the city. Nachimoff went first to Gdansk (Danzig), and from there to Kaunas (Kovno) and Vilna. Between Kaunas and Vilna he was arrested and held for several hours for not having the proper papers. From Vilna he went to Bialystok and was stranded by an epidemic. A cousin gave him a special vest with many pockets, in which he carried $5,000 in small denominations, and another cousin, who worked for the Red Cross, helped him to get to Volkovysk. There he stayed for five weeks and distributed approximately $55,000 in American dollars. He returned with more than a thousand letters and presented a report at a rally at the Volkovisker Shul.[101] Nachimoff proved an honest and capable emissary, and his landslayt sent him on a second mission the following year.[102] According to instructions, he and an associate were to contact the local committee appointed to handle American relief and to distribute the private remittances first. Of the general relief moneys, $3,000 were to go to an interest-free loan fund, and the rest distributed according to the determination of the committee. The delegates also evidently arranged for the emigration of a group of children.

The boost that the delegates gave to the morale of devastated Jewish communities was often as important as the material aid they brought. For many Jews in Eastern Europe the delegates seemed to embody the hope and dynamism symbolized by America, in contrast to their own state of despair. Much of this perception, of course, had to do with America's material wealth, but it had an emotional element as well. In contrast to the ragged, terrorized, and demoralized local Jewish population, the very person of the American visitor seemed to radiate strength and confidence. The journalist Max Babitsh later wrote about meeting delegate David Sohn in Bialystok: "I saw before me a well-dressed young man, evidently from the rich America. His face expressed confidence and friendliness, his eyes were good-natured. What a contrast, as if from another more confident and proud world, he presented to us, so tortured and dispirited."[103] In addition to distributing money, Sohn raised the morale of the population by helping to reinvigorate Jewish communal life and reestablish the community's connection with the larger Jewish world. The Bialystok Yiddish daily *Dos naye lebn*, reopened with funds brought by Sohn himself, wrote of his mission, "Our American brothers and sisters have not forgotten us . . . We will not die . . . A mood of joy has broken out, salvation after the days of sorrows and despair. Tattered and hungry, with terror in their eyes, they crawled out of the courtyards and with joy passed on the news from neighbor to neighbor, that the delegate David Sohn from America is here."[104]

The Brisker, Volkovisker, and Bialystoker delegates all worked efficiently and constructively. Unfortunately, not all missions went so smoothly. Incompetent, unlucky, or dishonest delegates squandered money, fell victim to bandits and hostile authorities, and brought shame on themselves and their societies. Even in the best of circumstances, the difficulties in traveling to one's destination led to the waste of tremendous amounts of relief money. The needless expenditures, one returned emissary reported, began in Paris, where delegates paid a premium for scarce hotel rooms. Many lacked the proper Polish visas, for which they then paid heavily in bribes. Others bought tickets on the Orient Express to Warsaw for twenty times the normal price. Once in the Polish capital, the delegate had to acquire permission to go to his town, which often cost still more in graft. Moreover, during the Soviet-Polish war many towns were simply inaccessible, and delegates remained stranded in Paris, Warsaw, or Gdansk for weeks at a time.[105]

On the way to their hometowns the delegates faced considerable personal danger, from hooligans and Polish army troops alike. Bandits robbed a number of delegates and dishonest local Polish authorities arrested others on suspicion of being Bolshevik spies, confiscating their cash. Other delegates simply returned to America without having carried out their missions.[106] Delegates to Romania faced similar dangers, though one Beril Barer, the delegate of the Bar landsmanshaft, fought back by suing the Romanian government for $50,000 after he was held in jail for a week without being allowed to contact the American consul.[107]

The steep fees charged by some unscrupulous individuals further damaged the reputation of the delegates, as did reports of currency speculation. Swindlers on both sides of the ocean presented themselves as delegates and extracted money from both donors and recipients of aid. Some so-called delegates were simply self-appointed hustlers. Even legitimate delegates might try to make money by manipulating unstable exchange rates. The Kalusher relief committee charged its delegate with profiteering and had him arrested on his return. The most tragic was the story of Max Shatzman, delegate to the town of Macjow, who committed suicide in the wake of rumors that his brother and other relatives had been "implicated in all sorts of [shady] financial deals" with landsmanshaft money.[108]

The American and Polish governments both looked askance at the landsmanshaft delegates. The Polish government resented foreign interference in its affairs and harassed not only Jewish relief workers but others as well. As the American minister to Poland, Hugh S. Gibson, wrote, "The [Polish] Government appears to proceed on the assumption that it is a privilege for foreigners to spend their money on relief in Poland, and that foreign relief organizations must be prepared to put up with all sorts of affronts, difficulties and delays in return for being allowed the privilege of carrying on their charitable activities."[109] Anti-semitism played a role in the Poles' response as well, especially during their war with the Soviet Union. While Polish officials were prepared to tolerate the JDC and HIAS, they remained suspicious of the delegates from smaller Jewish relief committees. As one landsmanshaft delegate reported, Polish authorities simply "didn't understand why so many Jews were going to those areas. They suspected every one of making [pro-Soviet] propaganda in the Polish army."[110] This delegate noted that he received "no help" and "no sympathy" from the American consul, not surprising given the American mission's own negative atti-tude toward the delegates. Consul Gibson reported that many were engaged in "unsavory activities," and even those who were completely legitimate were simply a nuisance. "Ever since the Legation was founded in 1919," he wrote in a report to the State Department, "a large part of its time and energy has been devoted to getting Americans out of trouble and trying to secure redress for their wrongs."[111]

Inefficiency, scams by hustlers, victimization of legitimate repre-sentatives, and government opposition all convinced the JDC that the practice of sending delegates "should be discouraged as far as possi-ble." Unable to stop the flow, however, the Joint attempted at least to control it and do away with the worst abuses.[112] While doing so, the agency frequently found itself working together with the landsmanshaft representatives. At various times the JDC office in Warsaw assumed responsibility for delivering funds for delegates unable to reach their intended destinations. In other cases JDC workers accompanied dele-gates to their towns and helped them carry out their appointed tasks.[113] Beginning in the fall of 1920, a handful of landsmanshaftn even took advantage of an offer by the JDC Landsmanshaft Department to pro-vide delegates with JDC credentials and assistance under a set of very strict conditions. The majority of relief committees, however, either refused to submit to JDC discipline or were unable to raise the mini-mum amount of funds required by the Joint.[114]

Inevitably, the distribution of American relief funds became the ob-ject of intense politics within the Jewish communities of Poland. In places where traditional communal structures, already under attack by new social forces at the turn of the century, had been further damaged by the recent war, various socialist, Zionist, and Orthodox parties vied for control over the Jewish community in a highly ideologically charged atmosphere. Sometimes, the need to administer large amounts of relief money forced uneasy cooperation among otherwise hostile factions.[115] Often, however, contending parties had very different ideas as to how such funds should be used. In a letter to the United Brisker Relief in New York, for example, Brisk's prominent Rabbi Isaac Ze'ev Soloveichik requested money to aid householders who had been ruined by the war. Former members of the upper-middle class, he pointed out, were reluctant to utilize the free kitchens and other facilities set up by the general Jewish relief agencies for the poor.[116]

Conversely, members of radical circles saw things quite differently. In a letter to the Americans, they accused the established communal leadership of wanting to "continue in the old ways: using the money for hand outs, giving one person a mark or two, and a bourgeois five marks. We demanded that the money be used to establish nutritional and educational institutions like public kitchens, schools, and also medical aid."[117] Similarly, in Wyszkow American relief workers organized a committee consisting of four Zionists, four Orthodox, five "artisans," seven "workers," and one nonpartisan to distribute 460,000 marks sent from America. (Locals usually refered to such committees as "American committees.") When, after four hours of debate, the committee decided that 60 percent of the money should go to aid the poor, as opposed to supporting cooperatives, loan funds, and similar organizations, the labor representatives walked out.[118]

In some places the JDC and the landsmanshaftn lined up behind different local factions. In Bialystok, for example, the landsmanshaft delegate complained that the JDC had turned over its funds to a committee of wealthy "honorables," bypassing the democratic Jewish community council. The delegate reported that he had managed to revive the council, undoubtedly giving it the upper hand by providing it with more than thirty times the amount of money controlled by the committee of honorables.[119]

For the most part, though, the JDC and the landsmanshaftn shared a common agenda. Both had achieved an unprecedented level of unity among ideologically diverse elements, and they attempted to impose this practical nonpartisan ethos on the local committees charged with distributing American aid. In some places the JDC and the landsmanshaft delegates collaborated to ensure an equitable distribution of American funds. In Janowa, for example, there had been three "American committees"—one for the JDC, and one each for the New York and Chicago landsmanshaftn—until a local JDC official and a landsmanshaft delegate organized one common representative committee.[120] In Pinsk the regional JDC director got together with Joseph Breen, representing the Pinsker Relief, and they succeeded with great difficulty in establishing a committee of all of the local institutions to hammer out a common budget.[121]

Even in Brisk, where relations between the landsmanshaft delegates and the JDC were cool, the delegates attempted to effect a compromise among the various local parties. The Americans, arriving in 1921, found "friction among the leadership": the "American committee" and the town rabbi engaged in a struggle for power against the official Jewish community council. Kleinberg and Finkelstein attempted to unite the two factions with limited success. They were more successful in mediating peace within radical circles, where the Bund stood in opposition to the left and right factions of the Poalei Zion (labor Zionists). The delegates formed a "united workers' committee" and enforced that unity by threatening to withhold American assistance from dissidents. The by-laws of the Workers' Relief Committee in Brisk, devised while the Americans were in town, stipulated that "narrowly partisan" institutions (with the exception of schools) would receive no support, and "reserve[d] the right [of the New York Brisker Relief] to representation" in local deliberations.[122]

As relief work in Poland began to decline after 1921, the attention of the hometown societies and relief agencies shifted to the Soviet Union. Landsmanshaftn from towns now in Soviet territory were in much the same position in early 1922 as the Polish societies had been in 1919. According to one report, "The Soviet Russia Landsmanschaften . . . have in their treasuries over one million dollars, and as they are still very energetic, they will be able to raise big amounts for transmission."[123] But political considerations made relief work in the Soviet Union more complicated. Many of the ways in which Polish, Lithuanian, Latvian, and Romanian landsmanshaftn had aided their needy landslayt in the old country were simply not available to those whose hometowns lay within the new Soviet state. The USSR banned foreign currency, so societies were unable to arrange for payment of private relief in dollars.[124] The government also forbade landsmanshaft delegates in no uncertain terms. Noting that many delegates were attempting to enter Russia, the representative of the Jewish Commissariat in Tallinn (Revell) proclaimed that "our government will not admit any of these representatives, first of all because their separate activities would crush the relief work into little fragments, and, secondly, because the activity of many individual delegates would certainly lead to demoralization, speculation and swindles, and would put many Jewish communities in danger."[125] Neither would secularist authorities permit any sort of assistance for religious purposes. Aid to students of yeshivahs (advanced religious schools) was prohibited, as was the provision of special supplies for Passover.[126]

Unable to reach their hometowns directly, "Soviet" landsmanshaftn were forced to channel their aid through the established agencies. Starting in 1920, the JDC was able to carry out general relief work through an agreement with Moscow. Beginning in late 1921, the JDC distributed food packages on behalf of landsmanshaftn in cooperation with the American Relief Administration (ARA), which deducted 25 percent of each contribution for "mass child food" relief. Between November 1921 and May 1922, the JDC's Landsmanshaft Department transmitted about $85,000 worth of food aid on behalf of 130 landsmanshaftn. The JDC also remitted other types of relief funds on behalf of landsmanshaftn, transferring $125,000 in 206 transactions in the year between November 1921 and October 1922. Even for the JDC distribution of aid proved much more difficult in the Soviet Union than elsewhere, with a successful-delivery rate of just 50 percent in the USSR, compared to 95 percent in other countries.[127]

Communist authorities were wary of allowing rival organizations to operate within the Soviet Union. They would not allow landsmanshaftn to name local distribution committees, as they often did in Poland. Boris Bogen, then assigned to the JDC office in Moscow, warned that "very often some of the people who are appointed on the committees are persona non grata, and according to the opinion of the Soviet Government, the entire committee participating with them in these distributions may be considered as unloyal citizens." In several cases, reported Bogen, members of such committees were arrested and tried.[128] The government only grudgingly permitted the JDC to function, and offered it competition in the form of an official Jewish relief committee known as "Idgezkom" (Yiddish acronym for the Jewish Social Committee).[129]

The Idgezkom also competed with the Joint for the allegiance and funds of landsmanshaftn in America. In 1920 the Soviet agency opened an office in New York and attempted to woo the hometown societies. Later, Idgezkom created its own Landsmanschaften Bureau with an office on the East Side, and ran a regular landsmanshaft column in its publication.[130] Idgezkom's New York representatives waged a propaganda campaign in the radical Yiddish press to promote their services, pointing out that Soviet authorities would not permit the JDC to earmark funds for application in specific localities. Claiming to have exclusive authorization to instruct the Moscow committee on how and where to use American relief money, the New York Idgezkom office warned landsmanshaftn to work with it, rather than with the JDC, if they wanted their money to reach their towns.[131] The Idgezkom also claimed that its food parcels were exempt from the 25 percent deduction for "general relief" applied to ARA parcels.[132] When these inducements proved insufficient, New York Idgezkom was willing to punish those landsmanshaftn which remained loyal to the Joint. The first head of Idgezkom, Dr. D. Dubrovsky, refused to forward letters or packages to the Jews in Berdichev: "It is because the Berdichev Landsmanschaft here [in New York] has boycotted me and has declared that all my work is a fake. Let the Jews from Berdichev who live here compel their Landsmanschaft to send over the relief moneys which it has raised for all the needy Jews in that city; then I will accept from them letters and, later, parcels as well."[133]

The Idgezkom succeeded in damaging the faith of many landsmanshaftn in the JDC and in attracting some support for its own campaign. Dubrovsky even persuaded the People's Relief Committee, officially a constituent agency of the Joint, to cooperate directly with Idgezkom in forwarding landsmanshaft aid to the USSR.[134] In 1924, however, the Soviet agency abruptly shut down, succumbing to accusations in the Soviet Yiddish press that "bourgeois elements" aimed to turn it into a "Jewish kehillah."[135]

By that time it appeared that some semblance of normality had returned to Jewish Eastern Europe, and the American relief effort began to wind down. The JDC planned its own dissolution, looking "forward to the moment when its relief work for war sufferers [would] come to an end."[136] The JDC Landsmanshaft Department began to have trouble justifying its existence as early as 1922, as remittances to Poland diminished and work in the Soviet Union proved less productive. The Department survived until the spring of 1924, when it closed its doors.[137] Individual landsmanshaft relief committees also went into decline. This is not to say that Jews in America forgot about their landslayt in the old country. Many landsmanshaftn continued to send regular support for institutions and individuals in their hometowns throughout the interwar period. Societies also continued to support the general relief agencies such as JDC (which never did close), HIAS, and ORT. Moreover, after a lull in the late 1920s, many united relief committees revived to meet the new economic and political crises of the 1930s. Nevertheless, by 1924 the period of feverish activity had subsided.

Their hometown relief effort brought home to the American landslayt just how American they had become. As the president of the Erste Shendishower Galizianer Chewra put it, "the members of the Chewra lost their greenness through the war."[138] Formal contact with landslayt in Europe only strengthened this impression, bringing out the contrast in demeanor between the American delegates and local populations, and between the American nonpartisan pragmatism and the politically charged European relief committees. Members of the United Horodyszczer Relief Organizations, while expressing faith in their town's distribution committee, also indicated clearly that they had developed a way of thinking different from that of their European brothers and sisters. As viewed by the American landslayt, these differences went beyond the imbalance of material wealth and the communities' contrasting fortunes during the war. "We look at things and people a little differently than they do," wrote one American Horodishtsher. "They don't understand our way of thinking. Their psychology is very different."[139]

The "heroic period" of World War I and its aftermath thus proved to be a turning point in the history of the landsmanshaftn. The war itself, followed by the enactment of restrictive immigration laws, all but cut off the influx of Eastern European Jews to America. The American landslayt were therefore increasingly distanced from the actual experience of immigration and especially from their East European origins. In this context the work of maintaining the link between the landslayt and the old country became increasingly abstract and formalized. Ironically, however, as the members became more conscious of their Americanness, their organizations devoted more and more of their time to their old hometowns. While relief work provided a much more concrete connection between the landsmanshaftn and their hometowns than they had ever had before, it also served as an organized arena for the expression of nostalgia for the lost Old World.

⌣ 8 ⌐

Looking Backward

Landsmanshaftn continued to play an important role after 1924, despite the lull in overseas relief work and the restriction of immigration to America. Throughout the 1920s and 1930s members benefited from the support of their organizations in times of unemployment or illness, received treatment from their society doctors, and arranged for low-cost loans. They still socialized together and attended funerals. And, through their organizations, they still participated in the broader Jewish community and responded to the events of the day in the community, the nation, and the world.

Nevertheless, the end of immigration, the Great Depression, the rise of Fascism in Europe, and, finally, the destruction of East European Jewry and the establishment of the State of Israel all affected the hometown associations. Ultimately, these events contributed to the marginalization and decline of the societies as a significant force in the Jewish community. In the interwar years, however, this had not yet come to pass. Rather, new political developments and changes in the demographic structure of the immigrant population directed the landsmanshaftn toward new forms of organization and activity.

Most important for the interwar period was the cessation of mass immigration. This meant that the landsmanshaftn no longer had a large pool of recent arrivals from which to draw new members. Growing older, and ever more removed from the actual experience of their Old-World origins, the landslayt turned increasingly to commemorating their shared experiences, first in their European hometowns and later in the early years of resettlement in America. Paradoxically, the hometowns' distance in time and space made them a more central focus of formal society activity than they had been before. At the same time, the new exercises in memory actually sharpened the landslayt's growing sense of themselves as a community distinct from the one they had left behind in Europe.

Demographic shifts within the societies contributed directly to the new emphasis on memory. By the 1930s, the landslayt were beginning to show signs of age. Though this had not yet led to a serious decline in landsmanshaft membership, the day was not far off when, as one observer warned, "only gray and bald heads will be seen at a society meeting."[1] Societies urged members to recruit their adult children, and a few had some success in luring American-born or raised young people into the ranks by offering them discounts on initiation fees and dues. A handful of young Americans even assumed leadership positions. But while some 15 percent of society members were American-born in 1938, most young people joined their parents' landsmanshaftn only to please them. Few participated actively.[2] While American Jews might attend landsmanshaft social events or pay their dues, their parents' identities as natives of a particular town in Eastern Europe no longer seemed particularly relevant to their own American-Jewish identity.

Shifting demographics also led to new forms of organization. The "family circle" was a new type of society, close in spirit to the landsmanshaftn but more successful in attracting American-born Jews. Consisting of male and female descendants (and their spouses) of a common ancestor, these organizations were primarily a product of the 1920s and 1930s. In 1939, the WPA Yiddish Writers' Project identified 166 family circles, 52 percent of whose members were America-born, with the majority in either business or the professions. While some such groups offered benefits similar to those of the landsmanshaftn, others were purely social, their periodic meetings providing a structured op-portunity for family members to get together in each other's homes or in public halls. The number of family circles continued to grow in the decades after World War II, and the new groups placed less and less emphasis on material benefits. In this respect they reflected the altered needs of their middle-class membership, which was more interested in reinforcing family ties strained by social and geographic mobility than in mutual aid.[3]

Within the landsmanshaft world itself, the growing involvement of women proved to be the most important demographic change. Women, many of them wives of members of men's groups, formed hundreds of landsmanshaft auxiliaries in the 1920s and 1930s. By 1938 the WPA Project surveyed 287 women's auxiliaries, only 11 of which dated their founding to before 1918.[4] With the membership aging, and with few new immigrants to infuse the societies with fresh blood, women formed the most important reserve of new forces for the landsmanshaftn. Their energy often helped lend new purpose and breathe life into otherwise tired organizations.[5]

Following on the heels of the Nineteenth Amendment in 1920, this expansion of women's formal role in the landsmanshaftn reflected the growing presence of women in public life generally.[6] Like the institutions of American civic culture they so admired, the landsmanshaftn had always been open mainly to men. Now, they actively sought to find a place for women as well—albeit largely in separate auxiliaries. Thus brothers from the First Bratslow Podolier Sick Benefit Society chaired the founding meeting of the First Bratslower Ladies Auxiliary. The brothers spoke on the importance of the women's group and helped induct its first seventeen members.[7] Paradoxically, the aging of the landslayt may also have enabled the women to become more involved in landsmanshaft affairs. By the 1920s, there must have been a sizable cohort of women who had finished bearing and rearing their children and had more time than before to engage in organizational activities.

The women's auxiliaries closely paralleled the men's societies in many ways, sharing an organizational structure, a meeting format, and a vocabulary. The "sisters" engaged in many of the same activities as the "brothers," including the general round of landsmanshaft social activities. Like the brothers, they also raised funds for charitable enterprises in New York and in their hometowns. Indeed, the women's groups invested more energy in charity work than did the men's. The Ladies' Auxiliary of the Bialystoker Center and Bikur Cholim, for one, devoted itself wholly to raising thousands of dollars to build and maintain the Bialystoker Home for the Aged in New York. Meanwhile, the Rakower Ladies Club, founded in 1931, sent $300 annually to Jewish institutions in its hometown.[8]

Like the men's groups, the ladies' auxiliaries found ways ro confer honor and prestige, though among the women recognition often centered on domestic skills and accomplishments. Baking and needlework frequently brought honor to individual members of the Bratslower Auxiliary. The organization occasionally auctioned off cushions or cakes contributed by sisters to benefit the hometown or a needy compatriot. The minutes often mention the importance of food in the auxiliary's meetings. Indeed, many gatherings ended as did the one on October 8, 1933, when "our sisters brought various cakes and strudel and candy and our sisters did not neglect to bring coffee and the tables were spread and the treats served and the crowd enjoyed itself." Success in raising offspring also brought recognition: six members celebrated the weddings of their children in 1933 alone.[9]

The ladies' auxiliaries offered some material benefits, though fewer than the men's organizations. The Bratslower Ladies Auxiliary, for example, sent committees to visit sick and mourning members—as well as new mothers in the hospital. It aided needy members with grants of up to five dollars and maintained a small loan fund. It did not, however, provide regular sick or death benefits. Nor did it engage a society doctor. For these services, the women presumably relied on the men's society.[10]

The First Bratslower Ladies Auxiliary maintained close social ties with the First Bratslow Podolier Sick Benefit Society. The women's and men's groups met on the same day and members sometimes attended the others' meetings. (In one case, the sisters reported getting little done at their own meeting because the members were anxious to adjourn and go to the brothers' gathering, where a Dr. Hofman was showing a "picture" on tooth care.) Bratslover brothers and sisters also helped out with each other's social events, at which nostalgic reminiscing became a central focus of landsmanshaft activity.[11]

In the 1920s and 1930s, the landslayt turned increasingly to formal evocations of the old country, as well as of the histories of the societies themselves. Not surprisingly, landsmanshaft members began to express their longing for the far-off places of their formative years at a time when their collective identity was in danger of waning. During the immigrant period, it had seemed natural for newcomers in New York to seek out compatriots whom they already knew from their hometowns. After decades in America, the former immigrants had accumulated enough other affiliations so that the need for landsmanshaftn no longer seemed quite so obvious. The social philosopher Maurice Halbwachs commented on the tendency of groups separated from their places of origin to maintain unity by "think[ing] of the old home and its layout."[12] Landsmanshaft reminiscing fit firmly into this pattern.

Indeed, memory, and continuity with the past, are important elements in the construction of a sense of both individual and collective identity.[13] But while continuity is problematic for everybody in the modern world, it can be particularly so for immigrants, whose formative pasts occurred in places and cultures different, often drastically so, from those in which they live in the present. As Halbwachs pointed out, however, memory is very much a social construct of the present even as it provides a link to the past. Moreover, even individual memory is the product of social processes, the work of groups of individuals who share not only the same past experiences but also the same current needs.[14] As organizations of people who had, by definition, experienced places and events that others in American society had not, the landsmanshaftn constituted an ideal arena for the recall and reconstruction of memories of childhoods and youths spent in faraway places.

The landsmanshaftn engaged in several different exercises in memory during the interwar years, each with its own flavor and purpose. Each exercise in memory strengthened on an abstract level the ties of the landsmanshaftn to the old country, but at the same time could not help but emphasize the growing sense of separation between the American landslayt and the old home. Nostalgia was the most pervasive attitude, as landslayt reminisced collectively about their old homes and lost youths. A few societies found it necessary to engage in a more somber and traumatic form of memory as they memorialized the destruction of their towns during and after World War I. Finally, the landslayt recounted the histories of the societies themselves, celebrating their rise from obscure and difficult beginnings to their present exalted (or so it seemed to the members) states.

Much nostalgic reminiscing took place at society balls and banquets, which by the 1920s and 1930s often marked significant anniversaries for organizations celebrating twenty, thirty, or even more years of existence. These were lavish affairs with elaborate formal programs, including concerts of classical, popular, and folk music, comedy, children's performances, dancing, and dinner. Some banquets still featured the "traditional" members' march, and opened with the American and Zionist anthems. (One ecumenical society began its event by singing the "Star Spangled Banner," "Hatikvah," and the "International.") But despite their formal aspects, these gatherings were often lively parties of people who had known each other for much of their lives and felt comfortable together. They were times for the landslayt to relax and have a good time.[15]

In conjunction with their anniversary celebrations, landsmanshaftn issued souvenir journals which ranged in format from a few pages of advertisements and greetings to richly produced volumes with histories of the respective societies, reminiscences of the hometowns, and all manner of homegrown literary material. Together with the balls and banquets, the journals proved an outlet for what Irving Howe called the "venting of nostalgia" about the old hometown.[16]

In keeping with the spirit of nostalgia that pervaded these celebrations and publications, journal writers portrayed their towns in glowing terms, describing landscapes, recounting local legends, and eulogizing local characters and prominent figures. One landsman recalled Horodyszcze as a "joyous town," and another described his teacher in Lipkan, Bessarabia, as a "wonder of creation." Members of the Progressive Society of Yaruga longed for

> Peaceful Yaruga . . . beautiful Yaruga, overlooking the Dniester River in whose shimmering waters she casts her reflections, she stands high on a lofty peak, like a proud mother watching over her loved ones. Her streets were warmed with the sunshine of hospitality . . . with the smile of friendship. Jews were the backbone of its very existence. Its influential citizens, its businessmen were Jews . . . Happy-go-lucky Yaruga, besprinkled with gaiety and splendor . . . honored and cherished by all who knew her.[17]

With sentiments like these, landsmanshaft nostalgia restored some of the word's original meaning as a "yearning for home."[18]

Like much nostalgia, landsmanshaft reminiscences of the old home often in fact represented longing for a time when the landslayt themselves were young. As one insightful memoir-writer admitted, nostalgia paints an idealized portrait of a place colored by its association with the rememberer's youth. "Physically," he wrote, "Boslev looked like an old pock-marked peasant, a victim of past Russian epidemics . . . full of ditches and hills, built without a plan. And the mud? Don't ask!. . . And yet one longs for Boslev. For us, for the youth, Boslev was full of charm."[19] Rarely, however, did a journal writer have the kind of perspective that would allow him to view his hometown critically and at the same time to recognize the reasons for its continued attraction as an object of nostalgia.

For many immigrants, then, their image of their hometown was, at least in part, a product of their own desires, longings, and memories.

The writers were quite conscious that the towns they described were things of the past, if they had ever existed at all in the way memory saw them.[20] More sophisticated landslayt recognized that the towns that appeared in the journals sprang as much from the writers' imaginations as they did from real life. As Paul (Pesakh) Novick, Brisker landsman and editor of the Yiddish Communist daily *Freiheit,* put it, "Just what is Brisk? The truth is that Brisk is what we want it to be."[21]

Despite, or maybe because of, their successful adjustment to American life, many of the former immigrants began to feel that their present lives were in some way deficient. In particular, after decades in America, the landslayt had come to feel that they had lost touch with their "true selves," which they identified with their old-country origins.[22] Abraham Cahan's fictional character spoke for many when he confessed that "David, the poor lad swinging over a Talmud volume at the Preacher's Synagogue [in Antomir], seems to have more in common with my inner identity than David Levinsky, the well-known [New York] cloak-manufacturer."[23]

Landsmanshaft gatherings enabled the members to air their inner identification with their old-country towns among others who shared the same feelings. When Communist journalist Novick wrote that "somewhere among the cells of our hearts . . . a special cell is found where our youthful years are hidden, a Brisker cell, so to speak, an eternal cell," he could be sure that his Brisker landslayt would understand him, whether or not they agreed with his politics.[24] Nostalgia therefore also reassured the former immigrants that their individual experiences and feelings were not odd or abnormal, but shared by many others.

As the examples of both the fictional David Levinsky and the real Paul Novick imply, landsmanshaft expressions of nostalgia by no means indicated that the members were living in the past. In fact, the landslayt turned their organizations into forums for the airing of certain aspects of their "inner identities" precisely because they no longer experienced these identities as keenly in everyday life. Moreover, by venting their nostalgia within their hometown societies, the landsayt freed themselves to deal more effectively with their contemporary lives. In Dovid Keshir's story "Landslayt," another fictional character, more modestly successful than Levinsky, serves as an illustration. Morris owns a drugstore in a non-Jewish neighborhood on Staten Island, where he lives with his American-born wife. The last time he attended a meeting of his society was fifteen years earlier, and he has no interest in its ongoing business. Yet he is drawn to a society meeting by the announcement that recently taken films of the hometown would be shown. The prospect of seeing images of his boyhood home exerts a strong attraction on Morris, one he finds difficult to explain to his Irish-American neighbor. While watching the film, he feels as if he has been transported home and rejuvenated, that the "soles of his childish feet burned once again on the warm earth of home." As the story makes clear, however, only Morris's distance from the old home in daily life enables him to experience nostalgia for it. And the landsmanshaft, where the other members have similar feelings, is the arena where he can indulge that yearning without compromising his hard-won integration into his current environment.[25]

Nostalgia sometimes merged with a more traumatic sense of loss to impel the landsmanshaftn to starker and more somber expressions of memory, particularly in cases where the old hometown had suffered especially harshly during World War I and its aftermath. In publications like *Khurbn Proskurov* (Destruction of Proskurov), American landslayt memorialized their ravaged towns, focusing particularly on the terrible events of the recent past. Published in 1924 by the United Proskurover Relief, *Khurbn Proskurov* commemorated the catastrophic pogrom that left 1,500 Jews dead in 1919.[26] In both form and function, the book was a prototype of the many memorial books *(yizker bikher)* published by groups of landslayt after the even greater destruction of World War II.

The format of *Khurbn Proskurov* made clear that its purpose transcended mere nostalgia. The word *khurbn,* traditionally used to describe the fall of the Temple in Jerusalem and used later in Yiddish to refer to the Holocaust, conveyed a sense of great national disaster. The use of Hebrew on the title page and in some sections of the text was unusual in landsmanshaft publications, and together with funereal iconography, black borders on the pages, and frequent scriptural quotes, emphasized the sacred nature of the project.

In many ways the Proskurov account conformed to traditional modes of expressing Jewish memory of disaster: conflating the most recent events into preestablished paradigms of catastrophe.[27] The book's main article, the chronicle of the pogrom, was called a *kinah* (lamentation), linking it not only to the Bible's Lamentations, which mourned the destruction of Jerusalem and the exile of Israel, but with Talmudic and medieval laments as well. Similarly, the authors referred to the Ukrainian Republican Army troops of Semyon Petlura, who perpetrated the pogrom, as *haidemaks,* after the Ukrainian paramilitary bands that had carried out similar attacks in the eighteenth century. The 1919 pogrom in Proskurov thus appears as another episode in the long tragic history of Jewish persecution.

At the same time, *Khurbn Proskurov,* like other landsmanshaft publications, exhibited a pronounced concern with specificity and detail in the recording of local events. In addition to its chronicle of the pogrom, printed in both Yiddish and Hebrew, the book includes a complete list of the victims and their ages, with pictures and short eulogies for the most prominent among them. It also names the hundreds of orphans living in three asylums supported by the American landslayt, and gives a history of the United Proskurover Relief.

The memorialization of their devastated former hometowns revealed the deep emotional connections the landslayt retained to their places of origin. Nevertheless, even more starkly than nostalgia, memorialization pointed toward the widening social and cultural gap between the Americans and their landslayt abroad. When the landsmanshaft writers described the destruction of their towns, they acknowledged that the towns, even when rebuilt, were no longer the same places they had known personally. Moreover, the vivid descriptions of pogroms, famine, and destitution could not help but drive home to the former immigrants just how different their fate was from that of their brothers and sisters left behind.

When some former residents returned home to visit, either privately or as landsmanshaft delegates, their experiences only confirmed the ambiguity of their relationships to their places of origin. Many were surprised by how exotic their old homes had come to seem. After ten or twenty years abroad, the emigrants had become much more American than they realized. Indeed, their trips were more likely to convince them that they had made the right choice in becoming American than to encourage them to reestablish ties with their hometowns. The dismal economic conditions they frequently encountered merely reinforced this conclusion, which the travelers then communicated to their landslayt in America.[28]

Landsmanshaft souvenir journals also included recollections of their American past. In recounting the histories of the societies themselves, however, immigrant memoirists turned the nostalgic viewpoint on its head; while accounts of the hometown described a decline from idyll to wretchedness, the story of the society generally followed a path in the opposite direction, from hardship to glory. Journal writers compared the societies' humble beginnings with their impressive accomplishments and stressed the great difficulties they had overcome to reach their current status. Members of the Mayaker Aid Society contrasted their organization's obscure birth "in a back room somewhere in the Bronx" to its current "broad, many-sided activity." Society history, as portrayed by landsmanshaft historians, was the story of eventual triumph over early adversity. In the words of one such writer, "The royal poet King David put it correctly—he who sows with tears will reap with a song."[29]

Society histories thus paralleled the biographies of the former immigrants themselves, serving as a metaphor for the members' own successful struggle to establish themselves in America. Landsmanshaft writers often described their organizations as "mighty fortresses," "big families," or "great trees," all metaphors for rootedness and security. Trees in particular sometimes appeared as journal illustrations representing the societies, their trunks firmly planted in the soil, bountiful leaves representing the organizations' many accomplishments. In looking back, the landslayt expressed particular pride in the important role their societies had played in building the larger American Jewish community.[30]

The stark contrast between the bleak conditions in their hometowns and their own comparative well-being moved the American landslayt to aid their less fortunate brothers and sisters overseas. Though the massive relief campaigns of the World War I era tailed off by the mid-1920s, many societies regularly sent funds to institutions in their hometowns throughout the interwar period. The urgency of these efforts grew in the face of the deepening economic crisis of the 1930s, the effects of which were magnified by mounting antisemitism, especially in Poland. In the mid-1930s many united relief committees revived after a decade or more of inactivity.[31]

Renewed relief work once again led the landsmanshaftn into wider affiliations. The United Galician Jews of America and the Federation of Lithuanian Jews of America both came into existence in 1937, largely to encourage aid to Jewish communities in their respective homelands.[32] The Joint Distribution Committee (JDC, Joint) established a new Landsmanshaft Department in 1937 and offered free lectures and slide shows on Jewish life in Poland to any society requesting one. The JDC also matched landsmanshaft donations of up to $2,000, with the total amount to be earmarked for the free-loan fund in the contributing society's hometown. In the first fifteen months of the campaign, 130 towns received $44,683 from their American landslayt and an equal amount from Joint.[33]

Other communal institutions also turned to the landsmanshaftn for support. The Hebrew Immigrant Aid Society (HIAS) remained among the most popular causes, with some 800 New York societies organized in a Council of Organizations. The Federation for the Support of Jewish Philanthropic Societies formed a similar council to attract organizational contributions.[34] A few landsmanshaftn continued to maintain their own social service institutions, as they had done in the years before World War I. The types of institutions they now favored reflected the changing demographics of the immigrant generation: the Bialystok, Warsaw, and Mohilev landsmanshaftn all sponsored homes for the aged.[35]

The societies responded to the political challenges of the time, most notably the rise of Fascism and Nazism in Europe. Many supported the boycott movement against German goods and helped mobilize their members for anti-Nazi rallies. Some affiliated with the American Jewish Congress, others (mainly Workmen's Circle branches) with the Jewish Labor Committee, and a smaller number with the pro-Communist Jewish People's Committee.[36]

Political events also influenced the composition of the landsmanshaft sector itself. Communists and their allies left the Workmen's Circle in 1930 to form the International Workers' Order (IWO). By 1938, 53 New York IWO branches were landsmanshaftn, most of which had emerged from corresponding units of the Workmen's Circle.[37] Landsmanshaft IWO branches shared fully in the culture of the pro-Communist left. When the Chmelniker Podolier Branch 179 published a souvenir journal in 1937, for example, slogans printed in the margins read, "Help build the United Front," "Defend the Spanish People's Republic," and "Fight Against War! Defend the Soviet Union!"[38] Yet IWO landsmanshaftn remained committed to aiding their hometowns, and they participated in the united relief committees of the late 1930s. In addition, many left-wing landsmanshaftn had their own committees known as *patronatn,* which assisted political prisoners in their hometowns in Poland.[39]

In the late 1930s, then, the landsmanshaftn still constituted an active and visible element in the Jewish community, with hundreds of thousands of members in thousands of individual societies. However, a number of factors were already apparent that would soon lead to their decline. The depression itself took its toll, as members dropped out and claims for relief severely taxed society treasuries. Conversely, the institution of such government programs as unemployment insurance and social security promised to diminish the value of mutual aid in the future. Most importantly, the end of mass immigration and the societies' inability to attract large numbers of the native-born meant that it was only a matter of time before membership began to fall.

World War II opened the final chapter in the history of the landsmanshaftn with the complete destruction of the Jewish communities from which the immigrants had come. Scholar Hannah Kliger has found a "relative disengagement" from events in Europe on the part of the landsmanshaftn during the first years of the war (1939–1941). She suggests that this apparent unconcern stemmed from a previous turning away from involvement with the hometown, lack of information, a feeling of helplessness, and a belief that resposibility for relatives abroad lay with individual families. Even later in the war years, landsmanshaftn primarily participated in the general war effort rather than in any special efforts on behalf of their landslayt in Europe.[40]

In fact landsmanshaft interest in the old hometowns had been growing in the late 1930s, as we have seen; hence other factors may have been just as significant in conditioning the immediate landsmanshaft response to the German war against European Jewry. Specifically, their World War I experience taught the societies that war conditions made it difficult, if not impossible, to reach their towns with the money they had raised for relief. After that war, however, they had contributed vitally to the reconstruction of devastated Jewish communities in Eastern Europe. On the basis of this experience, some landsmanshaftn clearly expected to aid in the reconstruction of their hometowns after World War II as well. This time, however, the destruction was so complete that there was nothing to rebuild.[41]

After the war, the landsmanshaftn once again came to the aid of surviving landslayt, a few of whom had found their ways back to their old homes, but more of whom landed in displaced persons' camps and other far-flung places. The societies sent food parcels and monetary assistance, and helped locate relatives. As after World War I, they worked both independently and through the central relief agencies. The JDC once again set up a special office to deal with the societies, and once more struggled to "harness the energies" of the landsmanshaftn to the general relief campaign.[42]

Many societies also received one last small infusion of new members from among the 137,450 Jewish immigrants who arrived in the United States between 1945 and 1952.[43] Many of the new arrivals joined the established societies, where they often came into conflict with the well-settled veterans, who were too Americanized for their taste. The two generations of immigrants found even their experiences of their common hometowns to be at variance, for the places had changed greatly in the decades between the old migration and the Second World War. In some societies the newer immigrants retained loyalties to their own subgroup, eventually out-lasting the old-timers to take control. A few postwar immigrants by-passed the old associations entirely and formed their own organizations.[44]

The landsmanshaftn's final important function was to memorialize their obliterated hometowns and their landslayt who had fallen victim to the Nazis. Some did this by erecting monuments in the towns themselves, in Israel, or in their own cemeteries in New York. Many held annual commemorations on the anniversaries of their communities' destruction. In a few cases, American landsmanshaftn memorialized their native towns and cities by funding projects in Israel.[45] By far the most interesting and significant memorials, however, were the books published by hundreds of landsmanshaftn in honor of their towns.

Taken together, the *yizker* (memorial) books form a vast project of memorialization and documentation of the vanished Jewish life in the towns and cities of Eastern Europe.[46] Beginning in 1943 with a volume devoted to the industrial center of Lodz, some 1,000 yizker books appeared in the United States, Israel, Latin America, and Europe. Ranging in format from small pamphlets to large multivolume works, most of them were about towns in (interwar) Poland, with other areas less well represented. In various combinations of Yiddish, English, and Hebrew, they recounted local history and folklore, with special emphasis on the interwar and Holocaust years through which their authors had lived. Some also included sections on the towns' "diasporas" abroad.

In addition to the wealth of information they contained, the yizker books had a kind of sacred quality which reflected their status as monuments. As the anthropologists Jack Kugelmass and Jonathan Boyarin have pointed out, the volumes often served as substitute grave-stones and included lists of the names of the dead along with illustrations of tombstones and other funereal iconography. The books' titles also reflected their sacred character, often including Hebrew elements normally associated in Yiddish with holy texts.[47] Furthermore, the yizker books relied on a number of precedents in Jewish documentary tradition, from the *memorbücher* recording the martyrdom of medieval Jewry, to the memorial volumes published by some landsmanshaftn for their towns after World War I and the pogroms of 1919. The post-World War I Yiddish literature of destruction, a few previously published landsmanshaft-sponsored town histories, and even some of the more elaborate landsmanshaft souvenir journals served as additional models.

The yizker books provided the societies with a sense of mission as the organizations' other functions became increasingly obsolete. Some societies hired professional historians or writers to compose their books. Others relied on their own amateur talent. Decisions on content became subjects of controversy, straining relations between society members and hired professionals. Hundreds of landslayt served on editorial committees, thousands contributed articles and photographs, and many more raised funds for the books' publication. Moreover, the effort was international, frequently involving landslayt in North and South America, Israel, and Western Europe. In some cases, societies even attracted new members through work on the memorial books.

Nevertheless, by the closing decades of the twentieth century the landsmanshaftn had fallen into a serious state of decline. Many folded as their members died or moved to Florida.[48] Others maintained a paper existence, primarily to distribute burial plots as the need arose. A few remained active, but they met less often, provided fewer benefits, elected fewer officers, and demanded less involvement on the part of members. Societies that survived the longest were those which managed to attract the most second- and even third-generation members. But these people often had only the haziest concept of the old hometowns which had originally furnished the societies with their central identities. One investigator heard American-born members of a Lodzer group refer to the major industrial center of Lodz as a shtetl.[49]

Even in decline, the societies adapted to circumstances as best they could in an effort to survive. Some groups, particularly synagogues and others with their own buildings, continued to function with memberships drawn from non-landslayt. Women, in the early days excluded from formal membership, now formed the majority of active members of many societies, even the "young men's" organizations. Finally, Israel replaced the old hometowns as the focal point of society activity and recipient of financial support. While the landsmanshaftn continued to play an important role in the lives of a handful of aging immigrants and an even smaller number of American-born Jews, they had become marginal to the Jewish community as a whole.

The Jewish landsmanshaftn of New York were a one-generation phenomenon. They had little attraction for most of their members' American children, who had developed their own sense of Jewish-American identity and to whom their parents' parochial loyalties seemed irrelevant at best. The fact that the aging societies continued to utilize Yiddish and Yiddish-accented English as their official languages made them seem all the more old-worldly. Even the material benefits, so important to the immigrant community, lost their appeal for a Jewish population become increasingly middle-class and made secure by private insurance and government programs.

It was hard for subsequent generations to comprehend the vital role that the landsmanshaftn had once played in immigrant life. In their heyday at the beginning of the century, the societies offered hundreds of thousands of immigrants a secure place to which to retreat from the strange environment; a place to "pour out their hearts," as they might have said, among familiar faces from home. At the same time, the societies provided the tools, from information to health care and capital, for dealing with that environment effectively. In so doing, they helped their members settle in and adjust to their adopted country. The immigrants created in the societies a medium for the expression of all of the levels of their complex identities, from the narrowest identification as natives of individual towns to the broadest interest in American or Jewish affairs.

Indeed, the landsmanshaftn's association with specific European towns, together with their use of Yiddish and occasional Old-World ways, only obscured the degree to which the societies constituted an American phenomenon. Patterned after organizations which their members first encountered in the New World among native-born Americans and other immigrant groups, landsmanshaftn helped initiate the immigrants into the culture of democratic citizenship and ideals. In their hometown societies the Jewish immigrants strove to integrate traditions and innovations from the Old World with New-World discoveries to create a Jewish identity appropriate to American life. The multiplicity of types of society mirrored the conflicts and divisions of the immigrant Jewish community as a whole.

Finally, the landsmanshaftn reflected the historical times of which they were a part. All of the debates in the Jewish world over the nature of Jewish identity had their echoes within the hometown associations. Such American elements as secret ritual found acceptance in many societies during the "golden age" of American fraternalism, only to lose their attraction later. Most importantly, the societies reflected the changing needs and aspirations of their own members. They therefore expended much of their energies during the period of mass immigration toward helping their members adapt to American life. Later, when the problems of adjustment had lost some of their immediacy, the societies provided an arena for nostalgia and participated in the emergence of American Jewry as the chief provider of assistance to poorer and endangered Jewish communities around the world.

The Jewish landsmanshaftn have nearly passed from the scene, but their accomplishments cannot be denied. In the 1930s, when the members of many societies took stock of their achievements in the pages of their anniversary journals, few of the amateur writers expressed as well as Louis Leybovits both a sense of accomplishment in the past and optimism about the future.[50] Leybovits reported that he and his brothers in the Shedlowtzer Benevolent Association had been so busy in the previous quarter century that they had hardly noticed the years going by. The members and their wives had become old and gray in America; their children had grown and started families of their own. "But how dear it all is to us," he wrote. "We have experienced much joy in the time we have worked together. Yes, brothers, the world does not stand still. It moves forward, and we move with it."

Notes

Introduction

1. The Yiddish WPA writers published their findings in 1938. Their book, still the best on the subject, includes analyses of the data collected from the societies, essays on various aspects of landsmanshaft activity, a historical evaluation of the role played by the societies in Jewish life, excerpts from landsmanshaft publications, and a roster of organizations. Nearly 80% of the 1,841 societies (not counting united relief committees) which responded fully to the project's survey had been founded before 1924. The major exceptions were women's societies and auxiliaries, family circles, and branches of the International Workers' Order, all of which came in the late 1920s and the 1930s. On the number of societies, see especially Isaac E. Rontch, "Der itstiker matsev fun di landsmanshaften," in Rontch, ed., *Di idishe landsmanshaften fun Nyu York* (New York: Yiddish Writers' Union, 1938), pp. 10–11, 15–16; tables in ibid., pp. 26–32. For a history of the project and abridged English versions of some of the book's articles, see Hannah Kliger, ed., *Jewish Hometown Associations and Family Circles in New York: The WPA Yiddish Writers' Group Study* (Bloomington: Indiana University Press, 1992). For other estimates on the number of landsmanshaftn in New York, see I. Silberstein, "Jewish Fraternal and Benevolent Societies," *Jewish Charities* 2 (December 1911): 14; Rosaline Schwartz and Susan Milamed, *From Alexandrovsk to Zyrardow: A Guide to YIVO's Landsmanshaftn Archives* (New York: YIVO Institute for Jewish Research, 1986), p. v; Nathan M. Kaganoff, "The Jewish Landsmanshaftn in New York City in the Period Preceding World War I," *American Jewish History* 76 (September 1986): 57; Michael R. Weisser, *A Brotherhood of Memory: Jewish Landsmanshaftn in the New World* (New York: Basic Books, 1985), p. 287 n.14. A comprehensive study of the New York Jewish community carried out in 1917 found 1,016 mutual aid societies and 617 Yiddish-speaking congregations in the city, together with several hundred fraternal lodges, many of which were landsmanshaftn. *The Jewish Communal Register*

of New York City 1917–1918 (New York: Kehillah (Jewish Community) of New York City, 1918), table following p. 122, and pp. 145–285, 735–864, 869–985. Regarding the Jewish population of New York at about the time of the WPA study see Ira Rosenwaike, *Population History of New York City* (Syracuse: Syracuse University Press, 1972), p. 128.

2. For these and other examples see Salo Baron, *The Jewish Community: Its History and Structure to the American Revolution* (Philadelphia: Jewish Publication Society of America, 1942), vol. 1, pp. 66, 81, 120, 168, 348, 350–351.

3. Sidney Sorkin, *Bridges to an American City: A Guide to Chicago's Landsmanshaften, 1870 to 1990* (New York: Peter Lang Publishing, 1993); Edmund James et al., *The Immigrant Jew in America* (New York: B. Buck, 1906), pp. 83–84, 162, 174–175, 233; Louis Wirth, *The Ghetto* (Chicago: University of Chicago Press, 1928), pp. 168–169, 223; Daniel A. Nadelman, "An Analysis of Voluntary Associations among Immigrant Groups with Particular Reference to Eastern European Jews of Philadelphia, 1870–1930" (B.A. thesis, University of Pennsylvania, 1983), pp. 52–69; Judith E. Smith, *Family Connections: A History of Italian and Jewish Immigrant Lives in Providence, Rhode Island 1900–1940* (Albany: SUNY Press, 1985), pp. 136, 140; Samuel Koenig, "The Social Aspects of the Jewish Mutual Benefit Societies," *Social Forces* 18 (December 1939): 268–274.

4. Z[ôsa] Sz[ajkowski], "Dos yidishe gezelshaftlekhe lebn in Pariz tsum yor 1939," in E. Tcherikower, ed., *Yidn in Frankraykh* (New York: Yiddish Scientific Institute-Yivo, 1942), vol. 2, pp. 218–234; Nancy Green, *The Pletzl of Paris: Jewish Immigrant Workers in the Belle Epoque* (New York: Holmes and Meier, 1986), pp. 87–91; Jonathan Boyarin, *Polish Jews in Paris: The Ethnography of Memory* (Bloomington: Indiana University Press, 1991); P. Wald, "Di landslayt-fereynen," *Der avangard* (Buenos Aires), November 1916, pp. 31–35; L. Losh, ed., *Landsmanshaftn in Yisroel* (Tel Aviv: Hitahdut ole Polin be-Yisrael, 1961). English-speaking North Americans also formed a kind of landsmanshaft in Israel—based on continent of origin. See Ava F. Kahn, "They Came, They Saw, They Organized: The Association of Americans and Canadians in Israel," *American Jewish Archives* 43 (Spring/Summer 1991): 41–54.

5. Deborah Dash Moore, *At Home in America: Second Generation New York Jews* (New York: Columbia University Press, 1981), p. 21.

6. Wirth, *The Ghetto*, pp. 203–204.

7. Wald, "Landslayt fereynen"; "Federatsie," *Parizer haynt*, 11 February 1926.

8. Maurice Freedman, "Immigrants and Associations: Chinese in Nineteenth-Century Singapore," pp. 35–41; Marjorie Topley, "The Emergence and Social Function of Chinese Religious Associations in Singapore," pp. 57, 60; W. T. Morrill, "Immigrants and Associations: The Ibo in Twentieth Century Calabar," pp. 174–181, all in L. A. Fallers, ed., *Immigrants and Associations* (The Hague: Mouton, 1967).

9. Robert F. Harney, "Unique Features of Fraternal Records," in *Records of Ethnic Fraternal Benefit Associations in the United States: Essays and Inventories* (St. Paul: Immigration History Research Center, University of Minnesota, 1981), p. 21. See also Stanley Nadel, *Little Germany: Ethnicity, Religion, and Class in New York City, 1845–1860* (Urbana: University of Illinois Press,

1990), pp. 3–7; June Granatir Alexander, *The Immigrant Church and Community: Pittsburgh's Slovak Catholics and Lutherans, 1880–1915* (Pittsburgh: University of Pittsburgh Press, 1987), p. 116; Lizabeth Cohen, *Making a New Deal: Industrial Workers in Chicago, 1919–1939* (New York: Cambridge University Press, 1990), p. 95; Susan Greenbaum, "Economic Cooperation among Urban-Industrial Workers—Rationality and Community in an Afro-Cuban Mutual Aid Society, 1904–1927," *Social Science History* 17 (Summer 1993): 173–193.

10. Alixa Naff, *Becoming American: The Early Arab Immigrant Experience* (Carbondale, Ill.: Southern Illinois University Press, 1985), p. 307; "Washington Heights Journal: Dominican Club Offers Home in a Foreign Land," *New York Times,* 5 August 1991. On late-twentieth century ethnic hometown associations, see also Pam Belluck, "Distant but Loyal: Little Sicily in Queens," *New York Times,* 17 July 1995.

11. The classic statement of the former view is, of course, Oscar Handlin, *The Uprooted* (Boston: Little, Brown, 1951). For a synthesis of the scholarship of the 1960s through the mid-1980s, placing more emphasis on continuity, see John Bodnar, *The Transplanted: A History of Immigrants in Urban America* (Bloomington: Indiana University Press, 1985). For a survey of changing views on Americanization and assimilation, see Russell A. Kazal, "Revisiting Assimilation: The Rise, Fall, and Reappraisal of a Concept in American Ethnic History," *American Historical Review* 100 (April 1995): 437–471.

12. Kathleen Neils Conzen et al., "The Invention of Ethnicity: A Perspective from the U.S.A.," *Journal of American Ethnic History* 12 (Fall 1992): 6.

13. Ibid., pp. 4–5. Conzen and her coauthors represent a moderate "inventionist" position which recognizes that ethnic identifications are "grounded in real life context and social experience." Their statement portrays well the dynamic quality of ethnic identity, and the history of the landsmanshaftn bears out many of their arguments. Werner Sollors's more radical contention that ethnicity is nothing more than a set of "collective fictions" is less useful, since it dismisses the reality of ethnic cultures and affiliations and underestimates their determining impact on people's lives. His argument is based largely on literature created by second and subsequent-generation ethnic Americans in command of mainstream Anglo-American cultural resources, and seems much more relevant to that milieu than to the experiences of first-generation immigrants. All invention theorists tend to underplay what they term the "primordial" aspects of ethnicity—those elements of culture and consciousness which older generations transmit to their children. There is no reason to assume, however, as Sollors does, that recognition of the primordial element in ethnicity presupposes that such identity is "eternal, stable, and static." One generation's social innovation may become the next generation's received tradition. Moreover, even recent cultural innovations are primordial to the American context when they are brought from abroad by immigrants. Werner Sollors, ed., *The Invention of Ethnicity* (New York: Oxford University Press, 1989), pp. ix–xx; Sollors, *Beyond Ethnicity: Consent and Descent in American Culture* (New York: Oxford University Press, 1986).

14. See Eric Hobsbawm, "Mass-Producing Traditions: Europe, 1870–1914," in

Eric Hobsbawm and Terence Ranger, eds., *The Invention of Tradition* (Cambridge: Cambridge University Press, 1983), pp. 283–288.

15. See Gary Mormino and George E. Pozzetta, *The Immigrant World of Ybor City: Italians and Their Latin Neighbors in Tampa, 1885–1985* (Urbana: University of Illinois Press, 1987); Dino Cinel, *From Italy to San Francisco* (Stanford: Stanford University Press, 1982), pp. 103–104, 199–200.

16. Lawrence Fuchs, *The American Kaleidoscope: Race, Ethnicity, and the Civic Culture* (Hanover, N.H.: University Press of New England, 1990), especially pages 1–75; Philip Gleason, "American Identity and Americanization," *Harvard Encyclopedia of American Ethnic Groups* (Cambridge, Mass.: Harvard University Press, 1980), pp. 31–34.

17. Michael Kammen, *Mystic Chords of Memory: The Transformation of Tradition in American Culture* (New York: Alfred A. Knopf, 1991), pp. 216–253; Gleason, "American Identity and Americanization," pp. 38–43; John Higham, *Strangers in the Land: Patterns of American Nativism 1860–1925* (1955; New York: Atheneum, 1981); Werner Sollors, *Beyond Ethnicity*, pp. 88–89.

18. Fuchs, *American Kaleidoscope*, p. 64.

19. Z. Tygiel, "Avrom Rozenberg," *Der farband*, 1 July 1925, p. 9.

20. For comments on the relationship of Jews to the American civic culture, see Hasia Diner, "From Covenant to Constitution: The Americanization of Judaism," in M. L. Bradbury and James B. Gilbert, eds., *Transforming Faith: The Sacred and Secular in Modern American History* (New York: Greenwood Press, 1989), pp. 11–24; Jerold Auerbach, *Rabbis and Lawyers: The Journey from Torah to Constitution* (Bloomington: Indiana University Press, 1990); Naomi Cohen, *Jews in Christian America: The Pursuit of Religious Equality* (New York: Oxford University Press, 1992). For a comparison of Jewish and Slavic responses, see Ewa Morawska, "Changing Images of the Old Country in the Development of Ethnic Identity among East European Immigrants, 1880s–1930s: A Comparison of Jewish and Slavic Representations," in *YIVO Annual* 21 (1993): 273–341.

21. David M. Potter, *People of Plenty: Economic Abundance and the American Character* (Chicago: University of Chicago Press, 1954); Andrew R. Heinze, *Adapting to Abundance: Jewish Immigrants, Mass Consumption, and the Search for American Identity* (New York: Columbia University Press, 1990).

22. Potter, *People of Plenty*, p. 105; Michael B. Katz, *In the Shadow of the Poorhouse: A Social History of Welfare in America* (New York: Basic Books, 1986), pp. xi–xii; Daniel Levine, *Poverty and Society: The Growth of the American Welfare State in International Comparison* (New Brunswick, N.J.: Rutgers University Press, 1988), pp. 15–17.

23. Paula E. Hyman, "Gender and the Immigrant Experience in the United States," in Judith Baskin, ed., *Jewish Women in Historical Perspective* (Detroit: Wayne State University Press, 1991), pp. 222–242.

24. Conzen et al., "Invention of Ethnicity," p. 5.

25. Higham, *Strangers in the Land*, pp. 234–263; Gerd Korman, *Industrialization, Immigrants and Americanizers: The View from Milwaukee, 1866–1921* (Madison: State Historical Society of Wisconsin, 1967); Robert Carlson, *The*

Quest for Conformity: Americanization through Education (New York: John Wiley and Sons, 1975); Elizabeth Ewen, *Immigrant Women in the Land of Dollars: Life and Culture on the Lower East Side, 1890–1925* (New York: Monthly Review Press, 1985); Rivka Shpak Lissak, *Pluralism and Progressives: Hull House and the New Immigrants, 1890–1919* (Chicago: University of Chicago Press, 1989); James R. Barrett, "Americanization from the Bottom Up: Immigration and the Remaking of the Working Class in the United States, 1880–1930," *Journal of American History* 79 (December 1992): 996–1020. Stephan F. Brumberg recognizes the degree to which the immigrants themselves shaped the institutions of Americanization in his *Going to America, Going to School: The Jewish Immigrant Public School Encounter in Turn-of-the-Century New York City* (New York: Praeger, 1986).

26. See, for example, two articles by Samuel Margoshes, himself a landsmanshaft leader: "The Verband Movement in New York City," *Jewish Communal Register,* pp. 1328–1336; "Der ferband un di organizirung fun'm gemeynde leben," in *Tsvishen blut un fayer* (New York: Federation of Galician and Bucovinean Jews of America, 1916), pp. 37–41.

1. The Old World

1. Others came under the control of Prussia. Bernard D. Weinryb, *The Jews of Poland: A Social and Economic History of the Jewish Community in Poland from 1100 to 1800* (Philadelphia: The Jewish Publication Society of America, 1982), pp. 9–11, 27–32; Salo Baron, *The Russian Jew Under Tsars and Soviets* (New York: Macmillan, 1976), pp. 13–14.

2. Baron, *Russian Jew,* pp. 32–33, 63; Michael Stanislawski, *Tsar Nicholas I and the Jews: The Transformation of Jewish Society in Russia 1825–1855* (Philadelphia: Jewish Publication Society, 1983), p. 36; S. M. Dubnow, *History of the Jews in Russia and Poland* (1918; rpt. New York: Ktav Publishing House, 1975), vol. 2, pp. 39–40.

3. Weinryb, *Jews of Poland,* pp. 113–114; Ezra Mendelsohn, *Class Struggle in the Pale: The Formative Years of the Jewish Workers' Movement in Tsarist Russia* (Cambridge: Cambridge University Press, 1970), p. 3.

4. Baron, *Russian Jew,* pp. 21, 25, 33–34; Dubnow, *History of the Jews,* vol. 2, pp. 30–31, 40.

5. On the origins of the shtetl, see Weinryb, *Jews of Poland,* pp. 112–118, 120–123, 134–137; Gershon David Hundert, *The Jews in a Polish Private Town: The Case of Opatow in the Eighteenth Century* (Baltimore: Johns Hopkins University Press, 1991); M. J. Rosman, *The Lords' Jews: Magnate-Jewish Relations in the Polish-Lithuanian Commonwealth during the Eighteenth Century* (Cambridge, Mass.: Harvard University Press, 1990).

6. For the development of the image of the shtetl in Yiddish and other literatures, see Dan Miron, *Der imazh fun shtetl* (Tel Aviv: Y. L. Perets Farlag, 1981); Ruth Wisse, ed., *A Shtetl and Other Yiddish Novellas* (1973; rpt. Detroit: Wayne State University Press, 1986), especially the introduction, pp. 1–21; Ruth Gay, "Inventing the Shtetl," *American Scholar* 53 (Summer 1984): 329–349; Ben-

jamin Harshav, *The Meaning of Yiddish* (Berkeley: University of California Press, 1990), pp. 94–95, 153–156.

7. Abraham Ain, "Swislocz: Portrait of a Jewish Community in Eastern Europe," *YIVO Annual of Jewish Social Science* 4 (1949): 87. On Svisloch see also Moshe Mishkinski, "Svislotsh—shem ehad, rav-tsurot, ayarot shtayim (mikro-historiyah ba-ri hatoponimikah)," *Gal-Ed* 9 (1986): 287–297.

8. David Roskies and Diane Roskies, *The Shtetl Book* (New York: Ktav, 1979), p. 2; Ghitta Sternberg, *Stefanesti: Portrait of a Rumanian Shtetl* (Oxford: Pergamon Press, 1984), p. 16.

9. A. Z. Levin-Epstein, quoted in Avrom Menes, "Di mizrakh-eyropeishe tkufe in der yidisher geshikhte," in *Algemeyner entsiklopedie: yidn daled* (New York: Central Yiddish Cultural Organization, 1950), p. 300.

10. Samuel Kassow, "Community and Identity in the Interwar Shtetl," in Yisrael Gutman et al., eds., *The Jews of Poland Between the Two World Wars* (Hanover, N.H.: University Press of New England, 1989), p. 200; Mark Zborowski and Elizabeth Herzog, *Life Is with People: The Culture of the Shtetl* (New York: Schocken, 1951), pp. 151–158.

11. As the *Encyclopedia Judaica* notes, "the real criteria for the size of a shtetl were vague and ill-defined." The encyclopedia argues that the population of a shtetl could range up to "20,000 or more." However, a settlement of such size, in the context of Eastern Europe, would probably have been considered a full-fledged city, not a town. "Shtetl," *Encyclopedia Judaica* (Jerusalem: Keter Publishing House, 1972), vol. 14, p. 1466.

12. Ain, "Swislocz," p. 87.

13. See, for example, P. Tikotshinski, "Dos shtetl Zhager mit a fuftsik yor tsurik," *Yivo bleter* 14 (May 1939): 476; Sternberg, *Stefanesti*, p. 14.

14. Jack Kugelmass and Jonathan Boyarin, *From a Ruined Garden: The Memorial Books of Polish Jewry* (New York: Schocken, 1983), pp. 30–34.

15. *Encyclopedia Judaica*, vol. 14, p. 1472.

16. Ain, "Swislocz," pp. 103–104.

17. Tikotshinski, "Dos shtetl Zhager," p. 478.

18. Ain, "Swislocz," p. 101.

19. Menes, "Di mizrakh-eyropeishe tkufe," pp. 297–298; Kugelmass and Boyarin, *Ruined Garden*, pp. 37–40; Sternberg, *Stefanesti*, p. 9.

20. A. Litwin, *In der poylisher shtetl*, quoted in Joshua Rothenberg, "Demythologizing the Shtetl," *Midstream* 27 (March 1981): 26.

21. Ain, "Swislocz," p. 87; Tikotshinski, "Dos shtetl Zhager," p. 477; Roskies and Roskies, *Shtetl Book*, pp. 26, 28.

22. Sternberg, *Stefanesti*, p. 17.

23. Jacob Lestchinsky, "The Jews in the Cities of the Polish Republic," *YIVO Annual of Jewish Social Science* 1 (1946): 161, 165.

24. Israel Cohen, *Vilna* (Philadelphia: Jewish Publication Society, 1943), p. 92.

25. Arcadius Kahan, *Essays in Jewish Social and Economic History* (Chicago: University of Chicago Press, 1986), p. 119.

26. Ain, "Swislocz," p. 101; Roskies and Roskies, *Shtetl Book*, pp. 45–46;

Zborowski and Herzog, *Life,* pp. 229–230; Menashe Vakser, "Folklor fun idishe yishuvim," in Isaac E. Rontch, ed., *Di idishe landsmanshaften fun Nyu York* (New York: Yiddish Writers' Union, 1938), pp. 61–63.

27. Jacob Katz, *Tradition and Crisis: Jewish Society at the End of the Middle Ages* (New York: Schocken, 1971), pp. 84, 128; Weinryb, *Jews of Poland,* pp. 35–37, 74; Avrom Menes, "Di kemerlekh fun tsiber-lebn bay yidn," *Yivo bleter* 2 (November-December 1931): 194–198; Salo Baron, *The Jewish Community: Its History and Structure to the American Revolution* (Philadelphia: Jewish Publication Society of America, 1942), vol. 2, p. 3.

28. Stanislawski, *Tsar Nicholas I and the Jews,* pp. xi–xii; Eli Lederhendler, "The Decline of the Polish-Lithuanian Kahal," *Polin* 2 (1987): 150–160; Baron, *Russian Jew,* pp. 20–21, 102; Isaac Levitats, *The Jewish Community in Russia, 1772–1844* (New York: Columbia University Press, 1943), pp. 16–57; Levitats, *The Jewish Community in Russia, 1844–1917* (Jerusalem: Posner and Sons, 1981), pp. 23–25.

29. Baron, *Russian Jew,* pp. 31–32, 110–111; Stanislawski, *Tsar Nicholas,* pp. 13–34; Eli Lederhendler, *The Road to Modern Jewish Politics: Political Tradition and Political Reconstruction in the Jewish Community of Tsarist Russia* (New York: Oxford University Press, 1989), pp. 50–51, 64–68.

30. Levitats, *Jewish Community, 1772–1844,* p. 68. In some places the kahal continued to exist secretly or with the knowledge of local authorities who preferred not to enforce the law. Levitats, *Jewish Community, 1844–1917,* p. 58. On the complicated issue of Jewish communal leadership after the abolition of the kahal, see Azriel Shochat, "Hahanhagah bekehillot rusia im bitul hakahal," *Zion* 42 (1977): 143–233.

31. Katz, *Tradition,* p. 158; Levitats, *Jewish Community, 1772–1844,* p. 105; F. Baer, "Der Ursprung der Chewra," *Zeitschrift für jüdische Wohlfahrtspflege und Sozialpolitik* 1 (September-October 1929): 241–247; Baron, *Jewish Community,* vol. 1, p. 349.

32. Levitats, *Jewish Community, 1772–1844,* pp. 121–122. Baron argues that this was true even before the final decline of the central communities. Baron, *Jewish Community,* vol. 1, p. 349.

33. Katz, *Tradition,* p. 166; Levitats, *Jewish Community, 1772–1844,* pp. 107–108, 121; Jacob Shatzky, *Geshikhte fun yidn in Varshe* (New York: Yiddish Scientific Institute-Yivo, 1947), vol. 1, pp. 123–124; Baron, *Jewish Community,* vol. 2, pp. 146–148, 155–156.

34. Katz, *Tradition,* p. 159.

35. Levitats, *Jewish Community, 1772–1844,* pp. 109–110; Hundert, *Jews in a Polish Private Town,* p. 88; L. Tsomber, "A bild fun yidishn kultur-lebn in a poylisher shtot in onheyb fun 19tn yorhundert (di kutner khevre kadishe in onheyb fun 19tn y'h)," *Yunger historiker* 1 (1926): 58–65.

36. Levitats, *Jewish Community, 1772–1844,* p. 108; S. Vinter, "Pinkeysim fun khevres," *Yivo bleter* 13 (January-February 1938): 77–78; Moyshe Fraykind, "Di khevre kadishe in Petrikov," *Lodzer visnshaftlekhe shriftn* 1 (1938): 56, 60.

37. Hevrah constitutions and by-laws were often written with the help of the local rabbi or other learned man, or copied from the documents of already existing societies of similar nature. As Benjamin Harshav has pointed out, Hebrew served to record in written form even those transactions which took place orally in Yiddish. Harshav, *Meaning of Yiddish,* pp. 22–23.

38. Roskies and Roskies, *Shtetl Book,* pp. 182, 184; M. Hendel, "Mezritsher pinkeysim," *Yivo bleter* 8 (January 1935): 61–67.

39. Katz, *Tradition,* pp. 161–165; Levitats, *Jewish Community, 1772–1844,* pp. 116–117; P. Z. Gliksman, "Tsvey alte khevres in Lodzh," *Lodzer visnshaftlekhe shriftn* 1 (1938): 268; Cohen, *Vilna,* pp. 127–128; Kugelmass and Boyarin, *Ruined Garden,* pp. 40–41.

40. Katz, *Tradition,* p. 158; Sara Rabinowitsch, *Die Organisationen des jüdischen Proletariats in Russland* (Karlsruhe, 1903), p. 45; Levitats, *Jewish Community, 1844–1917,* p. 115; Shatzky, *Geshikhte,* pp. 151–152; Baron, *Jewish Community,* vol. 1, pp. 351–352.

41. Natalie Joffe, "Dynamics of Benefice Among Eastern European Jews," *Social Forces* 27 (March 1949): 242.

42. Celia S. Rosenthal, "Social Stratification of the Jewish Community in a Small Polish Town," *American Journal of Sociology* 59 (July 1953): 2–5; Theodore Bienenstock, "Social Life and Authority in the East European Shtetl," *Southwestern Journal of Anthropology* 6 (Autumn 1950): 244.

43. Levitats, *Jewish Community, 1844–1917,* p. 80; Gliksman, "Tsvey alte khevres," p. 268; Vinter, "Pinkeysim," pp. 79–80; Levitats, *Jewish Community, 1772–1844,* p. 118.

44. For example, the Psalm-sayers' Society in Brisk. See Vinter, "Pinkeysim," p. 81.

45. Mark Wischnitzer, *A History of Jewish Crafts and Guilds* (New York: J. David, 1965), p. 253; Rabinowitsch, *Organisationen,* pp. 49–52; Ezra Mendelsohn, *Class Struggle,* p. 8.

46. Gliksman, "Tsvey alte khevres," p. 273; Vinter, "Pinkeysim," pp. 81, 83, 87; Levitats, *Jewish Community 1772–1844,* pp. 113–115.

47. Gliksman, "Tsvey alte khevres," pp. 269, 274.

48. Hundert, *Jews,* pp. 116–117; Levitats, *Jewish Community, 1772–1844,* pp. 116–117, 248; Baron, *Russian Jew,* p. 115.

49. Levitats, *Jewish Community, 1772–1844,* pp. 110–111; Gliksman, "Tsvey alte khevres," p. 268; Vinter, "Pinkeysim," p. 82; Fraykind, "Khevre kadishe," p. 56; Cohen, *Vilna,* p. 125.

50. Levitats, *Jewish Community 1772–1844,* pp. 130–131; Vinter, "Pinkeysim," p. 82; Fraykind, "Khevre kadishe," p. 58; Cohen, *Vilna,* p. 125.

51. Raphael Mahler, "Froyen, kinder un yugntlikhe mitglider fun amolige khevres," *Tsukunft* 43 (March 1938): 163–166; Levitats, *Jewish Community, 1772–1844,* pp. 112–113; Levitats, *Jewish Community, 1844–1917,* p. 82; Cohen, *Vilna,* p. 126.

52. Rabinowitsch, *Organisationen,* p. 44.

53. Samuel Joseph, *Jewish Immigration to the United States, 1881–1910* (New

York: Columbia University Press, 1914), pp. 79–81; Baron, *Russian Jew,* pp. 80–84; Kahan, *Essays,* p. 37; Stanislawski, *Tsar Nicholas,* pp. 174–175; Mendelsohn, *Class Struggle,* pp. 20–22; Klaus Hödl, *Vom Shtetl an die Lower East Side: Galizische Juden in New York* (Wien: Böhlau Verlag, 1991), pp. 23–26, 32; Raphael Mahler, "The Economic Background of Galician Jewish Emigration to the United States," *YIVO Annual* 7 (1952): pp. 259, 261.

54. Kahan, *Essays,* pp. 1–27, 44–45; Simon Kuznets, "Immigration of Russian Jews to the United States: Background and Structure," *Perspectives on American History* 9 (1975): 78; Aryeh Tartakower, "The Migration of Polish Jews in Recent Times," in S. Federbuch, ed., *Yearbook 1* (New York: American Federation of Polish Jews, 1964), pp. 11–12.

55. Shaul Stampfer, "The Geographical Background of Eastern European Jewish Migration to the United States Before World War I," in Ira A. Glazier and Luigi De Rosa, eds., *Migration Across Time and Nations: Population Mobility in Historical Contexts* (New York: Holmes and Meier, 1986), p. 223; Baron, *Russian Jew,* p. 64; Kuznets, "Immigration," pp. 66, 91; Lloyd P. Gartner, "Jewish Migrants en Route from Europe to North America: Traditions and Realities," in Moses Rischin, ed., *The Jews of North America* (Detroit: Wayne State University Press, 1987), pp. 26–27.

56. Baron, *Russian Jew,* p. 82.

57. Ibid., pp. 67–69; Jacob Lestchinsky, "Jews in the Cities of the Polish Republic," pp. 161, 169. In these new cities, as in the old, Jews left a distinctive mark on certain neighborhoods and influenced the shape of the city as a whole. See Peter J. Martyn, "The Undefined Town within a Town: A History of Jewish Settlement in the Western Districts of Warsaw," *Polin* 2 (1987): 19–36; Stanislaw Liszewski, "The Role of the Jewish Community in the Organization of Urban Space in Lodz," *Polin* 6 (1991): 27–36; Julian Janczuk, "The National Structure of the Population in Lodz in the Years 1820–1939," *Polin* 6 (1991): 20–26; Wieslaw Pus, "The Development of the City of Lodz (1820–1939)," *Polin* 6 (1991): 3–19.

58. Kahan, *Essays,* p. 33.

59. Baron, *Russian Jew,* pp. 67–69; Kahan, *Essays,* p. 33; Kuznets, "Immigration," p. 117.

60. Steven J. Zipperstein, *The Jews of Odessa: A Cultural History, 1794–1881* (Stanford: Stanford University Press, 1985), pp. 33, 36–37.

61. Celia Stopnicka Rosenthal, "Deviations and Social Change in the Jewish Community of a Small Polish Town," *American Journal of Sociology* 60 (September 1954): 180.

62. Joseph Zelkovitch, "A Picture of the Communal Life of a Jewish Town in Poland in the Second Half of the Nineteenth Century," *YIVO Annual* 6 (1951): 253–265.

63. Wischnitzer, *Crafts and Guilds,* pp. 274–275; Mendelsohn, *Class Struggle,* pp. 10, 63–72; Rabinowitsch, *Organisationen,* pp. 54–75.

64. Levitats, *Jewish Community, 1844–1917,* pp. 152, 173.

65. Vinter, "Pinkeysim," pp. 90–92.

66. Mendelsohn, *Class Struggle*, pp. 43, 80; Shatzky, *Geshikhte*, p. 159.

67. Levitats, *Jewish Community, 1844–1917*, pp. 71–78; Katz, *Tradition*, pp. 263–264.

68. Jonathan Frankel, *Prophecy and Politics: Socialism, Nationalism and the Russian Jew, 1862–1917* (Cambridge: Cambridge University Press, 1981).

69. Henry J. Tobias, *The Jewish Bund in Russia: From Its Origins to 1905* (Stanford: Stanford University Press, 1972).

70. Arthur Hertzberg, *The Zionist Idea* (New York: Atheneum, 1972).

71. Zvi Gitelman, *Jewish Nationality and Soviet Politics: The Jewish Section of the CPSU, 1917–1930* (Princeton: Princeton University Press, 1972), pp. 46–56.

72. Kuznets, "Immigration," pp. 42–43, 48–49; Gartner, "Jewish Migrants," p. 31. Kuznets notes that the United States probably received an even higher percentage of Jewish migrants, since many went elsewhere before moving on to America.

73. Kuznets, "Immigration," pp. 42–43, 49–52, 94–100; Gartner, "Jewish Migrants," p. 26; Joseph, *Jewish Immigration*, pp. 127–139. Gartner points out that it was not unusual for minority groups, or nationalities living under foreign rule, to have higher emigration rates.

74. Dubnow, *History of the Jews*, vol. 2, pp. 312–341; Baron, *Russian Jew*, pp. 49–50; Kuznets, "Immigration," p. 92; Gartner, "Jewish Migrants," p. 27.

75. Samuel Joseph, *Jewish Immigration*, pp. 73–74.

76. Joseph Kisman, "Di yidn in Rumenie un di emigratsie keyn Amerike," in E. Tcherikower, ed., *Geshikhte fun der yidisher arbeter bavegung in di fareynikte shtatn* (New York: Yiddish Scientific Institute-Yivo, 1943), vol. 1, pp. 134–136.

77. Kuznets, "Immigration," p. 39; Joseph, *Jewish Immigration*, pp. 94–96.

78. Kuznets, "Immigration," pp. 117–119; Stampfer, "Geographic Background," p. 227; Jacob Lestchinsky, "Di yidishe imigratsie in di fareynikte shtatn (1870–1900)," in Tcherikower, *Geshikhte*, vol. 1, p. 39.

2. The New World

1. Alexis de Tocqueville, *Democracy in America* (New York: Vintage Books, 1945), pp. 114, 118. See also Lawrence Fuchs, *The American Kaleidoscope: Race, Ethnicity and the Civic Culture* (Hanover, N.H.: University Press of New England, 1990), pp. 3–4.

2. Lynn Dumenil, *Freemasonry and American Culture, 1880–1930* (Princeton: Princeton University Press, 1984), p. xi. The "golden age" label was originally applied by W. S. Harwood, a contemporary observer. Quoted in Mark C. Carnes, *Secret Ritual and Manhood in Victorian America* (New Haven: Yale University Press, 1989), p. 1.

3. See Mary Ann Clawson, *Constructing Brotherhood: Class, Gender and Fraternalism* (Princeton: Princeton University Press, 1989), pp. 53–83.

4. Carnes, *Secret Ritual*, pp. 22–24.

5. Clawson, *Constructing Brotherhood*, pp. 79–80; Dumenil, *Freemasonry and*

American Culture, pp. 14–17, 23, 31–39; Albert Stevens, *Cyclopedia of Fraternities,* 2nd ed. (1907; rpt. Detroit: Gale Research, 1966), pp. 86–97.

6. Dumenil, *Freemasonry,* p. 7; Mark C. Carnes, "Middle Class Men and the Solace of Fraternal Ritual," in Mark C. Carnes and Clyde Griffen, eds., *Meanings for Manhood: Constructions of Masculinity in Victorian America* (Chicago: University of Chicago Press, 1990), p. 38.

7. Clawson, *Constructing Brotherhood,* pp. 118–123; Carnes, *Secret Ritual,* pp. 24–27; Carnes, "Middle Class Men," p. 38.

8. E. J. Dunn, *Builders of Fraternalism in America* (Chicago: Fraternal Book Concern, 1924), vol. 1, pp. 91–106; Myron Ward Sackett, *Early History of Fraternal Beneficiary Societies in America* (Meadville, PA: Tribune, 1914), pp. 219–223, 231–232.

9. Clawson, *Constructing Brotherhood,* pp. 126–129; Noel Gist, "Secret Societies: A Cultural Study of Fraternalism in the United States," *The University of Missouri Studies* 15 (October 1940): 45–46, 112–128.

10. Carnes, "Middle Class Men"; Gist, "Secret Societies," pp. 81–104, 120–121.

11. Gist, "Secret Societies," pp. 55–57, 65–79, 106–111.

12. Clawson, *Constructing Brotherhood,* pp. 13, 228.

13. Carnes, *Secret Ritual,* quote on p. 14; Carnes, "Middle Class Men."

14. Carnes, *Secret Ritual,* pp. 85–88; Clawson, *Constructing Brotherhood,* pp. 188–205; Stevens, *Cyclopedia,* pp. v–vi, 98–101; Gist, "Secret Societies," pp. 61, 133; Dunn, *Builders,* vol. 2, pp. 25–32, 47–52, 91–98, 187–208, 313–344.

15. William Muraskin, *Middle Class Blacks in a White Society: Prince Hall Masonry in America* (Berkeley: University of California Press, 1975), pp. 31–38, 109; Loretta Williams, *Black Freemasonry and Middle Class Realities* (Columbia, Mo.: University of Missouri Press, 1980), pp. 14–16, 44–45; Stevens, *Cyclopedia,* pp. 72–75.

16. Stevens, *Cyclopedia,* pp. 235–237, 266; Williams, *Black Freemasonry,* pp. 78–80; Charles Wright Ferguson, *Fifty Million Brothers: A Panorama of American Lodges and Clubs* (New York, 1937), pp. 184–196; Elsa Barkley, "Womanist Consciousness: Maggie Lena Walker and the Independent Order of St. Luke," *Signs* 14 (Spring 1989): 610–633; Edward Nelson Palmer, "Negro Secret Societies," *Social Forces* 23 (December 1944): 207–212; Betty M. Kuyk, "The African Derivation of Black Fraternal Orders in the United States," *Comparative Studies in Society and History* 25 (October 1983): 559–592. Kuyk argues that black fraternal ritual derived primarily from West African forms, but ignores closer parallels with other American fraternal orders.

17. The second Klan was formed after 1915 by a salesman who was a member of no fewer than fifteen fraternal orders. It carried fraternal ritual to a ludicrous extreme at a time when ritualism in the mainstream orders was on the wane. Stevens, *Cyclopedia,* pp. 290–320, 365–369, 402–409, 416–419; David Annan, "The Ku Klux Klan," in Norman MacKenzie, ed., *Secret Societies* (New York: Collier Books, 1971), pp. 222–237; Ferguson, *Fifty Million Brothers,* pp. 58–61, 175, 320–321; Gist, "Secret Societies," pp. 35–39.

18. Henry Joseph Browne, *The Catholic Church and the Knights of Labor* (Wash-

ington, D.C.: Catholic University Press, 1949), pp. 36; Stevens, *Cyclopedia,* pp. 378–385, 388–395. Farmers' organizations such as the Patrons of Husbandry and the National Farmers' Union also incorporated secret ritual. The National Farmers' Union was at first a nonsecret organization, but "found something was lacking" and adopted a ritual similar to that of the Patrons. Stevens, *Cyclopedia,* pp. 385–388, 395–399.

19. Abraham Rosenberg, *Di kloukmakher un zeyere yunyons: erinerungen* (New York: Cloak Operators Union, Local 1, 1920), pp. 10–11. After the ceremony, those who knew English explained the significance of the symbols to those who hadn't understood.

20. Fergus McDonald, *The Catholic Church and Secret Societies* (New York: United States Catholic Historical Society, 1946), quotes on pp. 13–14, 63.

21. Sean O Luing, *The Catalpa Rescue (Freemantle Mission)* (Tralee, County Kerry: Anvil Books, 1965), pp. 46–47. The AOH attempted to mollify its Catholic critics by presenting itself as one of the Catholic societies recommended by the Pope as an alternative to secret societies. Nevertheless, episcopal opinion remained divided concerning the Hibernians. Stevens, *Cyclopedia,* pp. 211–212; McDonald, *Catholic Church,* pp. 49, 54–55, 86–90.

22. Christopher Kauffman, *Faith and Fraternalism: The History of the Knights of Columbus 1882–1982* (New York: Harper and Row, 1982), quotes on pp. 139, 154.

23. Dale T. Knobel, "To Be American: Ethnicity, Fraternity and the Improved Order of Red Men," *Journal of American Ethnic History* 4 (Fall 1984): 62–87; Gerhard Wiesinger, "Orden der Herrmanns-Sohne and Deutscher Orden der Harugari: Two Antinativist Fraternal Orders in the United States 1840–1910," *In Their Own Words* 3 (1986): 135–157; Stevens, *Cyclopedia,* pp. 234–235, 238, 262, 282–284; Nadel, *Little Germany,* p. 111; Kathleen Neils Conzen, *Immigrant Milwaukee: Accommodation and Community in a Frontier City* (Cambridge, Mass.: Harvard University Press, 1976), p. 168.

24. Roy Rosenzweig, "Boston's Masons 1900–1935: The Lower Middle Class in a Divided Society," *Journal of Voluntary Action Research* 6 (July-October 1977): 120, 122; Dumenil, *Freemasonry,* p. 11; Hasia Diner, *A Time for Gathering: The Second Migration 1820–1880* (Baltimore: Johns Hopkins University Press, 1992), pp. 160–163; Tony Fels, "Religious Assimilation in a Fraternal Organization: Jews and Freemasonry in Gilded Age San Francisco," *American Jewish History* 74 (June 1985): 369–403.

25. Edward E. Grusd, *B'nai B'rith: The Story of a Covenant* (New York: Appleton-Century, 1966), p. 97; Stevens, *Cyclopedia,* pp. 206–210; *Jewish Communal Register* (New York: Kehillah (Jewish Community) of New York City, 1918), p. 869; "Groyse idishe organizatsionen," *Amerikaner,* 24 November 1905, 22.

26. Grusd, *B'nai B'rith,* pp. 90, 108; Deborah Dash Moore, *B'nai B'rith and the Challenge of Ethnic Leadership* (Albany: State University of New York Press, 1981), pp. 55–56; Hyman Grinstein, *The Rise of the Jewish Community in New York, 1654–1860* (Philadelphia: Jewish Publication Society of America, 1947), p. 112; Stevens, *Cyclopedia,* pp. 206–210.

27. Grusd, *B'nai B'rith*, especially pp. 12–15, 18–21; Moore, *B'nai B'rith*, especially pp. 6–7, 9, 12–13; Diner, *Time for Gathering*, pp. 109–112.

28. The limits of B'nai B'rith's universalism were first established when non-Jews were denied membership. Moore, *B'nai B'rith*, pp. 4–7, 14; Grusd, *B'nai B'rith*, pp. 29–31. On the differentiated social composition of B'nai B'rith lodges see William Toll, "Mobility, Fraternalism, and Jewish Cultural Change: Portland, 1910–1930," in Moses Rischin, ed., *Jews of the West: The Metropolitan Years* (Waltham, Mass.: American Jewish Historical Society, 1979).

29. Diner, *A Time for Gathering*, p. 109; "Groyse idishe organizatsionen," *Amerikaner.*

30. Beginning in 1869, B'nai B'rith undertook a number of reforms in an effort to stave off a crisis stemming from the inadequacy of its assessment structure. Finally, in the face of falling membership, some districts adopted graduated rates. In 1890 insurance was made optional, a move probably made easier by the increasing affluence of the order's members. Grusd, *B'nai B'rith*, pp. 27, 72, 86–87, 105–108.

31. Dumenil, *Freemasonry*, pp. 19–20, 81, 103–107; Stevens, *Cyclopedia*, pp. 112–113.

32. Stevens, *Cyclopedia*, pp. v, 128–130; Gist, "Secret Societies," p. 39; Dunn, *Builders of Fraternalism*, pp. 13–23, 43–80; Walter Basye, *The History and Operation of Fraternal Insurance* (Rochester: The Fraternal Monitor, 1919), pp. 9–14, 41–61; Sackett, *Early History.*

33. Viviana A. Rotman Zelizer, *Morals and Markets: The Development of Life Insurance in the United States* (New York: Columbia University Press, 1979), especially pp. 91–95, 115–116; Abb Landis, "Life Insurance by Fraternal Orders," *American Academy of Political and Social Science Annals* 24 (November 1904): 475–488; B. H. Meyer, "Fraternal Beneficiary Societies in the United States," *American Journal of Sociology* 6 (March 1901): 649–650.

34. Quoted in Clawson, *Constructing Brotherhood*, p. 225.

35. Stevens, *Cyclopedia*, p. 118; Landis, "Life Insurance," pp. 479–480; Meyer, "Fraternal Beneficiary Societies," pp. 651–652.

36. Stevens, *Cyclopedia*, pp. 116, 160–167; Meyer, "Fraternal Beneficiary Societies," pp. 652–653, 658–659; Basye, *History and Operation*, pp. 71–99; Sackett, *Early History*, pp. 226–231.

37. Stevens, *Cyclopedia*, p. 158.

38. Dumenil, *Freemasonry*, p. 81. The exclusivity of orders varied considerably, of course, with the Masons being the most prestigious. Not all orders required unanimous approval, though a minority could still "blackball" a candidate. See Gist, "Secret Societies," pp. 105–106.

39. Alexander, *Immigrant Church*, pp. 17, 19, 24–25; Judith E. Smith, *Family Connections: A History of Italian and Jewish Immigrant Lives in Providence, Rhode Island 1900–1940* (Albany: SUNY Press, 1985), p. 133; Frank Renkiewicz, "The Profits of Non-Profit Capitalism: Polish Fraternalism and Beneficial Insurance in America," and M. Mark Stolarik, "A Place for Everyone: Slovak Fraternal-Benefit Societies," both in Scott Cummings, ed., *Self-Help in Urban America* (Port Washington, N.Y.: Kennikat Press, 1980); Gary

R. Mormino and George E. Pozzetta, *The Immigrant World of Ybor City: Italians and Their Latin Neighbors in Tampa, 1885–1985* (Urbana: University of Illinois Press, 1987), pp. 192–200; Francis X. Blouin, Jr., "'For Our Mutual Benefit': A Look at Ethnic Associations in Michigan," *Chronicle* 15 (Summer 1979): 12–15; Bert J. Thomas, "Historical Functions of Caribbean-American Benevolent/Progressive Associations," *Afro-Americans in New York Life and History* 12 (July 1988): 51; Margaret E. Galey, "Ethnicity, Fraternalism, Social and Mental Health," *Ethnicity* 4 (March 1977): 19–53.

40. Smith, *Family Connections,* p. 133; Mormino and Pozzetta, *Immigrant World,* pp. 247–252.

41. Blouin, "For Our Mutual Benefit," pp. 14–15; John Bodnar, "Ethnic Fraternal Benefit Associations: Their Historical Development, Character, and Significance," in *Records of Ethnic Fraternal Benefit Associations,* pp. 5–12; Galey, "Ethnicity, Fraternalism, Social and Mental Health," pp. 24, 30–31; Noel Chrisman, "Ethnic Persistence in an Urban Setting," *Ethnicity* 8 (September 1981): pp. 257–259, 274–275.

42. Alexander, *Immigrant Church,* p. 21; Barton, "Eastern and Southern Europeans," in John Higham, ed., *Ethnic Leadership in America* (Baltimore: Johns Hopkins University Press, 1978), pp. 160, 166–167; John Bodnar, *The Transplanted: A History of Immigrants in Urban America* (Bloomington: Indiana University Press, 1985), p. 130; Mormino and Pozzetta, *Immigrant World,* pp. 191–192. Evidently, Romanian immigrants were an exception, with a very small percentage affiliated with societies. Gerald Bobango, "The Union and League of Romanian Societies: An Assimilating Force Reviewed," *East European Quarterly* 12 (Spring 1978): 85–92.

43. John Briggs, *An Italian Passage: Immigrants in Three American Cities* (New Haven: Yale University Press, 1978), p. 142. See also Virginia Yans-McLaughlin, *Family and Community: Italian Immigrants in Buffalo, 1880–1930* (Ithaca: Cornell University Press, 1977; Urbana: University of Illinois Press, 1982), p. 131. Significantly, Anne Firor Scott hardly mentions mutual aid societies at all in her book, *Natural Allies: Women's Associations in American History* (Urbana: University of Illinois Press, 1992).

44. Josef Barton, *Peasants and Strangers: Italians, Rumanians, and Slovaks in an American City, 1890–1950* (Cambridge, Mass.: Harvard University Press, 1975), pp. 59–60. See also Smith, *Family Connections,* pp. 133, 136, 140, 168; Robert Ernst, *Immigrant Life in New York City, 1825–1863* (1949; repr. New York: Octagon, 1979), p. 122; Yans-McLaughlin, *Family and Community,* pp. 130–131; Conzen, *Immigrant Milwaukee,* pp. 169, 190; Sucheng Chan, *Asian-Americans: An Interpretive History* (Boston: Twayne, 1991), pp. 63–64, 68; Him Mark Lai, "Historical Development of the Chinese Consolidated Benevolent Association/Huigen System," in *Chinese America: History and Perspectives* (San Francisco: Chinese Historical Society of America, 1987), pp. 13–14, 33; Briggs, *Italian Passage,* p. 146.

45. Nadel, *Little Germany,* pp. 110–111. Quote is on p. 111.

46. Barton, *Peasants and Strangers,* pp. 60–61; Bodnar, *Transplanted,* pp. 121–124.

47. Galey, "Ethnicity, Fraternalism, Social and Mental Health." For a typical meeting agenda see M. Mark Stolarik, "A Place for Everyone," p. 135. Chinese associations were significant exceptions. While different from traditional organizations in China, they were more centralized and oligarchical than most ethnic associations, at least until the 1920s. See Lai, "Historical Development."

48. Susan D. Greenbaum, "A Comparison of African-American and Euro-American Mutual Aid Societies in 19th-Century America," *Journal of Ethnic Studies* 19 (Fall 1991): 95–119; Gist, "Secret Societies," pp. 163–164, n.18; Robert Harris, "Early Black Benevolent Societies, 1780–1830," *Massachusetts Review* 20 (Autumn 1979): 603–628; C. A. Spencer, "Black Benefit Societies and the Development of Black Insurance Companies in Nineteenth-Century Alabama," *Phylon* 46 (September 1985): 251–261. See also several society-related documents in Dorothy Porter, ed., *Early Negro Writing, 1760–1837* (Boston: Beacon Press, 1971).

49. Dino Cinel, *From Italy to San Francisco* (Stanford: Stanford University Press, 1982), pp. 199–200.

50. Nadel, *Little Germany,* p. 2. On the influence of Czech and Polish fraternals on Slovaks in Pittsburgh, see Alexander, *Immigrant Church,* p. 20; and on the influence of the Centro Español on L'Unione Italiana in Ybor City, Florida, see Mormino and Pozzetta, *Immigrant World,* pp. 188–189.

51. Alexander, *Immigrant Church;* Renkiewicz, "Profits of Non-Profit Capitalism"; Donald Pienkos, *PNA: A Centennial History of the Polish National Alliance of the United States of North America* (Boulder: Westview, 1984); Helen Lopata, "The Function of Voluntary Associations in an Ethnic Community: Polonia," in Ernest Burgess and Donald Bogue, eds., *Contributions to Urban Sociology* (Chicago: University of Chicago Press, 1964), pp. 203–223; Daniel J. Walkowitz, *Workers' City, Company Town: Iron and Cotton Worker Protest in Troy and Cohoes, New York 1855–1884* (Urbana: University of Illinois Press, 1978); Mormino and Pozzetta, *Immigrant World,* especially pp. 175–209; Smith, *Family Connections,* pp. 153–156.

52. Robert Anthony Orsi, *The Madonna of 115th Street: Faith and Community in Italian Harlem, 1880–1950* (New Haven: Yale University Press, 1985), especially pp. 51–53; Kathleen Neils Conzen, "Ethnicity as Festive Culture: Nineteenth-Century German America on Parade," in Werner Sollors, ed., *The Invention of Ethnicity* (New York: Oxford University Press, 1989), pp. 44–76; April Schultz, "'The Pride of the Race Had Been Touched': The 1925 Norse-American Immigration Centennial and Ethnic Identity," *Journal of American History* 77 (March 1991): 1265–1295; John Bodnar, *Remaking America: Public Memory, Commemoration and Patriotism in the Twentieth Century* (Princeton: Princeton University Press, 1992), 41–77.

53. Bodnar, "Ethnic Fraternal Benefit Associations," pp. 8–11; Barton, *Peasants and Strangers,* pp. 82–85; Barton, "Eastern and Southern Europeans," pp. 162, 170; Bodnar, *The Transplanted,* p. 127; Cohen, *Making a New Deal: Industrial Workers in Chicago, 1919–1939* (New York: Cambridge University Press, 1990), pp. 68–70; Jose Amara Hernandez, *Mutual Aid for Survival: The Case of the Mexican American* (Malabar, Fla.: Robert E. Krieger, 1983). Some

groups were more centralized than others. The Sons of Italy, for example, did not have national benefits and never became as dominant a force among Italians as the Polish fraternals did among Poles. See Briggs, *An Italian Passage,* pp. 152–153, 161. In extreme cases, fraternals even exercised quasi-governmental powers. This was the case in the Southwest, where Mexican-American fraternal organizations filled a vacuum of authority at a time when an indigenous ethnic group refused to recognize the legitimacy of the new Anglo-American rulers. In both the Chinese and Japanese communities associations had the power, honored by steamship companies, to deny exit permits to compatriots wishing to return to the homeland. Chan, *Asian Americans,* pp. 65–66, 68–69; Lai, "Historical Development," pp. 19–20.

54. Jacob Rader Marcus, *United States Jewry 1776–1985* (Detroit: Wayne State University Press, 1991), vol. 2, pp. 197, 238; Diner, *Time for Gathering,* pp. 87, 92–99.

55. Grinstein, *Rise of the Jewish Community,* pp. 104–105. See also Eli Faber, *A Time For Planting: The First Migration, 1654–1820* (Baltimore: Johns Hopkins University Press, 1992), especially pp. 52–83.

56. Grinstein, *Rise of the Jewish Community,* pp. 48–50, 170–173, 401; Abraham J. Karp, "Overview: The Synagogue in America—A Historical Typology," in Jack Wertheimer, ed., *The American Synagogue: A Sanctuary Transformed* (New York: Cambridge University Press, 1987), pp. 5–14.

57. Grinstein, *Rise of the Jewish Community,* pp. 106–108, 313; Marcus, *United States Jewry,* vol. 2, p. 223; Diner, *Time for Gathering,* p. 74; Isaac E. Rontch, ed., *Di idishe landsmanshaften fun Nyu York* (New York: Yiddish Writers' Union, 1938), p. 319; *Jewish Communal Register,* pp. 761, 823.

58. Grinstein, *Rise of the Jewish Community,* pp. 184–185; Marcus, *United States Jewry,* vol. 2, p. 275.

59. Nathan M. Kaganoff, "The Jewish Landsmanshaftn in New York City before World War I," *American Jewish History* 76 (September 1986): 59–61; *Jewish Communal Register,* pp. 180, 241; Rontch, *Idishe landsmanshaften,* p. 283.

3. Landsmanshaft Culture and Immigrant Identities

1. "Vos galitsianerkes zogen vegen rusishe vayber," *Forward,* 16 January 1906.

2. David Blaustein, "The Different Peoples of the Lower East Side," *Seventeenth Annual Report of the University Settlement Society of New York* (1903), p. 8. See also Judd L. Teller, *Strangers and Natives: The Evolution of the American Jew from 1921 to the Present* (New York: Dell, 1968), pp. 5–9.

3. "Pinsk, Karlin—Karlin, Pinsk," in Anshey Pinsk, *25 yohriger yubiley-zhurnal* (1928), reprinted in Isaac E. Rontch, ed., *Di idishe landsmanshaften fun Nyu York* (New York: Yiddish Writers' Union, 1938), p. 166.

4. Elias Tcherikower, *Geshikhte fun der yidisher arbeter bavegung in di fareynikte shtatn* (New York: Yiddish Scientific Institute-Yivo, 1943), vol. 1, p. 320; Bernard Weinstein, *Di idishe yunyons in Amerika: bleter geshikhte un erinerungen* (New York: United Hebrew Trades, 1929), pp. 268–270, 276. Even radicals and nationalists who believed in Jewish or international prole-

tarian unity found it expedient to organize by country or region of origin. On the early radical Am Olam movement, which broke up into communes based on their members' European origins, see A. S. Sachs, *Di geshikhte fun arbayter ring 1892–1925* (New York: National Executive Committee of the Workmen's Circle, 1925), pp. 41–43. On Zionist organization by region of origin see Avyatar Friesel, *Ha-tnuah ha-tsionit ba-artsot-ha-brit ba-shanim 1897–1914* (Tel Aviv: Hakibbutz Hameuchad, 1970), pp. 39–40, 112.

5. Moses Rischin, *The Promised City: New York's Jews 1870–1914* (Cambridge, Mass.: Harvard University Press, 1962), pp. 76–78; Blaustein, "Different Peoples of the Lower East Side," p. 8.

6. Klaus Hödl, *Vom Shtetl an die Lower East Side: Galizische Juden in New York* (Vienna: Böhlau Verlag, 1991), pp. 117–119.

7. Editorial, "Di rumenishe iden," *Tageblat,* 29 March 1908.

8. Z. Kotler, "Di galitsishe iden in Amerika," *Tageblat,* 28 May 1916. A writer in the socialist *Forward* thought the Galician quarter "backwards" and under-developed in comparison with other sections of the Lower East Side. He also remarked on the large numbers of saloons where one could drink mead, the Galicians' favorite beverage. (Russians preferred tea, Romanians wine.) A. Gonikman, "Interesante zakhen in galitsianer kvartal," *Forward,* 23 March 1904.

9. "Farshidene landslayt hoben zeyere farshidene restoranen," *Forward,* 17 January 1914.

10. A. Lemberger, "Di landslayt-korners fun galitsianer kvartal," *Forward,* 17 January 1906; William Bakst (Velfke Rokhl Mikhls), "Ikh bin an oshmener fun Oshmene," in Oshmener B.M.A. un B.A., *45-yoriker yubileum zhurnal* (1937), reprinted in Rontch, *Idishe landsmanshaften,* p. 170; Gershon Tartatski, "Di geshikhte fun yetsies Mitsrayim bay di brikleyers," *Bialistoker fundament* (1935), also reprinted in Rontch, p. 184.

11. S. W., "Draysik yor kalushiner sosayti (di geshikhte fun kalushiner landslayt in Amerika)," in Independent Kalushiner Benevolent Association, *30th Anniversary Banquet* (New York, 1935); Shater Progressive Benevolent Association, *Souvenir Album: 25th Anniversary Jubilee Banquet . . . 1909–1934* (New York, 1934), pp. 16–17; Yankev Hurvits, "Erinerung," in Kamenets Litovsker Untershtitsung Fareyn, *30 yoriker yubiley zhurnal* (1928), and Leon Slonimski, "Historishe iberblik (1888–1938)," in Progressive Brethren of Nieshviez, *50 yoriger yubiley zhurnal* (1938), both reprinted in Rontch, *Di idishe landsman-shaften,* pp. 170, 173.

12. Irving Howe, *World of Our Fathers* (New York: Harcourt Brace Jovanovich, 1976), p. 183.

13. "Shishlivitser landslayt vakht oyf," advertisement, *Tageblat,* 17 March 1909; "Kaminetser podolier landslayt," advertisement for the Kaminetser Podolier Lodge, Knights of the Modern Maccabees, *Tageblat,* 21 May 1909. See also Minutes, 16 September, 7 October 1906, Records of the Satanover Benevolent Society, RG 818, YIVO; Minutes, 24 April 1897; 7 July 1898, Records of the Gluboker Benevolent Association, RG 1111, YIVO.

14. Minutes, 16 September, 7 October 1906, Satanover Benevolent Society.

15. Avrom Ellis, "Di Tshigriner progresiv benevolent asosieyshon," in Chigriner-Alexandrowker Benevolent Society, *Twentieth Anniversary* (New York, 1936).

16. There is no record that such a society ever actually existed. Lemberger, "Landslayt-korners."

17. For a comment on organizations with funny names, see Alexander Harkavy, "Khevres un fareynen mit komishe nemen," *Minikes yom-tov bleter: shvues,* June 1902. Harkvay mentions the Orders of the Garter, the Bath, the Fleece, and the Thistle, as well as the Kit-Kat Club, the Know Nothings, and the Odd Fellows.

18. Samuel Schoenfeld, *Zikhroynes fun a shriftzetser* (New York: Yiddish Scientific Institute-Yivo, 1946), p. 50.

19. Ellis, "Tchigriner progresiv benevolent asosieyshon"; Samuel Tucker, "A Little History from a Pioneer," Louis Tentchin, "Erinerungen fun a grinder," and I. S., "Half a Century," in Progressive Slutzker Young Men's Benevolent Association, *50th Anniversary Banquet* (New York, 1954), pp. 24, 95, 14–15; Minutes, 3 October, 11 October 1903, Satanover Benevolent Society.

20. Nathan Kaganoff, "The Jewish Landsmanshaftn in New York City in the Period Preceding World War I," *American Jewish History* 76 (September 1986): 64; Bakst, "Ikh bin an oshmener," p. 170.

21. For the Proskurover see Susan Milamed, "Proskurover Landsmanshaftn: A Case Study in Jewish Communal Development," *American Jewish History* 76 (September 1986): 40–55.

22. Some historians, most notably Michael Weisser, have suggested that immigrants from large cities were less likely to combine in landsmanshaftn than the less sophisticated natives of small towns. This is clearly not the case. See Michael R. Weisser, *A Brotherhood of Memory: Jewish Landsmanshaftn in the New World* (New York: Basic Books, 1985), pp. 18–20.

23. "Farshiedene landslayt hoben zeyere farshiedine restoranen," *Forward,* 17 January 1914. Concerning organizational politics in the landsmanshaft cafes see also Gershom Bader, "Di galitsishe-ungarishe 'kibetsarnie,'" *Tageblat,* 28 August 1913.

24. For the Bialystoker landsmanshaftn see D. S., "Di bialistoker landsmanshaften fun Nyu York," in Rontch, *Idishe landsmanshaften,* pp. 121–122; see also pp. 259–260 for a list. On incorporations, see Kaganoff, "Jewish Landsmanshaftn," p. 60. Twenty-one Cracow societies, nineteen Warsaw groups, and sixteen Bialystok organizations incorporated in the same period. Of course, many societies never incorporated at all. On the large Minsker societies, see "Yontef baym minsker fareyn," 20 March 1912, and "Groyser yontef bay minsker landslayte," 23 June 1912, both in the *Tageblat.*

25. On periodization, see B. Rivkin, "Di sotsiale role fun di landsmanshaften," in Rontch, *Idishe landsmanshaften,* p. 72. For a somewhat more complex scheme of categories see Isaac E. Rontch, "Der itstiker matsev fun di landsmanshaften," in the same volume, pp. 9–23. For an English version of the latter, see Hannah Kliger, ed., *Jewish Hometown Associations and Family Circles in New York: The WPA Yiddish Writers' Group Study* (Bloomington: Indiana University Press, 1992), pp. 31–34.

26. Tcherikower, *Geshikhte*, p. 322; *The Jewish Communal Register of New York City 1917–1918* (New York: Kehillah (Jewish Community) of New York City, 1918), table following page 122. The governmental census of religious institutions in 1910 found 720 Jewish congregations in New York. See "Idishe kongregeyshons un shulen in Amerike," *Tageblat*, 23 September 1910.

27. For example, the Odesser congregation which Samuel Schoenfeld's father joined in the 1890s. Schoenfeld, *Zikhroynes*, p. 43.

28. Jo Renee Fine and Gerard R. Wolfe, *The Synagogues of New York's Lower East Side* (New York: Washington Mews Books-New York University Press, 1978), p. 31. Fine and Wolfe cite a 1905 survey which made an actual count of 350 congregations, including 48 in buildings originally built as synagogues and 12 in converted churches. Similarly, the New York Kehillah found in 1917 that only 77 of the 435 congregations on the Lower East Side had buildings of their own. *Jewish Communal Register*, table following page 122.

29. Minutes, 30 June 1906; 27 February, 27 March 1909; 1 October 1910; 29 January 1916, Records of Congregation Ahavath Zedek Anshei Timkowitz, RG 840, YIVO; *Jewish Progress* (in English, New York, n.d. [ca.1906]); *Jewish Communal Register*, pp. 155, 228. Congregation Bnai Jacob Anshai Brzezon, with its own building at 180 Stanton Street, hosted at least three smaller Galician societies. This building was still in use as a synagogue in 1993. *Jewish Communal Register*, pp. 181, 194, 200, 208.

30. "Khanukas habayis un a vinkelshteyn," 22 February 1909; "Khanukas habayis der nayer shul fun khevre makover ov Poyln," 21 May 1909; "Khanukas habayis fun di makover shul," 29 May 1909, all in *Tageblat; Jewish Communal Register*, 218. For a similar event, see "Khanukas habayis fun bialistoker shul," 9 September 1910, and "Der khanukas habayis bay di bialistoker," 12 September 1910, both in *Tageblat*.

31. "Der Payk Strit shul," *Tageblat*, 7 March 1904. See Fine and Wolfe, *The Synagogues of New York's Lower East Side*.

32. Y. R. Rips, "Di geshikhte fun unzer kongregeyshon," Congregation of the People of the City of Bobruisk, *30th Anniversary* (New York, 1929).

33. Jonathan Sarna, *People Walk on Their Heads: Moses Weinberger's Jews and Judaism in New York* (New York: Holmes and Meier, 1982), p. 44.

34. Quoted in E. Verschleiser, "Di konstitutsies fun di landsmanshaften," in Rontch, *Idishe landsmanshaften*, p. 50.

35. Gershom Bader, "Funm amerikaner Galitsien," *Tageblat*, 30 August 1912.

36. *Tsvishen blut un fayer* (New York: Federation of Galician and Bucovinean Jews of America, 1916), p. 70; Teller, *Natives and Strangers*, p. 73.

37. Minutes, 20 April, 3 August 1907; 8 August 1908; 7 August 1909, Congregation Ahavath Zedek Anshei Timkowitz.

38. Regarding rabbis, see Menahem Blondheim, "The American Orthodox Rabbinate, 1881–1914: Pages from the Book of Numbers," unpublished paper, Scholars' Conference on American Jewish History and Life, Waltham, Mass., June 1994.

39. *Yudishe gazeten*, 31 July 1891. See also Jeffrey Gurock, "The Orthodox Synagogue," in *The American Synagogue: A Sanctuary Transformed*, ed. Jack

Wertheimer (New York: Cambridge University Press, 1987), pp. 49–50; Sarna, *People Walk on Their Heads,* p. 99.

40. Verschleiser, "Di konstitutsies," p. 50. See also Gurock, "Orthodox Synagogue," pp. 51–52; Zvi Hirsch Masliansky, *Maslianski's zikhroynes: fiehrtsig yohr leben un kemfen* (New York: Farlag Zerubavel, 1924), p. 195.

41. It is interesting to compare this assurance with efforts by Catholic fraternalists to reconcile their interest in similar rituals with their loyalty to the church. *Konstitutsion di ershte radimnoer khevre bney Mordkhe Menakhem* (New York, 1910), pp. 5–10. See also Verschleiser, "Di konstitutsies," p. 44; an English translation appears in Kliger, *Jewish Hometown Societies,* p. 59.

42. Sarna, *People Walk on Their Heads,* pp. 43–44.

43. See, for example, the election of a shamas by a vote of 60–23 in the Timkovitser Congregation. Minutes, 2 March, 9 March, 25 May 1907, Congregation Ahavath Zedek Anshei Timkowitz. See also Verschleiser, "Di konstitutsies," pp. 50–51.

44. Sarna, *People Walk on Their Heads,* p. 45.

45. Minutes, 8 November 1913, Congregation Ahavath Zedek Anshei Timkowitz.

46. On the crisis of Orthodoxy, see Gerald Sorin, *A Time for Building: The Third Migration 1880–1920* (Baltimore: Johns Hopkins University Press, 1992), pp. 174–181. One contemporary social worker estimated that 40% of the adult Jewish population of the Lower East Side were members of a congregation, but this is probably an exaggeration (even if only men are counted). James T. Gerould, "The Social Side of Synagogue Life," *Yearbook of the University Settlement Society of New York* (1899), p. 29. The Kehillah survey in 1917 found a synagogue membership on the Lower East Side of just over 50,000. This may very well have been an undercount, since not all congregations were recorded. *Jewish Communal Register,* table following page 122.

47. Isaac Levitats, "The Jewish Association in America," in *Essays on Jewish Life and Thought* (New York: Columbia University Press, 1959), pp. 344–345. There are twelve national orders listed in *Jewish Communal Register,* pp. 865–985. The twelve orders, including the Workmen's Circle and the Jewish National Workers' Alliance, claimed a total membership of 456,000 nationwide and 162,000 in New York City.

48. Deborah Dash Moore, *B'nai B'rith and the Challenge of Ethnic Leadership* (Albany: SUNY Press, 1981), pp. 7, 55–56; Edward E. Grusd, *B'nai B'rith: The Story of a Covenant* (New York: Appleton-Century, 1966), pp. 88–90.

49. *Jewish Communal Directory* (New York: Jewish Community (Kehillah) of New York City, 1912), pp. 22–24; *Jewish Communal Register,* pp. 865–985; advertisements for Brith Sholom and Ahavas Israel, *Amerikaner,* 2 October 1908, p. 29.

50. B. Shelvin, *History of the Independent Order Brith Abraham 1887–1937* (New York: Independent Order Brith Abraham, 1937), pp. 24–27, 34. *Jewish Communal Register,* pp. 888–934.

51. Estimates of the annual dues vary and of course differ from year to year. In 1907 average dues in Order Brith Abraham were $16. In 1917 it cost a member $16 a year in Independent Order Brith Sholom and $15 a year in Independent

Order Brith Abraham. In that year the average dues for a local society were $6. *Jewish Communal Register,* pp. 735, 888, 935; Order Brith Abraham, *Brief History (Message from Samuel Dorf, Grand Master)* (New York, 1907), p. 5. See also Jacob Massel, "Di idishe ordens in Amerika—di materiele un gaystige nutsen vos di ordens brengen," *Amerikaner,* 12 February 1909, p. 5.

52. Richard H. Lane, "East Side Beneficiary Societies," *Yearbook of the University Settlement Society of New York* (1899), p. 28; Rivkin, "Di sotsiale role," pp. 75, 78.

53. Leo Wolfson, "Jewish Fraternal Organizations," in *Jewish Communal Register,* p. 865; Order Brith Abraham, *Brief History,* p. 3; Independent Order Brith Abraham, *Report of the Grand Master Max Stern to the XXI Annual Convention . . .* (New York, 1908), pp. 39–40. One journalist also referred to the orders as "schools" and "academies" for good citizenship. Y. Tsioni, "Di konvenshon fun ind. order bris Avrom," *Amerikaner,* 20 May 1910, p. 4.

54. Shneyerzohn, "Fun vanen shtamen di fri-meysons (fray-moyerer)," *Amerikaner,* 17 May 1907, p. 8.

55. Jacob Massel, "Idishe benefit sosayetis in Amerika," *Amerikaner,* 15 January 1909, p. 5.

56. The following description is based on the Yiddish version of the ritual, *Ritual fun dem independent orden bris Avrom* (New York, n.d.), which would have been used by many of the Eastern European landsmanshaft branches. Quotes are taken from the English edition, *Ritual of the Independent Order Brith Abraham* (New York, 1940), unless it differs from the Yiddish version, in which case the Yiddish version is followed. In general the two versions are similar, though there are some differences which cannot be attributed to translation. The English booklet includes an alternate initiation ritual not included in the Yiddish, which, though undated, appears to have been published earlier. In addition to the long initiation ceremony discussed here, both versions include a short initiation ceremony, a ritual for installation of officers, and funeral and memorial services.

57. "Kristlekhe tfiles un tseremonies fir a idishen orden," *Tageblat,* 4 June 1912. The ritual described in the editorial seems similar in most respects to the version presented here, though there are a few elements that seem to have been deleted from the above editions.

58. *Jewish Communal Register,* p. 869; Rontch, *Idishe landsmanshaften,* p. 32.

59. In 1917, the JNWA had 23 or 24 New York branches, and B'nai Zion, 21. *Jewish Communal Register,* pp. 961–964, 980–983; L. Shpizman, "Etapn in der geshikhte fun der tsienistisher arbeter-bavegung in di fareynikte shtatn," in *Geshikhte fun der tsienistisher arbeter bavegung in Tsofen Amerike* (New York: Yiddisher Kemfer, 1955), vol. 1, pp. 236–250.

60. See Sachs, *Geshikhte,* especially pp. 3–6, 77.

61. For example, see Y. V-B., "Fraternal sosayetis," in *Der arbayter ring zamel-bukh* (New York: Workmen's Circle, 1910), pp. 228–236.

62. Sachs, *Geshikhte,* pp. 76–77.

63. Report of National Executive Committee to the second convention, quoted in Sachs, *Geshikhte,* p. 181.

64. Ibid., pp. 134–136.

65. Ibid., p. 139; J. S. Hertz, *50 yor arbeter-ring in yidishn lebn* (New York: National Executive Committee of the Workmen's Circle), p. 69; Rivkin, "Sotsiale role," p. 84.

66. Of the 164 Workmen's Circle branches which responded to the 1938 WPA landsmanshaft survey, 25 were established between 1902 and 1905, and 85 between 1906 and 1910. See Rontch, *Idishe landsmanshaften,* p. 32 (statistical table), pp. 247–361 (roster with founding dates), pp. 379–382 (list of Workmen's Circle branches, in English). For Workmen's Circle membership figures, see Melech Epstein, *Jewish Labor in U.S.A.* (1950, rpt. New York: Ktav Publishing House, 1969), vol. 1, p. 304.

67. See Hertz, *50 yor,* pp. 65–66.

68. Z. Shpayer, "Fuftsik yor dvinsker bund brentsh 75 arbeter ring," Dvinsker Bundisher Brentsh 75, Arbeter Ring, *50 yoriger goldener yubiley* (New York, 1954).

69. Meyer Kushner, *Lebn un kamf fun a kloukmakher* (New York: A Committee of Local 9, ILGWU, 1960), pp. 70–73.

70. Minutes of the Golter-Bogopolier Yugnt, 19 July 1908 to 13 December 1908, included in the minutes of Branch 301, Records of the Workmen's Circle, RG 575, YIVO.

71. Ben-Eliezer, "Vi azoy unzer brentsh iz gegrindet gevorn," in *Lodzer almanakh* (New York: Workmen's Circle, Lodzer Branch 324, 1934), pp. 5–6.

72. Kushner, *Lebn un kamf,* p. 81.

73. By 1938, 50% of the members of Branch 301 were non-Zherdover, while, despite Meyer Kushner's recollections, only 7% of the "friends" in Branch 63 were non-Kremenchuger. Minutes, 15 January, 22 January, 30 April 1909; 20 October 1911, Branch 301, Records of Workmen's Circle. Rontch, *Idishe landsmanshaften,* pp. 290, 347.

74. Ben-Eliezer, "Vi azoy unzer brentsh iz gegrindet gevorn," p. 6–7.

75. S. Rudovski, "Di amolike tetikeytn fun brentsh," and Kon, "Finf un tsvantsik yor," in *Bialistoker fraynd* (February 1930), pp. 12–13, 35.

76. S. W., "Draysik yor kalushiner sosayti," and "Thirty Years of Organized Kalushiner."

77. Bakst, "Ikh bin an Oshmener," p. 168.

78. For passwords, see minutes, 11 October 1903; 15 March 1908; 18 July 1909; 5 February, 2 July 1911, Satanover Benevolent Society. The First Mikulinzer Lodge 556, IOBA, also used Hebrew passwords. Minutes, 9 March 1910; 6 January 1912, Records of First Independent Mikulincer Sick Benevolent Association, RG 828, YIVO.

79. Bakst, "Ikh bin an Oshmener," p. 168.

80. Minutes, 11 October 1903, Satanover Benevolent Society. The hand signals remained virtually unchanged and are included in the printed constitution issued by the society in 1937. The Gluboker Benevolent Association had identical gavel signals. Its password was "order," perhaps an admonition to keep it. Minutes, 28 October, 25 November 1893, Gluboker Benevolent Association.

81. Minutes, 12 November, 3 December, 31 December 1905; meeting mistakenly dated 8 March 1906, probably actually 8 April, 18 November, 2 December, 16 December 1906; 2 July 1907, Satanover Benevolent Society.

82. This Germanic Yiddish came to be known as *"daytshmerish."* Leon Kobrin, *Fun daytshmerish tsu yidish in Amerike* (New York: YCUF, 1944); Christopher Hutton, "Normativism and the Notion of Authenticity in Yiddish Linguistics," in David Goldberg, ed., *The Field of Yiddish: Studies in Language, Folklore, and Literature* (Fifth Collection, Evanston: Northwestern University Press and the YIVO Institute for Jewish Research, 1993), pp. 14–28; Benjamin Harshav, *The Meaning of Yiddish* (Berkeley: University of California Press, 1990), pp. 61–73.

83. Jacob Pfeffer, "Meshoynediger idish in di fereynen un lodzhen," *Amerikaner,* 22 November 1907, p. 18. On daytshmerish in the orders, see Jacob Massel, "Di id. ord. in Amerika—di frage fun 'idish' bay di konvenshons," *Amerikaner,* 5 March 1909, p. 14.

84. Bakst, "Ikh bin an Oshmener," pp. 168–169.

85. Rontch, "Der itstiker matsev," pp. 18–19; M. Berger, "History of the Society"; Lynn Dumenil, *Freemasonry and American Culture 1880–1930* (Princeton: Princeton University Press, 1984), pp. xiii, 148, 161–164, 187–189, 216.

86. See, for example, *Konstitushon fun di ershte komarover untershtitsungs fareyn* (New York, n.d.), pp. 49–52, and *Konstitushon der ind. mlaver kranken unt. fareyn* (New York, includes amendments made 1917), pp. 40–42. Rontch even includes a hybrid category, "mutual aid societies connected with synagogues," of which there were 41 in 1938. Rontch, *Idishe landsmanshaften,* p. 29.

87. Minutes, 23 August 1895; 11 July, 1 August 1896, Gluboker Benevolent Association.

88. Minutes, 1 October 1905, Satanover Benevolent Society.

89. The comment on the private nature of religious practice and belief came in the course of a debate over the fate of a Torah scroll evidently owned privately by a group of brothers who met together to pray. Minutes, 7 August, 21 August, 2 October 1910, Satanover Benevolent Society.

90. *Konstitushon fun gluboker untershtitsungs fareyn* (New York, as amended 1926), p. 7. See also *Constitution of the Satanover Benevolent Society* (New York, 1937), p. 19.

91. On landsmanshaft constitutions, see Verschleiser, "Di konstitutsies," pp. 43–51, or the English version in Kliger, *Jewish Hometown Associations,* pp. 58–66. It was some time before the Satanover Society actually adopted a constitution. For its particularly long and drawn out process, see Minutes, 3 March, 7 April 1907; 18 September 1910; 2 July, 20 August, 5 November, 19 November, 9 December, 17 December 1911; 7 January, 3 March, 17 March, 5 May 1912, Satanover Benevolent Society.

92. Arlekin, An., *Far yeden member: a noytvendig hand-bukh far members fun lodzhen, sosayetis, yunyons, a.r. brentshes, soyrkls, klubs un ale meglikhe fareynen* (New York: Progress Publishing, 1914). *Far yedn member* was 36 pages long and sold for 12 cents.

93. See the series by the pseudonymous Avner in *Amerikaner:* "Vi azoy men darf fihren a miting," 18 June; "Organizatsion un konstitushon," 25 June; "Der prezident," 2 July; "Di beamte," 9 July; "Di mitglider," 16 July; "Spetsiel farzamlungen," 23 July; "Di debate," 30 July; "Forshlege un amendments," 6 August; "Fershidene forshlege," 20 August; "Vider vegn forshlege," 27 August 1905.

94. Avner, "Vi azoy men darf fihren a miting"; *Koshing's hand-bukh fun parlamentarishe rulings: regelen un forshriften vi tsu fihren farzamlungen un mitingen fun lodzhes, fareynen, khevres, sosayetis un organizatsionen,* trans. A. Tanenbaum (New York: Hebrew Publishing Company, 1914); advertisement in *Minikes Yom-tov bleter: shvues blat,* June 1900, p. 27, headed "Der kompus fir mitingen," for *Kushings hantbukh far parliamentarishes praktis.* Published by Yehudah Katsenelenboygn at 66 Canal Street, this edition sold for 25 cents. Journalist and historian Judd Teller comments on the use of Cushing's rules among the landsmanshaftn: "Its proceedings followed Cushing's Manual of Parliamentary Rules, although it is a mystery how they discovered its existence." Teller, *Natives and Strangers,* p. 15. E. Verschleiser also singles out Cushing's in "Di konstitutsies," p. 49, in English in Kliger, *Jewish Hometown Associations,* p. 65.

95. *Parlamentarishe ruls: vi tsu fihren mitingen fun yunyons, lodzhen un andere fareynen, bearbaytet nokh di beste bikher mekoyekh parlamentarizmus* (New York: Arbeiter Zeitung, 1891). Quotes are from pages 3, 5, and 4 respectively.

96. Bernard Modell, *Parliamentarishe gezetse. Klalim un erklerungen vi tsu organiziren sosayetis, vi tsu zayn prezident oder sekretar, es erklert oykh iber der farvaltung fun der amerikanisher regirung, ales daytlekh erklert un in a ontsiender shprakhe geshriben* (New York: Printed by A. Zunser, n.d.). Quote is from page 4.

97. See a number of articles in *Amerikaner:* Jacob Massel, "Idishe benefit sosayetis in Amerika—di stsenes bay mitings," 22 January 1909, p. 5; J. Pfeffer, "Halt zikh in ordenung!," 12 January 1906 (misdated 1905), p. 4; Y. Tsioni, "Di konvenshon fun ind. order bris Avrom," 20 May 1910, p. 4. The Socialist *Forward* was almost gleeful when it could report on disorder in conservative societies and saw that as evidence of their depravity. See "Klep in 'vilner fereyn,'" 23 December 1897.

98. *Minikes yom-tov bleter: shvues blat,* June 1900.

99. Circular, "An oyfruf tsu ale shpoler landslayt," 8 October 1902, Landsmanshaft Subject Collection, RG 123, YIVO. For recollections of similar situations, see "Bagrisung fun vays prezident, Chaim Schnitzer," and other greetings in Chmielniker Sick and Benevolent Society of Poland, Inc., *Suvenir zhurnal* (New York, 1931); Yoysef Blushteyn, "Di grindung un entviklung fun der independent loytsker eyd sosayeti," *Independent Lutzker Untershtitsung Fareyn,* 1927.

100. Minutes, 31 December 1905, Satanover Benevolent Society.

101. Minutes, 31 December 1905, Satanover Benevolent Society; Meretzer Relief Association, *Konstitushon* (New York, adopted 1919), p. 19.

102. Minutes of Congregation Ahavath Zedek Anshei Timkowitz. Slonimer and Grodner examples from 14 October 1916 and 22 September 1918, respec-

tively. Similarly, between 1903 and 1916, of the 89 applicants to the Satanover Benevolent Society whose places of origin are listed, 63% were Satanover, 6% "Satanover sons-in-law," and 33% non-landslayt, though many of these were from nearby areas. When the WPA carried out its survey in 1938, some 30% of all landsmanshaft membership consisted of non-landslayt. Rontch, "Der itstiker matsev," p. 17; Kliger, *Jewish Hometown Associations,* p. 36.

103. Verschleiser, "Di konstitutsies," pp. 47–48; Kliger, *Jewish Hometown Associations,* pp. 62–63; Independent Dobriner Benevolent Society of New York, *Konstitutsion* (New York, n.d.), pp. 8–10; Meretzer Relief Association, *Konstitushon,* pp. 17–19; Ershte Komorover Untershtitsungs Fareyn, *Konstitushon,* pp. 11–15; Independent Mlaver Krankn Untershtitsungs Fareyn, *Konstitushon,* pp. 7–10; Minutes of Congregation Ahavath Zedek Anshei Timkowitz, 1906–1916. Of 166 candidates only two were rejected by the doctor, four reported not suitable by committee, one blackballed, and four rejected for other reasons. Of 110 candidates for the Satanover Society who were clearly recorded as accepted or rejected, only seven were rejected, including only one blackballed. Minutes of Satanover Benevolent Society, 1903–1916.

104. Kh. Malits (Dr. Meyerson), "Idishe lodzhen un khevres," *Amerikaner,* 16 November 1906, p. 5; Anzia Yezierska, *Bread Givers* (1925; rpt. New York: Persea Books, 1975), 89–90, 257–268.

105. *Constitution of the Independent Order Brith Abraham of the United States of America* (1904), p. 56.

106. Lane, "East Side Benefit Societies," p. 27.

107. *Jewish Communal Register,* pp. 888–934, chart following page 108.

108. Ibid.; Rontch, *Idishe landsmanshaften,* p. 30; "Minsker leydis benevolent ass'n," *Tageblat,* 9 March 1916; *Jewish Communal Register,* p. 750.

109. Certificate of Incorporation, Nowoselitzer Ladies' Sick and Benevolent Society, Landsmanshaft Subject Collection.

110. The WPA group surveyed 23 ladies' auxiliaries founded before 1920, and 264 between 1920 and 1937. Rontch, *Idishe landsmanshaften,* p. 29.

111. Minutes, 2 November 1912; 23 May, 2 December 1914; 16 January 1915; 13 January 1917, Congregation Ahavath Zedek Anshei Timkowitz.

112. The *Forward* editorial announced the paper's shift to a position in favor of the Workmen's Circle especially. *Forward,* 9 May 1902.

113. Malits (Dr. Meyerson), "Idishe lodzhen un khevres."

114. Minutes of Branch 301 (including the Golter-Bogopolier Yugnt), 1908–1916, Records of the Workmen's Circle.

4. Brothers in Need

1. Michael B. Katz, *In the Shadow of the Poorhouse: A Social History of Welfare in America* (New York: Basic Books, 1986), pp. xi–xii. Daniel Levine makes a similar point in *Poverty and Society: The Growth of the American Welfare State in International Comparison* (New Brunswick, N.J.: Rutgers University Press, 1988), pp. 15–17.

2. On issues of gender in relation to attitudes toward poverty, dependence, and social welfare, see the essays in Linda Gordon, ed., *Women, the State, and Welfare* (Madison: University of Wisconsin Press, 1990); Linda Gordon, "Social Insurance and Public Assistance: The Influence of Gender in Welfare Thought in the United States, 1890–1935," *American Historical Review* 97 (February 1992): 19–54. Despite the efforts of some scholars to create a state-centered approach to the history of social welfare, the state, unlike private charity, was conspicuously absent from landsmanshaft considerations. See Theda Skocpol, *Protecting Soldiers and Mothers: The Political Origins of Social Policy in the United States* (Cambridge, Mass.: Harvard University Press, 1994). For a view of mutual aid societies as an alternative to government programs, see David T. Beito, "Mutual Aid for Social Welfare: The Case of American Fraternal Societies," *Critical Review* 4 (Fall 1990): 709–736.

3. M. Berger, "History of the Society," in First Yezierzaner Sick Benevolent Association, *Fortieth Anniversary Banquet* (New York, 1938). For a similar statement see Gershon Sherman, "Dos lebn fun kongregeyshon pukhovitser," reprinted in Isaac E. Rontch, ed., *Di idishe landsmanshaften fun Nyu York* (New York: Yiddish Writers Union, 1938), p. 164.

4. "Unzere shterer," *Idisher gayst*, October 1910, p. 1. *Idisher gayst* was the organ of the Federation of Roumanian Jews.

5. Jacob Massel, "Idishe benefit sosayetis in Amerika," *Amerikaner*, 1 January 1909, p. 5; 8 January 1909, p. 4.

6. A. Liessin, "Der arbayter ring, zayn vuks un zayne oyfgaben," in *Der arbayter ring zamelbukh: sovenir der tsehnter konvenshon gevidmet* (New York, 1910), pp. 6–7.

7. Massel, "Idishe benefit sosayetis," 1 January 1909, p. 4.

8. Jonathan Sarna, *People Walk on Their Heads: Moses Weinberger's Jews and Judaism in New York* (New York: Holmes and Meier, 1982), pp. 87–88.

9. Bernard Weinstein, *Fertsig yohr in der idisher arbayter bavegung (bletlakh erinerungen)* (New York: Farlag Veker, 1924), pp. 214–215.

10. Y. Weintraub, "Inshurens sosayetis un zeyer grund-gedank," *Forward*, 14 October 1908; "Geshprekhen mit forshtehers fun di vikhtigste idishe ordens," *Forward*, 7 December 1908. For similar arguments by other Workmen's Circle activists, see Liliput, "Der arbayter-ring: zayn vuks, zayn oyftu un zayne vaytere oyfgaben," and Y. Salutsky, "Kranken-benefit un klasen-kamf," in *Der arbayter ring zamelbukh*, pp. 200–203, 39–51 respectively. Rabbi Mayer Berlin, leader of the Religious Zionist movement, even argued that world Jewry should organize itself like one big mutual aid association. M. Berlin, "Gegenzaytige hilf," *Tageblat*, 14 May 1915.

11. Independent Drobniner Benevolent Society, *Konstitutsion* (New York, n.d.), p. 29 (Yiddish section), p. 25 (English section); E. Verschleiser, "Di landsmanshaft konstitutsies," in Rontch, *Idishe landsmanshaften*, p. 49, in English in *Jewish Hometown Associations and Family Circles in New York: The WPA Yiddish Writers' Group Study*, ed. Hannah Kliger (Bloomington: Indiana University Press, 1992), p. 64.

12. Z. B. Komayko, "A farbrekhen fun lodzhes," *Amerikaner*, 1 May 1908, p. 12.

For several such instances see minutes, 22 June 1912; 10 March 1917; 22 February 1919, Records of Congregation Ahavath Zedek Anshei Timkowitz, RG 840, YIVO.

13. Susan A. Glenn, *Daughters of the Shtetl: Life and Labor in the Immigrant Generation* (Ithaca: Cornell University Press, 1990), 64–67, 76–79.

14. Samuel Schoenfeld, *Zikhroynes fun a shriftzetser* (New York: Yiddish Scientific Institute-Yivo, 1946), p. 47.

15. Minutes, 4 June 1905; 15 May 1910, Records of Satanover Benevolent Society, RG 818, YIVO; minutes, 28 May 1910, Congregation Ahavath Zedek Anshei Timkowitz; Congregation B'nai Rappaport Anshei Dombrowa, *Konstitutsion und neben gezetse* (New York, as amended 1917), p. 31; Independent Mlaver Kranken Unt. Fereyn, *Konstitushon* (New York, includes amendments of 1917), p. 26; Ershte Komarover Untershtitsungs Fereyn, *Konstitushon* (New York, n.d.), pp. 35–36.

16. A. S. Sachs, *Di geshikhte fun arbayter ring, 1892–1925* (New York: National Executive Committee of Workmen's Circle, 1925), vol. 1, pp. 214–215, 232, 253, 320, 411.

17. Frank F. Rosenblatt, "Mutual Aid Organizations," in *The Jewish Communal Register of New York City 1917–1918* (New York: Kehillah (Jewish Community) of New York, 1918), pp. 732–734.

18. P. Wiernik, "Tsu keyn fareyn belang ikh nit," *Amerikaner,* 4 June 1909, p. 1.

19. See Arthur Goren, "Traditional Institutions Transplanted: The Hevra Kadisha in Europe and in America," in Moses Rischin, ed., *The Jews of North America* (Detroit: Wayne State University Press, 1987), pp. 65–66.

20. Zvi Hirsch Masliansky, *Maslianski's zikhroynes: fiehrtsig yohr leben un kemfen* (New York: Farlag Zerubavel, 1924), p. 195.

21. Robert Chapin, *The Standard of Living Among Workingmen's Families in New York City* (1909, rpt. New York: Arno Press, 1971), p. 194.

22. Louise Bolard More, *Wage Earners' Budgets: A Study of Standards and Costs of Living in New York City* (New York: H. Holt, 1907), pp. 42–43, 103–105, 145.

23. Yankev Hurvits, "Erinerungen," in Kamenets Litovsker Untershtitsung Fareyn, *30 yoriger yubiley-zhurnal,* 1928, reprinted in Rontch, *Idishe landsmanshaften,* p. 170.

24. See James J. Farrell, *Inventing the American Way of Death, 1830–1920* (Philadelphia: Temple University Press, 1980), quote on pp. 106–107.

25. *Yudishe gazeten,* 11 June 1891, p. 8.

26. Leon Slonimsky, "Historisher iberblik (1888–1938)," in *50 yoriger yubiley zhurnal progresiv bredren ov Nieshviez,* 1938, reprinted in Rontch, *Idishe landsmanshaften,* p. 174.

27. Farrell, *Inventing the American Way of Death,* pp. 115, 133.

28. Other ethnic groups also used their cemeteries as social centers. See the example of the Bohemian National Cemetery in Chicago, in Farrell, *Inventing the American Way of Death,* p. 219.

29. Minutes, undated special meeting in April or May 1905, 4 June, 2 July 1905, Satanover Benevolent Society.

30. Y. L. Dolidanski, "Farshvekhung fun kvorim," *Tageblat* (?) 9 August 1911, clipping in Papers of Judah L. Magnes, folder P3/1912, Central Archives for the History of the Jewish People.

31. Resolution of 1912 Kehillah convention; letter, Bernard Richards to cemeteries, 8 July 1912; letter, Samuel B. Hamburger to Bernard Richards, 11 July 1912, all in folder P3/1913, Magnes Papers. See also an article in the *Forward*, which almost gleefully reports a fight between a Galician society and a Russian group which had stolen the Galicians' food. The radical *Forward* enjoyed pointing out the depravity of conservative societies. "A milkhome tsvishen Estraykh un Rusland oyf a higer semeteri," *Forward,* 9 July 1904.

32. The arch was to carry the society name in raised Hebrew letters, while the name in English was to appear on the fence. Contract, May 1914, Landsmanshaft Subject Collection, RG 123, YIVO.

33. Minutes, 17 August, 7 September 1913; 18 January, 1 February, 5 April, 19 April, 21 June 1914; 5 November, 19 November, 3 December 1916; 7 January, 18 March, 15 April, 6 May, 17 June, 1 July 1917, Satanover Benevolent Society.

34. Independent Mlaver, *Konstitushon,* pp. 24–26. These provisions were typical. See Verschleiser, "Di konstitutsies," pp. 46, 49; minutes, special meeting in April or May 1905 (meeting number 37, undated), Satanover Benevolent Society. Estimates vary concerning how much a working-class funeral in New York might cost. In 1897 a writer for the *Evening World* reckoned that expenses might amount to $140 (including $70 for the casket, $30 for five coaches, and $10.50 for the hearse). Cited in Irving Howe, *World of Our Fathers* (New York: Harcourt Brace Jovanich, 1976), p. 221. However, the following year, another writer, an advocate of cremation and therefore likely to overestimate the cost of burial, figured that burial for the poor in New York should cost about $55 ($27 for grave and coffin, $16 for hearse and coach, $9 for shroud and ice, and $3 for the undertaker and miscellaneous). Cited in Farrell, *Inventing the American Way of Death,* p. 165. More found an average cost of $115 ($94 for Americans, $135 for foreigners). More, *Wage Earners' Budgets,* p. 103. But Chapin found a range for an adult's funeral from $65 to $130. Chapin, *Standard of Living,* p. 222.

35. Minutes, 1 December 1912, Satanover Benevolent Society.

36. Records of the First Soroker Bessarabier Mutual Aid Society, RG 832, YIVO. See also minutes, 4 May 1907, 6 November 1909, 2 December 1911, 2 November 1912, Congregation Ahavath Zedek Anshei Timkowitz; Congregation B'nai Rappaport Anshei Dombrowa, *Konstitutsion,* pp. 37–38; Verschleiser, "Konstitutsies," p. 51.

37. When a hevrah kadisha member did do his duty, he could be assured that incidental personal damages would be taken care of by the Congregation. For example, when Shimon Dovid Grinberg dropped his "specs with gilded frames" into an open grave, the Congregation reimbursed him for his loss. Minutes, 15 December 1906; 7 September 1907; 15 February 1913, Congregation Ahavath Zedek Anshei Timkowitz.

38. Goren, "Traditional Institutions Transplanted," p. 71; Judd Teller, *Strangers and Natives: The Evolution of the American Jew from 1921 to the Present*

(New York: Dell, 1968), p. 93; minutes, 28 December 1918, Congregation Ahavath Zedek Anshei Timkowitz.

39. Like the sick committee, the shivah committee was also charged with making sure that the mourning member was actually sitting shivah and therefore missing work and in need of the benefit. Verschleiser, "Di konstitutsies," pp. 48–49; minutes, 20 February 1910, Satanover Benevolent Society; minutes, 16 June 1906; 6 July 1907; 21 November 1908; 31 July 1909, Congregation Ahavath Zedek Anshei Timkowitz.

40. Quoted in Farrell, *Inventing the American Way of Death,* p. 133.

41. Independent Drobniner, *Konstitutsion,* 20–21; Ershte Komarover, *Konstitushon,* pp. 33–34; minutes of special meeting in April or May 1905 (meeting number 37, undated), Satanover Benevolent Society; Verschleiser, "Di konstitutsies," p. 49; notarized receipt, 25 January 1915, First Prailer Benevolent Association, Landsmanshaft Subject Collection; minutes, 27 April 1912; 28 April 1918, Congregation Ahavath Zedek Anshei Timkowitz; Farrell, *Inventing the American Way of Death,* pp. 71–73; Chapin, *Standard of Living,* pp. 191–193.

42. Leo Wolfson, "Jewish Fraternal Organizations," in *Jewish Communal Register,* p. 866. Also pages 871, 888, 935, 950, 956, 957, 958, 961, 965, 980, 984 in the same volume.

43. See B. Rivkin, "Di sotsiale role fun di landsmanshaften," in Rontch, *Idishe landsmanshaften,* p. 76; Rosenblatt, "Mutual Aid Organizations," p. 733; H. Plotkin, *Fraternalizm un inshurens: populer-visnshaftlekhe ophandlung* (New York: Farlag Brudershaft, 1938), p. 35.

44. Wolfson, "Jewish Fraternal Organizations," p. 867.

45. F. Rosenblatt (Ben Yakir), *Der arbeter ring un fraternal reyts,* 2nd ed. (New York: General Executive Committee, Workmen's Circle, 1915), pp. 21–23.

46. Many articles on the issue appeared in the Yiddish press. See "Tsu vos tsefalen zikh fiele benefit sosayetis," 13 October 1908, "Inshurens sosayetis un zeyer grund-gedank," 14 October 1908, "Geshprekhen mit di forshtehers fun di vikhtigste idishe ordens," 6 December and 7 December 1908, all in *Forward;* "Di idishe ordens in Amerika—vi di benefits in di ordens veren gefirt," *Amerikaner,* 19 February 1909, p. 5; "Inshurens sistem in idishe ordens" 22 March 1911, "Di gefar fir idishe ordens" (editorial), 23 March 1911, Jacob Massel, "Inshurens sistem in idishe ordens," 3 April 1911, "A lebens frage fir ale ordens," 1 April 1912, "Di oysgeshpilte role fun di alte idishe ordens" (editorial), 25 May 1913, Y. L. Dolidanski, "Der krizis in di ordens," series, 15 June, 19 October, 26 October, 2 November, 11 November, 18 November, 25 November, 2 December, 16 December 1917, all in *Tageblat.*

47. "Geshprekhen mit di forshtehers fun di vikhtigste idishe ordens," *Forward,* 6 December and 7 December 1908.

48. Minutes, 20 August, 30 December 1915; 2 February, 2 March, 7 September, 16 November 1917, Branch 301, Records of the Workmen's Circle, RG 575, YIVO; Sachs, *Geshikhte,* pp. 455–456, 532, 590, 624–659; B. Shelvin, *History of the Independent Order Brith Abraham 1887–1937* (New York: Independent Order Brith Abraham, 1937), pp. 35–44.

49. George Rosen, *The Structure of American Medical Practice 1875–1941* (Phila-

delphia: University of Pennsylvania Press, 1983), quotes on pages 99–100 and 36, respectively. According to Rosen, this practice grew out of earlier forms of arrangement with individuals and families. See Rosen, "Contract or Lodge Practice and Its Influences on Medical Attitudes to Health Insurance," *American Journal of Public Health* 67 (April 1967): 374. See also Paul Starr, *The Social Transformation of American Medicine* (New York: Basic Books, 1982), pp. 206–209.

50. Rosen, *Structure of American Medical Practice,* pp. 19–25, 35–36, 102; A. J. Rongy, "Half a Century of Jewish Medical Activities in New York City," *Medical Leaves* 1 (1937): 151–163.

51. Minutes, 17 April 1909; 6 January 1912; 14 July, 27 October, 10 November 1917, Congregation Ahavath Zedek Anshei Timkowitz.

52. Edmund James et al., *The Immigrant Jew in America* (New York: B. Buck, 1906), pp. 106–107.

53. Rosen, *Structure of American Medical Practice,* p. 102; Rongy, "Half a Century," pp. 158–159; Howe, *World of Our Fathers,* p. 188; minutes, 21 January 1912, Bolshowcer Arbeiter Lodge 517, IOBA, in Records of the Ershte Bolshowcer Sick and Benevolent Society and Lodge 517, IOBA, RG 872, YIVO. The anecdotes are from Morris Joseph Clurman, "The Lodge-Practice Evil of the Lower East Side," *Medical Record* 78 (22 October 1910): 718, and Yisrolik Der Yenki, "Pilen un politiks," *Tageblat,* 25 June 1909. In an earlier article, the pseudonymous Yisrolik ("Israel the Yankee") estimated that doctors might serve up to a dozen societies and see 100 patients each day. Yisrolik Der Yenki, "Lodzh-doktoyrim," *Tageblat,* 22 June 1909.

54. Albert T. Lytle, "Contract Medicine Practice: An Economic Study," *New York State Journal of Medicine* 15 (March 1915): 106; Clurman, "Lodge Practice Evil," 378; "Di idishe benefit sosayetis in Amerike—di mayles un khisroynes fun fareyns-doktoyrim," *Amerikaner,* 29 January 1909, p. 5; Rongy, "Half a Century," p. 158; Rosen, "Contract or Lodge Practice," p. 376. The anecdote is from M. A. Lipkind, "Some East Side Physicians at the Close of the Nineteenth Century," *Medical Leaves* 4 (1942): 104.

55. Yisrolik, "Lodzh-doktoyrim."

56. "Idishe benefit sosayetis in Amerike—di mayles un khisroynes fun fareyns-doktoyrim," p. 5.

57. See Alan M. Kraut, *Silent Travelers: Germs and the Immigrant Menace* (New York: Basic Books, 1994), pp. 140–141, 149.

58. These included Dr. J. Barsky, who later served as attending physician at Beth Israel Hospital, and Dr. Nathan Ratnoff, by the 1930s "directing a great hospital." Rongy, "Half a Century," p. 152; Lipkind, "Some East Side Physicians," p. 105; Rosen, "Contract or Lodge Practice," p. 376.

59. Yisrolik Der Yenki, "Dispensari doktoyrim," *Tageblat,* 28 September 1909; David Rosner, *A Once Charitable Enterprise: Hospitals and Health Care in Brooklyn and New York 1885–1915* (Cambridge: Cambridge University Press, 1982), pp. 146–163; Charles E. Rosenberg, *The Care of Strangers: The Rise of America's Hospital System* (New York: Basic Books, 1987), pp. 317–320; Charles Rosenberg, "Social Class and Medical Care in Nineteenth-Century

America: The Rise and Fall of the Dispensary," *Journal of History of Medicine and Allied Sciences* 29 (January 1974): 32–54; Elizabeth Ewen, *Immigrant Women in the Land of Dollars: Life and Culture on the Lower East Side, 1880–1925* (New York: Monthly Review Press, 1985), pp. 141, 143.

60. Starr, *Social Transformation of American Medicine,* especially pp. 21–28; Lytle, "Contract Medical Practice," pp. 103–108; Rosen, *Structure of American Medical Practice,* pp. 103–107. Rosen cites medical condemnations of the practice as far back as 1869, but also other statements calling for acceptance and the assertion of control over the practice. See Rosen, "Contract or Lodge Practice," pp. 374–377.

61. Clurman, "Lodge Practice Evil," p. 717.

62. Ibid., pp. 717–719; "Idishe benefit sosayetis in Amerike—di mayles un khisroynes fun fareyns-doktoyrim"; Yisrolik, "Lodzh-doktoyrim"; Solomon Schwartz, "Der politisher yarid in bostoner lodzhes," *Amerikaner,* 31 July 1908, p. 2 (deals with a similar situation in Boston); Rongy, "Half a Century," p. 159; minutes, 21 July, 4 August 1906; 18 April, 9 May 1908; 10 April, 17 April 1909, Congregation Ahavath Zedek Anshei Timkowitz; minutes, 19 December 1909, Bolshowcer Arbeiter Lodge 517, IOBA.

63. Minutes, 25 April 1914; 23 June 1917, Congregation Ahavath Zedek Anshei Timkowitz; minutes, 3 February, 3 March, 17 March, 9 April 1915, Records of Henry Clay Lodge 15, IOBA, RG 784, YIVO.

64. Minutes, undated special meeting (April or May 1905), 16 July, 13 August, 14 September, 24 September, 1 October 1905; 23 January, 11 February, 20 May 1906, Satanover Benevolent Society. Dr. Morris Joseph Clurman, who later railed against lodge-doctor practice, and the Satanover's Dr. S. Klurman (whose name appears in the records only once in Roman characters) were apparently not the same person.

65. The reasons for their dissatisfaction with Klurman are unclear. Minutes, 4 August 1907, Satanover Benevolent Society.

66. Dr. Seidler's first name is never given. Minutes, 1 September, 15 September, 1 December, 15 December 1907; 5 January, 2 February 1908, Satanover Benevolent Society.

67. Minutes, 2 February 1908, Satanover Benevolent Society.

68. Minutes, 2 August, 16 August, 6 September 1908, Satanover Benevolent Society.

69. Minutes, 7 February 1909; 2 January, 16 January, 6 March, 16 April, 1 May 1910, Satanover Benevolent Society.

70. Minutes, 1 January, 15 January, 5 February, 19 February 1911, Satanover Benevolent Society.

71. The minutes do not record exactly when, though at the meeting of November 17, 1912, it was decided to seek a new doctor. For subsequent elections see minutes, 20 June, 19 December 1915; 18 June, 17 December 1916; 17 June 1917, Satanover Benevolent Society.

72. Minutes, 1 April 1917, Satanover Benevolent Society.

73. Jacob Massel, "Inshurens sistem in di ordens," *Tageblat,* 11 March 1911.

74. During the inflationary period around World War I, many societies raised the

benefit to $7 per week. Minutes, 2 July 1911, Satanover Benevolent Society; minutes, 20 April 1907; 28 April 1917, Congregation Ahavath Zedek Anshei Timkowitz; Meretzer Relief Association, *Konstitushon* (New York, 1919), pp. 20–22; Independent Mlaver, *Konstitushon*, pp. 20–22, (also, amendments of 1917, n.p.); Ershte Komarover, *Konstitushon*, pp. 28–32; Verschleiser, "Di konstitutsies," p. 48; Kliger, *Jewish Hometown Associations*, pp. 63–64.

75. Sh. Dolinski, "Benefit," *Amerikaner*, 9 August 1907, p. 8; Jacob Massel, "Idishe benefit sosayetis in Amerika," *Amerikaner*, 15 January 1909, p. 5.

76. Rosenberg, "Social Class," p. 36.

77. Howe, *World of Our Fathers*, pp. 149–150.

78. Minutes, 17 April, 26 June 1909. The congregation also lobbied on behalf of needy brothers. For example, when one member fell ill with tuberculosis, the Congregation sent a committee to ask the prominent preacher Zvi Hirsch Masliansky if he could get the brother a place in a sanitorium. Minutes, 8 July 1911, Congregation Ahavath Zedek Anshei Timkowitz.

79. Sachs, *Geshikhte*, vol. 1, pp. 258, 357–373, 384. Fortunately, use of this benefit was infrequent. Only 12 members of Minsker Progressive Branch 99, for example, received this benefit between 1907 and 1931, and only twice did as many as two members use it in a given year. Minsker Progressive Branch 99, Workmen's Circle, *Yubileum oysgabe* (New York, 1931), p. 89.

80. Levine, *Poverty and Society*, pp. 151–166; Katz, *Shadow of the Poorhouse*, pp. 191–205.

81. Gerald Sorin, *A Time for Building: The Third Migration 1880–1920* (Baltimore: Johns Hopkins University Press, 1992), p. 79. For a discussion of the precarious condition of even those workers who lived above the poverty threshold, see James T. Patterson, *America's Struggle Against Poverty 1900–1980* (Cambridge, Mass.: Harvard University Press, 1981), pp. 8–12.

82. Patterson, *America's Struggle*, p. 23.

83. Ershte Komarover, *Konstitushon*, pp. 32–33; Independent Drobniner, *Konstitutsion*, pp. 16–17.

84. Minutes, misdated 22 March, actually 22 April 1906, 6 May 1906, 6 October, 20 October, 15 December 1907; 5 January 1908, Satanover Benevolent Society. See also minutes, 23 November and 7 December 1907, Congregation Ahavath Zedek Anshei Timkowitz; Richard H. Lane, "East Side Benefit Societies," *Yearbook of the University Settlement Society of New York* (1899), p. 27.

85. Minutes, 7 June, 5 July 1908, Satanover Benevolent Society.

86. Minutes, 19 August 1911, Congregation Ahavath Zedek Anshei Timkowitz.

87. Minutes, 16 August 1908, Satanover Benevolent Society. A similar request was granted Brother Frankfeld, whose dues were forgiven "until better times," 5 September 1909. See also minutes, 14 March, 6 June 1908; 10 June, 4 November 1911; 27 February, 16 April 1915, Congregation Ahavath Zedek Anshei Timkowitz.

88. See Jacob Billikopf, "Free Loans," *Jewish Charities* 2 (September 1911): 6–7; Samuel Steinfels, "Free Loan Societies," *Jewish Communal Register*, p. 689;

Shelly Tenenbaum, *A Credit to Their Community: Jewish Loan Societies in the United States, 1880–1945* (Detroit: Wayne State University Press, 1993). Tenenbaum discusses the ideological basis for free loans in the Bible and the Talmud. For several Yiddish proverbs on the preferability of loans over alms see Nahum Stutchkoff, *Der oytser fun der yidisher shprakh* (New York: Yiddish Scientific Institute-Yivo, 1950), p. 511 (entry 491).

89. The *Jewish Communal Register*'s survey of 632 mutual aid societies (not all of them landsmanshaftn) showed that 34.3% had free loan funds (page 735). A list of 50 affiliates of the Federation of Galician and Bucovinean Jews of America shows a similar proportion. *Tsvishen blut un fayer* (New York: Federation of Galician and Bucovinean Jews of America, 1916), pp. 62–98.

90. *Tsvishen blut un fayer,* p. 65.

91. Meretzer Relief Association, *Konstitushon,* pp. 38–46 (Yiddish), pp. 34–40 (English).

92. Deborah Dwork, "Health Conditions of Jews on the Lower East Side of New York 1880–1914," *Medical History* 25 (January 1981): 1–40; Jacob Jay Lindenthal, "*Abi Gezunt:* Health and the Eastern European Jewish Immigrant," *American Jewish History* 70 (June 1981): 420–441; Kraut, *Silent Travelers,* pp. 152–155; James et al., *Immigrant Jew in America,* pp. 282–303; "Iden un krankhayten" (editorial), *Tageblat,* 13 January 1909.

93. Morris Waldman, "Jewish Philanthropy in New York City," in *Jewish Communal Register,* pp. 989–993, quote on p. 993. Cyrus Sulzberger, the head of the New York Kehillah's Committee on Social and Philanthropic Work, agreed that "no single instrumentality in our community is more useful than these bodies in keeping people self-dependent in time of stress." Memo to the Executive Committee of the Kehillah, 11 October 1915, folder P3/1421, Magnes Papers. See also I. Silberstein, "Jewish Fraternal and Benevolent Societies," *Jewish Charities* 2 (December 1911): 14–15; James et al., *Immigrant Jew in America,* pp. 70–71.

94. Belle L. Mead, "The Social Pleasures of East Side Jews," M.A. thesis, Columbia University, 1904, pp. 2–3; Richard Lane, "East Side Benefit Societies," *University Settlement Society of New York Report* (1899), p. 28.

95. See flyer of Chevra Bnai Jacob Yitzhak Anshei Zabne, Landsmanshaft Subject Collection; minutes, 7 November, 26 December 1908, Congregation Ahavath Zedek Anshei Timkowitz.

96. Lane, "East Side Benefit Societies," p. 27. As historian Kathy Peiss notes, the degree of gender segregation varied from ethnic group to ethnic group, and immigrant men generally spent more leisure time with their families than did native Americans. Kathy Peiss, *Cheap Amusements: Working Class Women and Leisure in Turn-of-the-Century New York* (Philadelphia: Temple University Press, 1986), pp. 30, 32.

97. William Bakst, "Ikh bin a Oshmener fun Oshmene!" in Oshmener B.M.A. and B.A., *45 yoriger yubileum-zhurnal,* reprinted in Rontch, *Idishe landsmanshaften,* p. 168.

98. Minutes, 16 December 1906, Satanover Benevolent Society.

99. Mead, "The Social Pleasures of East Side Jews," p. 16.
100. James T. Gerould, "The Social Side of Synagogue Life," *Yearbook of the University Settlement Society of New York* (1899), pp. 29–31.
101. James et al, *The Immigrant Jew*, p. 231.
102. *Forward*, 21 November 1908. Belle L. Mead counted posters advertising 19 different balls on a three-block stretch on Grand and Clinton Streets. See Mead, "The Social Pleasures of East Side Jews," p. 7.
103. A. Tanenboym, "Beler un maskaraden," *Amerikaner,* 18 January 1907, p. 6.
104. "Groysartiger banket bay di brayler yong mens benevolent asosieyshon," *Idisher gayst,* April 1910, p. 20.
105. "Groysartiger banket." See also "Der fest fun di yunayted minsker," *Tageblat,* 25 June 1912; Andrew Heinze, *Adapting to Abundance: Jewish Immigrants, Mass Consumption, and the Search for American Identity* (New York: Columbia University Press, 1990), p. 121.
106. Regarding the age of dance hall patrons, see Peiss, *Cheap Amusements,* pp. 88–89.
107. "Der yontef fun di minsker," *Tageblat,* 15 December 1902.
108. Quoted in Ewen, *Immigrant Women,* p. 210. See also Peiss, *Cheap Amusements,* pp. 88–92.
109. "Der yontef"; "Der fest."
110. Minutes, 6 November 1910; 5 November 1911; 13 October 1913, Satanover Benevolent Society.
111. "Der yontef."
112. Minutes, 7 August, 21 August, 4 September, 6 November, 19 November 1910; 4 June, 18 June, 16 July, 6 August, 17 September, 5 October, 15 October 1911; 7 December 1913; 6 September, 18 October 1914, Satanover Benevolent Society.
113. See Peiss, *Cheap Amusements,* pp. 117–118, 121.
114. Z. Libin, "Ay, a piknik," in *Gezamelte shriften* (New York: Forward, 1916), vol. 3, p. 41.
115. See Y. Y. Yudsovitsh, "Khaym der kostomer pedler: er fohrt tsu a piknik," *Tageblat,* 7 August 1908.
116. See for example, minutes, 2 October, 13 October 1917, Congregation Ahavath Zedek Anshei Timkowitz.
117. *Yudishe gazeten,* 15 July 1892, p. 10. The following week there was a similar advertisement by the Thalia Theater, 22 July 1892, p. 6.
118. The 480 performances devoted entirely to benefits were a major proportion of the 1,100 performances given annually by the Yiddish theaters then in existence. Jacob M. Gordin, "The Yiddish Stage," *Fifteenth Annual Report of the University Settlement Society of New York* (1901), 27. On benefit performances, see also minutes, 20 November 1905 (arrangement committee); 6 March 1910; 19 November 1911, Satanover Benevolent Society; minutes, 13 October 1917, Congregation Ahavath Zedek Anshei Timkowitz; Howe, *World of Our Fathers,* pp. 479–480; James et al., *The Immigrant Jew,* p. 229; Hutchins Hapgood, *The Spirit of the Ghetto* (1902; rpt. Cambridge,

Mass.: The Belknap Press of Harvard University Press, 1967), pp. 114–115; Nahma Sandrow, *Vagabond Stars: A World History of the Yiddish Theater* (New York: Harper and Row, 1977), p. 82.

119. Gordin complained that management "was less attentive" to benefit performances since it could expect less of a profit, and that therefore "the greatest disorder prevails on the stage and among the audience." Furthermore, many people attended the theater only because of pressure from friends and colleagues, rather than out of proper "voluntary desire." Gordin, "The Yiddish Stage," pp. 27–28. For the *Tageblat*'s view, see "Ver iz shuldig?" 29 October 1903.

120. James et al., *The Immigrant Jew,* pp. 229–230. The book's individual sections, written by different people, are not signed.

121. As of June 3 the society had collected $58.95 of the $88.90 owed it for tickets sold—a profit of at least $21.45 and perhaps as much as $51.40, depending on how many buyers actually made good on their pledges. Minutes, 12 November, 3 December 1905; 3 June 1906; minutes of arrangement committee, 16 November, 20 November 1905; 29 January 1906, Satanover Benevolent Society.

122. Minutes, 4 November, 18 November, 16 December 1906; 6 February, 20 February, 6 March, 18 December 1910; 1 January, 7 May, 5 November, 19 November 1911; 17 March 1912, Satanover Benevolent Society.

123. For example, see minutes, 5 November 1910; 6 May 1911, Congregation Ahavath Zedek Anshei Timkowitz.

124. For example, Meretzer Relief Association, *Konstitushon,* p. 4; Independent Mlaver, *Konstitushon,* p. 4; Ershte Komarover, *Konstitushon,* p. 3.

125. B. Rivkin, "Di sotsiale role," p. 77.

126. Minutes, 18 November 1906, Satanover Benevolent Society.

127. Minutes, 12 October 1907; 13 February, 1 May 1909; 2 November 1912, Congregation Ahavath Zedek Anshei Timkowitz.

128. Since the immigrants believed that not all laws or convictions were just, the societies also felt free to retain jailed members. Independent Mlaver, *Konstitushon,* p. 32; Meretzer Relief Association, *Konstitushon,* pp. 31–32; Independent Drobniner, *Konstitutsion,* p. 29; Minutes, 16 February 1908, Satanover Benevolent Society; Verschleiser, "Konstitutsies," p. 48.

129. Abraham Karp, "Overview: The Synagogue in America—A Historical Typology," in *The American Synagogue: A Sanctuary Transformed,* ed. Jack Wertheimer (New York: Cambridge University Press, 1987), p. 18. Karp is writing specifically about immigrant synagogues, but the same could be said of other societies as well.

130. Minutes, 15 December (both meetings which carry this date), and 29 December 1906; 15 July, 26 July 1913, Congregation Ahavath Zedek Anshei Timkowitz.

131. See Howe, *World of Our Fathers,* pp. 186–187. Later, many cases went to the Jewish Conciliation Board. See Menashe, "Landsmanshaften far'n idishen gerikht," in Rontch, *Idishe landsmanshaften,* pp. 127–130.

5. The Building Blocks of Community

1. Edmund James et al., *The Immigrant Jew in America* (New York: B. Buck, 1906), pp. 14–15, 149–150; M. Blechman, "Di landsmanshaften un di tsentrale organizatsies," in Isaac E. Rontch, ed., *Di idishe landsmanshaften fun Nyu York* (New York: Yiddish Writers Union, 1938), p. 35; Irving Howe, *World of Our Fathers* (New York: Harcourt, Brace, Jovanovich, 1976), p. 189. For similar views, see Judd L. Teller, *Strangers and Natives: The Evolution of the American Jew from 1921 to the Present* (New York: Dell, 1968), p. 123; Michael Weisser, *A Brotherhood of Memory: Jewish Landsmanshaftn in the New World* (New York: Basic Books, 1985). Only recently have historians begun to accord the landsmanshaftn more respect for the role they played in building the community. See Gerald Sorin, *A Time for Building: The Third Migration 1880–1920* (Baltimore: Johns Hopkins University Press, 1992), pp. 97–98.

2. For a sampling of the contributions of two societies, see Minutes, 1 September, 17 November, 15 December, 29 December 1906; 27 July, 24 August, 7 September, 23 November, 7 December, 21 December 1907; 4 January, 18 January, 5 September, 11 October, 12 December 1908; 30 January, 27 February, 12 June, 6 November, 11 December, 25 December 1909; 19 November, 3 December, 17 December 1910; 4 February, 21 October, 4 November, 18 November, 2 December 1911; 11 May, 8 June, 12 October, 2 November, 7 December 1912; 4 January, 24 May, 22 November, 6 December, 20 December 1913; 17 January, 25 July, 12 September, 14 November, 28 November 1914; 30 January, 13 February, 28 February, 12 June, 25 September, 30 October, 27 November, 11 December 1915; 28 October, 11 November, 25 November, 9 December 1916; 27 July, 14 September 1918; 3 May 1919, Congregation Ahavath Zedek Anshei Timkowitz, RG 840, YIVO; minutes, Zerdover Branch 301, 16 July, 3 December 1909; 25 February, 6 May, 29 May, 3 June, 15 July, 21 October 1910; 3 February, 17 February, 17 March, 2 June, 16 June, 21 July, 18 August, 11 October, 1 December 1911; 19 January, 16 February, 5 April, 17 May, 4 October, 20 December 1912; 7 November, 21 November, 19 December 1913, Records of the Workmen's Circle, RG 575, YIVO.

3. The congregations carrying city or country names included Mishkan Israel Anshei Suwalk, Chevrah Kadisha Anshei Kalwaria, Congregation Machzikei Torah Anshei Senier, Bnai Emes Anshei Mariampol, Congregation Tiphereth Israel Anshei Neustadt, Talmud Torah Anshei Agustow, Kol Israel Anshe Polin, Beth Hamedrash Anshe Ungarn, and Knesset Israel Anshe Russia. Abraham J. Karp, "New York Chooses a Chief Rabbi," *Publications of the American Jewish Historical Society* 44 (1954–1955): 129–198; Judah David Eisenstein, *Otsar zikhronotai* (New York, 1929), pp. 252–254.

4. Karp, "New York Chooses a Chief Rabbi," pp. 154, 162–167.

5. Ibid., pp. 173–175.

6. Ibid., pp. 176–179.

7. It was common for lodges of the same fraternal order to aid each other in times of need. See Minutes of Branch 301, 30 July, 13 August, 20 August, 3 Septem-

ber 1909; 18 February, 25 February, 11 March, 25 March, 10 April 1910, and many other instances; Minsker Progressive Branch 99, Workmen's Circle, *Yubileum oysgabe* (New York, 1931), p. 88; Jacob Massel, "Inshurens sistem in idishe ordens," *Tageblat,* 14 March 1911; Leo Wolfson, "Jewish Fraternal Organizations," in *The Jewish Communal Register of New York City 1917–1918* (New York: Kehillah (Jewish Community) of New York, 1918), p. 867.

8. Independent Order Brith Abraham, *Report of the Grand Master Max Stern,* (New York, 1908), pp. 27–28; "Konvenshon shlist in harmonie," *Tageblat,* 12 May 1909; Order Brith Abraham, *Brief History (Message from Samuel Dorf, Grand Master)* (New York, 1907), pp. 6–7; B. Shelvin, *History of the Independent Order Brith Abraham 1887–1937* (New York: IOBA, 1937), pp. 33, 48–52 (quote on p. 33); Jacob Massel, "Di idishe ordens als politishe un gezelshaftlikhe makht," *Tageblat,* 28 November 1915.

9. Kh. Malits, "Di ideale konvenshon fun ind. order ahoves yisroel," *Amerikaner,* 9 September 1910, p. 6; "I.O.B.A. konvenshon nemt on vikhtige reformen," *Tageblat,* 27 May 1913; "Ershter tog fun bris sholem konvenshon endigt zikh in sholem," 15 June 1914, and "Letster tog fun konvenshon fun ind. order bris sholem," 17 June 1914, both in *Tageblat.*

10. *Jewish Communal Register,* pp. 1337–1339.

11. S. Margoshes, "The Verband Movement in New York City," in *Jewish Communal Register,* p. 1329.

12. The history of the individual federations, together with their sponsored institutions, is treated in Chapter 6.

13. Josef J. Barton, "Eastern and Southern Europeans," in John Higham, ed., *Ethnic Leadership in America* (Baltimore: Johns Hopkins University Press, 1978), p. 150.

14. Arthur Goren, *National Leadership in American Jewish Life: The Formative Years* (Cincinnati: University of Cincinnati Press, 1986), quotes on page 3. See also Victor Greene, *American Immigrant Leaders 1800–1910: Marginality and Identity* (Baltimore: Johns Hopkins University Press, 1987); John Higham, "Leadership," in *Harvard Encyclopedia of American Ethnic Groups* (Cambridge, Mass.: Harvard University Press, 1980), pp. 642–647; Nathan Glazer, "The Jews," in Higham, *Ethnic Leadership,* pp. 19–35.

15. "Di pflikht fun di galitsianer" (editorial), *Tageblat,* 7 June 1910.

16. *Jewish Communal Register,* pp. 154, 1337–1339.

17. "Der Galitsianer farband un der 'har hamoria,'" *Tageblat,* 18 March 1909.

18. "Di konvenshon fun 'ferband',￼" *Amerikaner,* 18 May 1906, p. 14.

19. "Di konvenshon fun ferband," *Amerikaner,* 25 May 1906, p. 4; "Der ferband," *Amerikaner,* 20 August 1906, p. 20.

20. Ploni ve-Kohen, "Di dray idishe konvenshons," *Amerikaner,* 1 May 1908, p. 4. Likewise, the Russian-Polish Federation, at its 1909 convention, resolved always to "take an active part in all Jewish interests and affairs." "Konvenshon fun poylishen ferband," *Tageblat,* 17 May 1909.

21. Yankev Kirshenboym, "Galitsie in Nyu-York," *Togblat* (Lvov, no date), clipping in Landsmanshaft Subject Collection, RG 123, YIVO. Concerning the Romanians, the conservative and nationalistic Yiddish daily *Tageblat* wrote

that they had not "given a large percentage to local 'comradism.'" "Di ru-menishe iden" (editorial), *Tageblat,* 29 March 1908. Concerning the Galicians, see also "Di pflikht fun di galitsianer" (editorial), *Tageblat,* 7 June 1910; "Der ferband fun di galitsianer iden," *Tageblat,* 28 May 1915.

22. The Russian-Polish Farband endorsed Zionism in 1916, by which time the movement had expanded tremendously under the leadership of Louis Brandeis. "Di konvenshon geshlosen," 23 May 1906; "Konvenshon fun rumenishe iden," 18 June 1911; "Poylisher ferband erklert zikh far Tsien un idishen kongres," 19 June 1916, all in *Tageblat.*

23. Yehoshua Pelovits, "Idishe ordens un tsienizm," *Tageblat,* 15 January 1912. The 600 societies attributed to the Galician Federation was something of an exaggeration. During the 1913 controversy within the Federation, another Zionist writer expressed disappointment in the organization for not living up to its original goals, which he believed (incorrectly) to have been to "acquaint the Jewish inhabitants of the Galician quarter with the national idea, instill in them the love of our ancient fatherland, agitate and propagandize in these circles for joining the general Zionist movement, from which these Jews still stand apart." On the other hand, he believed that the Galician Jews were ripe for Zionism because they were "clean of the other 'isms' whose influence is so damaging to the nationalism of the other quarters." Kh. A. Hafner, "Iz a fareynigung unmeglikh?" *Tageblat,* 3 July 1913.

24. "Ershter bal fun rumenishen ferband," 7 December 1908; "Rumenishe iden begrisen Rusland," 16 April 1917; "100,000 doler far Har Hamoria," 29 May 1916; "Konvenshon geshlosen," 6 June 1911; "Konvenshon fun rumenishe iden," 18 June 1911; "Galitsianer ferband makht sholem mit di raykhe tuer," 25 May 1914; "Ferbanden nehmen on dem 'tageblat' kongres forshlag," 31 May 1915, all in *Tageblat.*

25. Certificate of Incorporation for Federation of Galician and Bucovinean Jews of America (vol. 48, 1905, doc. 1093), Incorporation Papers: Items of Jewish Interest, American Jewish Historical Society.

26. "A rizen demonstratsion," *Amerikaner,* 17 November 1905, p. 24. See also "In galitsianer krayzn," 3 November 1905, p. 10; "Tsu di masenfarzamlung," 24 November 1905, p. 2; "A rizige demonstratsion," 1 December 1905, p. 3, all in *Amerikaner.*

27. "Ayndruksfoler troyer miting fun estraykh-ungarishe iden," *Tageblat,* 1 December 1916.

28. The Romanian and the Polish federations each offered the government the use of its medical facility—the Romanians' Home for Convalescents, and the Poles' Beth David Hospital. "Rumenishe iden bagrisen Rusland," 16 April 1917; "Ferband fun poylishe iden far patriotizm un Erets-Yisroel," 21 May 1917; "Rumenishe-idishe konvenshon dankt Amerika un England," 31 December 1917, all in *Tageblat.*

29. *American Jewish Year Book,* 1907, p. 331; Arthur Goren, *New York Jews and the Quest for Community: The Kehillah Experiment 1908–1922* (New York: Columbia University Press, 1970), pp. 21–24, 40.

30. Minutes, 3 June, 18 November 1906; 6 January, 3 February, 7 April, 4 August,

4 September, 17 November 1907; 20 June 1908; 6 June 1909, Records of Satanover Benevolent Society, RG 818, YIVO.

31. Goren, *New York Jews*, pp. 25–42, quote on page 36. Calls for unity within the Eastern European Jewish community predated the Kehillah. The journalist Jacob Pfeffer, first president of the Federation of Galician and Bucovinean Jews, called for an organization which would unite all American Jews. He hoped the Independent Order Brith Abraham, the largest Jewish fraternal order, would take the lead in forming a federation of all orders, lodges, societies, congregations, and other organizations, which would be more representative than the German-Jewish American Jewish Committee. Jacob Pfeffer, "Ver vil unz fareynigen?" *Amerikaner*, 4 May 1906; "Vegn fareynigen iden" (editorial certainly written by Pfeffer), *Amerikaner*, 18 May 1906, p. 14.

32. Flyer, "Oyfruf tsu der konferents . . . in klinton hall," folder P3/1389 Papers of Judah Magnes, Central Archives for the History of the Jewish People.

33. Call dated 14 January 1909, P3/1389, Magnes Papers; "Oyfruf," *Tageblat*, 28 January 1909; Goren, *New York Jews*, pp. 44–49.

34. "List of Delegates to the Constituent Convention," P3/1389, Magnes Papers; Goren, *New York Jews*, p. 49; "Konstitushon ongenumen," *Tageblat*, 1 March 1909; "The New York Kehillah Organized," *American Hebrew*, 5 March 1909, p. 467. The *Tageblat* and the *American Hebrew* reported that 218 organizations had attended.

35. "Vote for Executive Committee," P3/1389, Magnes Papers; "Di beamte fun kehile," *Tageblat*, 8 April 1909; "The Jewish Community of New York," *American Hebrew*, 19 March 1909; Goren, *New York Jews*, p. 54.

36. *American Hebrew*, 19 March 1909; Goren, *New York Jews*, pp. 65, 69, 127, 215, 274, 283; *Jewish Communal Register*, pp. 72, 373; "Di beamte fun kehile," *Tageblat*, 8 April 1909; *Report of the Executive Committee and Proceedings of the Fourth Annual Convention of the Jewish Community (Kehillah)* (New York, 1913), pp. 5–6. Minutes of the Kehillah Executive Committee, 9 June 1909, P3/1397; List of Advisory Council members elected 10 April 1909, P3/1389; "Report of the Election for Executive Committee and Advisory Council," 1912, P3/1464; Minutes of Fifth Annual Convention, 25–26 April 1914, P3/1472; "Executive Committee Members," 1916, P3/1498, all in Magnes Papers.

37. "The Jewish Community of New York," *American Hebrew*, 19 March 1909; Goren, *New York Jews*, pp. 38, 54, 65, 127, 208, 240, 283; *Jewish Communal Register*, pp. 72–73; "In gezelshaftlekhe krayzn," *Amerikaner*, 12 January 1906 (misdated 1905), p. 8; *Tsvishen blut un fayer* (New York: Federation of Galician and Bucovinean Jews of America, 1916), p. 95; Ts. H. Rubinshteyn, "Bernard Zemel," *Tog*, 16 November 1928; J. L. Magnes, "My Friend, Bernard Semel," *Tog* (English section), 18 November 1928.

38. E. V. Levin-Epstein, "Arbayt far der kehile," *Tageblat*, 18 March 1909; minutes of unidentified meeting, 14 September 1909, press release and notice for meeting in Brownsville on 21 December 1909, poster for meeting in Brownsville, 1 February 1910, press release "Jewish Community of New York City," 21 November 1909, and flyer "Important Mass Meetings of Jewish Commu-

nity (Kehillah) of New York City," 15 September 1912, all in P3/1608, Magnes Papers; Secretary's reports to Executive Committee, 14 December 1909, 11 January and 8 February 1910, P3/1397, Magnes Papers; "Forberaytungen tsu a kehile konvenshon," *Tageblat,* 9 February 1910.

39. Advertisement, "Vehlt delegaten tsu der kehile konvenshon," *Tageblat,* 21 February 1910.

40. "Report of the Executive Committee and Proceedings of the Fourth Annual Convention of the Jewish Community (Kehillah), New York April 12 and 13, 1913," p. 9; Y. Vortsman, "Vos di 'kehile' hot biz itst oyfgeton," *Tog,* 13 January 1918, clipping in P3/1512, Magnes Papers; Goren, *New York Jews,* pp. 80–83, 191, 196, 206–207.

41. "Report of the Executive Committee Presented at the Third Annual Convention of the Jewish Community (Kehillah), New York April 27–28, 1912," P3/1464, Magnes Papers.

42. "Kehile konvenshon nehmt on patriotishe milkhome rezolushon," *Tageblat,* 26 April 1914.

43. List of organizations at 1911 convention, P3/1463, Magnes Papers; List of organizations at 1913 convention, P3/1468, Magnes Papers; List of societies, including societies in arrears, 1916, P3/1500, Magnes Papers; "Analysis of Organizations and Delegates Sent to the Kehillah Convention in 1915 and 1916," P3/1504, Magnes Papers.

44. See for example, Rabbi Joffa's complaint at the 1911 Convention that "The Kehillah is supposed to be democratic, but its actions are not democratic." Minutes of the Second Annual Convention of the Jewish Community of New York City, 25–26 February 1911, P3/1463, Magnes Papers; Goren, *New York Jews,* pp. 60–61.

45. Joel Limon, "An der kehile konvenshon fun 1915," 21 April 1915, P3/1490, Magnes Papers; Minutes of the sixth convention of the Kehillah, 24–25 April 1915, P3/1491, Magnes Papers. In 1911, the Kehillah secured funds from the Galician and Romanian federations to provide Jewish prisoners with matzot and bologna through the Jewish Protectory and Aid Society. This is one of the few times that the Kehillah seems to have enlisted the support of its constituent organizations in a particular project. But even here it seems to have acted primarily as a broker between the federations and the Society. Minutes of Executive Committee, April 10, 1911, P3/1400, Magnes Papers.

46. Memo to the Executive Committee of the Kehillah, 11 October 1915, P3/1421; letter addressed to Felix Warburg, 15 June 1915, P3/923; minutes, Executive Committee, 9 March 1915, P3/1415, all in Magnes Papers.

47. Minutes, Executive Committee, 13 February 1912, P3/1401, Magnes Papers. The Kehillah opposed the orphanage even though its own Executive Committee had expressed concern about Jewish children in non-Jewish orphanages. See minutes of Executive Committee, 11 January, 8 February, 12 June 1910, P3/1397, Magnes Papers.

48. Minutes of the fifth annual Kehillah convention, 25–26 April 1914, P3/1472, Magnes Papers; "Kehile konvenshon nemt on vikhtige beshlise," *Tageblat,* 27 April 1914.

49. Statement, "Jewish Community (Kehillah) of New York City," 3 May 1910, P3/1397, Magnes Papers.

50. Minutes, Executive Committee, 12 May 1910, P3/1399, Magnes Papers.

51. The Romanian dispute began in 1909, shortly after the founding of both the Roumanian Federation and the Kehillah. The problem seemed to reside in the personalities of the leaders, and the conflict continued intermittently until 1917. The Kehillah made a number of unsuccessful attempts to resolve it. Minutes, Executive Committee, 11 May 1909, P3/1397, Magnes Papers; "Di konvenshon fun farband fun rumenishe iden," *Tageblat,* 26 April 1909; "Konvenshon apoyntet a sholem komitee," *Tageblat,* 28 April 1909; minutes of the Second Annual Convention of Jewish Community of New York City, 25–26 February 1911, P3/1463, Magnes Papers; minutes, Executive Committee, 10 April 1911, P3/1400, Magnes Papers; "Konvenshon fun rumenishe iden," *Tageblat,* 18 June 1911; minutes, Executive Committee, 12 September 1911; 9 September, 8 October 1912; 14 January, 9 April, 14 October, 17 November, 9 December 1913, P3/1400, 1401, 1408, 1409, 1410, Magnes Papers; "Kehile fir sholem in rum. ferb.," *Tageblat,* 4 July 1912; "Di kehile un der rum. ferband," *Tageblat,* 11 August 1912; "Kehile konvenshon nehmt on vikhtige beshlise," *Tageblat,* 27 April 1914; minutes of Kehillah Convention, 29 April 1917, P3/1508, Magnes Papers; minutes of Executive Committee, 3 May, 12 June, 17 July 1917, P3/1442, 1443, 1444, Magnes Papers.

52. Judah L. Magnes, "A Statement Presented to the Eighth Annual Convention of the Kehillah (Jewish Community) of New York City," in *What the Kehillah Has Given New York Jewry* (New York, 1917), pp. 14–15; Goren, *New York Jews,* pp. 61–62, 65–66, 231–244.

53. Goren, *New York Jews,* p. 214; Judah L. Magnes, "Address at the Opening Session of the Sixth Annual Convention of the Jewish Community (Kehillah) of New York City, April 24, 1915," P3/1486, Magnes Papers. See also a proposed resolution that the Kehillah urge the American Jewish Relief Committee to send a delegation to the "war stricken area" to distribute relief, P3/1487, Magnes Papers.

54. "Delegaten kritikiren kehile," *Tageblat,* 22 February 1915.

55. Gerald Sorin, *A Time for Building,* pp. 211–214; Goren, *National Leadership,* pp. 11–17.

56. Goren, *New York Jews,* pp. 218–227; minutes, Convention of the New York Kehillah, 24–25 April and 23 May 1915, P3/1491, 1492, Magnes Papers; minutes, Convention of New York Kehillah, 1916, P3/1500, Magnes Papers; "Shif entfert zayne ferloymder," *Tog,* 5 June 1916, clipping in P3/1503, Magnes Papers. Call for caucus of delegates to Kehillah in support of Congress, 1915, P3/1485, Magnes Papers; minutes of Kehillah Convention, 1915, P3/1491, P3/1492, P3/1495, Magnes Papers; A. D. Katcher to J. L. Magnes, 19 August 1915, and circular from Jacob Massel (in Yiddish), dated 8 Tishrei 5676 (16 September 1915), P3/1475, Magnes Papers; "Appeal to the Delegates to the New York Kehillah Convention," 1916, P3/1500, Magnes Papers; "Bevegung optsuraysen di Nyu York kehile fun der dzshuish komite," *Jewish Morning Journal,* 31 May 1916, and "Attacks Jewish Community Work as

Undemocratic," *New York Herald,* 4 June 1916, clippings in P3/1503, Magnes Papers.

57. "Educational Work in the Bolechower Association," unidentified sheet, possibly from anniversary journal, misdated 1911 by later hand, Subject Collection on Landsmanshaftn; "Ferbanden nehmen on dem 'tageblat' kongres forshlag," *Tageblat,* 31 May 1915; "Ferband fun rumenishe iden shtitst tsienizmus un kongres," *Tageblat,* 28 June 1915; "Ferbands 'ruf' tsu kongres-konvenshon," *Tageblat,* 17 February 1916; minutes, 12 February 1916, Congregation Ahavath Zedek Anshei Timkowitz.

58. Advertisement, 10 May 1917; "Galitsianer fereynen shtitsen kongres bavegung," 6 September 1915; "Delegaten fun ferband reden tsu gunsten fun kongres," 14 September 1915; "Galitsianer fereynen far a kongres," 8 November 1915; Gershom Bader, "Der galitsianer kvartal un der farband," 10 November 1915; "Konferents vegn hilf far galitsianer," 22 February 1917; "Konferents fun galitsianishe fereynen," 23 February 1917; "Estraykh-ungarishe fareynen shtelen foderungen tsum kongres," 26 February 1917, all in *Tageblat.*

59. Sorin, *Time for Building,* pp. 212–213; Goren, *National Leadership,* p. 16.

60. *Report of Proceedings of the American Jewish Congress, Philadelphia December 1918* (New York: American Jewish Congress, 1919), pp. 76–78. On landsmanshaft campaigning for the elections, see *Tageblat,* 8 June and 10 June 1917.

61. *Report of Proceedings,* pp. 5, 23, 36, 41, 43, 53, 68–71.

62. Henry L. Feingold, *A Time for Searching: Entering the Mainstream, 1920–1945* (Baltimore: Johns Hopkins University Press, 1992), pp. 158–159.

63. Goren, *New York Jews,* p. 189.

64. See Moses Rischin, *The Promised City: New York's Jews 1870–1914* (1962; Cambridge, Mass.: Harvard University Press, 1978); Howe, *World of Our Fathers;* Will Herberg, "The Jewish Labor Movement in the United States," *American Jewish Year Book* 53 (1952). For an attempt to show that modern Jewish radicalism sprang directly from traditional values and teachings, see Gerald Sorin, *The Prophetic Minority: American Jewish Immigrant Radicals 1880–1920* (Bloomington: Indiana University Press, 1985). For the influence of European developments on the American Jewish labor movement and organized labor's participation in Jewish communal politics, see Jonathan Frankel, *Prophecy and Politics: Socialism, Nationalism and the Russian Jews 1862–1917* (Cambridge: Cambridge University Press, 1981), pp. 453–551.

65. Minutes of Branch 301, 4 June 1909; 19 January, 16 February 1912; 7 February 1913, Records of the Workmen's Circle.

66. Minutes of Branch 301, 5 March, 4 June, 31 December 1909; 25 March, 6 May, 20 May, 29 May, 21 October, 4 November, 18 November, 16 December 1910; 6 January, 3 March, 19 May, 4 August, 1 September 1911; 19 January, 5 April, 17 May, 19 July 1912; 2 May, 19 September 1913, Records of the Workmen's Circle.

67. Samuel Tucker, "A Little History from a Pioneer," Louis Tentchin, "Erinerungen fun a grinder," and I. S., "Half a Century," in Progressive Slutzker Young Men's Benevolent Association, *50th Anniversary Banquet* (New York, 1954), pp. 24, 95, 14–15.

68. *Der Kolomear,* (New York, 1929); B. Rivkin, "Di sotsiale role fun di landsman-shaften," in Rontch, *Idishe landsmanshaften,* pp. 80, 85.

69. Weisser, *Brotherhood,* p. 82; Rischin, *Promised City,* 182; Abraham Cahan, *The Rise of David Levinsky* (1917; rpt. New York: Harper Torchbooks, 1960), p. 378; Sholem Ash, *Onkl Mozes* (1918; rpt. Buenos Aires: Ateneo Literario en el Instituto Científico Judío, 1973), pp. 85–86.

70. Z. Sher, "Di Vaynshteyn brider velkhe hoben oyfgeboyt di rifer biznes in Amerika," *Forward,* 22 January 1938; Rischin, *Promised City,* p. 183; Melech Epstein, *Jewish Labor in U.S.A.* (1950; New York: Ktav Publishing House, 1969), vol. 1, pp. 383–385; "Ver di rifer boses zaynen," *Forward,* 3 April 1907; *15 yohr leben: rifer-makher yunyon lokal num. 17 ILGWU* (New York, 1920), p. 31. For general accounts of the strike, see Rischin, *Promised City,* p. 246; Bernard Weinstein, *Di idishe yunyons in Amerika* (New York: United Hebrew Trades, 1929), pp. 347–348, 354–355; Louis Levine, *The Women's Garment Workers: A History of the International Ladies' Garment Union* (New York: B. W. Huebsch, 1924), pp. 128–133.

71. Weinstein, *Idishe yunyons,* pp. 347–348.

72. Transcript of interview with Abraham Belson, 7 December 1963, pp. 3–4, Oral History Collection, RG 113, YIVO. Belson could not actually remember the 1905 strike since he arrived in the United States two years later. But as a local officer and landsman, he was well versed in union lore.

73. "A dzsheneral strayk in di tshildren klouk treyd," *Forward,* 23 March 1907, gives the figure as 2,000; Rischin, *Promised City,* p. 246, writes 1,500; and Levine, *Women's Garment Workers,* p. 130, gives the figure as 1,200 "joined by others."

74. "Folshtendiger zieg fun di rifer meykers, hurrah!" *Forward,* 16 May 1907.

75. Quotes in "Ver di rifer boses zaynen," 7 April 1907; "Geshikt a bandit tsu ermorden an onfihrer fun rifer makher strayk," 14 April 1907. See also "Nokh 5 rifer boses setlen," 28 March 1907; "Hoben fon mit di boses," 5 April 1907, all in *Forward.*

76. Abraham Rosenberg, *Erinerungen fun di kloukmakher un zeyere yunyons* (New York, 1920), p. 159.

77. "Shtitsen di rifer makher," *Forward,* 23 April 1907.

78. Other directly involved landsmanshaftn which gave money to the strike included the Shmilevitzer Benevolent Society, Dukorer Brothers Benevolent Society, and Shmilevitzer Women's Benevolent Society. Minsker groups which contributed included the American Benevolent Minsker Association, Minsker Brotherly Benevolent Association, Minsker Young Friends Benevolent Association, and Minsker Regional Benevolent Society-RSDWP.

79. Levine, *Women's Garment Workers,* p. 132; Weinstein, *Idishe yunyons,* p. 354; "Der gantser kvartal kokht mit der rifer-makher strayk," *Forward,* 17 April 1907.

80. *Forward,* 14 April to 28 May 1907.

81. Epstein, *Jewish Labor,* vol. 1, pp. 411, 441. For histories of the "Great Revolt" see Epstein, *Jewish Labor,* vol. 1, pp. 387–420; Rischin, *Promised City,* pp. 247–257; Levine, *Women's Garment Workers,* pp. 144–195; Weinstein, *Idishe yunyons,* pp. 357–377; Howe, *World of Our Fathers,* pp. 295–304.

82. Epstein, *Jewish Labor,* vol. 1, p. 441.

83. "Hunderter sosaytis miten haynt un morgen," *Forward,* 8 January 1910.

84. "Vos di sosayetis kenen ton in foriers strayk," *Forward,* 18 July 1912.

85. *Forward,* 4 August to 14 September 1910.

86. "Ihr kont bevayzen ver es iz shtarker," *Forward,* 11 August 1910.

87. "Itst kumt di vikhtigste arbayt," *Forward,* 25 August 1910.

88. "Ihr kont bevayzen ver es iz shtarker," *Forward,* 11 August 1910.

89. Minutes, 30 July 1910; 15 February 1913, Congregation Ahavath Zedek Anshei Timkowitz. For more examples see articles in the *Forward:* "Ihr kont bevayzen ver es iz shtarker," 11 August 1910; "Fun gantsen land ruft men op mit shtitse," 16 August 1910; "Men vet morgen shafen mitlen vi azoy beser oystsuhalten di straykers," 23 August 1910; "Di boses blofen mit fonds fun toyzender dolar," 11 August 1912.

90. Minutes, 12 February, 26 February 1913, 26 March 1913, Records of Stabiner Young Men's Benevolent Association, RG 1037, YIVO. For more examples of weekly benefits, lump-sum grants, and other aid, see *Forward,* 13 August to 31 August 1910, 16 July to 11 August 1912.

91. Quoted in I. Silberstein, "Jewish Fraternal and Benevolent Societies," *Jewish Charities* 2 (December 1911): 15.

92. "Kontsert un bal" (advertisement), 22 December 1909; "Steyt bord ov arbi-treyshon vil makhen sholem," 4 January 1910; "Der kloukmakher strayk," 18 August 1910; "Der kloukmakher strayk," 29 August 1910; "Vos di sosayetis kenen ton in foriers strayk," 18 July 1912; "Oyfruf" (advertisement), 27 November 1909; "Di foriers," 17 July 1912; "Di foriers," 22 July 1912, all in *Forward.*

93. Minutes, 16 September 1913, Records of Zgierzer Sick Benevolent Association, RG 1064, YIVO; "Rezolutsion," 6 February 1900; "Rezolutsion fun dem brisker untershtitsung fereyn," 3 March 1907; "Tsu smuken sigarets nor mit yunyon leybl," 19 March 1907; "Rezolutsion," 23 April 1907, all in *Forward.*

94. "Di foriers," *Forward,* 29 July 1912.

95. Isaac Metzker, ed., *A Bintel Brief: Sixty Years of Letters from the Lower East Side to the Jewish Daily Forward* (New York: Ballantine Books, 1971), pp. 109–110. The president wanted to take the prerogative to make donations in the name of the society anyway. The editors sagely advised him that no matter how laudable the cause, a society officer should not make disbursements without permission of the members.

96. Roger Waldinger, "Another Look at the International Ladies' Garment Workers' Union: Women, Industry Structure and Collective Action," in Ruth Milkman, ed., *Women, Work, and Protest: A Century of U.S. Women's Labor History* (Boston: Routledge and Kegan Paul, 1985), p. 98. See also Meredith Tax, *The Rising of the Women: Feminist Solidarity and Class Conflict 1880–1917* (New York: Monthly Review Press, 1980), pp. 205–240; Nancy Schrom Dye, *As Equals and as Sisters: Feminism, Unionism, and the Women's Trade Union League of New York* (Columbia: University of Missouri Press, 1980), pp. 88–109.

97. *Forward,* 15 December 1909 to 21 February 1910. Over $43,000 was raised through the *Forward.*

98. "Di bevegung far'n halben tog veydzsh fond," *Forward*, 12 January 1910.

99. Minutes, 21 July, 1 September 1912; 7 December 1913, Satanover Benevolent Society; Roster for Federation of Jewish Organizations of New York State, ca.1907 (misdated 1905 by a later hand), Records of Satanover Benevolent Society. The Gluboker Benevolent Association also contributed generously to striking members but only after protracted debate, as both workers and employers belonged to the society. Minutes, 13 August, 16 August, 27 August 1910, Records of Gluboker Benevolent Association, RG 1111, YIVO. Tabulated from minutes of the Gluboker Benevolent Association, 1908–1914.

100. Minutes, 21 August 1910; 16 April 1911; 21 April 1912, Satanover Benevolent Society.

101. "Rumenien hibru eyd sosayeti," *Tageblat*, 9 December 1903; Announcements, *Tageblat*, 17 March 1909, 5 February 1915; *Jewish Communal Register*, pp. 741, 1006, 1009.

102. Z. Kotler, "Tsvishen fereynen un anshtalten," *Tageblat*, 23 August 1915; *Jewish Communal Register*, pp. 370–371.

103. For the significance of HIAS as an institution sponsored mainly by the Eastern European community, see Goren, *National Leadership*, pp. 10–11.

104. Mark Wischnitzer, *Visas to Freedom: The History of HIAS* (Cleveland: World Publishing, 1956), pp. 33–35; Ronald Sanders, *Shores of Refuge: A Hundred Years of Jewish Immigration* (New York: Henry Holt, 1988), pp. 184–186, 252–253. For early subscription lists with organizational supporters of the Sheltering House, see *Yudishe gazeten*, 11 September, 23 October, 6 November 1891.

105. Accounts concerning the origins of HIAS in 1902 differ. Wischnitzer mentions both Rabbi Jochanon Lodge and a Voliner Zhitomirer Aid Society, but the relationship between the two is unclear. Sanders credits the Voliner Zhitomirer Aid Society, which he says met at the Brith Abraham hall. Both Wischnitzer and Sanders cite an article by John L. Bernstein, a HIAS leader, which mentions the Brith Abraham lodge but not the Zhitomirer society. B. Rivkin and Irving Howe appear to conflate the foundings of the Hebrew Sheltering House Association and the original HIAS. According to Rivkin, the *Ezra* Lodge of IOBA, responding to a similar report of a death of an immigrant at Castle Garden, established the sheltering house sometime in the 1880s. Howe attributes the founding to an unnamed landsmanshaft and dates it to 1892. A perusal of the Yiddish press for 1902 did not resolve the issue, and neither do early HIAS publications. The Rabbi Jochanon Lodge appears in many lists and directories, but the Voliner Zhitomirer Aid Society does not. It appears likely that the lodge had a hand in HIAS's founding, and that it may, in fact, have been a lodge made up of landslayt from Zhitomir. Wischnitzer, *Visas to Freedom*, p. 38; Sanders, *Shores of Refuge*, pp. 187–188; John L. Bernstein, "HIAS Then and Now," *Rescue*, July-August 1944, p. 5; B. Rivkin, "Di sotsiale role," pp. 79–80; Howe, *World of Our Fathers*, p. 47; *Jewish Communal Register*, p. 925.

106. "Hibru imigreyshon eyd sosayeti," *Forward*, 23 December 1902, and *Tageblat*, 23 December 1902; "5 ordens tsuzamen," and "Oyfruf fun di grend masters," *Yudishe gazeten*, 26 December 1902, pp. 15, 16; "Hibru emigrey-

shon eyd sosayeti," and "Kaminets-Podolier untersht. fareyn," *Forward,* 31 December 1902. Other organizations also stepped up their activities for new immigrants at this time. See "Emese hilf far aynvanderer," concerning the work of the Roumanian Emigrant Aid Society, *Idishe velt,* 25 December 1902.

107. Concerning the work of HIAS, see Wischnitzer, *Visas to Freedom,* p. 41. Concerning the merger see Sanders, *Shores of Refuge,* pp. 252–264, Waldman quote on page 256.

108. "Statistical Report of Activities from 1909 to 1918 Inclusive," folder I-37, Records of HIAS, RG 245.4, YIVO; Hebrew Sheltering and Immigrant Aid Society, *First Annual Report—1909* (New York, 1910), pp. 13–18; Wischnitzer, *Visas to Freedom,* pp. 48–74; Sanders, *Shores of Refuge,* pp. 274–275; Bernstein, "HIAS Then and Now," p. 10. For HIAS political activities see *Jewish Immigration Bulletin,* January 1915, a "special immigration number" devoted to lobbying for a veto of the recently passed literacy bill.

109. Hebrew Immigrant Aid Society, *Fourth Annual Report, 1906–1907* (New York, 1907), p. 20; Hebrew Sheltering and Immigrant Aid Society, *Annual Report—1914* (New York, 1915), p. 18.

110. "A forshteyer fun hakhnoses orkhim redt in hatsiler fareyn," *Tageblat,* 17 June 1915.

111. Minutes, 1 December, 15 December 1912, Satanover Benevolent Society. For continued aid to HIAS, see minutes, 1 February 1914.

112. "Konferents fun fereynen," *Der idisher imigrant (The Jewish Immigrant),* January 1909, p. 26.

113. Minutes, 18 January, 6 June 1908; 1 March 1913; 31 January 1914; 13 February 1915; 12 February 1916; 27 January 1917, Congregation Ahavath Zedek Anshei Timkowitz; Minutes of Branch 301, 6 February 1914; 5 March 1915; 21 January, 4 February, and 3 March 1916; 5 October 1917, Records of the Workmen's Circle.

114. Hebrew Sheltering and Immigrant Aid Society, *Annual Report—1913* (New York, 1914), pp. 42–44. For various lists of societies contributing to HIAS see Hebrew Immigrant Aid Society, *Fourth Annual Report 1906–1907* (New York, 1908), pp. 24–26; *The Jewish Immigrant,* August 1908, pp. 22–25, November 1908, pp. 16–17, and January 1909, pp. 9–10; Hebrew Sheltering and Immigrant Aid Society, *First Annual Report—1909* (New York, 1910), pp. 107–123.

6. Institutional Dilemmas

1. *The Jewish Communal Register of New York City 1917–1918* (New York: Kehillah (Jewish Community) of New York City, 1918), pp. 1019, 1339; "Di geshikhte fun unzer farband," in *Poylishe iden* (New York: Federation of Polish Jews in America, 1933), pp. 56–57; Shmuel Schwartz, "Di landsmanshaft farbanden," in Isaac E. Rontch, ed., *Di idishe landsmanshaften fun Nyu York* (New York: Yiddish Writers' Union, 1938), p. 52; Dovid Tratman, "Di

federeyshon fun di poylishe iden in Amerika," *Der farband,* 1 May 1924, p. 16; and the following articles in *Tageblat:* "75 toyzent dolar hospital far ferband fun poylishe iden," 18 January 1909; "Poylisher ferband nehmt iber Yorkvil hospital," 23 May 1910; "Apil far'n beys Dovid hospital," 10 June 1910; "Der poylisher ferband un zayn hospital," 30 May 1911; "Shafen geld far dem nayem beys Dovid hospital," 1 June 1911; "Konvenshon fun poylishe iden," 26 June 1911; Z. Kotler, "Der eyntsiger kosherer hospital in Harlem," 27 December 1914.

2. On the Bessarabian Federation, see M. Schwartz, "Bessarabier farband-historisher iberblik," *Idisher gayst,* February 1914, pp. 25–26; *Jewish Communal Register,* pp. 1062–1063, 1337. On the Romanian Federation, see *Jewish Communal Register,* pp. 1021, 1339; User Marcus, "Historisher iberblik fun dem farband fun rumenishe iden in Amerika," January 1910, p. 2, and "Der rumenisher farband bashlist tsu grindn a vikhtike institushon," October 1913, p. 15, both in *Idisher gayst;* Solomon Diamant, "Federation of Roumanian Jews," *Jewish Charities* 4 (July 1914): 21; and the following articles in *Tageblat:* "Ferband fir rumenishe iden," 6 March 1908; "Ferband fir rumenishe iden in Amerika," 15 March 1908; "Rumenisher ferband vert shtarker," 23 March 1908; "Di rumenishe iden," 29 March 1908; "A vikhtiger masmiting," 29 March 1908; "1te konvenshon fun rumenishen ferband," 4 April 1908; "Di konvenshon fun ferband fun rumenishe iden," 26 April 1909; "Konvenshon apoyntet a sholem komitee," 28 April 1909; Z. Kotler, "Tsvishen fereynen un anshtalten," 20 June 1915; "Ferband fun rumenishe iden shtitst tsienizmus un kongres," 28 June 1915; Z. Kotler, "Tsvishen fereynen un anshtalten," 23 August 1915; "Shehne khanukas habayes fun nayem anshtalt fun rumenishe iden," 18 June 1917.

3. "Unzer program," January 1910, p. 3; S. Diamant, "Farband!" January 1910, p. 9; "Der konvenshon," June 1910, p. 3, all in *Idisher gayst;* and the following articles in *Tageblat:* "Di konvenshon fun ferband fun rumenishe iden," 26 April 1909; "Konvenshon apoyntet a sholem komitee," 28 April 1909; "Konvenshon fun rumenishe iden," 18 June 1911; "3te konvenshon fun rumenishen ferband," 26 May 1910; "Rumenishe iden muzen emigriren— farband hert a barikht," 30 May 1910. The Galician Federation occasionally also engaged in overseas work, for example by funding the defense led by Thomas Masaryk in the Hilsner blood-libel trial, contributing to Jewish nationalist candidates in the Austrian elections, and helping to establish free-loan funds for artisans and small merchants in Galicia. But these were a small part of its activities. See "Konvenshon fun ferband," 4 June 1911; "Konvenshon geshlosen," 6 June 1911; "Far di iden in Galitsien," 26 January 1912; "Krizis bay nomineyshons fun galitsianer ferband," 20 May 1912, all in *Tageblat.*

4. This continued to be true even after the establishment of Har Moriah and several other small hospitals. See an article on a State Board of Charities report on the shortage of hospital beds in New York City, "Engshaft in di hospitals," *Tageblat,* 29 January 1912.

5. *Jewish Communal Register,* pp. 1014–1015, 1022, 1023; "Di erefenung fun pipls hospital," *Tageblat,* 27 June 1910.

6. See Charles E. Rosenberg, *The Care of Strangers: The Rise of America's Hospital System* (New York: Basic Books, 1987), pp. 104–105, 264–268.

7. "Har Hamoria hospital," *Tageblat,* 10 May 1909.

8. Minutes, 25 March 1916, Records of Congregation Ahavath Zedek Anshei Timkowitz, RG 840, YIVO. See also "Vos men tut in a idishen hospital," *Tageblat,* 26 June 1914. This story relates a beard-cutting incident at a St. Louis Jewish hospital.

9. "Konvenshon fun poylishe iden," *Tageblat,* 26 June 1911.

10. Rosenberg, *Care of Strangers,* p. 299.

11. More concretely, the Russian-Polish and the Romanian Federations both offered use of their facilities as a regular benefit of membership. Members of the Federation of Russian-Polish Hebrews paid one dollar a year and received a card entitling them to free care at the hospital. Since patients unable to pay were treated gratis anyway, it is unclear what the practical effect of this arrangement might have been. But it probably helped raise money even as it removed any stigma of charity which still adhered to free hospital care. "Di geshikhte fun unzer farband," pp. 58–59; "Poylisher ferband erklert zikh far Tsien un idishen kongres," *Tageblat,* 19 June 1916; Tratman, "Di federeyshon fun di poylishe iden in Amerika"; "9te yerlikhe konvenshon fun rumenishen ferband," *Tageblat,* 23 April 1916.

12. See Rosenberg, *Care of Strangers,* pp. 109–113; Robert Ernst, *Immigrant Life in New York City, 1825–1863* (1949; rpt. New York: Octagon, 1979), p. 56; David Rosner, *A Once Charitable Enterprise: Hospitals and Health Care in Brooklyn and New York, 1885–1915* (New York: Cambridge University Press, 1982), pp. 3, 36–52, 57–59, 69, 105–111, 122–145.

13. "Nit freylekh in poylishen ferband," 16 June 1913; "Konvenshon shlist zikh in harmonie," 17 June 1913; "Di makhloykes in dem rumenishen farband," 28 June 1912, all in *Tageblat.*

14. The sources do not make clear just how the doctors seized control of Beth David, but it is interesting to compare this example with that of Brooklyn's Methodist Hospital, where David Rosner has described a similar coup by the medical staff against the board of managers. Beth David survived under various names and at various locations until 1963. Rosner, *A Once Charitable Enterprise,* pp. 119–120; Tina Levitan, *Islands of Compassion: A History of Jewish Hospitals of New York* (New York: Twayne Publishers, 1964), pp. 272–273; "Di geshikhte fun unzer farband," p. 58; Tratman, "Di federeyshon fun di poylishe iden in Amerika."

15. From a letter in the *Forward*'s famous advice column, "A bintel brief." The editor responded that the young woman's colleague was an "idiot." Letter from 1906, reprinted in *A Bintel Brief,* ed. Isaac Metzger (New York: Doubleday, 1971), pp. 52–53.

16. A. Gonikman, "Vifiel galitsianer zaynen do in Nuyork?" *Forward,* 24 March 1904. See also "Meynungen fun ongezehene menshen fun dem galitsianer kvartal," *Forward,* 20 February 1906.

17. Letter from a reader quoted in "Galitsianer un rusishe iden hasen zikh nit" (editorial), *Tageblat,* 17 July 1908. See also S. Neumann, "Di ershte teg fun'm

ferband," in *Tsvishen blut un fayer* (New York: Federation of Galician and Bucovinean Jews of America, 1916), p. 57.

18. Gershom Bader, "Der galitsianer ferband in Amerika," *Togblat* (Lvov?), n.d., clipping in Landsmanshaft Subject Collection, RG 123, YIVO. Similarly, journalist Z. Kotler regarded Galician resentment as a "foolish fantasy." Z. Kotler, "Der galitsianer ferband un zayn rikhtiger veg," *Tageblat*, 16 May 1912.

19. Bader, "Der galitsianer ferband in Amerika."

20. "Di galitsianer iden un zeyer konvenshon" (editorial), *Tageblat*, 4 June 1908.

21. "3 kehiles in flamen," 2 October 1903; "Shnele hilf fir galitsishe nisrofim," 4 October 1903, both in *Tageblat*.

22. "Di noyt in tsvey lender," *Tageblat*, 4 October 1903.

23. J. Pfeffer, "Tsu galitsianer fereynen," *Tageblat*, 1 May 1904. Concerning the fire in Buchach, see "Nisrofim—Vitebsk un Butshatsh," *Tageblat*, 29 April 1904.

24. "Konvenshon fun estraykhishe iden," *Tageblat*, 31 May 1904.

25. "Fareynigt," *Tageblat*, 13 June 1904.

26. *Tageblat*, 11 July 1904.

27. Neumann, "Di ershte teg fun'm ferband," p. 58; Bader, "Der galitsianer ferband in Amerika."

28. "An erklerung: Mr. Y. Pfeffer tsu zayne landslayte," 28 May 1905, p. 2; "Tetikeyten in ferband," 4 June 1905, p. 24; "Pfeffer vider ervelt," 30 July 1905, p. 1; "Dem 'ferbands' konvenshon," 23 July 1905, p. 1, all in *Amerikaner*. "Konvenshon fun ferband," *Tageblat*, 24 July 1905.

29. "A mekhtige bavegung," *Amerikaner*, 11 June 1905, p. 2.

30. "Dem ferband's prezent," 13 October 1905, p. 22; "In gezelshaftlekhe krayzn," 25 June 1905, p. 17, both in *Amerikaner*.

31. "In galitsianer krayzn," *Amerikaner*, 3 November 1905, p. 10; "Konvenshon fun galitsianer ferband," *Tageblat*, 21 May 1906.

32. "Di konvenshon fun ferband," *Amerikaner*, 25 May 1906, p. 4; "Di konvenshon geshlosen," *Tageblat*, 23 May 1906.

33. "Der ferband," *Amerikaner*, 20 August 1906, p. 20.

34. For Pfeffer's position see J. Pfeffer, "Di pflikht fun galitsianer iden," *Amerikaner*, 31 August 1906, p. 14.

35. Z. Kotler, "Der galitsianer ferband un zayn rikhtiger veg," *Tageblat*, 16 May 1912.

36. "Estraykhishe iden fareynigt in a groysen un shtarken ferband," *Amerikaner*, 8 February 1907, p. 6; "Konvenshon fun 'ferband' haynt," *Tageblat*, 2 June 1907. Four fraternal orders were represented among the branches: Independent Order Brith Abraham, Order Brith Abraham, Independent Order Ahavas Israel, and Independent Order Free Sons of Judah. Significantly, no Workmen's Circle branches were affiliated. *Report of the Financial Secretary to the Fifth Annual Convention of the Federation of Galician and Bucovinean Jews of America* (New York, 1908). See also "4te konvenshon fun 'ferband,'" *Tageblat*, 8 June 1908, which reported 275 affiliates.

37. "Konvenshon fun 'ferband' haynt," *Tageblat*, 2 June 1907.

38. "Nayer prezident far'n 'ferband,'" *Tageblat*, 4 June 1907.

39. This description of the opening ceremonies is based on the following reports in the *Forward*: "Haynt di erefenung fun Har Hamoria hospital," 15 November 1908; "A groyser yontef oyf der Ist Sayd," 16 November 1908; "2ter tog in Har Hamoria hospital," 17 November 1908; "Har Hamoria hospital hot shoyn a tsharter," 18 November 1908; "Der yontef fun Har-Hamoria," 19 November 1908; "44 brentshes martshen," 22 November 1908; "2te vokh in Har Hamoria," 23 November 1908; "5,000 martshen baym Moria hospital," 26 November 1908; "Oukshon-tog in Har Hamoria," 27 November 1908; "Haynt der letster tog in Har Hamoria," 29 November 1908; and the following from the *Tageblat:* "Har Hamoria hospital erefent mit glants," 16 November 1908; "Martshen tsum nayem hospital," 17 November 1908; "Groyser parad tsum 'Har Hamoria,'" 15 November 1908; "Martshen tsum hospital," 18 November 1908.

40. "Erefnung fun Har Hamoria," *Yudishe vokhenblat,* 1 January 1909, p. 1–2.

41. The opening of the Russian-Polish Federation's Beth David Hospital was similar. "Khanukas habayis fun beys Dovid hospital," 26 May 1913; "Haynt der khanukas habayis fun dem beys Dovid hospital," 1 June 1913; "Beys Dovid hospital erefent mit a glentsende tseremonie," 2 June 1913, all in *Tageblat.*

42. "Estraykhishe iden fareynigt in a groysen un shtarken farband," *Amerikaner,* 8 February 1907, p. 6; "Har Hamoria hospital," *Tageblat,* 10 May 1909; Z. Libin, "A hospital oysgehalten fun penis in idishen kvartal," *Forward,* 6 June 1909.

43. "Helft dem Har Hamoria hospital," 11 March 1908; "Talente oyf'n 'Har Hamoria' bal," 24 March 1908, both in *Tageblat.*

44. "Haynt di erefenung fun Har Hamoria hospital," *Forward,* 15 November 1908.

45. "Erefnung fun 'Har Hamoria' hospital" (editorial), *Tageblat,* 6 November 1908.

46. "Har Hamoria hospital," *Tageblat,* 10 May 1909; Libin, "A hospital oysgehalten fun penis in idishen kvartal."

47. "Har Hamoria efent zikh dem 17ten yanuar," *Tageblat,* 24 December 1908. It is not clear whether this rule was enforced.

48. The *Forward* reported space for 85 patients, while the *Tageblat* claimed there were 90 ward beds and 30 private beds. "Har Hamoria hospital," *Tageblat,* 10 May 1909; Libin, "A hospital oysgehalten fun penis in idishen kvartal." Quote from "A vikhtiger shrit fun 'Har Hamoria' hospital," *Tageblat,* 27 December 1908.

49. Libin, "A hospital oysgehalten fun penis in idishen kvartal"; "Laboratorium in Har Moria," *Tageblat,* 12 May 1910.

50. "Har Hamoria nehmt oyf patsienten," *Yudishe vokhenblat,* 29 January 1909, p. 1.

51. "Har Hamoria hospital," *Tageblat,* 10 May 1909; "A vikhtiger shrit fun 'Har Hamoria' hospital," *Tageblat,* 27 December 1908.

52. *Souvenir Journal: Concert and Ball . . . Har Moriah Hospital of the Galician and Bukovinean Federation* (New York, 1910), n.p.; *Jewish Communal Direc-*

tory (New York: Jewish Community (Kehillah) of New York City, 1912), pp. vii–viii; "Har Hamoria hospital," *Tageblat,* 10 May 1909; on the opening of the dispensary, see "Dispensari in Har Hamoria hospital," *Tageblat,* 31 August 1909.

53. Bernard Semel, "Prezidents bagrisung," *Souvenir Journal . . . Har Moriah Hospital,* n.p. (Yiddish section).

54. *Report of the Financial Secretary . . . to the VII Annual Convention of the Federation of Galician and Bukovinean Jews in America* (New York, 1910).

55. "Bagaysterte konvenshon fun galitsianer ferband," 6 June 1910; "Di pflikht fun di galitsianer" (editorial), *Tageblat,* 7 June 1910. On the conventions for 1909–1911, see additional reports in the *Tageblat:* "Di konvenshon fun ferband fun galitsianer iden," 7 June 1909; "Konvenshon fun ferband geshlosen," 9 June 1909; "Bagaysterte konvenshon fun galitsianer ferband," 5 June 1911; "Konvenshon geshlosen," 6 June 1911.

56. "Helft dem Har Hamoria hospital," 11 March 1908; "Der galitsianer ferband un zayn hospital" (editorial), 23 March 1908; "Talente oyf'n 'Har Hamoria' bal," 24 March 1908; "Di tsvey beler," 30 March 1908; "10,000 doler far Har Hamoria," 21 February 1910; Advertisement for ball, 24 December 1914, all in the *Tageblat.*

57. "Tsu der konvenshon fun ferband," 4 June 1909, p. 8; "Konvenshon fun ferband," 11 June 1909, p. 2; "In ferband," 3 September 1909, p. 8, all in *Yudishe vokhenblat.* For an account of the hospital controversy based mostly on Pfeffer's viewpoint, see Klaus Hödl, *Vom Shtetl an die Lower East Side: Galizische Juden in New York* (Vienna: Böhlau Verlag, 1991), pp. 186–192.

58. Both Dr. Neumann and his brother, Dr. William Neumann, had recently left Har Moriah's staff, though accounts differed as to whether they had quit or been fired. The *Tageblat* called the uproar "incomprehensible" and concluded, "How this bunch came to such a conclusion when the documents are so clear remains a question." Nevertheless, the paper aired the views of both sides. "Makhloyke vegen Har Moria hospital," 6 March 1911; "Di hospital makhloyke," 8 March 1911; "Der gantser emes fun der makhloykes," 9 March 1911; "Der tsveyter tsad" (open letter from Dr. Neumann), 12 March 1911, all in *Tageblat.* See also "Protest bevegung in galitsianer fereynen," 13 May 1910, pp. 2, 13; "Tsvey hundert ferband brentshes baym konferents," 27 May 1910, p. 2; "Protest miting gegen der fervaltung fun'm ferband," 10 March 1911, p. 7, all in *Yudishe vokhenblat.*

59. "Di makhloyke vegen Har Hamoria hospital," *Tageblat,* 7 March 1911; Certificates of Incorporation for the Federation of Galician and Bucovinean Jews in America (Vol. 48, 1905, doc. 1093), and Har Moriah Hospital of the Federation of Galician and Bucovinean Jews (Vol. 56, 1909, doc. 2057), in Incorporation Papers: Items of Jewish Interest, American Jewish Historical Society; "Bagaysterte konvenshon fun Galitsianer farband," 5 June 1911; "Konvenshon geshlosen," 6 June 1911, *Tageblat.*

60. J. Pfeffer, *Yudishe vokhenblat,* 24 December 1909, p. 3; "Bagaysterte konvenshon fun galitsianer ferband," 6 June 1910; "Di pflikht fun di galitsianer" (editorial), 7 June 1910, both in *Tageblat.*

61. "An erklehrung," 1 July 1910, p. 6; "Tsvey hundert brentshes baym konfer-ents," 27 May 1910, p. 2; S. Margoshes, "Hot der ferband erfilt zayn oyf-gabe?" 17 June 1910, p. 4; S. Margoshes, "Vos iz fun ferband gevoren?" 24 June 1910, p. 2; G. Bader, "Gershom Bader vegen ferband," 1 July 1910, p. 4, all in *Yudishe vokhenblat*. To be fair, Pfeffer also had ideas about what the Farband should do. See his articles in the *Vokhenblat*, especially, "Vos hot der ferband gezolt zayn?" 10 December 1909, p. 3; "Vu iz ahingekumen der ferband?" 17 December 1909, p. 4; 24 December 1909, p. 3 (the title of this article is not legible); "Unzer erklehrung," 3 June 1910, p. 3–4; "Mir muzen boyen a hospital," 16 September 1910, p. 4. See also Gershom Bader, "Fun'm nuyorker Galitsien," *Tageblat*, 29 May 1913.

62. "Krizis bay nomineyshons fun galitsianer ferband," *Tageblat*, 20 May 1912.

63. Gershom Bader, "Di naye firung funm galitsianer ferband—naye memshole in ferband," 6 June 1913; "Di naye firung fun'm galitsianer ferband—hert dem tsveyten tsad—fun 'an ineveynigsten,'" 6 June 1913; Gershom Bader, "Naye administratsie fun ferband," 16 June 1913, all in *Tageblat*.

64. "Funm nyu-yorker Galitsien," 7 May 1914; "Galitsianer ferband makht sholem mit di raykhe tuer," 25 May 1914; "Konvenshon fun galitsianer fer-band geshlosen in harmonie," 26 May 1914, all in *Tageblat*.

65. "Farband makht hakhones tsu a yohr vikhtige arbayt," 28 May 1915; "Fer-banden nehmen on dem 'tageblat' kongres forshlag," 31 May 1915, both in *Tageblat*.

66. For the effects of the economic crisis and the war on Jewish institutions, see Z. Kotler, "Tsvishen fereynen un anshtalten," *Tageblat*, 19 September 1915.

67. "Galitsianer bal a groyser erfolg," *Tageblat*, 28 December 1914.

68. "Bal fun ferband iz morgen abend," *Tageblat*, 29 December 1916.

69. "Delegaten fun ferband reden tsu gunsten fun kongres," 14 September 1915; "100,000 doler far Har Hamoria," 29 May 1916; "'Har Hamoria' tsurik bay dem 'ferband,'" 2 February 1917; "Krizis in galitsianer kvartal," 21 February 1917; "Har Moria hospital un ferband," 15 March 1917, all in *Tageblat*.

70. "Galitsianer ferband zukht tsu reten Har Hamoria hospital," 21 May 1917; "Fundament far sholem in ferband fun galitsianer," 22 May 1917, both in *Tageblat*.

71. Z. Kotler, "Idishe tetigkeytn in Nuyork," *Tageblat*, 18 May 1917.

72. "Veln reten 'farband' un hospital fun untergang," *Tageblat*, 3 September 1917.

73. "Veln reten 'farband' un hospital fun untergang"; "Konvenshon breyngt akhdes un retung far dem ferband," 4 September 1917; "Di naye program fun Galitsianer ferband," 19 September 1917; "Galitsianer yugend organizirt zikh," 6 December 1916, all in *Tageblat*; *Jewish Communal Register*, pp. 1337–1338.

74. "Konvenshon breyngt akhdes un retung far dem ferband," *Tageblat*, 4 Septem-ber 1917. See also Z. Kotler, "Idishe tetigkayt in Nuyork," 24 August 1917; "Konvenshon zuntog fun dem 'ferband,'" 31 August 1917; Gershom Bader, "Der untergang fun a groyser idisher organizatsie," 2 September 1917; "Di organizatsion fun galitsianer un bukoviner iden in Amerika" (editorial), 4 September 1917, all in *Tageblat*.

75. "Vos men hert un vos men zeht in unzer idishen kvartal," *Tageblat,* 16 August 1914.

76. "Bukowinian Federation Opens Credit Banks," summary of report in *Tog,* "Digest of News in the Yiddish Press," 9 March 1920, folder 46, Archives of AJJDC; "Vegen galitsiener farband," February 1928, p. 5; "Far vos is noytig a fareynigung mit dem galitsiener farband?" June 1929, p. 3, both in *Der farband,* organ of the Polish Federation.

7. The Heroic Period

1. Henry Rosenfelt, *This Thing of Giving: The Record of a Rare Enterprise of Mercy and Brotherhood* (New York: Plymouth Press, 1924), p. 12; Salo Baron, *The Russian Jew Under Tsars and Soviets,* 2nd ed. (New York: Macmillan, 1976), pp. 158–162.

2. Borukh Rivkin, "Di sotsiale role fun di landsmanshaften," in Isaac E. Rontch, ed., *Di idishe landsmanshaften fun Nyu York* (New York: Yiddish Writers' Union), pp. 98, 100–105; M. Blekhman, "Di landsmanshaften un di tsentrale organizatsies," in ibid., pp. 35, 37–39; Sam Tunik, "Mayne zikhroynes fun 30 yohr," in Independent Stabtzer Benevolent Association, *Der stayptser shpigel* (New York, 1930), p. 13; Allan Bernstein, "Our Society," in Progressive Society of Yaruga, *Souvenir Journal 1917–1937* (New York, 1937).

3. "Ershte brief fun a shtetel vos daytshen hoben tsugenumen," 16 August 1914, "Stri, Galitsien, pust tsulib milkhome," 17 August 1914, "Brief fun Rusland tsu landslayt in Amerika," 8 October 1914, see also daily war news, especially August 3, 4, 10, 12, 1914, all in *Tageblat.*

4. "Di pflikht fun amerikaner iden" (editorial), *Tageblat,* 20 August 1914.

5. See Oscar Handlin, *A Continuing Task: The American Jewish Joint Distribution Committee, 1914–1964* (New York: Random House, 1964), pp. 12–14, 23.

6. "Tsu helfen iden in Galitsien," *Tageblat,* 16 August 1914.

7. See advertisements and announcements in the *Tageblat,* especially on September 13 and October 7, 8, 11, 16, 18, 23, 25, 27, 1914. Zalman Kotler reported regularly on relief activities for the *Tageblat.* In his column on 27 December 1914 alone, he noted the recent establishment of some 23 different landsman-shaft relief committees. See Z. Kotler, "Tsvishen fereynen un anshtalten," *Tageblat,* 27 December 1914.

8. "Minsker helfen zeyere milkhome korbones," 23 October 1914, and "Minsker kumen tsu hilf zeyere milkhome korbones," 26 November 1914, *Tageblat.*

9. "Pinsker un Karliner khevres apeliren far milkhome laydende," *Tageblat,* 5 November 1914.

10. "Di idishe khurbn in Eyropa," 4 September 1914; "Tsentral komite organizirt tsu helfen idishe milkhome korbones," 7 October 1914; "Dzshuish komite ruft konferents," 3 November 1914; "Plener tsu helfen di milkhome korbones," 16 November 1914; "7ner komite far relief fond," 17 November 1914; "Oyf-ruf fun folks hilf konferents," 24 August 1915, all in *Tageblat;* Zosa Szajkowski, "Private American Jewish Overseas Relief (1919–1938): Problems

and Attempted Solutions," *American Jewish Historical Quarterly* 57 (March 1968): 285.

11. Rosenfelt, *This Thing of Giving,* p. 22.

12. Minutes, 10 July, 24 July, 4 September, 25 September, 9 October 1915; 11 March, 9 September 1916; 27 January 1917; 31 August, 14 December 1918, Records of Congregation Ahavath Zedek Anshei Timkowitz, RG 840, YIVO.

13. "Press Notice," 3 January 1917, and letters from JDC to Samuel Goldstein, 2 July 1917 and 26 December 1917, in folder 53; statement, Provisional Executive Committee of the Federation of Hungarian Jews in America, 3 October 1916, and report of a meeting of Federation of Hungarian Jews, 22 January 1917, folder 56, Archives of AJJDC, 1914–1918. "Kayn bazunder relief fir Rumenien," 1 January 1917, "Konferents fun ungarishe iden," 18 January 1917, advertisement by the Galician Federation, 25 January 1917, "Haynt der ersther tog fun rakhmones vokh," 27 January 1917, all in *Tageblat.*

14. Letters, Leo Lerner to Felix Warburg, 9 June 1918, and Albert Lucas to Leo Lerner, 17 June 1918, folder 55, and "Report Upon Conditions in Roumania, Learned After an Interview with Mr. Edward Herbert, Secretary of the American Union of Roumanian Jews," 14 October 1917, folder 53, Archives of AJJDC, 1914–1918.

15. "Hilfe far Galitsien—an oyfruf fun'm galitsianer un bukoviner ferband," 30 August 1914; advertisement, 19 October 1914; "Estraykhishe ambasador dankt dem ferband," 30 November 1914; "Ferband shikt nokh 5,000 kronen far milkhome lender," 21 December 1914, all in *Tageblat.*

16. "Oyfruf tsu ale galitsianer un bukoviner iden in Amerika," *Tageblat,* 17 June 1915.

17. "Entlofene fun galitsien zukhen kroyvim in Amerika," 30 December 1914, 12 January 1915; "'Ferband' makht hakhones tsu a yohr virdige arbayt," 28 May 1915; Z. Kotler, "A yohr hilfs-arbayt," 8 September 1915, all in *Tageblat.*

18. "Shloykhim fun rumenishe iden brengen hertsraysenden grus," 10 October 1917, "Konferents zuntog fun rumenishe iden," 19 October 1917, "Shildern tsores fun iden in Rumenien," 22 October 1917, "Ershte barikht fun rumenishe komite," 30 November 1917, "Tsu helfen di iden in Rumenien," 19 December 1917, "Rumener mass-miting fir milkhome korbones," 26 December 1917, "Rumenishe iden loyal tsu Amerika," 28 December 1917, "Rumenish-idishe konvenshon dankt Amerika," 31 December 1917, all in *Tageblat;* Committee of Roumanian Jews, "Ershter barikht," flyer, Landsmanshaft Subject Collection, RG 123, YIVO.

19. Z. Kotler, "Tsvishen fereynen un anshtalten," *Tageblat,* 4 December 1914.

20. "Mezritsher iden shtitsen di milkhome korbones," *Tageblat,* 3 November 1914.

21. "Landslayt vilen helfen Kalvarie," *Tageblat,* 31 May 1916. For a similar report see the advertisement of the Goniandzer Relief Committee, *Tageblat,* 12 January 1917.

22. See "Vikhtig far brisker!" *Tageblat,* 21 February 1917.

23. "Bialistoker oyfmerkzam," 2 February 1916; advertisement, 25 January 1915; "Far di idishe milkhome korbones," 4 February 1916; "Minsker leydis benevolent assn'n," 9 March 1916, all in *Tageblat.*

24. Advertisement, *Tageblat,* 6 April 1917. For similar appeals see "Tsu landslayt fun Novoridok," 15 February 1917, and the advertisement of the Lubliner War Relief urging landslayt to "do your duty to the unfortunates in Lublin" and attend the upcoming "search-light dance 'til dawn," 19 April 1918, *Tageblat.*

25. Minutes, 25 December 1915, Congregation Ahavath Zedek Anshei Timkowitz; "The History of Zloczower Relief," in *Zloczower Relief Verband of America* (New York, 1935), p. 6.

26. Report on relief activities, 31 January 1915; "Berditshever landslayt," 19 March 1916; advertisement, 14 March 1916, all in *Tageblat.*

27. "842 dolar far korbones in Pinsk," *Tageblat,* 16 February 1917.

28. Handlin, *Continuing Task,* p. 29.

29. Gershom Bader, "Men ken nit shiken geld nokh Galitsien," *Tageblat,* 3 February 1915.

30. "Iden tog—di pinsker relief komite," *Tageblat,* 27 January 1916.

31. Minutes, 29 July, 23 December 1916, Congregation Ahavath Zedek Anshei Timkowitz.

32. Advertisements, *Tageblat,* 2 April, 16 April, 4 June 1916.

33. "Der miting fun ferband," 11 November 1914, and "Galitsishe ferband arbayt energish far milkhome korbones," *Tageblat,* 25 December 1914.

34. Z. Kotler, "A yohr hilfs-arbayt," *Tageblat,* 8 September 1915.

35. Handlin, *Continuing Task,* pp. 29–30.

36. M. Kaplan, "Brisker yidn in 19tn yohrhundert," in Elieser Steinman, ed., *Entsiklopedie fun di goles-lender: Brisk-Dlite* (Jerusalem: The Encyclopedia of the Jewish Diaspora, 1955), p. 102; "Brest-Litovsk," *Encyclopedia Judaica* (Jerusalem: Keter, 1972), vol. 4, cols. 1359–1362.

37. Avrom Kaplan, *Der khurbn fun Brisk in der velt milkhome* (Brzesc nad Bugiem, 1925).

38. Meeting notice, *Tageblat,* 19 December 1914; Jacob Finkelstein, "Geshikhte fareynigter brisker relif" (manuscript), and "Bletl geshikhte brisker relif—same onfang" (manuscript), both in folder 12, Records of United Brisker Relief, RG 898, YIVO; Jacob Finkelstein, "Di landsmanshaftn un di geshikhte fun fareyniktn brisker relif," in Steinman, *Entsiklopedie fun di goles-lender,* pp. 612–662; Jacob Finkelstein, "50 Years United Brisker Relief," in *50 Anniversary of United Brisker Relief* (New York, 1965), pp. 3–5; advertisement, *Tageblat,* 11 December 1914.

39. The organizations involved were the Brisker Bundist Fareyn; Brisker Branch 286, Workmen's Circle; Brisker Branch 85, Jewish National Workers' Alliance; Brisker Shul Tiphereth Israel; Brisker Ladies' Society; Brisker Young Men's; Brisker Lodge 337, Independent Order B'rith Sholom; Brisker Lodge 682, Independent Order Brith Abraham; Semiatisher Society; Rabbi Zuberstein Lodge; Brisker Untershtitsung Fareyn, Brisker Zelbstbildung Klub; and possibly the Brisk D'Lite Lodge. Finkelstein, "Bletl geshikhte brisker relif," p. 2.

40. Finkelstein, "Geshikhte," p. 6.

41. "Unzer thetigkeyt," in *Brisker Relief for the War Sufferers* (New York, 1917), n.p.

42. "Yehrlikher finans berikht," 1917, folder 10, Records of United Brisker Relief.

43. "Apiel fun brisker," 1 February 1917, "Tsu helfen di brisker heymloze," 16 February 1917, "Vikhtik far brisker," 21 February 1917, all in *Tageblat;* "Yehrlikher finans berikht."

44. "Unzer thetigkeyt."

45. "Yehrlikher miting," folder 10, Records of United Brisker Relief.

46. "Brisker hilfs ferband . . . a grus fun Brisk," folder 10, Records of United Brisker Relief.

47. The exact figures are disputed. See Baron, *Russian Jew,* pp. 183–185; Peter Kenez, "Pogroms and White Ideology in the Russian Civil War," in *Pogroms: Anti-Jewish Violence in Modern Russian History,* ed. John D. Klier and Shlomo Lambroza (Cambridge: Cambridge University Press, 1992), pp. 292–313, and Abraham Greenbaum, "Bibliographical Essay," in the same volume, especially pp. 380–382.

48. Handlin, *Continuing Task,* pp. 34–37.

49. Ibid., pp. 39–44; Joseph Hyman, *Twenty-Five Years of American Aid to Jews Overseas* (Philadelphia: Jewish Publication Society of America, 1939), pp. 19–25; Rosenfelt, *This Thing of Giving,* p. 139.

50. D. Davidovitch, *Der Weg* (Berlin), April 1923, p. 7, quoted in Zosa Szajkowski, "Private and Organized American Jewish Overseas Relief (1914–1938)," *American Jewish Historical Quarterly* 57 (September 1967): 61. The JDC figures are from page 63.

51. "Lithuanian Jews Appeal to America," *Tageblat,* 23 April 1920, and "Appeal from Lithuanian Jews," *Forward,* April 1920 (no date given), from "Digest of the Yiddish Press," folder 46, Archives of AJJDC, 1919–1921.

52. "Galician Commission Confers with Local Leaders," *Jewish Morning Journal,* 31 March 1920, "Commission from Galicia Discusses Its Plans," *Jewish Morning Journal,* 1 April 1920, "Galician Commission Confers with Representatives of Landsmanschaften," *Forward,* 30 April 1920, "Galician Commission to Sail Home on June 10th," *Jewish Morning Journal,* 5 May 1920, "Delegate of Ukrainian Relief Committee Here," *Tog,* 27 September 1920, "Warsaw Relief Conference to Be Held in New York," *Tog,* 14 April 1921, all in "Digest of News in Yiddish Press," folder 46; Flyer, "Dvinsker deneburger lezt dem brief tsu aykh fun Dvinsk," folder 79, all in Archives of AJJDC, 1919–1921.

53. "The Activities of the Landsmanschaften," 8 March 1920, folder 78, Archives of AJJDC, 1919–1921.

54. Circular letter on stationery of Poloner Relief, n.d., folder 80a, Archives of AJJDC, 1919–1921.

55. "Record of Landsmannschaft Committee," 12 August 1920, folder 23. Another estimate, probably low, put the number of relief committees at 300, with 1.5–2 million dollars accumulated. Joseph Gedalecia, "Statement on Landsmanschaften," 2 March 1920, folder 78, Archives of AJJDC, 1919–1921. See also Letter, Samuel Margoshes to Bernard Semel, 27 December

1918, and "Galitsianer ferband shikt a komisie keyn Galitsien," *Forward,* undated clipping, both in folder 76, Archives of AJJDC, 1919–1921.

56. Letter, Khaym Zev ben Ruveyn Kazan, et al., to Narever hilfs komitet, New York, 22 June 1920, folder 80, Archives of AJJDC, 1919–1921.

57. Letters, S. Margoshes to Bernard Semel, 27 December 1918 and 22 January 1919; S. Margoshes to Felix Warburg, 24 January 1919; Felix Warburg to Albert Lucas, 10 April 1919, all in folder 76, Archives of AJJDC, 1919–1921. In his letter of April 10, Warburg reported that he had told Semel, Fischman, and Margoshes to "go before their little societies and tell them that, in our opinion, it would be a crime if they insisted on keeping the funds given for the benefit of the Galicians in their treasuries."

58. Letters, Bernard Semel to Felix Warburg, 16 June 1919, and Felix Warburg to Bernard Semel, 27 June 1919, folder 76, Archives of the AJJDC, 1919–1921. The file copy letter from Warburg is unsigned, but bears the stamp of Kuhn, Loeb and Co., with which Warburg was associated.

59. Quoted by Frank F. Rosenblatt in his report, "To the Committee on Landsmanschaften," 6 June 1921, folder 23, Archives of AJJDC, 1919–1921.

60. Letter, Albert Lucas to Alexander Kahn, 17 September 1919, and "Report of Committee on Landsmanschaften" (based on meetings of 30 September and 6 October 1919), both in folder 23, Archives of AJJDC, 1919–1921. For a similar recommendation by the Reconstruction Committee, see memo, Frank Rosenblatt to Felix Warburg, 1 June 1920, folder 78, Archives of AJJDC, 1919–1921.

61. See letters of invitation to meeting, Judah L. Magnes to Pierre A. Siegelstein, F. Baron, and "President, Federation of Polish Jews," 11 March 1920, folders 74 and 76, Archives of AJJDC, 1919–1921. Marginal notes in the copy of the letter to F. Baron, who was President of the Galician Federation, indicate that the letter was sent to the Baltic, Bessarabian, Ukrainian, Lithuanian, Galician, Polish, Romanian, and Bukovinean federations, and to the Minsker and Pinsker societies.

62. "Kooperatsie mit landsmanshaften," part of Yiddish typescript marked (in English) "News Letter," 28 May 1920, folder 47, Archives of AJJDC, 1919–1921.

63. "Record of Landsmannschaft Committee, August 12, 1920," and "Minutes of the meeting on Landsmanschaften," 23 August 1920, folder 23, Archives of AJJDC, 1919–1921; *Information Service Letter* 7 of 7 September 1920, folder 45, Archives of AJJDC, 1919–1921.

64. "Report to the Committee on Landsmanschaft," 6 October [1920], folder 23; "Der department fun landsmanshaften vos iz geefent gevoren fun der dzshoynt distribushon komite," *Tog,* 2 October 1920, clipping, and full-page advertisement, "Landsmanshaften!," unidentified, undated clipping, both in folder 82 Archives of AJJDC, 1919–1921.

65. "Report to the Committee on Landsmanschaften," 22 March 1921, folder 23, Archives of AJJDC, 1919–1921; "Report of the Committee on Landsmanshaften to the Executive Committee," 30 September 1922, folder 82, and memo, 1 September 1922, folder 123, Archives of AJJDC, 1921–1932.

66. See *Information Service Letter* 18 of 1 April 1921; see also periodic reports on

Landsmanshaft Department activities, including "Report to the Committee on Landsmanshaftn," 31 January 1921, folder 23; memo, Joint Distribution Committee, Warsaw, to Joint Distribution Committee, Paris, 22 April 1921, folder 78; clippings, "Shif mit pesakh-mehl fohrt bald ob," *Tageblat*, 26 January 1921," "Bloyz getsehlte teg gebliben tsu bazorgen di heymishe shtedt mit matses," *Tog*, 26 January 1921, folder 82, Archives of AJJDC, 1919–1921; circular letter JDC Landsmanschaften Department, 13 January 1921, folder 7, Records of United Brisker Relief.

67. Memorandum to Dr. Magnes from Dr. Rosenblatt, no date, folder 23, Archives of AJJDC, 1919–1921. The general impression that the wave of missions abroad subsided after 1921 is reinforced by comments in the Yiddish press. See "The Mistaken Policy of the Landsmanschaften," *Jewish Courier* (Chicago), 31 January 1922; "Newspaper Approves Opening of Landsmannschaften Bureau of JDC on East Side," *Jewish Morning Journal*, 8 December 1922, in "Digest of News in Yiddish Press," folder 61, Archives of AJJDC, 1921–1932.

68. Leon Elbe, "Di shlikhim fun folk," *Tog*, 22 June 1920, clipping in folder 78, Archives of AJJDC, 1919–1921.

69. Szajkowski, "Private American Jewish Overseas Relief," pp. 301, 307.

70. See reports on a series of meetings called by Hershfield, *Tageblat*, 14 March, 16 March, 23 March, 2 April 1916. See also Gedalecia, "Statement on Landsmanschaften."

71. See Elbe, "Di shlikhim fun folk."

72. "Digest of News in Yiddish Press," report from *Tog*, 5 April 1920, folder 46, Archives of AJJDC, 1919–1921.

73. Memo to the Special Landsmanshaft Meeting from S. Schmidt, 12 November 1920, folder 23, Archives of AJJDC, 1919–1921.

74. Yosef Lipnik, "Dovid Sohn's rol in der landsmanshaft," in *Bialistoker yoyvel-zamlbukh* (New York: Dovid Sohn yubileum zhurnal komitet, 1961), p. 12.

75. See, for example, advertisements for upcoming meetings of First Kaliser Podolier Relief, unidentified clipping, 23 September 1920, and for Kalvarier Relief, unidentified clipping, n.d., folder 82, Archives of AJJDC, 1919–1921.

76. See, for example, the advertisement for a farewell meeting for the Kovler delegate, Mr. Gevirts, unidentified, undated clipping, folder 82, Archives of AJJDC, 1919–1921.

77. "Ven eyn amerikaner sheliekh kumt aheym," reprinted in *Tageblat*, 5 July 1920, clipping, folder 78, Archives of AJJDC, 1919–1921.

78. See, for example, "Landsmanshaften Delegates Reach Warsaw With $2,000,000," *Jewish Morning Journal*, 4 April 1921, "Digest of News in Yiddish Press," folder 46, Archives of AJJDC, 1919–1921.

79. S. V., "Draysig yor kalushiner sosayti," Independent Kalushiner Benevolent Association, *30th Anniversary Banquet* (New York, 1935).

80. Rivkin, "Sotsiale role," p. 102.

81. Letters, Ely Greenblat to Albert Lucas, 7 January, 8 January 1921; memo, JDC Paris to JDC New York, 18 February 1921; delegate questionnaire for Ely Greenblatt, folder 80, Archives of AJJDC, 1919–1921.

82. Statistical report by JDC Brisk office, 4 June 1921, folder 2, Records of United Brisker Relief; A. Verthaym, "Di tetikayt fun 'dzshoynt' in Brisk," in Steinman,

Entsiklopedie fun di goles-lender, pp. 657–659; Kaplan, *Der khurbn fun Brisk,* pp. 24–27.

83. "Synagogues of Brest-Litovsk: An Inferno of Human Suffering as Told by Miss Irma May," typescript, ca.1924, quote on page 4, folder 14/9–10, Records of United Brisker Relief. See also "Letste grusen fun Brisk," press release, 26 November [1920], folder 47, Archives of AJJDC, 1919–1921.

84. See letters to J. Finkelstein, 25 July 1919; from Rabbi Isaac Ze'ev Soloveichik to Nisn Liberman, 2 Heshvan 5680 (26 October 1919); from Kooperatywa to Corn (sic) Relief Committee, 8 April 1920, folder 2, Records of United Brisker Relief.

85. Flyer, "Tsu ale brisker!," 1919, folder 10, Records of United Brisker Relief.

86. Finkelstein, "Geshikhte," p. 14; series of receipts issued to the Brisker Relief by the Public Bank of New York City, the Irving National Bank, and the State Bank, folder 2, Records of the United Brisker Relief.

87. Letter, A. Williams to J. Finkelstein, 12 March 1920, folder 6, Records of United Brisker Relief.

88. This was a common development. See "The Activities of the Landsmanschaften," which mentions conferences of Bobruysk and Rovno landsmanshaftn from various cities, folder 78, Archives of AJJDC, 1919–1921.

89. Finkelstein, "Geshikhte," pp. 15–16; Finkelstein, "Landsmanshaftn," pp. 619–621.

90. Letter, Philip Rabinowitch to J. Finkelstein, 28 June [1920], folder 2, Records of United Brisker Relief.

91. Finkelstein, "Geshikhte," p. 16. Rabinowitch also brought back a kind of testimonial signed by over 100 residents of Brisk thanking him personally and the American landslayt in general for their assistance. This document surely impressed anyone who saw it both with the importance of continuing the relief work, and with the importance of Rabinowitch himself. "A grus fun Brisk," 15 June 1920, scrapbook, box 3, Records of United Brisker Relief.

92. Postcard meeting notice, "A grus fun Brisk," 1920, folder 10; telegrams and letter, A. Williams to J. Finkelstein, 25 August 1920, and Sol Weiss to J. Finkelstein, 1 September 1920, folder 6, Records of United Brisker Relief, YIVO.

93. Letters, Levengard et al. to Jacob Finkelstein, 8 November 1920, and Sol Weiss to Jacob Finkelstein, 17 January 1921, folder 6, United Brisker Relief.

94. Flyer, "Hilf oyf pesakh durkh di brisker shloykhim," folder 6, Records of United Brisker Relief; advertisement, "Brisker relief komite," unidentified, undated clipping, folder 82, Archives of AJJDC, 1919–1921.

95. See financial summary headed "Yor 1921," folder 1; letter on stationery of the Bank of United States to Brisker Relief Society, 9 March 1921, supplying two letters of credit for $110,868, in scrapbook, box 3, Records of United Brisker Relief. Expenses for the two delegates came to $1,984.25.

96. Concerning the 1921 Brisker delegates' trip see Finkelstein, "Geshikhte," pp. 17–19; Finkelstein, "Landsmanshaftn," pp. 623–627; Finkelstein, "A bagegenish mit mayn heymshtot," in Steinman, *Entsiklopedie fun di goles-lender,* pp. 251–254; "Ayndrukn fun mayn ershtn un tsveytn bazukh in Brisk," in Kopl Novik, *Di shtot Brisk* (New York, 1973), pp. 33–35.

97. Finkelstein, "Geshikhte," p. 17.

98. See receipts from various organizations to the delegates of the Brisker Relief, April and May 1921, and coded list of receipts and amounts, both in folder 2, Records of United Brisker Relief.

99. List of "letters from Brisk," 1921.

100. "Dankzogung," 1 June 1921, and receipt for photographer M. Zablud, folder 2, Records of United Brisker Relief, YIVO. The photographs are also in the collection. Delegates occasionally even made films of their towns, a practice which became more common in later years. See letter, H. Joseph Hyman to I. Rubenstein, 29 June 1921, which mentions that S. Wolos, delegate to the Latvian city of Daugavpils (Dvinsk), intended to make such a film, folder 79, Archives of AJJDC, 1919–1921.

101. Transcript of interview with Harry Nachimoff, n.d.; Unidentified clipping, n.d. [1920], Records of Wolkowysker Relief Society, RG 1042, YIVO. Concerning the practice of charging a commission for expenses and general relief, see also "Memo to the Special Landsmanschaften Meeting From Mr. [Samuel] Schmidt," 12 November 1920, file 23, Archives of AJJDC, 1919–1921.

102. Letter on Guaranty Trust Company of New York stationery, Harry Lawton to Bates Wyman, 25 February 1921; notebook with instructions headed, "Tsu Hery Nakhimof," Records of Wolkowysker Relief Society, YIVO. The Guaranty Trust Company, with offices on Grand Street, encouraged this sort of business among landsmanshaftn. The bank offered technical assistance to landsmanshaftn interested in sending delegates abroad, as well as letters of credit and travellers' checks. The bank's representatives would even make appointments to come to visit potential clients. See advertisement for Guaranty Trust Company of New York, unidentified clipping, folder 78, Archives of AJJDC, 1919–1921.

103. Maks Babitsh, "A rizikalishe shlikhes in a kritisher tsayt," *Bialistoker yoyvl-zamlbukh*, p. 19.

104. Ibid., pp. 19–20.

105. Yisroel Bernshteyn, "Fun Nyu York biz Buten," *Di Zeit*, undated clipping (hand-dated October 1920), folder 82; Joseph Schlossberg, "Landsmanschaft Delegations A Waste and A Source of Demoralization" (excerpts from an article in *Zeit*, 7 October 1920), in "Digest of News in the Yiddish Press," folder 46; memo from Boris Bogen to Committee on Landsmanschafts, 23 September 1920, folder 78, all in Archives of AJJDC, 1919–1921.

106. Bernshteyn, "Fun Nyu York biz Buten"; "In Re: Delegate of Society of Telechan," folder 81a; "Report to the Committee on Landsmanschaft," 6 October [1920], folder 23; list, "Delegates That Have Returned Without Reaching Destination," folder 78; "American Relief Delegate Jailed in Poland," *Tog*, 28 July 1920, in "Digest of News in Yiddish Press," folder 46, all in Archives of AJJDC, 1919–1921.

107. "Landsmanschaft Delegate Sues Rumanian Government for $50,000 Damages," *Zeit*, 31 January 1921, in "Digest of News in the Yiddish Press," folder 46, Archives of the AJJDC, 1919–1921. Concerning the case of four delegates to Proskurov and Yarmolintsy arrested for being "Bolshevik" spies, see letter,

Morris Weinberg to Felix Warburg, 23 February 1921, folder 80a, Archives of AJJDC, 1919–1920.

108. "Self-Appointed Relief Delegate Arrested," *Forward,* 19 March 1921; "American Relief Delegates in Bessarabia Deal in Diamonds," *Forward,* 22 March 1921; Bernshteyn, "Fun Nyu York biz Buten"; "Blames Irresponsible Delegates for Plight of Stricken Jews," *Tog,* 18 March 1921, all in "Digest of News in Yiddish Press," folder 46; memo, Morris Lewis to I. M. Kowalsky, 14 February 1921 (misdated 1920), folder 79a; "Kalisher relif sheliekh unter beyl," *Tageblat,* undated clipping, folder 82; list, "Delegates That Have Fulfilled Mission and Returned," 15 October 1920, folder 78; delegate questionnaire for Max Shatzman, and memos from JDC Warsaw to JDC Paris, 16 June and 23 June 1921, folder 80, all in Archives of AJJDC, 1919–1921.

109. Quoted in Szajkowski, "Private American Jewish Overseas Relief," p. 302.

110. Bernshteyn, "Fun Nyu York biz Buten."

111. Szajkowski, "Private American Jewish Overseas Relief," pp. 301, 302. See also memo from Boris Bogen to Joint Distribution Committee, New York, 25 September [1920], folder 78, and an unidentified and undated newspaper clipping based on this memo, "Ambasador Gibson vil obshtelen landslayt-shloykhim nokh Poylen," folder 82, Archives of AJJDC, 1919–1921.

112. "Report of Special Meeting of the Administrative Committee to Discuss the Question of Landsmanshaften," 19 October 1920, folder 23, Archives of AJJDC, 1919–1921. See also letter from Samuel Schmidt of the JDC to Gedaliah Bublick, editor of the *Tageblat,* advocating that the Yiddish press discourage the landsmanshaftn from sending delegates, 30 September 1920, folder 78, Archives of AJJDC, 1919–1921.

113. Memos, Boris Bogen to JDC New York, 26 September and 9 October 1920; Abraham Zucker to Boris Bogen, 16 October 1920; I. M. Kowalsky to JDC New York, 17 October 1920; JDC Poland to JDC New York, 9 November 1920, folder 80a, Archives of AJJDC, 1919–1921.

114. *Information Service Letter* 18 of 1 April 1921, folder 45; Press release, "Slonimer delegat fohrt op mit 167,000 dolar unter'n shuts fun der dzhoynt distribushon komite," n.d., folder 47; memo to William J. Mack from I. M. Naischtut, 8 May 1922, folder 123; "Report to the Committee on Landsmanshaften," 26 April 1921, folder 23, all in Records of AJJDC, 1919–1921; memo from I. M. Naischtut to F. Rosenblatt, 22 August 1921, folder 123; "Report on Delegates," 21 September 1921, folder 123, Archives of AJJDC, 1921–1932.

115. See, for example, the case of Terespol, a small town served by the Brisker Relief. "Protokol," 11 April 1921, folder 2, Records of United Brisker Relief.

116. Letter, Isaac Ze'ev Soloveichik to Nisn Liberman, 2 Heshvan 5680 (26 October 1919), folder 2, Records of United Brisker Relief.

117. Letter to Jacob Finkelstein, 25 July 1919, folder 2, Records of United Brisker Relief.

118. "Vi di gelder fun di hiege landsmanshaften veren oysgegeben in zeyere shtedt-lakh in Poylen," *Forward,* 26 June 1920, clipping, folder 78, Archives of AJJDC, 1919–1921.

119. "Relief Delegate Returns After Five Months' Stay in Bialystok," *Tog,* 16 February 1921, in "Digest of News in Yiddish Press," folder 46, Archives of AJJDC, 1919–1921.

120. Memo, Morris Lewis to I. M. Kowalsky, 14 February 1921 (misdated 1920), folder 79a, Archives of AJJDC, 1919–1921.

121. Memo, M. Raskin to JDC Warsaw, 22 May 1921, folder 82a, Archives of AJJDC, 1919–1921.

122. Finkelstein, "Geshikhte," p. 18; Finkelstein, "Landsmanshaftn," pp. 624–625; Petition of Jewish Artisans' Union, 2 May 1921, folder 2; "Reglamin fun a.h.k. in Brisk," folder 14/9–10, Records of United Brisker Relief, YIVO. The JDC Warsaw office, angry over lack of cooperation between the Brisker Relief and the JDC representative in Brisk, reported that it "was, of course, impossible" to establish harmony between the local factions. See memo, JDC Warsaw to Landsmannschaft Department, 23 June 1921, folder 79, Archives of AJJDC, 1919–1921.

123. "Report of Landsmanschaften Bureau," 14 February 1922, and memo to William J. Mack from I. M. Naischtut, 8 May 1922, folder 123, Archives of AJJDC, 1921–1932.

124. Minutes, 8 December 1922, folder 32, Archives of AJJDC, 1921–1932.

125. "Rusland vet nit araynlozen keyn delegaten fun landslayt," *Forward,* 18 October 1920, clipping, and "Relief organizatsies gevorent nit tsu shiken keyn shloykhim in sovet Rusland," *Zeit,* 9 October 1920, clipping, folder 82, Archives of AJJDC, 1919–1921.

126. Minutes, 8 December 1922, folder 32; "Memorandum of Meeting," 9 May 1923, folder 32; "Landsmanschaften May Send Money for All Kinds of Relief to Russia, Says Dr. Bogen," *Jewish Morning Journal,* 24 December 1922, translation in folder 123, Archives of AJJDC, 1921–1932.

127. "Landsmanshaften kenen shiken hilf un kleyder in zeyere shtedt in sovet Rusland," unidentified, undated clipping (fall 1920), folder 82, Archives of AJJDC, 1919–1921; "Report to Committee on Landsmanschaften," 20 June 1922, folder 32; memo to I. M. Naischtut from F. Rosenblatt, 15 November 1921; letters, B. Bogen to I. M. Naischtut, 14 May 1922, William J. Mack to David Bressler, 11 October 1922, I. M. Naischtut to B. Bogen and Joseph Rosen, 23 February 1923, folder 123, all in Archives of AJJDC, 1921–1932.

128. Minutes, 8 December 1922, folder 32, and letter, Bogen to Peter Wiernick, 17 March 1923, folder 125, Archives of AJJDC, 1921–1932.

129. Regarding the Idgezkom, see Zvi Y. Gitelman, *Jewish Nationality and Soviet Politics: The Jewish Sections of the CPSU, 1917–1930* (Princeton: Princeton University Press, 1972), pp. 236–239, 271. See also "What Does the 'Joint' Say to This?" *Freiheit,* 30 April 1922, in "Digest of News in the Yiddish Press," folder 61, Archives of AJJDC, 1921–1932.

130. "Idgeskom Opens Landsmanschaften Bureau on East Side," *Tog,* 25 February 1923; "Special Landsmannschaften Department in Organ of Local Idgeskom," in "Digest of News in Yiddish Press," folder 61, Archives of AJJDC, 1921–1932.

131. Memo to Albert Lucas from Mr. Menachem, August 1920, folder 84; "Dr.

Dubrovsky zogt 'dzshoynt' tor nit nemen gelder fun landsmanshaften," *Zeit,* 27 October 1920, clipping, "Dzshoynt ken nit onemen landsmanshaft gelder far Rusland," unidentified, undated clipping, folder 82; "Relief Work in Russia Can Be Done Only Through Him, Dr. Dubrovsky Asserts," *Zeit* and *Forward,* 26 October 1920, in "Digest of News in Yiddish Press," folder 46, Archives of AJJDC, 1919–1921.

132. "Important Announcement of Idgeskom for all Landsmannschaften," *Freiheit,* 8 August 1922, "Digest of News in Yiddish Press," folder 61, Archives of AJJDC, 1921–1932.

133. "Will Cooperate with People's Relief Provided It Secedes from JDC, Says Dubrovsky," *Zeit,* 11 November 1920, in "Digest of News in Yiddish Press," folder 46, Archives of AJJDC, 1919–1921.

134. "New Relief Action of American Landsmanschaften Through Idgeskom," *Tog,* 14 December 1922, in "Digest of News in Yiddish Press," folder 61, Archives of AJJDC, 1921–1932; *Di pipels relief fun Amerika: faktn un dokumentn 1915–1924* (New York: Special Book Committee, 1924), pp. 121, 184. The rapprochement between the PRC and Idgezkom coincided with a movement within the radical PRC to secede from the JDC.

135. Quoted in Gitelman, *Jewish Nationality,* p. 239.

136. Fund raising also declined, and although the JDC was forced to continue its work because an economic downturn in 1925 left 83% of Jewish workers unemployed in Warsaw, it raised only $200,000 in that year. Handlin, *Continuing Task,* pp. 46–55. The quote from a JDC publication is on page 46–47.

137. See memos to Mr. Strauss from Miss Morrissey, 22 August 1922, and to Mr. Menachem from Landsmanschaft Bureau, 13 March 1923; minutes, 27 February 1924; "Copy of Publicity Item Translated from Yiddish," 1 April 1924, all in folder 123, Archives of AJJDC, 1921–1932.

138. Letter from S. Tenzer, Records of Works Progress Administration Historical Records Survey—Federal Writers' Project, Box 3627, New York City Municipal Archives.

139. *Horodishtsher barg* (New York: United Horodyszczer Relief Organizations, 1920), p. 21.

8. Looking Backward

1. Yosef Rosenberg, "Der yunger element in unzere sosaytis," *Der idisher sosayti,* 6 January 1933, p. 5.

2. Not counting family circles, percentages ranged from a low of 6% for Workmen's Circle landsmanshaft branches to 16% in the lodges. I. E. Rontch, "Der itstiker matsev fun di landsmanshaften," in Rontch, ed., *Di idishe landsmanshaften fun Nyu York* (New York: Yiddish Writers' Union, 1938), pp. 17–18. For an English version see Hannah Kliger, ed., *Jewish Hometown Associations and Family Circles in New York: The WPA Yiddish Writers' Group Study* (Bloomington: Indiana University Press, 1992), pp. 36–37. For a society which claimed success in attracting young people see First Yezierzaner Sick Benevolent Association, *35th Anniversary* (New York, 1933), and *Fortieth*

Anniversary Banquet, (New York, 1938). See also Homler Brothers Society, *Souvenir Journal 1899–1936* (New York, 1936); Congregation of the People of the City of Bobruisk, *30th Anniversary* (New York, 1929).

3. A related form, the cousins' club, consisted of a "group of first cousins and their descendants." William Mitchell, *Mishpokhe: A Study of New York City Jewish Family Clubs* (The Hague: Mouton Publishers, 1978); I. E. Rontch, ed., *Idishe familyes un familye krayzn fun Nyu York* (New York: Yiddish Writers' Union, 1939), especially pp. 41–61 (for an English translation see Kliger, *Jewish Hometown Associations and Family Circles,* pp. 77–83); "Familye fareynen," *Di idishe sosayti,* 3 March 1933.

4. This does not include the independent women's societies, many of which were formed earlier. Rontch, *Di idishe landsmanshaften,* pp. 29–30.

5. "Di idishe froy un ihr ort in gezelshaftlikhen leben," *Di idishe sosayti,* 13 January 1933, p. 4.

6. The first female national officer of Independent Order Brith Abraham suggested that this was the case in her own order. Elizabeth Blume-Silverstein, "Women's Contribution in the Independent Order Brith Abraham," in B. Shelvin, ed., *History of Independent Order Brith Abraham* (New York: Independent Order Brith Abraham, 1937), p. 94.

7. Minutes, 24 January 1932, and subsequent meetings from 1932, Records of First Bratslower Ladies Auxiliary, RG 835, YIVO.

8. Rakower Ladies Club, *Di shtime fun rakover froyen klub* (New York, 1937); Ladies' Auxiliary Bialystoker Center and Bikur Cholim, *Bialystoker Ladies' Journal* (New York, 1930).

9. Minutes, 14 February, 20 March, 28 March, 26 June, 25 December 1932; 29 January, 26 February, 14 May, 28 May, 11 June, 25 June, 10 September, 1 October, 8 October, 22 October, 12 November 1933; 14 March 1937, First Bratslower Ladies Auxiliary.

10. Minutes, 22 May, 25 December 1932 (second meeting carrying this date); 26 March, 23 April 1933; 14 February, 14 March, 23 May, 13 June 1937, First Bratslower Ladies Auxiliary.

11. Minutes, 24 April, 8 May, 26 June 1932; 22 October, 5 November, 12 November 1933; 14 March 1937, First Bratslower Ladies Auxiliary.

12. Maurice Halbwachs, *The Collective Memory* (1950; New York: Harper and Row, 1980), p. 130. See also David Lowenthal, *The Past Is a Foreign Country* (Cambridge: Cambridge University Press, 1985), p. 42; Lowenthal, "Past Time, Present Place: Landscape and Memory," *The Geographical Review* 65 (January 1975): 6–9. Ewa Morawska provides a very interesting analysis of how images and memories of the old country contributed to the construction of Jewish and Slavic ethnicities in the Unites States. See her "Changing Images of the Old Country in the Development of Ethnic Identity among East European Immigrants, 1880s-1930s: A Comparison of Jewish and Slavic Representations," in *YIVO Annual* 21 (1993): 273–341.

13. See John R. Gillis, "Memory and Identity: The History of a Relationship," in Gillis, ed., *Commemorations: The Politics of National Identity* (Princeton: Princeton University Press, 1994), pp. 3–24.

14. See Halbwachs, *The Collective Memory;* Halbwachs, *On Collective Memory,* Lewis Coser, ed. and trans. (Chicago: University of Chicago Press, 1992).

15. For examples of programs and menus see Kartuz-Berezer Benevolent Association, *Sovenir zhurnal aroysgegeben tsum draysig-yehrigen yubileum* (New York, 1924); First Lutzker Benevolent Association, *25th Anniversary: Souvenir Journal* (New York, 1926); Voronover Young Men's Benevolent Association, *Souvenir Journal, Thirty-Fifth Anniversary Banquet and Ball* (New York, 1928); Kiever Independent Benevolent Association of Brooklyn, *Souvenir Journal: Twenty-Fifth Anniversary Banquet* (New York, 1933); Chvoniker Independent Aid Society, *Tsvantsig yohriger yubileum* (New York, 1933); United Winnitzer Young Men's Benevolent Association, *Twentieth Anniversary Banquet,* with "International" (New York, 1935); Lespezier Benevolent Society, *Second Annual Dinner and Dance* (New York, 1925); Newmark Young Men's Benevolent Association, *25th Anniversary Banquet* (New York, 1930). On the liveliness of the parties see the poem and cartoon in Vilner Branch 367, Workmen's Circle, *Der vilner* (New York, 1934), p. 4. See also the many photographs of society banquets in the YIVO archives.

16. Irving Howe, "Pluralism in the Immigrant World," in David Berger, ed., *The Legacy of Jewish Migration: 1881 and Its Impact* (New York: Brooklyn College Press, 1983), p. 152. On the souvenir journals, see G. Borekh, "Di suvenir-zhurnalen," in Rontch, *Di idishe landsmanshaften fun Nyu York,* pp. 152–157. An English version of this article appears in Kliger, *Jewish Hometown Associations and Family Circles,* pp. 67–70.

17. "Brider in noyt," *Der horodishtsher barg* (New York: United Horodyszczer Relief Organizations, 1920), p. 16; Abraham Horenstein, "The Significance of 'Gmilus Chessed' and Its Place in the Life of the Jewish People," in Lipkaner Bessarabier Progressive Society, *First Annual Banquet* (New York, 1936); Allan B. Bernstein, "Our Society," Progressive Society of Yaruga, *Souvenir Journal: Twentieth Anniversary Banquet* (New York, 1937).

18. On nostalgia in general see Fred Davis, *Yearning for Yesterday* (New York: Free Press, 1979); Suzanne Vromen, "The Ambiguity of Nostalgia," *YIVO Annual* 21 (1993): 69–86; Jean Starobinsky, "The Idea of Nostalgia," *Theory, Culture and Society* 4 (February 1987): 147–156; Christopher Shaw and Malcolm Chase, eds., *The Imagined Past—History and Nostalgia* (Manchester: Manchester University Press, 1989); Anthony Brandt, "A Short Natural History of Nostalgia," *Atlantic Monthly* 242 (December 1978): 58–63; Lowenthal, *The Past Is a Foreign Country,* pp. 4–13. On the importance of a sense of place in memory, see Simon Schama, *Landscape and Memory* (New York: Alfred A. Knopf, 1995).

19. D. R. Zaslavski, "Bohslev: der plats vu ikh hob gekholemt mayne kindershe nit farvirklekhte khaloymes (erinerungen un shtriken)," in Boslever Benevolent Association, *Thirty-Fifth Anniversary* (New York, 1935).

20. See, for example, Progressive Society of Yaruga, *Souvenir Journal 1917–1937: Twentieth Anniversary Banquet* (New York, 1937); Lipkaner-Bessarabier Progressive Society, *First Annual Banquet.*

21. P. Novick, "Vos iz Brisk?" in Brisker Branch 286 Workmen's Circle and Brisker

Czechanower Branch 15, International Workers Order, *Unzer vort* (New York, 1937), p. 3.

22. On the importance in nostalgia of the perception of a deficient present and the search for the "true self," see Chase and Shaw, "The Dimensions of Nostalgia," in *Imagined Past*, p. 3; Davis, *Yearning for Yesterday*, pp. 15, 39–41.

23. Abraham Cahan, *The Rise of David Levinsky* (1917; New York: Harper Torchbooks, 1960), p. 530.

24. Novick, "Vos iz Brisk," p. 2.

25. Dovid Keshir, *Tsvishn vent* (New York: Farlag Signal baym Proletpen and Proskurever Br. 54, IWO, 1939), pp. 121–124.

26. *Khurbn Proskurov* (New York, 1924); Susan Milamed, "Proskurover Landsmanshaftn: A Case Study in Jewish Communal Development," *American Jewish History* 76 (September 1986): 44–48.

27. See Yosef Hayim Yerushalmi, *Zakhor: Jewish History and Jewish Memory* (Seattle: University of Washington Press, 1982); David Roskies, *Against the Apocalypse: Responses to Catastrophe in Modern Jewish Culture* (Cambridge, Mass.: Harvard University Press, 1984).

28. See Chuna Gottesfeld, *Mayn rayze iber Galitsiye* (New York: Fareynikte Galitsianer Yidn in Amerike, 1937); Diary of Sidney Herbst, Herbst family file, Collection on Family History and Genealogy, RG 126, YIVO; Daniel Soyer, "The Travel Agent as Broker between Old World and New: The Case of Gustave Eisner," *YIVO Annual* 21 (1993): 345–368.

29. Harry Fein, "Mayak," and Samuel A. Lerner, "A vort fun'm grinder un ershtn prezident fun unzer sosayti," in Mayaker Aid Society, *Fifteenth Anniversary Banquet and Dance* (New York, 1937).

30. See for example, Shedlowzer Benevolent Association, *Souvenir Journal, Twentieth Anniversary Banquet* (New York, 1929); Independent Skerniewicer Benevolent Association, *25th Anniversary Celebration Banquet* (New York, 1935); Breziner Sick and Benevolent Society, *Fortieth Anniversary Banquet* (New York, 1936); United Winnitzer Young Men's Benevolent Association, *Twentieth Anniversary Banquet,* with tree illustration (New York, 1935); Lipkaner-Bessarabier Progressive Society, *First Annual Banquet . . . in Dedication of the Free Loan Fund,* with tree illustration (New York, 1936); Chmielniker Sick and Benevolent Society of Poland, *Fifth Annual Banquet and Dance,* with tree illustration (New York, 1931).

31. See, for example, Fareynikter Ostrover Hilfs-Komitet, *Tsu hilf* (New York, 1938); United Radomer Relief, *Third Anniversary Banquet* (New York, 1937); Chotiner Hospital Moshev Zkenim Relief, *Banquet and khanukes habayis* (New York, 1937); United Lubliner Relief, *Purim bol* (New York, 1938); United Czenstochover Relief Committee, *Grand Ball* (New York, 1937); reports of the annual Passover aid campaign of the Gross Moster Sick and Benevolent Association (1931, 1935, 1938), Landsmanshaftn Subject Collection, RG 123, YIVO. The Brisker Relief revived after the 1937 pogrom in Brisk. See J. Finkelstein, "Di landsmanshaftn un di geshikhte fun fareyniktn brisker relif," in Elieser Steinman, ed., *Entsiklopedie fun di goles-lender: Brisk-Dlite* (Jerusalem: The Encyclopedia of the Jewish Diaspora, 1955), pp. 628–629.

32. Other landsmanshaft federations, notably the Federation of Polish Jews, sur-

vived from the pre-World War I era and continued to carry out relief work. Shmuel Schwartz, "Di landsmanshaft farbanden," in Rontch, *Di idishe landsmanshaften,* pp. 52–60; United Galician Jews of America, *Der galitsianer* (New York, 1938).

33. M. Blechman, "Di landsmanshaften un di tsentrale organizatsies," in Rontch, *Di idishe landsmanshaften,* pp. 40–41; *Folkshilf* 1–3 (Warsaw, 1939): 49–50; Rubin Feldshuh, ed., *Yidisher gezelshaftlekher leksikon* (Warsaw: Yidisher leksikografisher farlag, 1939), pp. 794–795.

34. Blechman, "Di landsmanshaften un di tsentrale organizatsies," 33–35; Report of Morris Feinstone, chairman, "Zibeter yerlekher konvenshon fun dem hayas kounsil ov organizeyshons," n.d., folder I-34, Records of HIAS, RG 245.4, YIVO; list of "Organizations Affiliated with the Council of Fraternal Organizations of the Federation for Support of Jewish Philanthropic Societies," 1935, Landsmanshaftn Subject Collection.

35. Warschauer Haym Salomon Home for the Aged, *Souvenir Journal 1922–1938* (1938); Mohilev-on-Dnieper and Vicinity Home for the Aged, *Testimonial Dinner and Dance in Honor of Our President Oscar Jaroff and His Family* (New York, 1936), and *Souvenir Journal: Tenth Anniversary Banquet* (New York, 1937); D. S., "Bialistoker landsmanshaften," in Rontch, *Di idishe landsmanshaften,* p. 122.

36. "Der protest in medison skver garden," *Di idishe sosayti,* 31 March 1933, p. 1; M. Blechman, "Di landsmanshaftn un di tsentrale organizatsies," pp. 33–35, 39–40.

37. More than half of the New York membership was in landsmanshaft branches. Borekh Rivkin, "Di sotsiale role fun di landsmanshaftn," in Rontch, *Di idishe landsmanshaften,* p. 93, also table on page 26; Rubin Saltzman, *Tsu der geshikhte fun der fraternaler bavegung bay yidn* (New York: International Workers Order, 1936); Roger Keeran, "National Groups and the Popular Front: The Cause of the International Workers Order," *Journal of American Ethnic History* 14 (Spring 1995): 23–51.

38. Chmelniker Podolier Branch 179, IWO, *Souvenir Journal . . . Seventh Anniversary* (New York, 1937). See also Lukover Branch 153, IWO, *Finf-yoriker yubileum* (New York, 1937); Baltik-Vitebsker Branch 33, IWO, *7ter yubiley* (New York, n.d.).

39. Tshekhanov-Mlaver Patronat, *Der ruf fun polit-arestantn in Poyln* (New York, n.d.); United Relief Committee of the Nowo-Radomsker Society, *Souvenir Journal: Second Annual Ball* (New York, 1937); Rivkin, "Di sotsiale role," pp. 104–105.

40. Hannah Kliger, "Communication and Ethnic Identity: The Case of Landsmanshaftn," Ph.D. diss., University of Pennsylvania, 1985, pp. 125–131; Kliger, *Jewish Hometown Associations and Family Circles,* p. 127.

41. Finkelstein, "Di landsmanshaftn un di geshikhte fun fareyniktn brisker relif," p. 630; Kliger, "Communication and Ethnic Identity," pp. 58–59.

42. Kliger, "Communication and Ethnic Identity," p. 58; Michael Weisser, *A Brotherhood of Memory: Jewish Landsmanshaftn in the New World* (New York: Basic Books, 1985), pp. 183–213.

43. Of these, 85,128 or 62% settled in New York. Leonard Dinnerstein, *America*

and the Survivors of the Holocaust (New York: Columbia University Press, 1982), pp. 287–288.

44. Kliger, "Communication and Ethnic Identity," pp. 48, 62–63, 142–144; Kliger, "Traditions of Grass-Roots Organization and Leadership: The Continuity of Landsmanshaftn in New York," *American Jewish History* 76 (September 1986): 36–37; Kliger, *Jewish Hometown Associations and Family Circles,* p. 120.

45. L. Losh, *Landsmanshaftn in Yisroel* (Tel Aviv: Hitahdut Olei Polin be-Yisrael, 1961), pp. 61–62.

46. On the yizker books see Jack Kugelmass and Jonathan Boyarin, *From a Ruined Garden: The Memorial Books of Polish Jewry* (New York: Schocken, 1983), especially the introduction, pp. 1–19; Kugelmass and Boyarin, "Yizker Bikher and the Problem of Historical Veracity: An Anthropological Approach," in Yisrael Gutman et al., eds., *The Jews of Poland Between the Two World Wars* (Hanover, N.H.: University Press of New England, 1989), pp. 519–536; E. D. Wein, "'Memorial Books' as a Source into the History of Jewish Communities in Europe," *Yad Vashem Studies* 9 (1973): 255–272; Miriam Hoffman, "Denkmol un zikorn: an oysforshung funem tsuzamenshtel fun zvoliner yizkerbukh," *Yivo bleter* 1 (new series, 1991): 257–272; Philip Friedman, "Di landsmanshaftn-literatur in di letste tsen yor," *Jewish Book Annual* 10 (1951): 81–96 (Yiddish section); Elias Schulman, "A Survey and Evaluation of Yizkor Books," *Jewish Book Annual* 25 (1967–1968): 184–191; Jacob Shatzky, "Yizker-bikher," *Yivo bleter* 37 (1953): 264–282; Shatzky, "Yizker-bikher," *Yivo bleter* 39 (1955): 339–355; Kliger, "Communication and Ethnic Identity," pp. 98–111.

47. Kugelmass and Boyarin, *From a Ruined Garden,* especially pp. 3, 12.

48. There are no reliable estimates of how many landsmanshaftn continued to exist in 1990. Michael Weisser cites JDC officials who estimated in 1980 that there were fewer than 1,000 landsmanshaftn in existence, only 400–500 of which met regularly. The same officials believed that there would be fewer than 100 functioning societies by 1990. It is not clear whether they were referring just to New York or to the entire country. Weisser, *Brotherhood of Memory,* p. 221.

49. For the later years of the landsmanshaftn see studies by Hannah Kliger, "Communication and Ethnic Identity"; "Traditions of Grass-Roots Organization and Leadership"; *Jewish Hometown Associations and Family Circles,* pp. 119–131 (Lodz observation on page 128).

50. Shedlowtzer Benevolent Association, *Souvenir Journal 1909–1934* (New York, 1934).

Acknowledgments

This book originated as a dissertation in the History Department at New York University. I wish therefore to thank, first of all, the members of my doctoral committee, David Reimers, Daniel J. Walkowitz, and Jenna Weissman Joselit. Their close reading and critical comments on various drafts of this work contributed significantly to its final form. Each also presided over earlier stages of my research into New York's *landsmanshaftn,* but Professor Joselit deserves special mention for originally suggesting the topic during a seminar at the YIVO Institute for Jewish Research. Other friends and colleagues also read part or all of the manuscript. These include Paul Baker and Michael Lutzker, who served as additional members of my dissertation committee, as well as Barbara Bianco, Peter Eisenstadt, Arthur Goren, Ezra Mendelsohn, and my father, David Soyer. Each offered valuable comments and suggestions, for which I am grateful. My friend and fellow historian Peter Eisenstadt, in particular, provided emotional support and intellectual stimulation, mostly in the course of our many bicycle rides through Prospect Park in Brooklyn.

Much of the material in this work is drawn from the library and archives of the YIVO Institute in New York. My friends and former colleagues there, Dina Abramowicz, Zachary Baker, Leo Greenbaum, Herbert Lazarus, Fruma Mohrer, and Marek Web were of enormous assistance. I would also like to thank the staffs of the American Jewish Joint Distribution Committee Archives (New York, especially Denise Gluck and Regina Chimberg), the New York Public Library Jewish Division, the Central Archives for the History of the Jewish People

(Jerusalem), and the American Jewish Historical Society (Waltham, Mass.) for their help.

The Lucius N. Littauer Foundation and the National Foundation for Jewish Culture provided financial support for this project. Pamela Brumberg and William L. Frost of the Littauer Foundation also supplied invaluable logistical assistance and encouragement, as did my parents, David and Jane Soyer.

Parts of chapter 7 appeared in slightly different form in the *Journal of American Ethnic History,* and are used with the permission of the editors.

Index